THE DREYFUS CASE: A REASSESSMENT

By the same author

A PASSIONATE PRODIGALITY
BECKFORD: A BIOGRAPHY
CULTURE AND SURVIVAL

ALFRED DREYFUS
about 1894

THE
DREYFUS CASE

A REASSESSMENT

BY

GUY CHAPMAN

**SOMETIME PROFESSOR OF MODERN HISTORY
IN THE UNIVERSITY OF LEEDS**

"Fanaticism begins at the point where evidence stops short."
THIERRY MAULNIER

GREENWOOD PRESS, PUBLISHERS
WESTPORT, CONNECTICUT

Library of Congress Cataloging in Publication Data

Chapman, Guy.
   The Dreyfus case.

   Reprint of the ed. published by Reynal, New York.
   Bibliography: p.
   Includes index.
   1. Dreyfus, Alfred, 1859-1935. I. Title.
[DC354.C47 1979]   944.081'092'4 [B]   78-31754
ISBN 0-313-20980-4

Reprinted in 1979 by Greenwood Press, Inc.
51 Riverside Avenue, Westport, CT 06880

Printed in the United States of America

10 9 8 7 6 5 4 3 2 1

Contents

6   Contents

Illustrations

The pictures of Guérin, Esterhazy, Zola and André are from
L Illustration, those of Mercier, Lauth and Cavaignac, and
Dreyfus at Rennes are from *Quelques Dessous du Procès de
Rennes* by Ajalbert. The others are reproduced by per-
mission of Picture Post Library.

Preface

FOR some years I have been engaged on a study of the French Third Republic. As everyone knows who reads the history of France between 1870 and 1914, the Dreyfus case lies in his way, a vast and distracting maze, *una selva oscura*. It cannot be avoided. Unhappily much legend is attached to the Affair. To accept the conventional reading of a clerico-military conspiracy is to swallow the propaganda of the Dreyfusards. No conspiracy existed in military circles, none in clerical. The arrest of Déroulède and his allies in August 1899 was no more than the spectacular method of a shaky and nervous Government of rallying opinion to its side. This consideration led me back to a re-examination of the evidence from the beginning. It soon became apparent that much more is to be said for the War Office than has generally been admitted, that anti-semitism played little, perhaps no, part in the arrest of the unhappy victim or in his trial, that the accusations against the secular Church and, save the Assumptionists, against the religious Orders have the flimsiest foundations. In short, the conventional story is overlaid with propaganda put out by partisans on both sides.

To explain all this would occupy far more space than could be spared in a history covering seventy years. I therefore decided to treat this fragment in isolation and at greater length than I could in the context of the history of France. I have here dealt with nothing but the case and the internal politics connected with it. I have omitted everything touching foreign affairs save as they impinge on the case. I have omitted all questions of economics, finance, labour and so forth. I have sketched in, far more roughly than I hope to do later, the necessary background of party politics, the Army and the Church, and the changes wrought by the case.

Perforce I have had to disregard the many

> Rich windows that exclude the light
> And passages that lead to nothing.

9

The great Dreyfusist history of Joseph Reinach requires three and a half volumes, some two thousand pages, to reach August 1898, and those who wish to can pursue the details there. Except for the discussion of some still unsolved secondary problems at the centre of the case, for example, how the *bordereau* reached the War Office, I have been content to tell a plain story.

As far as possible, I have avoided annotation, most of which I have relegated to appendices. References, where necessary, have been placed in the text. It must be remarked that, during the twelve years from the beginning to the end of the case, some individuals testified as many as six or seven times at an ever lengthening period after the events they were speaking to, and that failure of memory often accounts to a far greater extent than ill-intention for the embroidery or omission of parts of their earlier evidence. I have read and compared the testimony of at least the main witnesses in the transcripts of the proceedings, so far as available, at the Esterhazy court-martial, at the Zola trial, before the Cour de Cassation in 1898–99, at the Rennes court-martial and again before the Criminal Chamber of the Cour de Cassation in 1904, and if I have failed to notice some admission that I should have seen, well—I am sorry. I hope never to have to read those transcripts again.

Readers will notice that I have used the words "Dreyfusist" and "Dreyfusard." The first distinguishes those who almost from the beginning suspected a judicial error and attempted to secure a reopening of the case by legal methods, long before it was brought into the political field. The word "Dreyfusard," which was coined by the opponents of revision as a term of opprobrium, I have reserved for those who saw in the case an opportunity for political or personal advantage, the late-comers whom Péguy stigmatised as the profiteers.

Much of this book was written in Bordeaux, Nice and Paris between the autumn of 1953 and the spring of 1954, and I have had the inestimable good fortune to talk with men who in their youth experienced the social upheaval of 1898–99 and were acquainted with some of the characters who appear in these pages. I should also like to offer my thanks to Mr. Wickham Steed, who was kind enough to throw light into several dark corners.

January, 1955

GUY CHAPMAN

CHAPTER ONE

The Background

I: POLITICAL, SOCIAL, RELIGIOUS

1

In the early eighteen-nineties France was not a happy country. For more than a decade the depression of trade which had hung over Europe had affected the French no less than Great Britain and Germany. There were falling prices, falling rents, unemployment, hunger in many towns, suicides. The phylloxera scourge was still marching through the vineyards, and where it had passed, replanting was on a smaller scale. There had been bad financial crashes which had hampered government finance—the Union Générale crisis of 1882, the Comptoir d'Escompte crisis of March 1889, the Panama Company crisis in February of the same year. Since trade unions, legalised only in 1884, were still weak and almost wholly local, since the majority of the industrial workers were confined to the few big cities—apart from Paris, only ten towns possessed a population of more than a hundred thousand—and of the industrial workers most were employees in small workshops, nothing was done to relieve distress. Hitherto only a few deeply religious Catholics had taken any interest in the social question, and that from the viewpoint of morals rather than of economics. Ministers had allowed themselves to be dominated by the financial Pangloss, Léon Say: they denied the possibility of remedies for unemployment, even of palliatives for distress, and left the problem to their successors. Hence came the first beginnings of Socialism, on the one side from a few Radical Deputies, some of them union secretaries from the Pas-de-Calais coalfield, the Montluçon iron-works, the soap and vegetable-oil factories of Marseilles and, outside the Chamber of Deputies, from such theoretical revolutionaries as Jules Guesde, the "Torquemada in spectacles" and apostle of Karl Marx.

At the same time, more sympathetic to the hungry casual workmen, who abounded in Paris, there appeared the Anarchists, relying on "the unquenchable spirit of destruction and annihilation, which is the perpetual revival of new life." From March 1892 onwards, bombs thrown into restaurants or left in buildings brought home the fact that there existed a problem for society to solve.

In the Chamber the majority group was that of the Republicans, who had been in power since 1877. At one time all powerful, it had been slowly eaten into. In the early nineties it balanced between the groups to Right and Left, always in a small minority against a coalition. Some fifteen Cabinets had been formed and fallen since 1881, but, as Clemenceau said, it was always the same Cabinet: the same twenty to thirty men appear, disappear and reappear. Defeat of the Republicans was possible only by an alliance of the Monarchists and Bonapartists with the Radicals, and there were fortunately few issues on which they saw eye to eye. Like all Governments by the Centre, the Republicans wished to preserve the structure of politics; hence their motto was " Neither revolution nor reaction." As Paul Cambon wrote (19, 355), [1] "For minds of this nature, parliamentary government does not consist in having ideas and applying them under the control of the Chambers, but in finding out the ideas of the majority, which for the better part of the time do not exist, and giving an appearance to this non-existence. . . . Our friend Léon Say belongs to this school. He was a member of the Cabinet which abandoned Egypt in 1882, and his mind is completely at ease because he is covered by a vote of the Chamber." Among the Republicans were few men of strong character. Constans, whose ruthlessness had broken the Boulangist Movement in 1889, was detested and distrusted. President Carnot refused to ask him to form a Ministry. It was characteristic of the regime that it feared forceful politicians and got rid of them—Gambetta in 1882, Ferry in 1885. Clemenceau, the Radical leader, waited thirty years to become a Minister. The typically safe man of the period

[1] The figures printed in the text are references. The first figure is the number of the book in the Bibliography (pp. 377–82); the subsequent figures refer to the page, or to the volume and page, from which the quotation is taken.

was Charles de Freycinet, Dilke's "little white mouse," intelligent, persuasive, eloquent, who invariably resigned as soon as he met resistance.

Serious danger from the Right had disappeared. Both claimants, the Comte de Paris for the royal throne, Prince Napoleon for the imperial, were in exile: both were soon to die, Prince Napoleon in 1893, the Comte de Paris in 1894. The Duc d'Orléans was young, headstrong and inexperienced, Prince Victor negligible and discreet. Their representatives in France had made the fatal blunder of supporting Boulanger, and thus surrendered seats in the Chamber; together they scarcely amounted to a hundred and fifty. The appeal of Royalism or Imperialism was dead: even the traditionally Royalist Brittany was returning Republicans. Right-wing Deputies were drifting into support for Republican measures, rallying tacitly to the Republic, so long as the Church was not attacked. The force on the Right was now not Royalism but Catholicism.

On the extremity of the Left had appeared in 1886 a small group of men, elected as Radicals, who had added the adjective Socialist and by now had dropped the Radical. There were only a dozen of them, all of working-class origin, and several of them secretaries of trade unions. As yet they had devoted themselves almost wholly to labour matters, their chief proposition being the eight-hour day, a proposal laughed at by the employers both inside and outside the Chamber as mere moonshine, but they had met with some sympathy from a few of the Radicals.

The main body of the Left opposition was formed by the Radicals. Exactly what Radicalism meant is difficult to define: it was, said one of the political correspondents of the *Revue Politique et Parlementaire*, "the most elastic of epithets," since many used the word for electoral purposes only.[1] The group extended

[1] All ascriptions of individuals to parties are uncertain. So far as I can see, some thirty-six Deputies who stood as Republicans in 1889 stood as Radicals in 1893. This may have been purely for electoral purposes, since the difference between an advanced Republican and a Right-wing Radical was very small. As André Siegfried says, the only way to be sure is to check their votes in the Chamber, but even the interpretation of these may be vitiated by other considerations.

from those hardly distinguishable from Republicans to those who
had added the word Socialist to Radical. Their nominal leader,
Clemenceau, would have nothing to do with Socialism; he had
debated with Jules Guesde and had insisted that Socialism spelt
tyranny, while Radicalism stood for integral liberty, the liberty
of the individual. The group claimed to have taken up the banner
of democracy let fall by Gambetta and to stand by the programme
the Tribune had subscribed to in 1869, that is to say, anti-clericalism and the separation of Church and State, the replacement of
the professional Army by a national militia, the abolition of the
Senate, decentralisation of government, and election for practically all public offices. During the last ten years Clemenceau had
been the overthrower of Republican Governments, but he had
never formed one. President Grévy had declared that he would
turn the country upside down, and President Carnot was adamant
against him. He had been the original sponsor of Boulanger, but
when he found the General uncontrollable and moving towards
anti-parliamentarianism, he had fought him tooth and nail, and
thus earned the undying enmity of Boulanger's followers. But
Clemenceau had as yet no practical policies, and by the nineties
his followers, now reinforced by younger men with ambitions, were
becoming tired of a leader without a programme. Some were toy-
ing with Socialism, others were recommending income-tax as the
answer to Socialism. Each Radical, in short, had his own colour
and his own specifics. The single question on which they were
united was anti-clericalism.

One other group remains, that of the late General Boulanger's
followers, a disunited body which agreed only on one thing, the
destruction of parliamentary government.

Boulanger had been War Minister in the Cabinets of Freycinet
and Goblet in 1886–87. It is said that he was forced on Freycinet
by Clemenceau, who believed the General to have Radical leanings.
Boulanger was a keen soldier, but he had no political knowledge
and no tact. He talked too much. In January 1887 Bismarck, in
order to secure increased military credits, had made a half-veiled
allusion to him in the Reichstag. A little later a minor frontier in-

cident led to a short-lived tension between the French and German Governments. The German Government having behaved with considerable restraint and correctness, the Paris mob was led to believe that Bismarck was frightened by Boulanger. His popularity increased and the Republicans, as always alarmed at the sight of a popular general, disposed of him by defeating Goblet's Ministry. Boulanger was not included in the next Government but given command of the army corps at Clermont-Ferrand. On his departure from Paris he was given a frenzied demonstration by the mob. At Clermont he behaved with the minimum of discretion, and after disciplinary measures had failed to bring him to reason, he was placed on the retired list. In the meantime all the dissident groups had begun to see in him the man they wanted. It was not only the Royalists and the Bonapartists, but also the younger Radicals, though Clemenceau had turned against Boulanger as soon as he found he could not control him. Boulanger was therefore put up as an independent candidate at every by-election, and immediately he had won, he resigned and stood for another seat. The Right found money for him, the Radicals the populace. The crisis arrived in January 1889 with an election for a Paris seat. Boulanger was elected by an overwhelming majority. His supporters and the mob believed he would carry out an immediate *coup d'état*, but Boulanger went off to bed. He knew very well that troops had been brought into the capital in case of an emergency and that the Military Governor, General Saussier, would not hesitate to act. His hesitation weakened the movement. Constans, the Minister of the Interior, let it be known that he intended to arrest the aspirant dictator, and Boulanger fled. The movement collapsed, and although a number of Boulangist candidates were elected in October, it was the end of the adventure. In 1891 Boulanger, an exile in Brussels, shot himself on the grave of his mistress.

The Boulangist alliance had been a movement of discontent and its only formula revision of the constitution. Hence it brought together men of different creeds and varied ambitions: violent Socialists, discontented Radicals, clericals, business men, ambitious lawyers and pure adventurers. The flight of the General had destroyed their coherence. Though they had won nearly fifty seats, they had not formed a parliamentary group, but had dispersed, some to the Right, others to the Left. How could the revolutionary working-man, Gabriel, who wrote for *Le Cri du Peuple*, sit cheek by jowl with Jules Jaluzot, owner of the great Printemps store, who controlled a paper called *La Patrie*? How could Jules Delahaye, the passionate Catholic, tolerate Naquet, the sponsor of the divorce laws? They thus sat in the Chamber as *frondeurs*, active, abusive, seeking and using every opportunity to bring discredit on the Government.

2

There was one problem which Governments since 1886 had been loath to touch, that of the Church, a question loaded with dynamite.

The Catholic Church in France consists of two bodies: the secular Church with its hierarchy of archbishops, bishops, down to the parish priests; and the regulars, or religious Orders. The secular Church was regulated by the Concordat with the Papacy of 26 Messidor, An IX (10 September 1801). By that instrument the Church was recognised as an organic institution of the State. In compensation for the loss of Church property in the Revolution, salaries—very modest salaries—were paid to the clergy. On the other hand, the Church was not a free agent. Every appointment had to be agreed and confirmed by the Ministry of Public Worship (*Cultes*), of which the key man was not the Minister, a transient who moreover invariably held the portfolio in conjunction with that of a major Ministry, the Interior, Justice or Public Instruction, but the permanent civil-service Director. During the period with which this book is concerned, the Director was Charles Dumay, who is said to have been a Freemason, who was indubitably a loyal Republican, and whose test for promotion to a bishopric or archbishopric was the subservience of the candidate to the regime rather than to the Vatican. No nonsense about the ability of the candidate as a man of piety, of impeccable doctrine, as an organiser, weighed with him; for example, Monsignor

Bourret, Bishop of Rodez, was recommended by Leo XIII for eight archbishoprics in succession, only to be met by Dumay's veto: finally he was made a cardinal in compensation. Not only this: the Ministry treated the Church with rough discourtesy. Protests at legislation directed against the Church brought down the wrath of the State. Priests who meddled in politics, bishops who denounced some new method of applying the screw to Church property, were brought before lay tribunals and deprived of their salaries.

What Dumay did not, or did not care to, recognise was the fact that a Republican bishop, or even one correctly neutral, would have considerable trouble in controlling his diocese. He would be opposed, spied on and denounced in the local press by laymen who wished to use the Church for political ends, or by priests who thought Republicanism synonymous with atheism. His clergy would ignore his instructions. Even men as close to him as his own Vicar-General might intrigue against him. His clergy would ignore his instructions and perhaps involve themselves in political activity for their conscience' sake. As Monsignor Duchesne once said: "Every time a curé, a bishop, a decent churchman says to you, 'I acted as my conscience told me,' you may be sure the worthy man has just committed a gross blunder." As perhaps Dumay in the end discovered, a bishop who intended to be master in his own diocese, be he ever so hostile to the State, was more suited to the work than one who had become a Republican either from interest or conviction. In the last days of the Concordat the great archbishops and bishops were those who defended the rights of the Church.

Yet, although the Church was forbidden to meddle in politics, and on more than one occasion a successful parliamentary candidate was unseated on the grounds of clerical pressure on the electorate, a priest was entitled to vote and to sit in the Chamber or Senate. For many years the militant Bishop of Angers, Monsignor Freppel, represented Quimper in the Chamber. The Christian Democrat, the Abbé Lemire, sat for Hazebrouck, of which he was also the Maire, from 1893 to his death in 1928.

The religious Orders—the Dominicans, the Marists, the Oratorians and the rest—being, as the description implies, supranational organisations of the Church, each with its own head, responsible only to the Vatican, were not controlled either by the French State or the French Church, although each congregation was supposed to follow the directions of the bishop in whose diocese its house lay. The Concordat does not mention them. They had various functions: preaching, teaching, nursing and even trading. They were split up into religious houses, congregations of men or women living in common. According to the census of 1896, they numbered 52,567 individuals, of whom a little over six thousand were men. Although the majority were French, there were numerous foreigners among them. The Order most detested and most feared by the Republic was the very conservative Society of Jesus, which was believed to be the enemy of the regime, hostile to modern thought and to democracy. No doubt these fears were exaggerated, deriving from tradition: expulsions and re-entries of the Jesuits had taken place on more than one occasion, and to Michelet, that exuberant and deleterious historian, the Jesuits, with England, had been the foremost enemy. Only a few of the Orders were authorised: the Sulpicians, the Lazarists, and two missionary Orders, the Fathers of the Foreign Missions and the Brethren of the Christian Schools, which were looked on as valuable agents in empire-building.

The presence of the Orders was winked at in the early seventies, since they fulfilled functions for which laymen were not available in sufficient numbers. The trouble began on the score of education. Education was regulated by the Law of 15 March 1850, known as the Loi Falloux, which had placed priests on all the educational committees, hitherto monopolised by the University, the body that controlled all State teaching agents from the Rector of the Sorbonne down to the humblest lay primary-schoolteacher. During the Second Empire the Church had had the protection of the Government, but with the arrival of the Republic the Rationalists had reopened the attack. Their plan of campaign was to laïcise education, then to expel the Orders, and finally to disestablish the

Church. There was some case for expelling clerical schoolteachers, but Gambetta and Ferry founded their opposition to them, not purely on the grounds of inefficiency, but on the charge that they were anti-democratic, royalist and superstitious. As the most ardent of Ferry's henchmen, Paul Bert, had said: "Bismarck made war on the Church. We will make it on God." Such declarations could not but create opposition. "The unpardonable stupidity of our Republicans," wrote Paul Cambon, "had been to combat the clergy, not in the name of the interests of the State, of public order, but in the name of free thought and positivism. . . . The clergy is thus in a position of legitimate defence when it fights the Republic, and the Republic does not persecute it from political motives, but for philosophical reasons" (19, 376).

Two things stood in the way. Many politicians, especially in the Senate, resented the attempt to drop religious teaching from the State schools, while, on a more material plane, there were not enough lay teachers to fill the posts designated by Ferry's legislation between 1880 and 1886. The number of State teachers between 1886 and 1896 rose only from a hundred and fifteen thousand to a hundred and thirty-three thousand. A half-hearted attempt to expel the members of the unauthorised Orders in 1880 was a failure. The Orders were merely scotched, and continued to exist: the women's Orders were not even touched. Moreover, the Catholics riposted by maintaining out of their own resources the so-called free schools and the five Catholic universities which had been brought into being under the Law of 12 July 1875. The number of teachers in these private establishments rose from fifty-eight thousand to a hundred and sixteen thousand between 1881 and 1896.

Ministers fought back with financial and legal weapons. The State refused to recognise degrees granted by Catholic universities. If a pious municipality voted a subsidy for a Church school, the Préfet disallowed it. Nevertheless about 1900 the failure of laïcisation was admitted, when it was shown that nearly a third of the school population was being taught in the free Catholic schools.

Similar attempts to get rid of the nursing Orders were no more successful. Economical municipalities could not, or would not, find the money to replace the nuns, and where the reform was carried out, as in certain hospitals in Paris, the substitution of untrained and ill-paid laywomen was soon found to be a failure.

Thus, through the eighties and nineties, a guerilla war between the anti-clericals and the clergy dragged on in a spirit of nagging intolerance, showing no sign of finality. Year after year Radical Deputies produced motions to abolish the Public Worship budget, or to withdraw the Vatican embassy, or to disestablish the Church. Year after year their motions were defeated.

3

From 1878, the year of his elevation to the Triple Tiara, Pope Leo XIII had set himself the task of discovering how the authority of the Catholic Faith could come to terms with a contemporary society in which the ancient beliefs were being almost daily challenged by biologists from one side and by Biblical exegetists from the other. It was not the facts that must be met, but the philosophical hypotheses developed from those facts. The three dangers for the Church were Modernism, Positivism or Rationalism, and Socialism. With Modernism Leo temporised, admitting the need for Biblical studies, but warning the scholars not to go too far: adaptation in reason would sum up his policy. For Socialism he had other prescriptions. Before his accession, as has been noted, attempts had been made to come to grips with the social problem of the condition of the poor by a group of French Catholics, who, until the beginnings of revolutionary Socialism in the early eighties, alone recognised its existence. In May 1891 appeared the encyclical *Rerum Novarum*, which has been called the charter of the workers under Catholicism. While condemning Collectivism and approving the maintenance of private property, the Pope claimed for the working classes fair wages, decent treatment by employers, State guarantees of welfare, and the right to form peaceful, non-revolutionary, associations. From these beginnings was to grow the Christian Democratic movement, of which the heir to-day is the Mouvement Républicain Populaire.

The third danger—Rationalism—had to be fought to the death, and that could be accomplished only by the Church making its weight felt in the State. The Republic must be captured.

As early as 1881, by the encyclical *Diuturnum*, Leo had warned Governments that war against the Church would eventually lead to war on the State, and he expressly declared that any form of regime, democratic or otherwise, that was compatible with justice, was not repugnant to Catholic doctrine. In 1885 he said much the same with even greater clarity. In that year he dissuaded the prominent Catholic Deputy, Albert de Mun, from forming a Catholic political party, and he abstained from meddling in French politics. The discredit brought to the Royalist cause by its alliance in 1889 with the Boulangist Movement indicated to the Vatican that the hour had come to advance to a more positive policy. In January 1890 yet another encyclical reaffirmed the political neutrality of the Papacy. Shortly afterwards, on his own initiative, the strenuous Archbishop of Carthage and Algiers, Cardinal Lavigerie, sounded President Carnot and several leading Ministers as to some kind of composition with the Church in return for an acceptance of the Republic. He then saw the Pope and attempted to persuade him to make a declaration in this sense. Leo seems to have resisted, but allowed Lavigerie to proceed as he thought fit, provided he did not in any way commit the Vatican. Thus, in November of the same year, on the occasion of the French fleet anchoring at Algiers, Lavigerie, at a banquet to the officers, toasted the Republic and as good as declared that the Church accepted the Republican regime. The incident was given wide publicity. The Royalists were aghast and the Comte d'Haussonville, whose family had in the past been notorious for changing its coat with each change of regime, claimed that, with all respect for His Holiness, this was a political matter for laymen and that the Royalists were not prepared to follow the advice. Very few of the French bishops publicly approved the Cardinal's action, and some even went so far as to invite Leo to disavow the untimely words. For the moment the Pope held his peace. On the Republican side, the reception of Lavigerie's speech was one of distrust: it was not believed that reconciliation boded any good to the Republic: two authoritarian regimes could not work side by side in amity.

During the year following the Algiers banquet, numerous agitated emissaries, both lay and clerical, travelled from France to Rome. To all of them the Pope made it clear that the Church could no longer attach itself to the moribund body of monarchism and was sooner or later bound to cut itself loose. Nevertheless, the French episcopate was divided. In January 1892 five French cardinals addressed a letter to the Pope, setting forth the grievances of the Church in France, particularly that of the cult of godless education. In spite of this, a month later, having given a special interview to Ernest Judet of the *Petit Journal*, the Pope issued, on February 16, the encyclical *Inter innumeras sollicitudines*, which in effect reaffirmed that all forms of government which pursued the common weal were good and should be accepted: that the Republic was said to be anti-Christian, but a distinction must be made between constitutions and legislation. Let Catholics bring to power men who within the constitution would make good laws. Thus what was to be known as the Ralliement was set on foot.

Two days later Freycinet's Ministry was defeated in the Chamber on a bill to regulate the standing of the religious congregations. For the Opposition, Clemenceau had reasserted the anti-clerical thesis that no compromise was possible with Rome. "There is one thing you cannot do, bring the Catholic Church to you except within the measure of its interest as a dominant power. . . . Because it is placed higher, because it sees further, because in the blink of an eye it can survey the vast stretch of a long history and that history is subsumed in the words:—the Church is nothing if it is not everything. . . . You say a hand is held out. Put your own in it: it will be so firmly held that you can never draw it back. . . . You will be the prisoner of the Church. The Church will never be in your power." Clemenceau was in fact voicing the thoughts of Leo XIII.

The Ralliement was greeted by the Right with mixed feelings. The older and more faithful men did not openly reject the Pope's counsel; they simply did not rally. In aristocratic circles His Holiness was dubbed "the old Jacobin." But among the younger men—those who had seen the successive failures of their elders over twenty years, their lack of political sense, their hopeless frivolity—there was a feeling that the experiment should be tried, that a Catholic party which put religion first was a worthy foundation. The leaders were Jacques Piou, who had long been the lay mouthpiece of Cardinal Lavigerie, and Albert de Mun, the Deputy for Pontivy. Among those who joined were a number of Deputies, conservative business men, Prince d'Arenberg of the Suez Corporation, Schneider of Le Creusot, Grandmaison the shipowner, the ex-Boulangist Jaluzot of Le Printemps, and with them the Baron Mackau, who had been the Conservative spokesman in the conversations with Boulanger and who was now disabused: "One has to act for [the Royalists], think for them and pay for them." Simultaneously there came forward among the clergy a few audacious priests who called themselves Christian Democrats.

In contrast to the refusals of the Royalists, some of the older members of the Republicans welcomed the Pope's counsel. They looked at Socialism rising on the Left of the Radicals and at the more violent Anarchism, and saw in the new group a useful ally But the Radicals did not disarm. They could put no trust in the Church. "You accept the Republic?" cried Léon Bourgeois to the Ralliés at Nantes; "well and good. Do you accept the Revolution?"

Since every movement, and particularly a political *volte-face*, requires a press, the Pope entrusted the propaganda for the Ralliement to the Augustin Fathers of the Assumption, an Order founded about 1850, which had built up over a number of years a great periodical-publishing business known as the Bonne Presse. The reasons for this choice were that the Order had been founded for the particular purpose of "going to the people." The Assumptionists had been one of the main founders of the series of spectacular pilgrimages organised in France following the Franco-Prussian War. After some success with a crude and simple weekly, *Le Pélerin*, the Fathers in 1883 launched a daily paper, *La Croix*. They were possessed of excellent business sense: "The board," wrote Father Lecanuet (71, 226), "neglected no means either

natural or supernatural. . . . Quite early they persuaded the curés
that they ought to become not merely subscribers, but apostles of
the Press." They printed local supplements and formed local committees, which would later be transformed into electoral agencies
under the title of "Justice-Egalité." *La Croix* was not what might
be called a judicious publication. The members of the Order were
scarcely intellectuals of the calibre of the Dominicans or Jesuits,
having been recruited in the main from the sons of peasants, but
they understood what they were about. *La Croix* was orthodox,
clerical, narrow, suspicious, exaggerated and violent: but its con-
scienceless brutality was effective. Father Vincent de Paul Bailly,
who wrote over the nom de plume of The Monk, was better served
by his strong will, simple childlike faith and audacious zeal than by
such intellectual subtleties as were distilled by the fashionable
preachers of Notre Dame. On the other hand, as an instrument of
the Church, the Assumptionists were dangerous. They did not understand the problem of Leo XIII, and they hated the policy of reconciliation with the Republic. Hence, while *La Croix* purported
to serve Vatican policy, the Fathers in fact opposed and did all they
could to undermine the Ralliement. "The purely clerical character
which the paper adopted prevented it from penetrating those
circles which should have been conquered or led back to the
Church. . . . [The Assumptionists] did not stigmatise only the anti-
religious laws, which was their right and their duty; they adopted
an aggressive attitude, throwing doubt and suspicion everywhere,
ridiculing the highest of public offices, carrying their hatred of the
enemies of the Church to the point of exasperation" (71, 231–33).
So violent did they become against the institutions of the Republic
that they increased the hatreds they were supposed to allay, with
the result that eventually they became the scarecrows used by the
anti-clericals to demonstrate to agnostics, to Protestants and to
Jews what Catholicism really stood for.

4

In the autumn of 1892 there came to light one of those scandals
which provided the enemies of the Republic with ammunition. For

long the finances of the Panama Canal Company had given cause
for anxiety. Founded in 1880, with inadequate capital, in the hey-
day of a boom period, on the strength of the reputation of de
Lesseps, the constructor of the successful Suez Canal, the Company had been struggling for years. Little progress had been made,
conditions at Panama were known to be appalling, and more and
more money had been sunk in the enterprise. Since the original
flotation, money had become tight: fresh capital was not readily
available and, since 1884, the public had shown reluctance to take
up further share issues. In 1888 Parliament had voted permission
for the Company, now in desperate circumstances, to issue what
amounted to a lottery loan of 720 million francs: but once more
investors held off, and little more than a third of the issue was subscribed. Finally in 1889 the Company failed and was put into liquidation by the Seine tribunal. The liquidation was slow. The share-
holders were suspicious and angry. It was not until January 1891
that the Procureur-Général, Quesnay de Beaurepaire, on receiving
the liquidator's report, laid the case before the courts. The examining magistrate took his time over the highly involved evidence,
and it was only in September 1892 that Quesnay was in a position
to ask leave of the Minister of Justice to prosecute the Panama
directors for false pretences and malversation of funds.

At this juncture, primed by certain disappointed financiers, and
perhaps also by the members of the Panama Board in the hope of
securing Government protection, Edouard Drumont, owner and
editor of the *Libre Parole*, started a series of articles accusing
Deputies and Senators of accepting bribes to vote the loan of 1888.

5

The French press of the eighties and nineties was turbulent and
undisciplined. Censored and dragooned by the Second Empire,
Opposition journalists had gradually devised methods of distilling
the subtle venom, which superficially appeared innocence itself.
Partly freed from restraint in 1871, owners, editors and contributors had campaigned for complete freedom, which they succeeded in winning by the Press Law of 1881. Of its many articles,

the vital clause was that which put actions for defamation to trial by jury. Paris juries were drawn largely from the stratum of small shopkeepers and artisans and were infinitely persuadable through what was often tantamount to press blackmail. There were of course the highly conservative leading papers, *Le Temps* and *Le Journal des Débats*, followed by the more militant political organs, Gambetta's *République Française*, the liberal-minded *Siècle* and the Radical *Rappel* and *Radical*. But below these lay a range of bitterly polemical journals of opinion, offering not news but comment. These were of all colours, Royalist, Bonapartist, Boulangist, Radical, Socialist, Anarchist, anti-parliamentarian, revolutionary.

In the eighties the most violent, most scurrilous and wittiest had been *l'Intransigeant*, owned and edited by Victor-Henri, Comte de Rochefort, who long before the days of Maurras and Léon Daudet made a feature of personal abuse. As owner of the *Lanterne*, Rochefort had been one of the terrors of the Second Empire and had gone to jail. Mixed up in the Commune, he had been arrested and only narrowly avoided being shot. Instead, he was deported to New Caledonia, whence he had escaped within three months. For these grievances he had never forgiven the Republicans. When after the amnesty of July 1880 he had come back to Paris, he had founded *l'Intransigeant* and attacked the regime with unfailing hatred, sparing none. His chief enemy had been Jules Ferry, and undoubtedly his campaign in 1887 was one of the factors in the defeat of that statesman for the Presidency of the Republic. Rochefort had been one of Boulanger's stoutest supporters, but when the movement failed he had fled to England, whence he continued to direct his paper. However, the years abroad had meant loss of touch. Though the abuse of politicians did not abate, the paper had grown stale. *L'Intran* was losing circulation to a newcomer with as ready and as bitter a pen as Rochefort's, and what Rochefort had never possessed, a creed. This was Edouard Drumont.

Drumont, in spite of the accusations of Socialists and others that he was a renegade Jew, a Hans Pfefferkorn, was in fact of peasant stock from the Ardennes. A small man with thick lips, a beard and

short-sighted eyes gleaming through thick spectacles, he was a
widely read and forceful writer of considerable humour, but a
monomaniac. He had once been in the employ of the Pereire
brothers, the Saint-Simonien railway financiers who in the fifties
and sixties had waged a campaign against Rothschild and been defeated. Drumont, on the death of Isaac Pereire, had written a
sympathetic *éloge* of his patron. In 1886 he had suddenly sprung
into notoriety with the publication of two volumes, *La France
Juive*, a violent polemic against the Jews, Jewish finance and the
social evils the author believed to derive from this source. But anyone who has read through these two tedious volumes, which include
all the mediæval anti-semitic legends, will be struck by the fact
that the contemporary Jews attacked are the very few prominent
ones, particularly the Rothschild family, and that the most
venomous assaults are made on the aristocratic Christians who
batten on Jewish finance.

The Jews in fact formed only a tiny fraction of the French population. Outside Paris there were two main groups: the old Papal
Jews of the Comtat Venaissin, and the descendants of the Portu-
guese exiles in Bordeaux, Toulouse and Nantes, both Sephardic,
long established and wholly assimilated. Most of the originally
Eastern Jews, the Askenazim, had been in Alsace, and save for
those who had come over to France after 1870 were now German
citizens. In Alsace alone was there any feeling of anti-semitism,
and that had existed before the Revolution. In 1880 there had
been not more than eighty thousand Jews in the whole of France,
of whom about half were in Paris.

Then two events occurred which did something to create anti-
semitic sentiment. After the murder of Alexander II in 1881 there
was considerable unrest in the Russian Empire, which led first to
anti-Jewish measures and then to a series of pogroms in Poland and
the Ukraine. A large Jewish exodus began, chiefly to the United
States, but refugees into Roumania and the Austrian Empire
found themselves unwelcome and a number pressed on westward.
In the mass their numbers were not great—by 1900 there were
less than two hundred thousand Jews in the country—but the

immigrants caused the Jewish committees in Paris anxiety. The Eastern European Jews, who spoke only Yiddish, were conspicuous and not easily assimilated.

The second event was the crash of the Lyonnais financial house, the Union Générale, in the first months of 1882. Founded in 1877 by one Eugène Bontoux, who had made a fortune in Austria and for a short time had been a Monarchist Deputy, the Union had been widely advertised as a Catholic corporation, to which the *bien-pensant* investor should entrust his money. Partly owing to the crookedness of the directors, partly to the superior strategy of its major enemy the Rothschild house, the Union, after a few months of spectacular boom, blew up in January 1882, with grave consequences for French public finance. How far this affected groups beyond the aristocratic and clerical circles is difficult to estimate, but undoubtedly the failure brought down a number of mushroom companies into which modest investors had put their savings.

Nevertheless, there was little substantial anti-semitism in France. In Paris, where the Jews formed a tenth of those occupied in law and finance—a high proportion in relation to their numbers—it existed. But it was on the whole confined to high society, where according to Brunetière (18, 428) it was more a paradox of conversation than a problem. Indeed, with so many families—Breteuil, Richelieu, Gramont, Rochechouart, Wagram, Faucigny-Lucinge—marrying into Jewish families, it was difficult to take anti-semitism seriously.

For Drumont however this was the very point. It was not the Jewish religion he attacked; he never insulted a rabbi. It was the Jewish financier—the Rothschilds, the Ephrussi, the Bambergers, the Cahens d'Anvers, the finance-capitalists—whom he hated, with as deep a fury as Lenin, for having destroyed what he believed to be the ancient French virtues and values: loyalty, religion, responsibility, modesty, work and thrift.

La France Juive had an immense success, which he had followed with other books, the best of which is perhaps *La Dernière Bataille*, a devastating exposure of the horrors of the Panama Canal area. In 1889, with the aid of an impoverished and athletic aristocrat, the Marquis de Morès, he founded the Anti-Semitic League, composed largely of youths from the slaughterhouses of La Villette. In April 1892, having made a great deal of money, he launched an anti-semitic daily paper, the *Libre Parole*.[1] Within a month, as a result of his attacks on Jewish officers in the Army, there took place a number of widely-publicised duels, in one of which Morès killed a Jewish officer, Captain Mayer, by means believed to be despicably unfair.[2] Now, in September, by a series of devastating articles, Drumont brought about the Panama crisis.

6

What was unknown at the outbreak of the Panama crisis was that for some time an unadvertised and complex battle had been going on between two Jewish company promoters, the Baron Jacques de Reinach and Dr Cornelius Herz, both French citizens of foreign origin. Reinach had acted for the Panama Company and had used much of the money from loans not only to bribe journalists to puff the Company, but also to sweeten his persuasions of parliamentarians to vote the loan of 1888. Reinach, a somewhat amateurish rascal of extravagant tastes, had become indebted to the more accomplished scoundrel Herz, who had used blackmail not only to screw money out of his debtor, but also to secure some evidence, by no means reliable, against a number of Deputies and Senators. Drumont and others were now on Reinach's track, as well as on that of the takers of bribes.

The crisis came with the reopening of the Chambers on November

[1] The Dreyfusards claimed that the capital had been provided by the Jesuits. Their ground for the accusation was that Odelin, who had been the lay administrator of the Jesuit school in the Rue des Postes, was an original partner in the *Libre Parole*. But Odelin had resigned from the school's board in 1890, and further, in 1894, he disagreed on policy with Drumont and resigned from the paper. Furthermore, though Drumont was a Catholic, he was by no means a clerical (51, 114 and 124).

[2] Later, Morès, in order to pay a gaming debt, involved Drumont, who seems to have loved him like a son, with one of the Jewish figureheads in the Panama scandal, Cornelius Herz. Morès eventually undertook an expedition on the Tunisian frontier, where in 1896 he was murdered by his escort, a crime cheerfully attributed to the British secret service. The Anti-Semitic League fell into the hands of a somewhat shady businessman, Jules-Napoleon Guérin, who had been one of Morès's seconds in the duel with Mayer.

19, when it was revealed that the President of the Chamber of
Deputies, Floquet, Prime Minister during the days of Boulanger,
had taken three hundred thousand francs from the Panama
Company in order to fight the Boulangist movement.

On the same day, Reinach, half mad with anxiety, had, in the
presence of Clemenceau and Rouvier, made an *ad hominem* appeal
to Herz to restrain the pursuing journalists. Herz had replied that
he was powerless. That night Reinach died either from a stroke or
by self-administered poison: the exact cause of death has never
been cleared up. When the news broke, the police for some un-
avowed, perhaps unavowable, reason neglected for three days to
have the body examined or to seal up the Baron's rooms and
property. During this time the Baron's nephew and son-in-law,
Joseph Reinach,[1] a Republican Deputy, had the free run of his
uncle's papers and appears to have destroyed a number, which one
must believe to have been compromising for members of the party.
This incident had certain repercussions on later events. Simultaneously, Herz, apprised of his enemy's death, flitted to England,
where he took up his residence at Bournemouth and proclaimed
himself to be dying.

Further exploration of these sooty corridors is unnecessary.
The point of the melodrama lies in the fact that almost all those
publicly accused of taking bribes were Republicans, hated alike
by the Conservatives, the Boulangists and the Left. To complicate
the issue, within the Republican ranks there was little love lost
between the veterans of 1877 and 1881, and the newer and younger
members such as Deschanel, Poincaré, Barthou and Jonnart, who
firmly supported a motion for enquiry into the accusations against
the members of their own group. The Prime Minister, Emile
Loubet, although in no way connected with the charges, considered it his duty to circumscribe the trouble. He failed, was defeated, and made way for the Right-wing Republican, Ribot, who
succeeded in holding the fort until the worst of the trouble had
blown over. It may be that Clemenceau intended a shattering cam-

[1] This is the prominent Dreyfusist, whose history of the Dreyfus case
(Bibliography, 47) is often quoted throughout this book.

paign against the Republican Centre. If so, he was surprised before he could mount it.

Among the Boulangist Deputies sat Paul Déroulède. He had fought very gallantly in the war of 1870–71, and after its conclusion had produced a volume or two of not very good patriotic poems calling for a renewal of the battle, *Chants du Soldat*. He had been one of the promoters of rifle and gymnastic clubs all over the country during the years when *revanche* was still considered a possibility, and had been taken up by Gambetta and Jules Ferry, who had placed him on one of the committees of the Ministry of Public Instruction. In May 1882 he founded the Ligue des Patriotes, but when the *détente* with Germany came in 1884, he turned against Ferry. On the appearance of Boulanger, he had thrown himself and his patriots into the movement. In 1889 he was elected as a Boulangist Deputy in the Charente, but his League had already been dissolved by the Government. Like all Boulangists, he hated Clemenceau and hoped to destroy him. In the Chamber he accused his antagonist of being a client of Herz, who was a shareholder in Clemenceau's paper, *Justice*, and of having procured the promotion of the blackmailer to the highest rank in the Legion of Honour. Clemenceau called Déroulède a liar and met him in a bloodless duel, but the accusation, of which only a minute part had any foundation, stuck. Clemenceau had now become a liability to the Radicals.

The accusations of parliamentary corruption were found to have little root—only one member, who was rash enough to confess, went to jail. But the rumours stirred up were effective, although a second attack on Clemenceau in June 1893, by Millevoye, a Boulangist Deputy, with the charge, based on obviously forged papers, that he was in the pay of the British Foreign Office, was swept away in a gale of laughter. A number of Members of Parliament disappeared from politics, or at least retired into the background. From now onwards the younger men began to come forward.

7

Although the Boulangists had done their utmost to use the Panama scandals to agitate public opinion in view of the approaching elections in the autumn of 1893, they had worsened their chances by their support of Millevoye's foolish attack on Clemenceau. Those who profited from their excesses were the Socialists, who themselves had a grievance to exploit. The Paris Bourse de Travail—an institution partly labour-exchange, partly working-men's club—had been closed, chiefly because it had fallen under Socialist control.

The elections were held at the end of August and beginning of September. In spite of all the troubles of the past twelve months it was comparatively easy for the Government, now headed by Charles Dupuy, Ribot's successor, to control constituencies of indeterminate colour, especially because, as Minister of the Interior, Dupuy had inherited the hard-trained Préfets of Constans. The minor Boulangists were swept out; at most sixteen came back. The Right had split over the Ralliement. Both Conservatives and Ralliés preferred a Republican to each other. Although some thirty Ralliés were returned, neither Piou nor de Mun was elected. The Radicals gained seats, but many of these were in fact Republicans changing their coats to the electoral wind, but not their politics. The new feature was the appearance of over fifty members calling themselves Socialists, eighteen from Paris, of whom sixteen were new. True, the Socialists were split into eight mutually suspicious groups, but among them were men of talent: Jean Jaurès, once the hope of the Republican centre; Jules Guesde, the disciple of Karl Marx; Vaillant, the successor of the old revolutionary, Blanqui; and the 'silver-tongued' Viviani.

One figure had disappeared, Clemenceau. His constituency—Draguignan in the Var—was invaded by Boulangists who promoted several Radical candidates against him. The Socialists of the district asked advice of Jaurès, who told them to support someone other than the Radical leader. After a bitter fight, Clemenceau was defeated, to the delight of the Republicans and to the less exultant satisfaction of the Radicals he had so long driven and bullied. They hoped they had seen the last of him.

8

As soon as Parliament opened in November 1893, the conservative colour of the new Chamber was shown by the election of Jean Casimir-Perier to the Presidency of that House. Nevertheless, all was not well with the Government. Charles Dupuy was not liked. He came from the barren country round Le Puy and had made his way upwards in the teaching profession. In politics he had been a colourless Republican; as Prime Minister he had not displayed any imaginative qualities. An Auvergnat, he was credited with all the qualities of that rapacious people: a burly man with a rough beard, he was said to resemble in physique and cunning a Balkan peasant. The chief reason for his being at the head of the Government seems to have been the desire to avoid the only alternative, Constans, the strong man of 1889–93. Dupuy's Ministry, which had survived since April, had in it a group of Radicals, of whom the chief was Peytral, the Minister of Finance and the champion of income-tax. These Radicals were uneasy colleagues. On November 25, on a minor matter, they withdrew and the Cabinet fell to pieces. Dupuy, on being challenged as to whether a Government existed, failed to carry the Chamber and resigned.

After the usual consultations with the Presidents of the two Chambers, Carnot called on Casimir-Perier to form a Government. Jean Casimir-Perier, now forty-five, was the son of one of the conservative founders of the Republic, and the grandson of Louis-Philippe's famous Minister. He came from the highest rank of the bourgeoisie; he was a hereditary director of the great Anzin coal-mine syndicate, one of the richest companies in France, to whose board were elected the most prominent men in the Republic. He was wealthy, he was conservative, he was independent. He had shown his independence by resigning his seat when the claimants to the throne of France were expelled in 1886. He was a member of that group of young and ardent Republicans, known as "the Family," guided and encouraged by Léon Say and the other members of the old Left Centre. Physically, he was a broad man of middle height, with drooping dark moustaches and a curiously flat-topped head.

He soon made up his Cabinet. He appointed his personal friend Burdeau to the Ministry of Finance, and three old Gambettists—Spuller, Raynal and Antonin-Dubost—to other ministries. He himself took the Foreign Office, while to the War Office he appointed General Auguste Mercier. The new Cabinet met the Chamber on December 3, and on the same day Charles Dupuy was elected to the presidency over the Radical leader, Brisson. Three days later the Anarchist outrages reached a new level, when a bomb was thrown from the gallery among the Deputies. Only one, the Abbé Lemire, was wounded, and the sitting continued. But on December 11 the Government brought forward a bill for the repression of crimes against the State, including the penalty of imprisonment for the propagation of Anarchism, together with the extension of the ordinary criminal law to Anarchists, hitherto treated as political prisoners, and the tightening up of the control over the manufacture of explosives. Violently and noisily attacked by the Socialists, the "lois scélérates" were passed by a huge majority.

Early in the New Year, 1894, the Cabinet was given a moral tonic by the news that, after many months of negotiation, Alexander III of Russia had at last initialled a secret military convention with France, which converted the somewhat platonic treaty of 1891 into an active alliance. Although the agreement was kept secret in accordance with the Russian request, the fact of its existence, though not its terms, slowly leaked out during the year and was welcomed by the great majority of publicists, who saw in the convention the lightening of the perpetual German menace, some going so far as to look on it as a pointer towards the early recovery of Alsace-Lorraine.

Casimir-Perier's Ministry came through the first four months of 1894 without difficulties. It fell on May 22 quite unexpectedly, on the question of whether State industrial employees should be given leave from their duties to attend trade union conferences.

The question of the relation of State servants to unionism had
escaped the notice of the legislature in the discussion of the law of
1884 which sanctioned the formation of trade unions. Jonnart,
Minister of Public Works, was opposed to the State railwaymen
belonging to the unions. In spite of its conservatism, the Chamber declined to follow the Minister; the Government was defeated
and Casimir-Perier resigned. A week later Charles Dupuy returned
as Prime Minister. With him he brought back several members of
his previous Cabinet: Guérin, Minister of Justice, and Poincaré,
moving him from Public Instruction to Finance. As before, he himself took the Interior, while to the Foreign Office, he appointed an
official, the Political Director of the Foreign Office, Gabriel Hanotaux. Beyond these, he invited several men of future note, Louis
Barthou to the Ministry of Public Works, Théophile Delcassé to
the Colonial Office, George Leygues to Public Instruction and
Félix Faure, a civilian, to the Ministry of Marine. Of the Casimir-
Perier Cabinet, the only important survivor was General Mercier.

This was on May 30. Less than a month later Anarchism struck
its final and worst blow, when an Italian, Caserio, stabbed the
President of the Republic, Carnot, during a ceremony at Lyon.
Carnot died an hour later.

In accordance with constitutional procedure, both Chambers
were immediately summoned to meet in National Assembly at Versailles on June 26. A group of conservative Republicans approached
Casimir-Perier, and after a long argument persuaded him, much
against his will, to stand. At the first poll he was elected. Of the
881 votes he was given 451, against 195 to Brisson, and 97 to
Dupuy, who had rashly stood. When the result was known,
Drumont, who had been attacking the new President, took refuge
in Brussels, whence he continued to direct the *Libre Parole*.

As soon as the new President was installed, Dupuy, according to
convention, resigned. The two men were not on good terms; they
had little in common, perhaps because of the unbridgeable gulf,
noted by Barrès, between heirs and scholarship boys. More
probably Casimir-Perier, having been persuaded by his friends to
accept the position, intended to bring the Presidency back to the

position of power it had held before 1877, when MacMahon surrendered to the Republicans the direction of policy and proclaimed
himself, as President, to be without responsibility. Casimir-
Perier, having accepted the office, had no intention of being a self-
effacing figurehead, as Carnot had been. Therefore he unwisely
accepted Dupuy's resignation, and asked his friend Burdeau to
form a Government. Burdeau, already a sick man—he died in
December—refused, whereupon Casimir-Perier recalled Dupuy.
Dupuy accepted the invitation to continue in office, but he may in
return for the snub have decided to make the life of the new President as disagreeable as possible. Even if he had not, it is almost
certain that he must have done so as soon as he saw the reaction to
the Presidential message to Parliament. In this Casimir-Perier did
not fail to tell the Chambers that they needed to reform themselves.
Both Senate and Chamber resented his vigorous criticism. Dupuy
saw that he could ignore Casimir-Perier without imperilling his
position with the legislature, and proceeded to do so. He saw him
as little as possible; he did not discuss current affairs with him; he
allowed the Extreme Left considerable licence in their attacks on
the large shareholder of the Anzin Company. Moreover, he permitted his Foreign Minister to snub the President. Although the
President was constitutionally entitled to see Foreign Office papers
and to discuss them at formal Cabinet meetings, Gabriel Hanotaux
refused to disclose documents, on the ground that the President's
entourage at the Elysée could not be trusted. Casimir-Perier should
have insisted on his resignation; he did not. Worse was to follow.

CHAPTER TWO

The Background

II: THE ARMY

IN spite of the overwhelming and rapid defeat of 1870, the Army remained both popular and respected. There was its long and glorious tradition from the days when it was said that no war could occur without the presence of the French, through the great period when the armies of the First Republic had overrun Europe—"*O Soldats de l'An II! O guerres! O épopées!*"—through the Napoleonic epoch, the Algerian conquest, the Crimea, Magenta and Solferino and finally, even in defeat, the memories of Mars-la-Tour and Patay. And there was the fact that at least two men in three had served in its ranks for three years and upwards, not only plebeians but also bourgeois and aristocrats. Few Frenchmen doubted that in the rooms of the War Office in the Rue Saint-Dominique the staff of the "silent service," *le grand silencieux*, were preparing the plans which in one invincible sweep would drive the Germans from the lost provinces.

On the other hand, the politicians of the Republic were torn between the popular sentiment, which as Frenchmen they shared, and the distrust they felt as Republicans. Republican histories showed a professional army which had supported Charles X in 1830, had shot down the workers in June 1848, had gone over to Louis Napoleon in 1851 against the Second Republic, and had massacred the Communards of Paris in 1871. They believed the Army to be a political instrument; they were wrong in their reading. The history of the Army shows it to have been non-political. Every time it had been drawn into civil crises, the officers had done no more than obey the orders of their highest authority, the Minister of War. That was why in 1851 Louis Napoleon on the eve of the *coup d'état* had placed at the head of the War Office the single

37

General on whom he could rely, Saint-Arnaud, "an obscure brigadier-general, whose *condottiere* spirit was unembarrassed by scruples" (75, 141). He knew that the War Minister would be obeyed.

For their suspicions the Republicans had themselves to thank. The legislature of 1877–81 had insisted on the purge of the non-Republican elements in the civil service, and had given the vacant places to their friends and parasites. That of 1881–85 did much the same with the judiciary. It had not become impossible, but it was certainly difficult, for a member of a Royalist family to enter the civil service. "Former pupil of the Jesuits, former abjuring member of a Republican committee, former active, though none the less sceptical, member of a Boulangist committee, my unworthiness seemed solidly established. And how heavily charged my ancestry: a great-grandfather shot at Quiberon and a great-grand-uncle dead in the September massacres." Thus M. de Saint-Aulaire on his attempts to sit—only to sit—the examinations for the Foreign Office (49, 13).

The single institution on which the Republicans had not laid their sacrilegious hands was the Army. For one thing, as in all armies in the late nineteenth century, the pay was abominable, while, with continuing peace, promotion was slow. It was thus not a career for the ambitious, but it could be one for those to whom the other departments of State were closed. Therefore the professional officers who had entered through Saint-Cyr tended to be drawn from what in England would be called the county families. Many Saint-Cyriens came from homes untouched by the ideas of the Great Revolution. It is noteworthy that after the Revolution of 1830, and again after the *coup d'état* of 1851, the sons of many famous military families no longer entered the Army, refusing to serve the usurpers. It was only after 1870 that they reappeared, possibly to some extent influenced by the decline in income from rents caused by the agricultural slump at the end of the seventies.

Most of these officers had been educated in Catholic, not in State schools, but this no more implies that they were devout than an education at Westminster or Winchester implies that an English boy is a classicist and a royalist. They were believing but not necessarily practising Catholics. Interested publicists were later to take up the theme that the General Staff was Jesuit-trained and controlled: but as the Comte de Mun wrote in *The Times* (17 January 1899), "Of the hundred and eighty officers who last year composed the General Staff, there were hardly as many as nine or ten belonging to that category." Major Ducassé, giving evidence at the final revision of the Dreyfus case (8, II, 347–48), said: "They say I acted under the orders of Father du Lac. Odd. I was not at a Jesuit school, but at a lay one. Though I am in fact a Catholic born, I am a free-thinker. I am so little clerical that I married a Protestant. Since the formalities of the Church are irksome, I married in a Protestant *temple*. I have one daughter, and she's a Protestant. That's how clerical I am."

It remains true that the officers were almost all nominal Catholics. The infantry and cavalry were less exposed to alien influences than the artillery and engineer officers, who had passed through the Polytechnic and rubbed shoulders with civilians and Republicans, and, generally speaking, did not reach the highest commands. In spite of the fact that a number of men well known to be Republicans did in fact reach the highest rank in the Army—Divisional General —it would be true to say that as a whole the officer class, particularly in the highest ranks, was at best neutral towards the regime. A convinced Republican officer was an anomaly. Almost alone, General Galliffet, whose birth, gallantry and competence were undeniable, made no bones about his loyalty to the Republic; but Galliffet was notoriously eccentric.

The technical cause of this state of affairs was the system of promotion. This was regulated by Soult's Law of 1832, by which, up to the rank of Commandant (Major), two-thirds of the vacancies were filled through seniority, but above that rank half the promotions were by selection carried out by the Classification Commission of the corps commanders under the authority of the Minister of War. The Minister up to 1888 was invariably himself a general, hence no difficulties arose. From 1888 to 1893 the Ministry was occupied by de Freycinet, a civilian who to all intents abdicated

from his control over the senior appointments. Gradually and very
naturally, the classification commission tended to select men of
their own way of thinking. Thus, by the nineties, the successive
changes in the upper hierarchy had produced on the whole a group
of conservative senior officers, in which the Republicans were a tiny
minority. At the height of the controversy over the Dreyfus case
and after, the politicos and press of the Left were to talk of a
"clerico-military plot"; but the situation had a simpler and far
more realistic cause, merely that like calls to like, and men elect
to their clubs men of their own kind. In spite of the legends,
clericalism played a minimal part in the promotions.

The officer cadre was not, however, filled wholly by those who
had passed through the military schools of Saint-Cyr and the Polytechnic. Owing to the reluctance of Republican families to send
their sons into the Army, it was necessary to draw men from the
ranks. Before the Franco-Prussian War this had been done by
selection; but in the reforming zeal of the seventies there had been
created the infantry school at Saint-Maixent, the cavalry school at
Saumur and the artillery school at Versailles, from which proven
non-commissioned officers were promoted. By the nineties these
schools provided possibly a third of the officer corps, but since these
officers as a rule lacked private incomes or social connections, and
moreover had already spent some years in the ranks, they could
scarcely hope to rise high. (A small and variable proportion were
usually members of the wealthier classes who had failed either the
baccalauréat or the entrance to Saint-Cyr (75, 188).) Their best
chances of promotion lay in service overseas in the frequent
frontier campaigns in Africa and Indo-China, a service neglected
by all but unusually serious officers from the upper classes. It was
common for a general, whose career had been made abroad and who
had received the thanks of the Government and the adulation of
the press, to be looked on as an outsider by those who had spent
their service lives in smart garrisons in France. One could not gain-
say the capacity of a Galliéni or a Lyautey in their own sphere, but
—after all, the colonies were the colonies.

Thus it may be said that those who officered the metropolitan

Army were a class apart, unaware of what was happening in the
country, reading mostly conservative and Right-thinking newspapers—General Messimy when a subaltern was told off by his corps
commander for subscribing to the *Figaro*—prejudiced, and to a
large extent ignorant. The Army had not seriously changed since
the days when Vigny wrote: "It is a body separated from the great
body of the nation, which seems the body of a child, so far does it
lag behind in intelligence, and so much is it forbidden to grow."

Yet in spite of its prejudices, the Army was, it must be emphasised, not a political body. As Pimodan wrote (45, 231): "In
spite of what has since been claimed, we in the Army did not go
in for politics": he adds that the half-yearly reports required statements on an officer's morality, education and behaviour, but not on
his politics or religion. The duty of the Army officer was to obey
his superior officer in all circumstances, however repugnant might
be the task, and whoever might be his commander. There had in
fact been few anti-Republican demonstrations, even at the height of
the sixteenth of May crisis of 1877. Nothing could be found against
generals known to be of Royalist or Bonapartist sympathies; they
were simply put on the retired list because they were suspected.
In the late eighties Boulanger received no backing from the Army;
he was considered an undisciplined officer, as well as an upstart.
The automatic resistance to a summons to act politically will be
seen in General Roget's behaviour after Félix Faure's funeral in
February 1899. The Army regarded itself as sacred, a thing apart
and, as Girardet says (75, 255), an officer who frequented civilian
circles often had this noted on his half-yearly report as a bad mark,
while those who advertised their Republicanism were frowned on for
playing politics.

Yet if the Army stood apart from the nation, the nation regarded the Army as part of itself. At the opening of the Dreyfus
case in 1894, in the country as a whole anti-militarism scarcely
existed. Some writers have tried to establish its existence earlier,
from the publication in 1887 of Abel Hermant's *Le Cavalier
Miserey* and Lucien Descaves' *Sous-Offs*. But neither book attacked
militarism, only the abuses and wretchedness of the conscript's

life in barracks. Although Descaves was prosecuted and later reduced from the rank of sergeant-major on the reserve to private, what he had written was well known to thoughtful officers, who from before 1870 had without effect been preaching reforms. One of the few things to the credit of the despised General Boulanger is that he did carry out certain improvements in the conscript's life.

That there lay a gulf between the professional officer and N.C.O. and the conscript is undeniable, the latter itching to return to civilian life, the professional lacking experience of what that life might mean. It was a problem which was recognised by thinking soldiers, yet no solution had been found. Lyautey, in a famous article published anonymously in the *Revue des Deux Mondes* in March 1891 (74), complained that officers knew far more about their troop-horses than about their men. The gulf existed.

Nevertheless, the criticism of the Army was in no way pacifist. The Army was regarded with esteem, even with affection, by those who had served in it. It was only in what might be called "intellectual" circles that war began to be discredited, for example in the well-known remark of Rémy de Gourmont that he would not exchange one of his little fingers, so useful for knocking the ash from one's cigarette, for the liberation of the "forgotten lands," Alsace and Lorraine. Such sentiments had not penetrated the masses. Guglielmo Ferrero in his study *Militarism* of 1899 [1] insisted that the pacifism of the workers was only superficial and described a meeting of railwaymen with the Socialist Deputy, Clovis Hugues, in the chair, at which all the speakers were outraged at the suggestion that they could be suspected of failing in their military duty, and where the final motion recommended close contact with the War Office in every strike so that it could be broken as soon as the necessities of national defence demanded.

If criticism of the Army of the nineties was valid, it should have been directed to professional shortcomings. In the agony of defeat immediately after 1870, the Army had flung itself into reconstruction in expectation of a renewal of the war. While Séré

[1] English translation 1902.

des Rivières was undertaking the new line of fortifications on the Meuse heights between Verdun and Toul and from Epinal to Belfort, the National Assembly were making a thorough investigation into the causes of defeat. They reached the conclusion that one of the most serious defects had been the inadequacy of the Staff. Under the Law of 1818 the members of the Staff had not been drawn from the fighting troops. The Staff Corps was a caste by itself. On leaving Saint-Cyr or the Polytechnic, bright young officers, after a very short period with the various arms, had gone directly into the the Staff Corps. It thus became a closed circle, inexperienced in warfare. In accordance with Berthier's precepts, staff officers were not the assistants, but the obedient tools, of generals. The Assembly laid it down that in future the Staff should be drawn from the whole Army, and that for appointment to the Staff only those would be eligible who had secured the brevet of the Ecole Supérieure de Guerre, the new military school for subalterns and captains. These officers would not remain permanently on the Staff, but at each promotion would return to their own arm for an appropriate period. Moreover, as he left the school, each brevetted officer would put in a two-year period as a staff learner (*stagiaire*) in the War Office or on a corps or divisional staff. The old Staff Corps was disbanded and its members sent to regiments, but nevertheless after a turn of penance, many of these, who lacked the brevet of the new school, worked their way back to the Staff again.

In 1888 Charles de Freycinet became War Minister and held the office until 1893, the first civilian War Minister in the history of the Republic. Once Gambetta's right hand in the national defence after Sedan, and already three times Prime Minister, Freycinet desired above all else to modernise the Army and to bring about an alliance with Russia. He was not a forceful character, but he had great charm and enormous persuasiveness. During these four years he tacked dexterously between political and military claims. "His consummate cleverness in the eyes of Parliament lay in his inserting military legislation into democratic evolution, and in the eyes of the soldiers in showing them the way to the stars, in other words, in creating those high positions towards which ambition

reaches" (76, 253). In concrete terms, he secured the reduction
of national service from five years to three, while to incorporate the
reserves he created a number of cadre units and formations and
staffed them with ten new divisional generals, twenty brigadiers
and a host of lower officers. "The officers became founder share-
holders" (76, 238), while the civilians profited from the reduction
in length of service. At the same time he continued the modernisa-
tion of arms, but he failed to improve the training. The Army was
and remained a barrack army: of every twelve months eight were
wasted. By now war seemed remote: the hopes of the seventies were disappointed. There was to be no crusade for Alsace-
Lorraine. The international crises passed without serious trouble
or alarm. Disbelieving in the probability of war, but reluctant
to admit an idea which would reduce their prestige, the generals
were becoming interested in other fields. "The Saint Petersburg
Embassy is vacant," said Galliffet to the Bixio dinner in 1890:
"now, of four generals commanding corps, three have asked for the
Embassy. . . . They have to lead a quarter of a million men, to
defend the country: they dream of a job" (21, 60).

CHAPTER THREE

The *Bordereau*

1

AUGUSTE MERCIER, the War Minister, who was to play a major part
in the Dreyfus case, was not a well-known soldier. A gunner, he
had had a slow career: he had not been a member of the Staff Corps.
He had served in the Mexican campaign of 1867 and the Franco-
Prussian War, but he had only reached the highest rank in the
French Army, Divisional General, in 1889. As a corps commander
he had done well at the manœuvres of 1892. On the strength of
this, coupled with a recommendation from General de Galliffet,
Casimir-Perier had selected him as Minister of War. Mercier had
never meddled in politics; his reputation was entirely professional.
He was no more than a conventional Catholic; indeed, he was
married to an English Protestant. A tall, slim man of sixty, with
sallow skin and harsh features, a bitter mouth between a grey
moustache and a grey mouche, he was reserved and courteous.
Whatever other virtues he possessed, he had one to a marked
degree: courage.

At first the Chamber had approved of him. He spoke clearly and
plainly, and he led the Deputies to believe that so far as the Army
was concerned, all was well. But in May he ran into unexpected
trouble. An inventor named Turpin, from whom the State had
bought certain rights in an explosive in 1885 and had decorated,
had claimed that he was cheated by the Director of Artillery, and
after much obscure quarrelling had eventually been given five years
for espionage. On his release he attempted to sell another invention to the War Office. That department, having had enough of
Turpin, closed its doors to him. He then publicly announced that
he would take himself and his invention to Germany. Interpellated
in the Chamber by the Extreme Left, Mercier mistook the temper

of the members and failed to please. This was at the end of May. In June Galliffet, always reckless in speech, was found to have made some caustic comments on the state of the Army to a journalist. Questioned in the Chamber, Mercier made a spirited defence of his senior. Although he was cheered by the majority, he was assailed with violent abuse by the Left and by all the mischief-making press, in particular by Rochefort and Drumont.

Two months later he clumsily laid himself open to further and more justifiable criticisms. On August 1, after Parliament had risen, he published in the Official Journal a circular ordering the release of 60,000 men from the 1891 and 1892 classes in November. Save that it left the garrisons somewhat short-handed, it was not important. But he had failed to notify the Army commissions of the Senate and Chamber of his intentions, and moreover he had not even deigned to inform the titular head of the armed forces, the President of the Republic, whose first knowledge of the order was the circular in the Official Journal. Casimir-Perier for once lost his temper and summoned a Cabinet meeting, at which Mercier was told to draft an amendment to retain twenty thousand of the sixty thousand with the colours. Thus at the end of August Mercier's situation was far from secure. He had insulted the President; he had shaken the confidence of his Cabinet colleagues; he had snubbed the Army commissions; he had naturally, by his counter-orders, confused and enraged the Army and, perhaps worst of all, he had not only given a lot more ammunition to the Rocheforts and Drumonts, but had drawn acid criticisms from the sober newspapers. He knew that when Parliament met in October he would have to face the wrath of the commissions and the Chambers, and he could be quite certain that Charles Dupuy was not of the stuff to defend him. Only a happy accident could save him.

2

Parallel with the reconstruction of the Army after 1870, the reorganisation of the War Office was undertaken in the setting up of four Bureaux: the First covering Administration; the Second, Intelligence; the Third, Operations and Training; and the Fourth,

Movements and Railways. Before becoming staff officers, the learners seconded to the War Office had to do six months with each branch, but in each year they must also be attached to units for three months.

The executive head of the War Office was the Chief of Staff, a position created in 1874. From May 1890 the post had been filled by General de Miribel, considered the best brain in the Army. The only criticism voiced was that he was, if not a Monarchist, at least a believing and practising Catholic, and inclined to select his staff officers on the recommendation of his confessor. Since the relevant accusation came from one of his successors, the Protestant, General Billot, given in 1897 to the Alsatian Protestant, Scheurer-Kestner—"since Miribel's passage here, the War Office has become a Jesuitry"—in order to gain sympathy for himself, the statement is prejudiced: there were in fact few officers in the War Office who had been educated at the Jesuit school in the Rue des Postes.

Miribel had been selected as Chief of Staff by Gambetta in 1881, a choice which brought unsympathetic comments from the Republicans in the Chamber. Freycinet, during his tenure of the War Ministry from 1888 to 1893, had brought Miribel back from command of the VI Corps at Nancy to put through the reorganisation of the Army after the reduction of the period of service from five to three years. Miribel, an indefatigable worker, was inclined to take too much on his own shoulders. As his sub-chief, he brought back with him from Nancy his chief staff officer, General Charles Le Mouton de Boisdeffre, a man from an old military family.

Reinach (47, I, 270–71) suggests that Miribel chose Boisdeffre because he was lazy and would not interfere. Boisdeffre, a tall, handsome man, with stately, courteous manners, had been sent to Russia in 1892 to work out with the Russian staff the terms of the military convention which was initialled by the Tsar, Alexander III, in January 1894. When Miribel died of a stroke in September 1893, Boisdeffre stepped into his shoes. Like Miribel, he was a practising Catholic. His confessor and, it is said, counsellor was none other than the well-known Jesuit preacher, Father du Lac. Boisdeffre's career had been very different from Mercier's. A member of the Staff Corps from his first commission, he had met no difficulties, and his rise had not been slow: five years junior to Mercier, he had reached the rank of Divisional General only fifteen months after his senior. His Russian contacts had given him a taste for politics, and he hoped that one day he would succeed the Marquis Lannes de Montebello in the Embassy at Saint Petersburg. As Chief of Staff in 1894, his work was devoted to the redrafting of the war plan as a result of the Russian military convention, and he left the current business of the War Office to his two assistant-chiefs, Generals Renouard and Gonse, the latter of whom had been attached to him at Nancy and was a lifelong friend.

3

The existence of the War Office revolved round the assumption of a renewal at some date of war with Germany. In the early years of the Republic there had been constant fear of another invasion, and all plans had been devoted to the defence of the new unfortified frontier. But with the late eighties the possibility of at least a counter-offensive began to take shape. Between 1887 and 1892 five new plans had been drafted. On the signature of the convention with Russia, yet another plan was undertaken, to come into force in the spring of 1895.

Now, in the early nineties, when new and improved weapons were continually appearing, it was the duty of the Intelligence branches of all the War departments in Europe to keep abreast of what their potential enemies were preparing in the way of defences, weapons, explosives, tactics and mobilisation. To this end, spies were employed, while to defend themselves against the enemy's spies counter-espionage sections were formed. In the French War Office in the Rue Saint-Dominique such a section had been created about 1876 under the cover-name of the Statistical Section. It had no relationship and no communication with the formal Intelligence branch, the Second Bureau. Its officers were unidentifiable on the War Office list, and its head communicated only with the Chief of Staff, or with his assistant.

Spy stories woven by novelists have rarely reached the level of unreality that the espionage sections of the European War Ministries rose to during these years. The strange ruffians they employed were often drawing money from two or three sources. Many of them were on familiar terms, advising each other of jobs to be done, or if need be denouncing their own sub-agents. No spy was wholly trustworthy, and thus, in an attempt to confuse the demiurges they themselves had created, counter-espionage staffs began an elaborate industry in the fabrication of false reports and misleading plans to be deliberately sold to the enemy. By 1893, so involved had the practice become in the Statistical Section, that it is doubtful if its members knew what documents were secret, which were genuine and which of the low-lived creatures they paid were in their own service or that of the enemy. Moreover the whole security system in the War Office was laughable. There appears to have been no central registry and no record of the movement of papers. In evidence before the Criminal Appeal Court (6, I, 305–6), Lt-Col. Cordier, late of the Statistical Section, stated that the Staff Warrant Officer in charge of the filing had sold an old strong-box in which the purchaser found a number of secret papers. Documents of vital importance were passed from hand to hand; no one knew who had read them. The Statistical Section had no certainty as to how or when papers reached their office. In all branches officers had documents copied for their private use and put them in their private files. Photographs were taken in the Statistical Section, but no record was kept of how many prints had been made or how they had been distributed.

The head of this somewhat amateurish section was Colonel Jean-Conrad Sandherr, an Alsatian, the son of a convert from Protestantism to Catholicism who, like so many converts, had become the hater of all subscribers to a creed other than his own. The son, who had made France his home after the annexation of his native region, had brought with him from Alsace, the one area in France where Jews formed a fairly large group, a strong anti-semitism. He had been appointed to the Section in 1886. Between 1890 and 1892 a few trials and condemnations of minor officials spying on behalf of foreign countries had roused the Chamber to ask about the disappearance of secret papers. General Loizillon, Mercier's predecessor, had assured the Deputies that the leakage had stopped; but, on his arrival at the Rue Saint-Dominique, Mercier was dismayed to hear from Sandherr that this was not the case. Whether such losses, apart from certain plans of fortresses, were of serious value is doubtful; but the weakness of security precautions meant that no one could be sure what had been stolen and what merely mislaid.

By 1894 Sandherr was already showing symptoms of the disease, creeping paralysis, which was to end his career in the following year, but he was still capable of working. His senior assistant, Lt-Col. Albert Cordier, who had joined the Section at the same time as Sandherr, was a bluff, free-spoken soldier, and also an anti-semite. But he disliked the work and only stayed in the department from his affection for Sandherr. The rest of the staff consisted of Major Henry, Captain Lauth, Captain Matton, and the filing clerk and copyist, Gribelin.

Hubert-Joseph Henry, a man in his late forties, was the dominant figure in the office. He came from the small village of Pogny on the Marne canal, a few miles south of Châlons. A peasant, he had enlisted in the Army in 1865 and made it his career. He had been commissioned from the ranks and in 1877 had somehow attracted the notice of Miribel, who took him on his personal staff. In 1879 Miribel had had Henry seconded to the Statistical Section, but the officer then in charge disliked the ranker, and in 1880 had him returned to the infantry. Posted to the 2nd Zouaves at Oran, Henry distinguished himself in the South Oran campaign, during which he was wounded and decorated. From Algeria he was sent to Indo-China, where he showed himself to be a bold and resourceful leader in the never-ending guerrilla war against the Tonkinese. When, in 1890, he returned to France, he was promoted to Major in the 120th Infantry Regiment, and employed as Town Major at Péronne. Two years later he married the daughter of a small innkeeper in his native village.

Then in January 1893, apparently through his old patron Miribel, he was once again posted to the Statistical Section. Henry possessed both the virtues and the defects of the peasant. He was at once brave and astute, but with the simple cunning of the uneducated. His bravery often turned to audacity; he was the kind of man, someone said, who should have been employed in buying cattle, an opinion confirmed by his appearance. He was a big man, bullet-headed, with a low forehead and an upturned nose above a short, heavy moustache: his eyes were small and protruding. He was ambitious, but within the limits of his capabilities; that is to say, he hoped to reach a rank which would allow him to retire with a pension, small but wealth in the poor village of Pogny. (Boisdeffre at Rennes said that Miribel, in the event of war, intended to make Henry camp-commandant of G.H.Q., a position far above his rank.) In Paris he and his wife lived modestly. Like all professional soldiers he had a high regard for the service, which was probably the lodestone of his life.

At the Statistical Section his chief duties were the provision of faked documents for the counter-spies to dispose of, and the examination and, where necessary, reconstruction of such papers as were brought in by the agents. His deficiency was a total ignorance of any language other than French. Thus the Italian and German documents had to be worked on by Captain Lauth, a cavalryman, much influenced by his senior, but, like Sandherr, an Alsatian, with therefore a ready command of German. The third officer, Matton, in 1894 was on the point of being posted elsewhere: he disliked the work and was on cold terms with Sandherr. As for Gribelin, he was altogether in Henry's pocket. In the Section there was coolness, not to say dislike, between the two senior officers who disliked the dirty police work, and the junior group who had to deal with the lowly agents and suppliers of raw materials.

When Mercier took over the War Office in 1893 he was warned by Sandherr that, apart from organisations beyond the frontiers, there existed in Paris foreign secret-service groups, and that the centres of these were the military attachés of the Triple Alliance within the immunity of their respective Embassies. The two important ones were Colonel Max von Schwartzkoppen, the German, and

the Italian, Colonel Panizzardi. Their activities were unknown to
their respective ambassadors; but since each attaché corresponded
directly with his own War Office, there was no occasion for Münster
or Ressmann to know. Münster, indeed, had sacked Schwartzkoppen's predecessor for being involved in espionage by a French administrative officer, tried in 1890, and had at that time promised
the Quai d'Orsay that in future there should be no attempts to
seduce French military or civil officials. Panizzardi and Schwartzkoppen worked hand in hand, often employing the same agents or
alternatively sharing the spoils they brought.

To counter these activities, Sandherr had bought the services of
French domestics employed in the Embassies. Among these, in
the German Embassy, was an elderly housemaid named Bastian
who came to the Embassy daily. Her business was to collect all
the fragments of writing from the wastepaper baskets and at intervals to hand them over to a French agent. This system was con-
ventionally known as "the ordinary route." Unfortunately, at the
end of 1893 the agent, one Martin Joseph Brücker, had been
gravely indiscreet, and this duty was taken from him and put into
the hands of Henry. Once or twice a month Henry met Bastian,
usually after dark, and took from her the paper bags into which she
had thrust, unsorted, the fragments of Embassy correspondence.
On his return home, Henry examined the pieces, separating those
in French from those in other languages. The former he kept for
himself, the rest he handed over to Lauth next day. Usually little of
interest emerged from the bags, though the writing of the military
attachés became familiar, and much of their private lives: it was
known, for example, that Schwartzkoppen was the lover of a French
lady, and that she frequently wrote letters at his dictation. However, enough was obtained to establish that from December 1892
someone was selling to Schwartzkoppen large-scale plans of the
fortification of the eastern frontiers of France, and that those of
the Alpine frontier were being passed on to Panizzardi. Among the
intercepted letters was one which opened: "Herewith twelve large-
scale plans of Nice, which that scum (*canaille*) D. has handed to me
for you." The letter was signed "Alexandrine," the pseudonym

both attachés used for this correspondence.[1] The letter was undated, and, since the Section was extremely casual in its work, no
record was made of the date it was received.[2]

Early in January 1894, however, a crumpled and torn ball of
paper bearing some notes in Schwartzkoppen's handwriting did
reveal that he was now in touch with a person of greater conse-
sequence than "*ce canaille de D.*" During the following March
one of Henry's creatures, a shady police-informer named Guénée,
had a conversation with a somewhat seedy but well-connected retired attaché of the Spanish Embassy named Val Carlos, who had
once or twice passed on minor information to the Statistical Section. Val Carlos dropped a hint that someone whom be believed
to be an officer in one of the War Office departments was handing
documents to a foreign power: but he had not identified him. "If
I did, I would tell you." A month later he again spoke to Guénée:
"There is a wolf, perhaps more than one, in your sheepfold. Look
for him." Val Carlos was not at this time in the pay of the Statistical Section, though he received occasional sums of money: it may
be he was trying to be placed, as he was by the end of the year, on
their regular pay-roll. Guénée reported these talks to Henry. In
June, this time to Henry himself, Val Carlos said that an officer,
either recently or now in the Second Bureau, was informing
Schwartzkoppen and Panizzardi, but he did not know his name.
However, during the rest of the summer nothing further was discovered.

4

According to his own narrative (53, 3–11), on the afternoon of
20 July 1894 Colonel von Schwartzkoppen was told that a Frenchman had come to the Embassy about a passport for Alsace, which

[1] The Statistical Section consulted the Foreign Office experts as to the writer
of the letter. Although the content showed it to be from Schwartzkoppen, the
Foreign Office, for some unexplained reason, assigned it to Panizzardi. It is odd
that the handwriting was apparently unknown.

[2] At the trials in 1898–99 various dates were given by Cordier and Lauth.
Cordier believed it dated from 1892, Lauth from December 1893. No photograph was taken of it until October 1894. In any case, other evidence tended
to show that D. was not an officer: he was badly paid—no more than ten francs
a sheet for the large-scale plans he purveyed. (See Appendix vi, p. 367.)

required the permit of the Governor of the Reichsland. Since these permits were frequently refused, French officers in the circumstances were used to claiming the help of the German military attaché. As Schwartzkoppen had guessed, the visitor proved to be a French army officer in mufti, a man in the middle forties, of middle height and slight build. "He had a lined face, a crop of grey hair, a long greying moustache, and deep-set dark eyes." In response to Schwartzkoppen's enquiry as to his business, he said that he was financially embarrassed owing to speculations which had gone wrong and to the serious illness of his wife. His choice lay between suicide and the offer of his services to Germany. He claimed to be able to give valuable information, since he had been a member of the Second Bureau and was friendly with Sandherr. He also claimed to be a friend of the well-known Deputy for Chambéry, Jules Roche, who had promised to make him Assistant Chief of Staff if he, Roche, became Minister of War. He was at the moment stationed outside Paris, but he expected an early transfer to the capital, when he would renew his connections with the War Office.

Schwartzkoppen indignantly repulsed the offer. Ready enough as he was to buy from the riff-raff, he was horrified that a commissioned officer should offer to sell his country. He sent the man away, but the latter, remarking that he was about to go to the artillery firing camp at Châlons for some trials, said he would call again. On the following day Schwartzkoppen received a note from his visitor. On this, the attaché swallowed his repugnance and wrote an account of the interview to his chief in Berlin. He was told to pursue the matter.

On the evening of July 27 the visitor returned and introduced himself as Major Count Walsin-Esterhazy, commanding a battalion of the 74th Infantry Regiment, stationed at Rouen. In earnest of this, he produced the mobilisation orders of his regiment, and demanded a salary of two thousand francs a month. As before, the embarrassed attaché tried to dissuade the man, and, having failed to do so, suggested that he should deal directly with Berlin. Esterhazy replied that the only way of doing business of this nature was by personal contact, which was less dangerous, since many people came to 78 Rue de Lille. Once more Schwartzkoppen dismissed him, but he felt that he must have personal confirmation of his orders from Berlin. Consequently he went off to Germany, and on August 4 saw the head of the German Intelligence Branch, Müller, who reiterated the original order. On his return to Paris two days later, he found a letter from Esterhazy saying that he would leave Châlons on August 10 and go to his wife's house at Dommartin-la-Planchette until the 12th. At 10 p.m. on August 13 he appeared again and told the attaché that he could let him have the recently revised General Instruction for Artillery on Mobilisation. Two days later, the 15th, he brought the document. Schwartzkoppen weakened: the Instruction was a document asked for by Berlin. He gave five thousand francs to Esterhazy, who went off saying he would shortly bring other papers.

At 6.30 p.m. on September 1, he reappeared, bringing (*a*) a list of covering troops for the frontier defences, (*b*) a description of the new short 120-millimetre gun, (*c*) the provisional "Firing Manual of Artillery in the Field." He said he had just come back from firing exercises at the Sissonne artillery range and would report what he had picked up. This he did on September 5, and on the following day he handed in a note on the proposed Madagascar expedition.[1]

What Schwartzkoppen did not know, and Esterhazy neglected to let fall, was that before going to Sissonne, perhaps on August 26 or 27, he had left with the concierge at the German Embassy a letter containing a list of the papers he intended to hand over.

This letter, subsequently known as the *bordereau*, or list (it will be called the *bordereau* in this narrative), reached the Statistical Section at the War Office during the last week of September. How it came there is a subject of controversy. There are two versions.

The first runs that Brücker, the agent now on reduced pay, was burning to get back into favour. Probably he was hanging about the Rue de Lille, watching the Embassy and hoping for something to turn up. One afternoon towards the end of August the Embassy

---

[1] See Appendix i, p. 361.

concierge went out with her husband for a drink and asked Bastian to take her place. Brücker, being well acquainted with the woman, who it seems had his uncle, a retired employee of the Sûreté, as a lodger, walked in. According to a later and third-hand account, Bastian looked into Schwartzkoppen's pigeon-hole and found in it a letter together with a thicker package. She took the former and handed it to Brücker. As to whether the letter had come by post or hand, there is no statement. Brücker slit open the envelope, and seeing that the content was apparently important, carried it to Henry.

The second version omits Brücker and runs that on the evening of September 26 Major Henry met Bastian and took from her the two paper bags containing the usual scraps and sweepings. On reaching home he began his normal sorting of the fragments. Mme Henry went to bed, but since her husband showed no signs of following her, came back and asked him: "Why are you working so much later than usual?" To which he answered: "I've found some interesting stuff which I must finish to-night." He had in front of him a letter which he showed to her. It ran:

Without news indicating that you wish to see me, nevertheless, Sir, I send you some interesting information:
1. A note on the hydraulic buffer of the 120 and the way in which this gun behaves (*s'est conduite*);
2. A note on the covering troops (some modifications will be made under the new plan);
3. A note on a modification to the artillery formations;
4. A note about Madagascar;
5. The preliminary Firing Manual of the Field Artillery (14 March 1894).

The last document is extremely difficult to come by and I can only have it at my disposal for very few days. The War Office has sent a fixed number to the Corps, and the Corps are responsible for them. Each officer holding one must return it after manœuvres.

If therefore you wish to take from it what interests you and then keep it for me, I will fetch it. Unless you would like me to have it copied in extenso and only send you the copy.

I am just off to manœuvres.

This letter, the *bordereau*, was written on what is known as *papier-pelure*, or onion-skin semi-transparent paper. It was not in small fragments, or crumpled, but partly torn across twice. It was unsigned and undated, and the envelope was missing. Before going to bed, Henry repaired it with the gummed transparent paper he employed for this kind of work.[1]

On the following morning, the 27th, instead of taking his normal ride, Henry went straight to the Rue Saint-Dominique. To Gribelin, the first to come in, he said: "Here, see what's been given me. It's pretty strong and I only hope we catch him." Lauth also was shown the paper on arrival. The three men discussed it for a few minutes and seem to have agreed that the writer must be on the staff and a gunner. During the morning the letter was taken to Sandherr. After showing it to Matton, the only artillery officer in the Section, who thought that a gunner must have written it, he carried it to his immediate superior, Gonse. Gonse in turn brought it to General Renouard, the other assistant Chief of Staff, who at the moment was acting for Boisdeffre, absent on leave. Renouard went with it to General Mercier. All the officers who saw the *bordereau* on the first day unanimously agreed that it was from an officer in the War Office itself, so much, according to Roget (6, I, 57), did it "use the language of the house."[2]

It was now circulated confidentially to the chiefs of all the War Office departments: all replied that they did not recognise the hand. This took some time. On October 4 the letter was photographed and prints distributed to the departmental chiefs, with a request that they should compare the writing with that of the officers serving under them. By October 6 the heads of the First, Second and Third Bureaux, as well as the Director of Artillery, General Deloye, were convinced that the *bordereau* was not the work of any

---

[1] See Appendix ii, p. 363, and Appendix vi, p. 368.

[2] Mazel (64, 29) is very caustic about the style of the *bordereau*, which he asserts could not have been written by a French officer. Yet no one involved in the case at the time saw anything wrong.

of their subordinates. But on that day there rejoined the Fourth
Bureau from leave the sub-chief, Lt-Col. Albert d'Aboville. On
being shown the print by his chief, Colonel Fabre, Aboville said
that it should be easy to run down the writer if he were in the War
Office. Because of the technical notes, he must be a gunner: Aboville himself had been at the Bourges Arsenal in the previous
January and had been refused all details of the new 120-milli-
metre gun. The writer must also be highly qualified. Further, since
the Bureaux were closed departments, it was only on matters
which concerned two or more that conversations took place, and
these invariably in the form of written minutes: therefore, a man
who could offer information on such a variety of subjects must be
a staff learner, because staff learners alone passed through all four
Bureaux. Fabre and Aboville then examined the writing of the
four or five artillery captains who were or who had recently been
attached to their Bureau. They hit on the name of Captain Alfred
Dreyfus, an Alsatian Jew, who had passed through the First,
Second and Fourth Bureau, and was now under Colonel Boucher
in the manœuvres section of the Third.

In the Fourth Bureau this officer had not been liked. Fabre's
report at the end of December 1893 had stated that while he was
very gifted and intelligent, yet from the point of view of character,
conscientiousness and obedience he was not ideally fitted to be
employed on the Staff; he was inclined to be critical of his superiors
and was not the pliant servant staff-duties required. As he later
admitted, the report was based on the reports of Aboville's predecessor, Lt-Col. Roget, and of the head of the railway section,
Major Bertin-Mourot, since Fabre himself had only come to the
Bureau in mid-November 1893, towards the end of Dreyfus's
attachment; but Aboville, who had known Dreyfus for some three
months, said he was secretive, inquisitive and little liked by his
brother-officers. Roget's sole complaint had been that Dreyfus,
having been given a fictitious troop-movement exercise to do, had
asked to be allowed to carry it out with two existing corps and real
transport. But Bertin-Mourot, under whose eye Dreyfus had
worked, had said that after initial enthusiasm he had become in-

different to the dull routine work of the department. At Rennes
(7, I, 560) Fabre added that Dreyfus had not the frankness of bearing to which the staff was accustomed; he ferreted about in corners,
took an exaggerated interest in the important parts of the railway
network, especially those on the Est Railway, and showed little
in day-to-day business. "In his examination [before the court-
martial in 1894] it appears that he said he only sought to learn; he
did indeed—even too much, but he did not do his duty."

From the point of view of Fabre and Aboville, Dreyfus was thus
not a good officer. He might be the man they were looking for,
but a difficulty lay in the fact that the author of the *bordereau*
had said that he was just off to manœuvres. Now, by a circular of
May 17 the second-year staff learners had been told that they would
do their attachment to the troops from October to December, and
thus would not attend manœuvres, which took place between July
and early October. Fabre turned this—it will be remembered that
the *bordereau* was not dated—by pointing to a staff ride that had
been held in June. On such frail reasoning the two went to the
Third Bureau and got hold of a sample of Dreyfus's handwriting.
In view of their expectations, it is not surprising that their suspicions were confirmed. The writing, they were honestly convinced,
was identical with that of the *bordereau*. Fabre reported to Boisdeffre, who had now come back. He was instructed to discuss the
matter in strict secrecy with Gonse. Gonse, keeping Fabre with
him, sent for Dreyfus's chief, Colonel Boucher, Colonel Lefort of
the First Bureau, and Sandherr. As soon as Dreyfus's name was
mentioned, Sandherr slapped his forehead and exclaimed: "I
ought to have thought of it." The five men examined the papers
and concluded that there was sufficient similarity between the
handwritings to warrant a searching enquiry. This was reported to
Boisdeffre, who sought Mercier.

5

Had Sandherr been a competent intelligence officer, certain
peculiarities about the *bordereau* should have struck him. First,
only one of the items offered was a printed document, No. 5, and

thus could possibly be identified. Had he verified this, he would
have found that the title was not the "Firing Manual of the Field
Artillery," but the "Firing Manual of Artillery in the Field," an
error no gunner was likely to make. Further, far from being difficult to procure, some three thousand copies had been distributed
to formations, that is down to at least section commanders; they
were not "confidential"; their return was not required, and in some
units copies had been made and put on sale at twopence apiece.
Again, had Sandherr enquired of a gunner about the hydraulic
buffer, he would have learned that there were two 120-millimetre
guns, of which the older one, a siege-gun in service for some years,
had a "hydraulic" buffer, but that the new one, a field-gun just
coming forward, had a buffer known as "hydro-pneumatic." No
gunner would have used the word "hydraulic" about the new gun,
and moveover, no gunner would have written "*s'est conduite*" which
implies human behaviour, but "*s'est comportée*".

As to the other three documents, a thorough consideration would
have raised a nice crop of conundrums, turning on the date of the
writing of the *bordereau* and what the "notes" contained.

If, as at this time was assumed, the *bordereau* was of April or
May, then the note on covering troops must refer to provisional
dispositions taken on March 1. If, on the other hand, it referred
to further work undertaken in June–August which would not be
made known to the corps commands until October 1, then it must
be at least of September.[1]

As regards the modification of artillery formations, this might
refer to the transfer of the bridging trains from the artillery to the
engineers, a subject which had been thoroughly discussed in Parliament and finally made official by the Law of June 20. On the other

---

[1] The date of April seems to have been adhered to throughout the trial of
1894. Although there seems to have been some argument between Demange
and Du Paty de Clam, Demange let the question drop (cf. his speech at Rennes,
7, III, 713–14). It was not until the end of 1897 that the mistake was seen and
August substituted. But since Dreyfus had known by the circular of May 17
that he, with the other second-year staff learners, would not go on manœuvres,
and thus could not have written, "I am just off, etc.," several officers were
called at Rennes in 1899 to show that the possibility still existed up to the end
of August.

hand, it might refer to the new and provisional artillery march formations, which were tried out at Châlons in August. As was to be known before the end of the trial from other documents secured from the German Embassy, the German War Office was asking for these regulations to be procured. Last, the note on Madagascar equally presented a problem, since the only work done on Madagascar before August was a purely geographical study, in no way confidential. The work on the expedition had been carried out, not in the War Office, but by an inter-services committee formed of one representative from each of the four Ministries concerned—Foreign Affairs, Navy, Colonies and War—between August 5 and 22, and had not yet been seen by the chief of the Operations Bureau to which Dreyfus was attached.

Finally, to the Criminal Appeal Court and the court-martial at Rennes, General Sébert declared categorically that no officer who had passed through the Polytechnic could have written in the terms and language of the *bordereau*. None of these contradictions was resolved.

Reinach thinks that Sandherr, bent on finding the culprit, allowed his anti-semitism to get the better of his judgment—he had refused to allow Dreyfus to be attached to his section—and thus became obstinate in his pursuit of this officer. It may be so: but it must be remembered that the running down of the traitor, if, as was believed, he was a member of the War Office staff, was a matter of serious urgency in view of the current work now being done on Plan XIII.[1] This is quite sufficient to account for the precipitancy with which action was taken. The fundamental error lay in ascribing to the "notes" a value far above their intrinsic worth,

---

[1] *Les armées françaises dans la Grande Guerre*, I, i, Ch. I (1922) gives the history of the series of war plans to 1914. The signing of the Russian Treaty in 1891 led to a revision of Plan XI. The new plan, XII, envisaged an immediate offensive against Germany. This came into force in February 1892. But the initialling of the military convention in December 1893–January 1894 called for further revision. A further plan, XIII, was put in hand, which was not ready until February 1895, but in the interval there was a reorganisation of the covering troops in March 1894, which seems to have been only partially carried out before September. It was no doubt to this that the writer of the *bordereau* was referring.

but this error is excusable in that no one could know—and in fact no one ever did know—what was contained in them.

6

The suspected man, Captain Alfred Dreyfus, came from a Jewish family long established in Alsace, that debatable land which the Germans had annexed in 1871. Under the Treaty of Frankfürt-am-Main, French nationals could, within eighteen months of the ratification of the treaty, choose the country to which they would owe allegiance, but those who preferred to remain French citizens must cross the new frontier. The Dreyfus family owned a cotton-spinning mill at Mulhouse. Like many Alsatians and Lorrainers, whether Jew or Gentile, they were passionately French, and like many Jewish families of long residence they were, bating their religion, more French than Jewish, completely assimilated. There were four Dreyfus brothers—Jacques, Mathieu, Alfred and Léon—and three sisters. In 1871 the whole family opted for French citizenship, except Jacques and Mathieu, who remained in Mulhouse to direct the factory: in 1897 Jacques moved part of the factory over the frontier into the Territory of Belfort.

Alfred Dreyfus had been born on 19 October 1859. In 1882 he had entered the Ecole Polytechnique and later had been commissioned in the artillery. Throughout his career, until he reached the War Office, the reports of his commanding officers had been uniformly excellent; their single unfavourable comment had been the tonelessness of his voice. He had entered the Ecole Supérieure at the end of 1890, sixty-seventh in the list, and had passed out nineteenth. He was then, in January 1893, seconded as a staff learner to the War Office. In 1890 he had married Lucie Hadamard, the daughter of a Paris diamond merchant, by whom he had two children. Some years earlier he had had a liaison with a young married woman, which he had broken off in response to an appeal by her parents. Beyond this, it seems, he had two brief liaisons of no serious character in 1893 and 1894. Moreover, he was rich. At this date he had a private income of twenty-five to thirty thousand francs and could look forward to inheriting at least fifty thousand francs a year. Everything in his existence cried out against the probability of his being in the pay of Germany.

At the War Office he had passed his first six months in the First Bureau, his second in the Fourth, his third in the Second, and at this date he was attached to the Third. During the staff ride in June, with the other officers he had dined in Boisdeffre's mess on the last evening. Something having arisen about the new guns, Dreyfus described some recent trials at Bourges and Calais so effectively that Boisdeffre after dinner spent an hour walking up and down the Moselle bridge at Charmes in conversation with him. Dreyfus believed that he made a friend of the Chief of Staff. As has been seen, his report from the Fourth Bureau stated that he was unsuited to staff employment. The report from the First Bureau, while stressing his intelligence and width of knowledge, ended: "Desires to and should succeed." From the Second Bureau (Intelligence) Colonel de Sancy, while praising his intellect and adaptability to the work, thought him possibly a little too sure of himself. In this Bureau, however, Sandherr had specially requested that he should not be attached to the Statistical Section. The report from the Third Bureau was not due until December, but Major Picquart, ordered to post the staff learners, had not put him in the Operations Section dealing with secret and confidential matters, but in that of manœuvres.

Generally, it emerges from the testimony given by his brother-officers that Dreyfus was not liked. He was admitted to have an excellent brain, but he was inclined to boast. "I thought his manners," wrote Pimodan, a contemporary in the Rue Saint-Dominique (45, 225), "not very agreeable, and altogether hardly suited to our society, although I attached no importance to it." Other officers with whom he served said he put his nose into matters which did not concern him, especially mobilisation plans, and talked about them too much (7, II, 92–98). It certainly appears that Drey fus had an extremely limited range of interests. He was ambitious and a passionate student of military affairs. He seems to have had few interests outside his family; neither literature, music, art nor sport made any appeal. His *Lettres d'un Innocent*, written from his confinement on The Devil's Island, even allowing for the exigencies of censorship, show a man of commonplace, even narrow imagination. It would seem that Dreyfus, with his ambition and self-sufficiency, possessed a simple vanity which made him show off his professional knowledge; this was in itself harmless, but, since talking shop was regarded with disfavour in the Army, it was enough to chill less ambitious men. G. W. Steevens, the English journalist who covered the Rennes trial for the *Daily Mail,* considered he had been "bumptious." Thus when those who had served with him were asked to give evidence, they recalled these trifles, which, in their cumulation, weighed with the judges.

Moreover, one officer (Duchâtelet, at the second trial at Rennes), to whom Dreyfus had been attached for a short time, stated on oath that the accused man had suggested that they should call on a *poule de luxe,* in whose house he said he had lost a large sum of money. Another (Lemonnier, also at Rennes) testified that Dreyfus had boasted to him of being present at German army manœuvres in Alsace. Dreyfus denied the fact of both these things, but Jean France (31, 218–19), a Sûreté agent present at the Rennes trial, was certain that both officers were speaking the truth, in so far that Dreyfus had made the statements. This somewhat foolish boasting by a young man, of things he had not done, took its revenge. Dreyfus was vain. He liked to display his capacity, his wide knowledge of secret or confidential topics. He talked ostentatiously of his wealth, perhaps of women. At Rennes (7, II, 86) an officer, Maistre, compared him with another, Captain Junck, "a very unpretentious lad, very sound, who is counted one of our best. He has a family to support and a sister to coach for her degree. Obviously, compared with him, Dreyfus was on velvet."

Reinach put this hostile evidence down to anti-semitism: that, in fact, is the theme of his history. But, save for Sandherr, who is known to have been a passionate anti-semite, there is no evidence to support this thesis. Anti-semitism no doubt existed, but it cannot be shown to have played a dominant part in the arrest and trial of Dreyfus. As General Lebelin de Dionne, Commandant of the Ecole de Guerre when Dreyfus was a student, said at the Rennes

trial, he did not wish the school to be a place of religious persecution, and a Christian would be sent back to his regiment for faults
which in a Jew were passed over. So far as the War Office was concerned, apart from Sandherr the only two identifiable anti-
semites were Major Picquart of the Third Bureau [1] and Major
Cordier of the Statistical Section, both of whom were to struggle on
behalf of Dreyfus. Picquart (7, I, 373) said that anti-semitism was
rife in the War Office and that in consequence he had taken care
to put Dreyfus in a section where he would have an unprejudiced
chief, Lt-Col. Mercier-Milon, and also would not have to deal
with security matters. On the other hand, Leblois (35, 14, f.n.1),
himself as deeply involved in the case as Picquart, remarks: "The
case appears essentially to have been an army mistake. . . . We
doubt that anti-semitism should be made responsible for the opening of the case, though it seems likely that, at the War Office, an
appeal was made to it from the beginning, and it is certain that the
case then at once found powerful reinforcement." Again, Bertin-
Mourot, the son of a Jewish mother, who wished, Reinach asserts
on no evidence, to have this racial stain forgiven, strenuously
resisted the accusation that he had desired to get rid of this Jew
(7, II, 158): "During my time at the War Office the question
[anti-semitism] never existed. I cannot give a better proof than
that Captain Dreyfus, a learner, was put to work on the most
important, the most secret, railway network. From the moment
Dreyfus came to us, he was a comrade to whom I handed all my
work, all my secrets, the secrets of all my files." Similarly, Aboville,
primarily responsible for pitching on Dreyfus, shows not a touch of
anti-semitism in his evidence.[2] Reinach says that the whole
General Staff, because Dreyfus was a Jew, "was astounded that

[1] When Gallet, one of the judges, remarked that he could find no motive for
the crime, Picquart replied, "Ah! but you don't know these Mulhouse Jews."
[2] On the other hand, when Aboville saw Forzinetti, the commandant of the
Cherche-Midi, on the business of Dreyfus's detention, he warned him not to
let the identity of the prisoner be discovered, and "warned me against the
approaches high Jewry would attempt" (7, III, 103). Aboville was the son of
a particularly militant Catholic representative from Loiret in the National
Assembly, and if twelve children be reckoned as evidence, he was a true son
of his father.

they had not earlier smelt the Judas" (47, I, 74), but in that case, how was it that rather more officers gave evidence as to character in Dreyfus's favour than gave evidence against him?

What it is important to recognise is that Dreyfus was accused of the cardinal sin against the Army and the country. The officers were asked to testify to facts and character, and it was their duty to give such evidence as they possessed. The anti-semitic shadow over the case came, not from the Army, but from the press.

CHAPTER FOUR

The Arrest

1

ON October 8 Boisdeffre laid the case before Mercier. All Mercier seems to have said was that, since neither Fabre nor Aboville was a graphologist, someone competent to pronounce on the papers should be found. Boisdeffre passed this on to Gonse, who sent for Major the Marquis Du Paty de Clam of the Operations branch, said to have some technical knowledge. Du Paty was not a fool: he had passed second out of Saint-Cyr and second from the Ecole de Guerre. He was looked on as one of the brilliant officers on the Staff: recently he had been the War Office representative on the joint committee planning the Madagascar expedition. But he had a frivolous and romantic mind. A tall man, with an upturned nose, a sprouting moustache, an eyeglass, and going bald, he looked like a figure from a German musical comedy. He had some taste for literature and thought the world of himself. On seeing the documents, he at once jumped to the conclusion that the hands were identical. But when Gonse warned him that the matter was one of treason he asked to be allowed to make a thorough study. Major Picquart, who was in the same branch and had had Dreyfus in his sub-section, was told to provide Du Paty with all the Dreyfus handwriting he could find. On looking at the *bordereau*, Picquart remarked that the divergences between the two hands were so numerous that one could not be sure. Du Paty thought otherwise, and in his report, delivered within the next twenty-four hours, he reaffirmed his first impressions.[1]

---

[1] Picquart asked Du Paty how Dreyfus had been paid for his treachery. Du Paty said that the Dreyfus family had been paid in the form of insurance money for a site at one of their factories in Alsace. This was later shown to be false. Picquart commented (7, I, 386) that he then formed a poor opinion of Du Paty's judgment and understanding, and from that moment distrusted his appre-

Boisdeffre and Mercier were persuaded. On this day therefore, the 9th, Mercier, at a meeting of the Cabinet, asked Guérin, Minister of Justice, if he knew a handwriting expert. Guérin suggested the Bank of France's man, Gobert. On the 10th Mercier told Casimir-Perier that a letter to the German Embassy had been discovered which demonstrated the treason of a member of the War Office staff, but that the documents which had been handed to the Germans were of little moment. From the Elysée Palace Mercier then sought Dupuy at the Ministry of the Interior in the Place Beauveau. Dupuy saw at once that more was involved than the misconduct of a single officer and recommended the utmost discretion: he summoned a meeting of the four Ministers who might be concerned: those of Justice (Guérin), Interior (himself), War (Mercier) and Foreign Affairs (Hanotaux). These met on Thursday, the 11th, at the Place Beauveau. Mercier told them that the *bordereau* had been found in the wastepaper basket of the German military attaché, torn in pieces, and had been reconstituted at the War Office; he was led to believe that a Staff officer was the culprit. But he withheld the name and merely asked for advice.

Hanotaux was never more than a second-rate Minister, a civil servant translated into politics; but his spirit of routine and his lack of character had not yet been perceived. However, he was at least well aware of the diplomatic complications which would follow the public accusation of a French officer trafficking with the German military attaché. He insisted that, without better evidence, it was impossible to open a prosecution, and anyhow it was not in the national interest to proceed: even an official investigation would be an error. Neither Dupuy nor Guérin appears to have offered opinions. Eventually Hanotaux wrung from Mercier an agreement to do nothing unless more weighty evidence was forthcoming.

At this juncture Mercier was pressed for time. During the next two days he must be at Limoges on army manœuvres; he must then

---

ciations. Moreover, the terms in which the *bordereau* was couched showed that the writer was not a professional spy: no spy sends documents without having first bargained and agreed the price.

return to Paris and go off at once on other manœuvres round Amiens on the 16th and 17th. He had Gobert, the expert, sent for, and at the same time despatched Sandherr and Du Paty to the Sûreté-Générale to obtain the co-operation of the police. When Gobert arrived he was handed over to Gonse, Sandherr, Lefort, Fabre and Henry, who all drew his attention to the similarity of the handwritings in the documents. Unimpressed by their exaltation, he asked a few questions and made a request for a photograph of the *bordereau*. Gonse, who knew that prints had been distributed among the departments a week earlier, refused, on the ground that if the War Office produced a photograph it would be all over Paris the next day. Gobert then asked that Alphonse Bertillon, of the Préfecture of Police, should be allowed to take one. To this Gonse agreed, thus unfortunately bringing Bertillon into the enquiry.

That evening Hanotaux, who had become uneasy, called on Mercier after dinner and once more tried to persuade him to drop the enquiry. Although he admitted that the most experienced and senior officer in the Army, General Saussier, Military Governor of Paris and Vice-President of the Conseil Supérieur de la Guerre, was also against prosecution ("No publicity," Saussier had said: "send him off to the colonial frontiers and see he doesn't come back "), Mercier refused, on the ground that the treason was by now too widely known, and that "we"—the Cabinet—"would be accused of making a pact with espionage." However, he left Hanotaux with the impression that nothing more than a search of the traitor's home, which had been agreed to by Dupuy, was intended. He did not reveal that he had already seen a *commissaire* from the Sûreté and had arranged for his presence at the arrest of the still unnamed accused on his return from Limoges.

With Mercier and Boisdeffre at Limoges, the enquiry was left to Gonse. He tried to hurry Gobert. Gobert asked for the name of the officer involved; the law required it. Gonse refused; but Gobert found enough evidence in Du Paty's file to identify Dreyfus from the Army List. On the morning of Sunday the 14th he sent in his report. Gonse, certain in his own mind that Dreyfus was the culprit, had already arranged with Du Paty to recall Dreyfus on

Monday from the regiment in Paris to which he was temporarily attached, and that he should come in civilian clothes, be given a handwriting test by Du Paty and, if necessary, arrested. To his chagrin, Gobert's report was negative: "the anonymous letter could well be from some other person than the suspect." Gobert stuck to his opinion. But in the meantime Du Paty had hurriedly sent over to the Police Préfecture to ask for the assistance of Bertillon. By now all the officers who had taken part in the investigation found their own reputations involved: should Dreyfus be proved innocent, what would Boisdeffre, what would Mercier, say?

The file was hurried over to Bertillon. Bertillon was not a handwriting expert, but head of the anthropometric department for the identification of criminals. Furthermore, from what had been let fall, he believed that other evidence against Dreyfus was available. He therefore set to work under the impression that he was dealing with secondary and supporting material. Nevertheless he, like Gobert, was uncertain, and reported to this effect during the afternoon, adding, however, that the *bordereau* might be a forgery.

Mercier got back to Paris on Sunday, and in the evening saw Boisdeffre, Gonse, Sandherr, Du Paty and Cochefert of the Sûreté. It was arranged that after the dictation and the subsequent arrest Dreyfus should be handed over to Major Henry to be taken to the military prison in the Rue de Cherche-Midi, and that his house would be searched. So besotted were the group that they expected an immediate confession of guilt from the prisoner, in which case he would be invited to commit suicide. However, should he not do so, Mercier planned to go forward, in spite of his promises of three days back to Dupuy, Hanotaux and Guérin. Remembering that Saussier, who also had preached discretion, was, as Military Governor of Paris, the commander of the Cherche-Midi, Mercier decided to avoid the chain of command by sending a message direct to the prison governor, Lt-Col. Forzinetti, to the effect that a senior officer would communicate with him on the next day, and he gave orders to Aboville to instruct Forzinetti to hold the prisoner in complete secrecy but not to inform Saussier.

It may be that Mercier accepted the opinions of the seven or eight officers he had heard a great deal too readily. In any case, in view of his conversations with Hanotaux and Saussier, he acted with immense recklessness: for if the case against Dreyfus broke down—and the evidence was extremely dubious—his own situation would not be improved. The Chambers would reopen on October 23; he well knew that many members, especially those of the Army Commission, would be sharpening their knives for him, and that Dupuy would not hesitate to drop him overboard. No doubt the conviction of a traitor would give him some kudos, but scarcely enough to weigh against his mishandling of the Army in August. In any case, the trial of the prisoner was not likely to take place before he was interpellated. Did he fear the press, which had had no mercy on him in August? He had told Hanotaux, on the evening of October 11, that the name of the traitor was known to practically every officer in the War Office and that this would undoubtedly leak out. He had rejected Saussier's advice.

Certainly Mercier's actions, when related to the abuse from Drumont and Rochefort, lend some colour to the supposition. Yet Mercier was a man of cold, almost insolent courage, who never feared to stand alone: years later he is to be found treating the press of both sides with equal disdain. From what he said to General André on the eve of the Zola trial in 1898, it is clear that at the time he was convinced of Dreyfus's guilt, and it may well be that he had been persuaded by Sandherr before Dreyfus's arrest (9, 229–33).

2

At the beginning of October Dreyfus had left the War Office to do his period of attachment to a regiment stationed in Paris. In accordance with the orders he had received from Du Paty, he reported at 9 a.m. on October 15 to Major Picquart at the rue Saint-Dominique.

Dreyfus was a man of medium height with broad, high shoulders. He had a prominent jaw, but except in profile his features were not Jewish. He had light hair and a light brown moustache and wore pince-nez over closely set eyes. His voice was reedy and weak.

Picquart showed him into Boisdeffre's room, where he found Du Paty and three men in civilian clothes: Cochefert and his secretary and Gribelin, the archivist of the Statistical Section. Du Paty, saying Boisdeffre would come later, asked him to take down a letter for Boisdeffre's signature: Du Paty had his hand bound up to demonstrate that he could not write. He then dictated to Dreyfus a letter based on the wording of the *bordereau*. After Dreyfus had written about ten lines, Du Paty sharply exclaimed: "What's the matter with you, Captain? You're trembling." "Not at all," Dreyfus calmly replied: "my fingers are cold." The dictation continued, and Dreyfus imperturbably took down the words. Again Du Paty tried to provoke some evidence of disquiet, but without effect. The letter finished, Du Paty rose, placed his hand on Dreyfus's shoulder and in a loud voice said: "Captain Dreyfus, in the name of the law I arrest you; you are accused of high treason." The victim of this masquerade stammered some words of protest. Du Paty then sat down again and, taking up the Code of Military Law, read out the article on espionage; in doing so, he deliberately uncovered beneath a file on the table a revolver. Dreyfus shouted: "I am innocent; kill me if you want to." Du Paty answered: "It is not our business to do the executioner's work; it is yours." To which Dreyfus returned: "I won't do it. I am innocent." Cochefert and his aide then searched the prisoner. "Take my keys," said Dreyfus: "open everything in my house. I am innocent." He now broke out into loud protests, claiming that he, an Alsatian, married, wealthy, could not be guilty of such a crime. He said he would have compensation for the insult, that he was the victim of a plot. Du Paty attempted to open an interrogation: "What have you to say?" Dreyfus asked of what he was accused, and Du Paty said nothing. He did not produce either original or print of the *bordereau*.

The interrogation was short. Du Paty hinted that there were documents, whereas there was only one, of which he refused to speak.

"Have you been on a staff ride, and when?"

"In the second fortnight of June."

Dreyfus was then asked what documents he had had in his hands on the covering troops, Madagascar etc. He answered that the only secret document he had handled was one on covering troops. "Have you had any contact with the artillery technical section?" "Yes, twice." Cochefert now took a hand, but all he got was: "If the facts alleged against me were established, I should be a villain and a coward. I wish to live to confirm my innocence." On this Du Paty called Henry, who was waiting outside. "Major, you have nothing to do but escort Captain Dreyfus to the Cherche-Midi."

In the carriage on their way to the Cherche-Midi, Henry and Dreyfus talked. Dreyfus said he was accused of treason. "The devil! Why?" "I have no idea. I'm going mad. I'd rather put a bullet in my head. I'm not guilty. This accusation is the end of my life." Henry comforted him. "If you are not guilty, don't lose your head. An innocent man is always strong. You will get justice." Dreyfus went on: "Major Du Paty told me I am accused of handing documents to a foreign power."

"Do you know what the documents are?"

"No. Major Du Paty spoke of secret and confidential documents without saying which."

Henry expressed astonishment and suggested that Dreyfus might have enemies who had forged them. Dreyfus replied that he had no enemies capable of such hatred.

After handing the prisoner over, Henry returned to the War Office, where he wrote out a report of the dialogue (6, II, 47), adding of his own volition that Dreyfus was making a wilfully lying statement, since from the next room he had heard Du Paty mention three of the documents in the *bordereau*. (It is possible that he had mistaken the documents mentioned in the dictation for part of the charge.) The statement went unchallenged. Next day Bertin-Mourot told Du Paty that in the Fourth Bureau Dreyfus had shown particular interest in the plans for mobilisation on the eastern frontier, and that in consequence, after his departure, the doors of the Bureau had been closed to him.

Immediately after the handing over of Dreyfus to Henry, Du

Paty, Cochefert and Gribelin went to Dreyfus's house in the Avenue du Trocadéro. They informed his wife of the arrest, but refused all information as to his whereabouts or the charge. Lucie Dreyfus wanted to telegraph for Mathieu Dreyfus. Again Du Paty refused. "A word, one single word, from you will bring about his certain ruin. The only means of saving him is silence." The three men searched the house. They found nothing, not even a sheet of paper resembling the *papier pelure* of the *bordereau*. Everything, even his accounts, were in perfect order, and his bank-book showed a balance of four hundred thousand francs. They took away a number of papers.

When questioned by Mercier, Cochefert said his personal impression of Dreyfus's behaviour was one of guilt: this derived only from the fact that he had been told that the *bordereau* was undoubtedly Dreyfus's work, and that there was other supporting evidence. But he was shaken by the accused's refusal to use the revolver and the fact that the search of the house had revealed nothing.

Du Paty was told to prepare the War Office brief against Dreyfus. On October 16 and 17 he and Cochefert went over the twenty-two bundles of papers they had taken from the house in the presence of Mme Dreyfus and her mother, Mme Hadamard. Not a thing to rouse suspicion was discovered. Next day, on Mercier's orders, Du Paty went to the Cherche-Midi.

Having been kept in solitary confinement for three days without any communication with the outer world, Dreyfus was on the verge of a breakdown. Forzinetti, alarmed at his condition, broke Mercier's injunction and informed his chief. Saussier told Forzinetti that but for their being old friends he would have punished him. To Mercier he repeated his earlier recommendation to hush the matter up and deal with Dreyfus on the frontiers of the Empire: a trial would only let loose the press.

Du Paty's proceedings during the examination of Dreyfus need not be examined in detail. Dreyfus was shown by faint lamplight one line of a photograph of the *bordereau*, which he failed to recognise. He was interrogated in involved sentences, of which he could no more than guess the meaning. On some days he was left in solitude, while Du Paty attempted to draw evidence from Lucie Dreyfus. From neither did he secure one admission that could help the prosecution.

In the meantime Bertillon had been set to work. As he understood the case, there were other proofs against Dreyfus besides the *bordereau*. A couple of years earlier a spectacular case of forgery of a will—the La Boussinière case—had been cleared up after the handwriting experts had been proved wholly wrong. With this in mind, he did not reject the theory of a plot. The handwriting of the *bordereau* and Dreyfus's were both of that commonplace sloping character which all French children were taught, but the writing of the *bordereau* was irregular.[1] He therefore reached the conclusion that Dreyfus had produced a forgery of his own hand. This was on October 20. Three more experts were now obtained from the Préfet of Police and were given prints of the *bordereau*. One, Pelletier, refused to talk with Bertillon, and on October 25 rejected any connection between Dreyfus's hand and the writing of the *bordereau*. The other two, Charavay and Teysonnières, were persuaded by Bertillon to accept his conclusions, though Charavay did so with considerable hesitation. These reports came in on October 29.

Du Paty was feeling frustrated. Turn where he might, he could find no evidence, though to his romantic mind this merely meant that Dreyfus had covered his tracks with devilish Jewish skill.

By Saturday October 27 Dreyfus was so ill that Forzinetti feared for his sanity. He reported to Mercier and was summoned to the War Office, where, Mercier being busy, he was seen by Boisdeffre. Boisdeffre asked him his opinion of Dreyfus, to which Forzinetti replied that he was as innocent as himself. Boisdeffre, saying that Mercier had to be away until Monday, asked Forzinetti to do his best to keep Dreyfus going till then, when the Minister would "get himself out of his Dreyfus case," thereby implying that he himself

[1] It is said that Esterhazy in fact had something wrong with his arm during August 1894 (57).

did not approve of what was going on. He allowed Forzinetti to send the prison doctor to Dreyfus under the seal of secrecy. That evening Mercier left Paris for Pau.

On the morning of Monday the 29th in the *Libre Parole* there ran a note: "Is it true that recently a highly important arrest has been made by order of the military authorities? The person arrested seems to be accused of espionage. If the information is true, why do the military authorities maintain complete silence?" In the War Office there was consternation. Who had disobeyed Mercier's instructions? The journalists who hurried to the Rue Saint-Dominique got the uniform reply: nothing was known.[1]

8

If up to this point there had been hesitations as to whether the hitherto fruitless examinations of Dreyfus should continue, those hesitations were brushed aside. That evening Du Paty showed the prisoner a print of the *bordereau* for the first time, and invited him to own himself the writer. Dreyfus indignantly replied: "I never wrote this infamous letter. Some of the words are like my handwriting, but it is not mine. The letter as a whole is not like my writing; they have not even tried to imitate it." Du Paty made him copy the *bordereau*, and the difference was so great that he did not even submit this copy to the experts.

Up to the morning of October 29 no hint of the arrest had been given to the general public. Outside the War Office and those investigating the case, it was known only to the President, Dupuy, Hanotaux and Guérin. It is unlikely that any one of the four Ministers, except Hanotaux, had realised what might arise out of the case. Casimir-Perier and Dupuy had both prescribed discretion to Mercier and relied on him to follow their advice. Hanotaux had also wrested a promise from the War Minister. To each of these, involved as they were in immediate and pressing problems of their own, the case was a minor matter.

Casimir-Perier had now been in office for four unhappy months. As Prime Minister he had enjoyed authority and respect. At the

[1] See Appendix iii, p. 364.

Elysée he was alone and found himself powerless. Ever since his election he had been attacked by the Socialist press in language as violent as that employed by Drumont against the Jews. He was spared nothing—water-closet vulgarity, abuse of himself, his father and grandfather—while from other sources came threats to murder him, his wife and children. The Socialist *Petite République* had been particularly fierce: in September one of its correspondents had been prosecuted and given two months in jail. In the same month Gérault-Richard had printed in the *Chambard* an article headed "Down with Casimir!" and was now awaiting trial. From the Ministers he received little support. Hanotaux's impudence in refusing to show him Foreign Office papers was infectious. Mercier's failure to inform him before producing the blundering decree of August 1, Dupuy's resentful neglect of him, were similar pieces of insolence. Casimir-Perier had not desired the Presidency; he had only yielded to the pressure of the conservative Republicans, and these now failed him. The fact was that he was not and had never been a Chamber politician. As President he was isolated and distressed.

In any case, Dupuy had his own boat to steer, and the water was rough. The Chambers had opened on October 23. On October 30 a storm blew up over the case of Mirman, the Independent Socialist Member for Reims. Mirman, a teacher at the Reims State Lycée, had been excused military service under the Recruiting Law of 1889, with the provision that he continue to teach as a State servant for ten years. On election to Parliament he had resigned his post, which was incompatible with the mandate of Deputy; but by so doing he fell under the Recruiting Law and must now do his military service: he had been called up for November 16. It was the kind of situation the Extreme Left loved—an opportunity for the Radicals and Socialists to twist the Government's tail. Regardless of the law, they clamoured that the electoral mandate took precedence over the decrees of the Minister of War. Mercier and Dupuy had no difficulty in rebutting the thesis, and the Chamber backed them by a majority of nearly a hundred, on which the Opposition broke loose, and the eminent philosopher and orator,

Jaurès, was heard shouting: "Servile Chamber! A slaves' vote! Down with dictatorship!" Nevertheless, the Government followers had not been warm with Mercier. The trouble over the August decree was about to come up, and he could see what was in store for him. If he did not quickly find a means of placating the distrustful majority, he would go.

Du Paty's report, handed in on October 31, while suggesting that Dreyfus's guilt was established, left the decision as to proceedings to Mercier. The account of what had been said by the prisoner during the examinations, if not completely falsified, was sufficiently distorted to make it appear that a case could be built up. It attributed to Dreyfus a hatred of Christians. It implied that he had bought his accelerated promotion. It gave him mistresses, including a rich middle-aged Austrian. But in spite of this loading, the case was transparently thin. The central, indeed the only solid fact was the *bordereau*; here Du Paty cast doubts on the credentials of the two experts who had refused to ascribe it to Dreyfus. But on the evidence which Du Paty had collected, no court could convict. Mercier hesitated.

That morning the *Eclair*, of which the political editor was an ex-Communard turned Nationalist, Alphonse Humbert, had said that the man in Cherche-Midi was not a high-ranking officer and that his examination had just been completed, while in the *Patrie* Millevoye, the Boulangist, said that the traitor was a Jewish officer attached to the War Office, who had tried to sell confidential papers to Italy. Both alleged he had confessed. Mercier contented himself with sending out through Havas, the official news agency, a note to the effect that an officer was under provisional arrest, that the documents, though confidential, had little importance, and that the case would soon be cleared up—a note scarcely calculated to damp down inquisitive journalists: moreover, it was issued too late. For next day, November 1, the *Libre Parole* headline ran: "High Treason. Arrest of the Jewish Officer, A. Dreyfus." The follow-up article asserted that the traitor had made a full confession, that there was ample proof he had sold "our secrets" to Germany, that he was in the Cherche-Midi under another name.

"But the case will be hushed up because the officer is a Jew. . . .
He will be allowed to find a shelter at Mulhouse, where his family
resides." At once the rest of the press was in the hunt: *Matin,
Journal, Petit Journal* and others, all had versions of the *Libre
Parole* statements. The *Figaro* contented itself with suppressing
the traitor's name and saying the charge was not yet clearly proved.
Alone, the violent Bonapartist polemist, Paul Granier de Cassagnac,
owner and editor of *L'Autorité* (he had sat for many years for
Mirande, but had lost on a split vote in 1893), refused to follow
Drumont's lead. "The arrest of a French officer on the charge of
high treason without serious proof would be a crime as abominable
as treason itself."

Only the four Ministers, who might be officially interested in the
case, had heard of Dreyfus. The first intimation the other seven
received was from the newspapers of November 1. Poincaré
telephoned to Dupuy, who, although it was All Saints' Day, hastily
collected those members of the Cabinet he could reach. Félix
Faure, Viger and Lourtice were not present. There arrived at the
Place Beauveau eight irritated and perhaps alarmed men, four of
whom knew nothing whatever of the case—Poincaré, Barthou,
Leygues and Delcassé. They complained that they had not been
informed. Hanotaux defended Dupuy on the ground of international relations. But the crux of the matter was what should be
done. Like the others, Mercier had seen the *Libre Parole* and knew
he must take decisive action one way or the other. He had brought
to the Place Beauveau a print of the *bordereau*. This he laid before
his colleagues and explained its significance, or rather the significance dictated to him by his own intentions. He told them that
Dreyfus was undoubtedly the writer, that he alone could have
had access to the five documents, that only he could have taken
them, and that therefore only he could have sold them. He
went on to say that the dictation test supported this view,
and that at it Dreyfus had shown his feelings. The motive was
disappointed ambition. He offered no other document than the
bordereau.

There was no reason for the Ministers to suspect Mercier's good faith. Thus deceived by the unambiguity of his statement, they unanimously voted that the prosecution should be undertaken; even Hanotaux, who had foreseen the diplomatic consequences. Dupuy took Mercier over to the Elysée to explain the case to Casimir-Perier, who had no *locus standi* at an informal Cabinet meeting. The case was then sent to Saussier, as Military Governor of Paris, the executive authority, who in turn communicated the matter to the *rapporteur* of the First (standing) Court-Martial of the Paris garrison, Major Bexon d'Ormeschville (November 3).

4

On October 31 Du Paty had at last granted Mme Dreyfus's plea to be allowed to inform her brother-in-law at Mulhouse. Mathieu Dreyfus, though ignorant of what had happened, arrived the next day. Naturally he was overwhelmed, indignant and full of misgivings that a great error had been made. He arranged for Du Paty to meet him at Alfred's house. Du Paty appears to have indulged his mania for pompous dramatics. Mathieu asked that he might be permitted to see his brother on any conditions: "If in a moment of madness he has committed an imprudence, he will tell me all, and I will put the pistol into his hand." Du Paty cried: "Never, never, never. One single word, and it would be war, a European war." So Alfred Dreyfus was left in solitary confinement.

During November the press raged. The most fantastic stories were built up by the imaginations of journalists, particularly in the *Libre Parole*, *l'Intransigeant*, the Assumptionists' organ *La Croix*, by Judet in the *Petit Journal* and Barrès in the *Cocarde*. Quite false but fully detailed accounts were given of the papers the traitor had sold: the Alpine fortifications, the complete mobilisation scheme. Every possible reason was found for his action: he hated France; he was not really rich, but took money either from Germany or else from wealthy Jews like the Rothschilds who wanted the ruin of France. It would be tedious to enlarge on these fantasies. But one note was struck again and again by Drumont—the note for Mercier to hear: again and again it was hinted that Mercier was sold to the Jews and that the case would be hushed up.

CASIMIR-PERIER

CHARLES DUPUY

MÉLINE

BRISSON

FÉLIX FAURE

LOUBET

SCHEURER-KESTNER

JOSEPH REINACH

CLEMENCEAU

JAURÈS

Dreyfusists

Anti-Dreyfusists

DRUMONT

ROCHEFORT

JULES GUÉRIN

And lest he should seek the support of the Right in the Chamber and Senate, they too were threatened, particularly those on the directorates of companies.

5

As the news leaked out and the uproar of the press rose, Schwartz-koppen was at first alarmed, but the headlines of the *Libre Parole* on November 1, naming Dreyfus, relieved him of anxiety; he was, however, puzzled by the press statement that the accused had made a full confession. So, too, was Panizzardi, since the majority of the newspapers said that Dreyfus was in the pay of Italy. Both attachés took it that Dreyfus had been in direct touch with their own War Offices. Panizzardi wrote to Rome assuring the Italian military authorities that neither he nor his German colleague knew anything of the prisoner. On November 2 he telegraphed in cipher: "If Captain Dreyfus has not had relations with you, it would be well to order the Ambassador to publish an official denial, in order to avoid press comment." The Italian War Office replied on the same day that it had had neither direct nor indirect contact with Dreyfus. At the same time the German War Office circulated an enquiry among its military attachés, all of whom replied that hitherto they had never heard of Dreyfus. Both War Offices were bewildered by the allegations. Schwartzkoppen and Panizzardi, with perfect honesty, assured their ambassadors of their ignorance of the prisoner.

The Panizzardi telegram of November 2 was intercepted by the French Post Office, and a copy sent to the Foreign Office. The cipher, a new one, had to be broken down. At the first trial the only certain word was "Dreyfus." Eventually the first part of the text was unravelled, but for the phrase "to avoid press comment" the Foreign Office version read "precautions taken"; the decipherer admitted that this reading was doubtful, and Sand-herr, who apparently was waiting eagerly beside the decipherer, was expressly cautioned. He took this version away to show Mercier, Gonse and Boisdeffre, to whom he said, according to Boisdeffre, "Well, General, here's another proof of Dreyfus's guilt." Before returning them to the Foreign Office, Sandherr made Henry take copies of the telegram in cipher and of the doubtful translation, in spite of their having been lent to him in confidence. Eventually the correct reading was discovered and within a week handed to Sandherr. Hanotaux also saw the final text, though he naturally attached no significance to it.[1]

The German Ambassador, Graf von Münster, an old-fashioned aristocrat, who had not feared Bismarck, and who hated spying, soon saw that some of the press were now claiming Germany as the traitor's paymaster. On November 10 he published an official denial in the *Figaro*, stating categorically that Schwartzkoppen had never had relations with Dreyfus, nor had ever received a letter from him. Two days later the Italians published a similar denial, as did the Austrians. The journalists treated the denials as lies. From Berlin the Chancellor Hohenlohe ordered Münster to repeat the denial to Hanotaux. Münster obeyed, once during an informal conversation, once officially. As Reinach says, "A more, intelligent man than Hanotaux, one less exclusively preoccupied with himself, knowing as he did the fragility of the proofs against Dreyfus, Dreyfus's protests, and the impossibility of discovering a motive for the crime, would have seen light in the darkness" (47, I, 254). But Hanotaux was not acute and was obsessed with form. The case was one for justice, and therefore, as a politician, remembering the doctrine of the separation of powers between the judiciary and the executive, he forbore to pry into the evidence. The file of evidence was never brought before the Cabinet, and he never asked to see it. With perhaps even greater nonchalance, he no more than mentioned Münster's *démarche* to Casimir-Perier, who constitutionally and by long custom should have been informed of what Münster had said. Nevertheless he told his fellow-Ministers, but they wholly failed to appreciate the denials of an ambassador who had never hitherto interfered in a case of spying. They believed that, if he were not lying, the relations between Schwartzkoppen and Dreyfus were simply unknown to him.

[1] See Appendix vi, p. 368.

Behind the scenes, the officers working on the case in the Rue Saint-Dominique had seen more clearly than the Minister of War that the prosecution's case, based solely on the *bordereau*, would be torn in shreds by a competent lawyer, and that further evidence must be found. Moreover the complete absence of motive must somehow be explained. Du Paty took it on himself to guide the *rapporteur*,[1] Bexon d'Ormeschville, and influence his presentation. Henry set on his agent Guénée to build up evidence of the prisoner's bad character. Guénée, recklessly seeking the very common name of Dreyfus among the low haunts of Paris, soon returned with information of a Dreyfus, an habitué of gambling dens, a pursuer of women of the *demi-monde*. The Préfet of Police, Lépine, who had also set enquiries on foot, at once recognised a confusion of identity, and officially informed Henry that Dreyfus neither gambled nor whored. Lepine's notes were not put into the record; Guénée's were.

Ormeschville, faced by the blank denials of Dreyfus, turned to his brother-officers for evidence of character. Even this was unsatisfactory. While Fabre, Aboville, Bertin and others gave more or less hostile evidence, a number of officers from other departments testified in his favour, or at least declared that nothing about him would lead them to foresee treason. All that remained were the contradictory reports of the handwriting experts, and Henry's tale of what he had heard through the door. By November 12 the case for the prosecution was crumbling. Sandherr ordered Henry to go through the Section's files and bring him such documents as might bear on the case. Henry found what he could—eight or nine pieces, he said later. Sandherr and Cordier went over them. There was the *canaille de D* letter, which Cordier believed to be "an antique"; it amounted to very little, but since there was an initial, it might as well go in. The rest offered even less: "All the dead heads in the

---

[1] The *rapporteur* of a military court-martial had the equivalent function of the *juge d'instruction*, the examining magistrate, in civil criminal trials. Up to the Law of 8 December 1897 the suspect was without legal assistance, nor could he even be present at the hearing of witnesses. The task of the magistrate was to build up the case, and this he often carried out to the prejudice of the prisoner.

files," said Cordier. They eventually made up weight with a letter from Panizzardi, warning Schwartzkoppen not to let Colonel Davignon, the War Office spokesman, know that the two attachés had any connection; "one must never let it be seen that one agent deals with another." [1] Then there was a letter, or rather a report, from Guénée relating to the visit of a foreign attaché to Switzerland on Schwartzkoppen's business, a document wholly irrelevant to Dreyfus. There was a report from Henry of his conversation with Val Carlos in June. There was the remains of a torn and crumpled ball of paper from Schwartzkoppen's wastepaper basket with notes for a letter. This last, which was in German, ran: "Doubt (*Zweifel*) —Proofs (*Beweise*)—Authority (*Patent*). Dangerous situation for me, relations with a French officer. To bring what he has. Absolute (word partly missing) Bureau de Renseignements [in French]. No relation with the troops. Importance only in coming from the Ministry. Already somewhere else." This note had reached the War Office in late December or early January. Dreyfus had only come to the Second Bureau on January 1.[1]

On November 6 Mercier's troubles with the Chamber began. The Chamber Army Commission unanimously found that he had acted unwisely, and by a majority that he had exceeded his powers. In the full Chamber he underwent bitter criticism from Le Herissé, Deputy for Rennes, a retired officer. Mercier's reply was heard in silence, and Dupuy, to save his Minister, accepted a "pure and simple" passage to the order of the day. Mercier by now knew only too well that, when the facts came out, his organisation of the Madagascar expedition would be even more severely attacked.

A week later, on November 13, Boisdeffre left Paris to represent France in Russia at the funeral of Alexander III and to be present at the marriage of his successor, Nicholas II. He did not return until November 30.

6

Ormeschville's interrogatory went slowly on. Prompted by Du Paty, he accepted every witness he could find: the evidence of those

[1] See Appendix vi, p. 369.

against Dreyfus he included, that of those who spoke in his favour, so far as he could, he omitted. But the length of the proceedings irked the journalists. Cassagnac, for all his anti-semitism, dared to say that the evidence rested on a single contested document, and that he was not happy to see the shooting of a French officer on the word of comedians professing to be experts in handwriting. Mercier felt he must reply. On November 28 an interview with the War Minister was printed in *Figaro*, in which he asserted that from the first day there were crying proofs against Dreyfus: that it was neither Italy or Austria to whom the papers had been offered; and that the only missing piece in the puzzle was whether Dreyfus had been paid. A few Deputies, a few editors, voiced their astonishment that Mercier should dare to publicise his views before the trial. Dupuy was even roused to tackle him. Mercier blandly denied that he had given the interview. The correspondent of *Figaro* was content to reaffirm all he had printed and to say that the General had said a good deal more. Five years later Mercier admitted the interview.

Münster read the interview and saw that by implication his own Embassy was the one involved, and that a responsible Minister had made the accusation. He once more protested to Hanotaux, who tried to placate him by sending a note to Havas that no foreign Embassy or Legation was involved. The War Office, knowing that the *bordereau* had in fact come from the German Embassy, were convinced the Ambassador was either lying or being deceived. The quicker journalists replied that of course Dreyfus's correspondent was the German military attaché in Brussels. William II, irritated that the good faith of his Minister was questioned, ordered Münster to protest more strongly. Münster, sick in bed, asked Hanotaux to call. Drumont at once pounced on Hanotaux as the lackey of Germany and said that the case would be hushed up. Barrès went so far as to say that Dreyfus would be decorated— he would be, but not for many years. The German press retorted acidly on the French idea of diplomatic conventions. The *Libre Parole* stated that one letter had been found among the papers of a military attaché of the Triple Alliance which overwhelmed Dreyfus, but it was so important that it would be suppressed. It followed this by claiming that the letter had indeed been suppressed, but that Mercier had a photograph of it.

This romance went on for several days and included an allegation that two vital letters had been returned to the Ambassador. (In these fantasies are to be observed the embryo of the story that the Kaiser had written to Münster about Dreyfus, and that Dreyfus had been writing directly to the Emperor.) Hanotaux, seeing his worst forebodings fulfilled, protested to Dupuy. Dupuy said that he found the Minister of War highly elusive and could never get to the bottom of things. On December 13 Hanotaux took to his bed, leaving another note for Havas to the effect that no documents had been handed back to the German Ambassador, and that Münster had done no more than protest against the allegations involving his Embassy.

7

Meanwhile Du Paty, instructed by Sandherr, had been working on the documents Sandherr had selected from the Section files. After long study he presented a commentary intended to show the connection between three of the documents and the *bordereau*. In this he identified Schwartzkoppen as the purchaser of the plans from the *canaille de D.* He interpreted Panizzardi's letter to Schwartzkoppen about Davignon as showing that the German had a friend in the War Office who was also his agent. He interpreted the Schwartzkoppen fragment "Doubt, Proofs" to mean that the German attaché had become involved in January with an officer who was important because he belonged to the Intelligence Bureau. This commentary he gave to Sandherr, who had a fair copy made. The fourth document—Guénée's report on the journey of a foreign attaché to Switzerland—was discarded, together with Henry's note of his conversation with Val Carlos.

The commentary was in fact a feat of wilful romancing, a highly ingenious, almost unintelligible rigmarole, though it is fair to say that Du Paty never committed himself to the statement that Dreyfus was D, or that he was the traitor; he merely said that he could be. Sandherr obviously saw that in this form the commentary was useless, since none of the judges would be able to understand it. As Davignon, by then a general, exclaimed on being shown it during the final revision of 1904: "I can't make head or tail of this nonsense; it's so complex and complicated that it's beyond my understanding." Sandherr decided to discard it, and handed back to Du Paty his original, telling him to keep it; he might one day need it as protection.

Someone, almost certainly Sandherr himself—who else could it have been?—then set to work to produce a group of documents of sufficient weight to convince the judges. It was in two parts: one, several original documents; the other, a biographical notice giving an account of all Dreyfus's treasonable activities. All we know of the contents of this file comes from the evidence of Captain Freystaetter, one of the judges at the court-martial of 1894, which he gave at the Rennes court-martial of 1899. It contained, he said, the *canaille de D.* and Davignon letters, and a biographical notice. He also remembered reading the words "Dreyfus arrested, emissary warned," and possibly also "precautions taken." The biographical notice appears to have stated that Dreyfus began his career as a spy at the Explosives School at Bourges in 1890. While he was there, a charred paper was found of instructions on the filling of shells with melinite; only two hundred copies had been issued. Dreyfus was alleged to have been copying it but failed to get rid of the original. Then, in 1894, the Statistical Section had got hold of part of the Ecole de Guerre course on the defences of Lyon copied out in the hand of a supernumerary attaché at the German Embassy. Dreyfus had been at the school from 1890 to 1892. The date was unimportant; Dreyfus had sold the information.

Freystaetter's memory in 1899 was not perfect; he was not sure as to the identity of the documents, but he was certain as to the allegations against Dreyfus. Until 1898 he had wholly believed in the guilt of Dreyfus. A highly honourable man, he had certainly not been prompted by anyone: he had no interest in falsifying his testimony and he could not have known any of these points except from the file submitted to the judges of 1894.

Sandherr had the biographical notice copied out and the file put together. At the Rennes trial Mercier said that he saw and approved the biographical notice, which he had had made for his personal use. It was agreed at Rennes by three other of the first court-martial judges that the *canaille de D* letter was also with it, probably the Davignon letter. As for the Panizzardi telegram, either the first erroneous version (with the invented addition: "precaution taken") was included in the file, or its content was written into the biographical notice. Mercier at Rennes denied this, but Freystaetter was immovable that somewhere during the court-martial he had read the words "Dreyfus arrested etc." (7, II, 399–403).

It seems that Mercier took this new file into his private keeping and put it in the safe of his private office, where it remained until it was brought out on December 22. The contents then, in the presence of Mercier and Boisdeffre, were put by Sandherr into an envelope, which was sealed and given to Du Paty to carry to the president of the court-martial.[1]

That Sandherr was the author of the biographical notice seems incontestable. Mercier had obviously neither the knowledge nor the time to compile it. It is unlikely that it was Henry, as yet a minor figure in the case. It was certainly not Du Paty, who did not see the document until 1897. Sandherr alone, except for Henry, knew all the papers. Furthermore, leaving aside both his anti-semitism and the fact that his professional *amour-propre* as head of the Section required the conviction of the prisoner, there is that cry uttered when Fabre first suggested Dreyfus by name: "I ought to have thought of it." More weighty are the two further facts. First: he had handed back to Du Paty the draft commentary with the hint that he should keep it as "protection," a hint repeated in January that he, Du Paty, might have to suffer heavy attacks. The second (see p. 96), after the verdict he did not obey Mercier's order to break up the file and return each piece to its original

[1] See Appendix iv, p. 366.

folder; he did not, as he knew Mercier had done, destroy his own copy of the biographical notice. This disobedience by a senior officer suggests that he, too, felt that he might later need "protection."[1]

[1] The various files should be distinguished. First, there is the judicial file, containing only Ormeschville's report and the original of the *bordereau*, which was sealed up in December 1894. Next there is the Secret or Little File, which contained the biographical notice and its accompanying documents in one part, and various other unused pieces, e.g. the Schwartzkoppen memo ("Doubt, Proofs") and photographs of the *bordereau* in another. Thirdly there is the Ultra-secret File referred to by Henry at the Zola trial, which nobody ever saw, which was supposed to hold the letter from Alsace identifying Dreyfus as the spy, and possibly the mythical letters from the Kaiser. This file probably never existed. The Secret or Little File was intact when Picquart saw it in August 1896. Thereafter it seems to have been monkeyed about with by a number of people, Henry, Gonse, Roget, Cuignet, until it was swollen to nearly four hundred exhibits.

CHAPTER FIVE

The Verdict and Sentence

1

BEXON D'ORMESCHVILLE completed his report on December 3. He identified all the papers on the *bordereau* as being secret or confidential documents, which must have been known to Dreyfus, while the evidence of his colleagues, coupled with his knowledge of several languages, "notably German," showed him to be of the spy type: everything pointed to his guilt. Prompted by Du Paty, he omitted everything favourable to the prisoner. He threw doubt on Gobert's motives and on Pelletier's capacity. This report he presented to General Saussier, and next day the Military Governor issued orders for the summoning of a court-martial.

Mathieu Dreyfus had hitherto been able to do little. He asked the most eminent barrister in Paris, Waldeck-Rousseau, to undertake the defence. Waldeck had given up criminal practice; his last appearance of this kind had been in defence of Eiffel in the Panama Company proceedings early in 1893. He recommended Edgar Demange, a barrister of fifty-three, bred in the highest traditions of the law, a believing and practising Catholic, who had behind him a long series of brilliant defences in criminal actions. Demange agreed to undertake the defence if, after seeing Dreyfus and reading the indictment, he believed him innocent. On December 5 he saw Dreyfus and went over the documents. They were not many: a copy (not a photograph) of the *bordereau*, the reports of the experts, of Du Paty and Ormeschville, with the statements of the witnesses. He at once perceived the hollowness of the case. He also saw no less clearly the odium and insults he would incur for his boldness in defending a Jewish traitor. He accepted the brief.

On December 13 Mathieu and Léon Dreyfus at last obtained an interview with Sandherr. The conversation displayed Sandherr as determined to do nothing whatever to assist the defence. He wilfully misunderstood what Mathieu said, or replied that he did not know the answer. They asked him about the trial *in camera.* Sandherr said that it was a matter for the court only. Du Paty, said Mathieu, was treating Alfred abominably: Sandherr rejoined that he knew no more honourable officer. When Mathieu said that they would do everything to discover the real traitor, and that their fortune was at Sandherr's disposal if he was able to help them, Sandherr took them up sharply and insinuated that they were trying to bribe him. And when finally they said: "We will find him. Can you help us?" Sandherr coldly answered: "I can do nothing, and I do not see how you could find this, according to you, other traitor. Believe me, if your brother has been arrested, it is because a long and serious investigation was made before a decision was reached. And then, to carry out your investigations, you would have to be installed in the War Office, have the Minister and all the officers at your disposal etc. That does not seem to me very practical" (7, II, 187–89). Fortunately for Mathieu, Sandherr wrote down the gist of the conversation that day, guaranteeing its exactitude; but talking to friends during the next months, he left them with the impression that Mathieu had attempted to bribe him.

Reinach alleges that Mercier did not dare to allow a public trial, since the emptiness of Ormeschville's report would cry aloud. It may be so; but since some of the documents on the *bordereau* dealt with secret matters, which must be explained to the court— for example, that on covering troops—normal security reasons are equally probable, as in all spy cases. The trial would be held *in camera.* But he could not order a secret trial: that was the pre-rogative of the judges. Nevertheless, the knowledge that the Minister desired a closed hearing would, if conveyed to the president of the court, be tantamount to an order. The Dreyfus family were aware of the danger. Demange asked Waldeck-Rousseau to approach Casimir-Perier. Joseph Reinach, the most prominent Jew in the Chamber, once head of Gambetta's secretariat, a staunch and patriotic Republican, but unhappily tainted by being the nephew and son-in-law of the defunct Baron de Reinach of scandalous memory, had, from the abnormal volatility of the anti-semitic press,[1] guessed that the evidence against his co-religionist was doubtful. He too feared a trial *in camera,* and also sought Casimir-Perier. To both the President said he would pass on their appeal, but that he himself was constitutionally impotent. Reinach also appealed to Mercier, who coldly refused him. The press broke out into a confused and virulent debate: the one side, those who stood on the grounds of decency and law for a public trial; on the other, those who either feared involving Germany and increasing the risk of war, or knew that Mercier wanted the trial to be secret. The Cabinet stood aside and let Mercier have his way. Someone dropped a hint to Colonel Maurel, the president of the court, that it would be better from all points of view to hold a public trial.

2

The trial opened on December 19 in an old building across the street from the Cherche-Midi. After the announcement that it was almost certain there would be no public audience, there were few sightseers. The judges were Colonel Maurel, Lt-Col. Echemann, Majors Gallet, Florentin and Patron, Captains Roche and Frey-staetter: all, except Gallet, who was a cavalryman, were infantry officers, Freystaetter of the Marines. There was no gunner member.

As soon as the accused had answered to his name, the military prosecutor, Major Brisset, asked for the case to be held *in camera* on the grounds of public policy. Demange protested that since the case rested on a single document . . . He was cut short by Maurel, who requested him not to speak of a single document, and con-tinued to prevent him from stating his argument. "The interests of the defence . . ." said Demange. "There are other interests than those of the defence and the accusation laid in this case," returned Maurel. Demange's mouth was closed. The judges retired, read his written submission against the closed court and rejected it. The court was closed: there remained only the judges and the three

---

[1] On November 6 the *Libre Parole* stated that he had through Freycinet forced Dreyfus on the War Office.

judges in waiting, the military prosecutor, the prisoner and his counsel, Lépine, Préfet of Police, and Major Picquart of the Third Bureau, detailed by Boisdeffre to report to him on the progress of the trial.

The Ormeschville report was gone over and Dreyfus replied in his usual toneless voice to the questions, with all the respect that an officer should show to his seniors. He protested against the charge of treason. His denials of precise statements were heard with indifference: if the statement was inaccurate, Major Brisset might nonchalantly suggest that its accuracy was unimportant: when he denied possessing any knowledge of changes in artillery formations the president rejoined that a gunner could not help but be interested. The examination was short. During the rest of the day and on the next two the witnesses were heard: Gonse, Henry, Du Paty, with seventeen officers called by the prosecution, Cochefert and the handwriting experts. For Dreyfus, the Chief Rabbi of Paris, a few friends and half a dozen officers, honourably risking their reputations, took the stand. One witness—Lt-Col. Jeannel, who had lent Dreyfus the artillery manual—was not called, in spite of the prisoner's request.

Gonse in evidence did his utmost to discredit the good faith of Gobert, who had refused to identify the writing of Dreyfus with that of the *bordereau*. It was pointed out that information about the covering troops was known to the copying clerks in the Ministry as well as to the officers: the point made no impression. Henry gave his version of the dictation scene and the subsequent interchanges. Du Paty gave his own account of the day of the arrest, asserted once more that Dreyfus had trembled when he heard the phrase about the hydraulic buffer. Demange offered him the piece of writing, and Du Paty had to admit that it showed no signs of agitation: but of course Dreyfus had been warned. By whom? He did not know. He was again confounded over the question of the date of the *bordereau*: if it was of April, as was alleged, then Dreyfus could not have had information available only in July, while if the *bordereau* was after July, then he could not, in view of the May 17 circular, have written that he was just going on manœuvres.

At the end of the second day the judges were shaken in their original belief in the prisoner's guilt. While they had been told that Mercier and Boisdeffre were convinced, the evidence was thin; it proved nothing. Picquart, reporting to Boisdeffre, said that if he did not know of the Secret File he would be very doubtful. Lépine thought acquittal probable. So too did Henry.

Henry had no illusions. Headquarters needed the conviction of a spy: so did the Statistical Section. In his thirty years' service he had seen much of the peculiarities of military justice. It was no matter to him who was condemned, so long as someone was. He was unscrupulous, and he was bold. He asked to be recalled.

In the box he told the judges that long before the arrival of the *bordereau* the Section had suspected a traitor in the War Office. They had had warnings from a man of honour as early as March. This man repeated his warnings in June that the traitor was a member of the Second Bureau. "And there is the traitor!" Dreyfus and Demange both loudly demanded the name of this informant, that he might be called. Henry replied brutally: "There are secrets in an officer's head which his cap mustn't know." Maurel weakly intervened: "You are not asked the name, but tell us on your honour whether this individual told you that the officer-betrayer was in the Second Bureau and was Captain Dreyfus." Henry raised his hand and in a loud voice cried: "I swear it."

Four experts were heard on the second day, two for, two against; on the third morning, Bertillon. He had now evolved a system largely based on his own method of measuring the heads of criminals. It was complex and needed a lot of explanation with the aid of diagrams and blackboards. He had thereby reached the conclusion that Dreyfus had forged his own handwriting. Mercier had been impressed. He had insisted on bringing Bertillon to explain it to Casimir-Perier. Casimir-Perier, after wasting much time on Bertillon, thought he was an argumentative lunatic. The court heard him through for an hour, stunned by his unintelligible verbosity. All they understood was that Bertillon believed that Dreyfus had forged the *bordereau* in a mixture of his own hand and those of his wife and brother.

By the end of the third morning the opinions of the judges were still wavering. Henry had made an impression, yet the material proofs were still absent, and no one had been able to divine any reason for the crime.

After lunch the prosecutor made a laconic speech, which Lépine thought empty of facts. Demange for the defence spoke for three hours, attacking the only substantial evidence he knew of, the *bordereau*. His policy as he saw it was to raise doubts in the minds of the court, and these doubts were already there. But, as someone in the court said, "He had not the trick of courts-martial"; he talked to them as he would to High Court judges. Brisset in his reply abandoned all attempts to show motive and relied solely on the single document.

At the luncheon interval Du Paty approached Maurel and handed him the sealed envelope he had received from Sandherr. At the conclusion of the speeches the court retired. Maurel, who was a sick man—it is said he was suffering from piles—produced the envelope he had been given by Du Paty and broke the seals. The members of the court were not versed in procedure; they did not know that the production of documents not shown to the defence was irregular and illegal in both civil and military law: they relied on their president, who himself relied on the Minister of War. The first document was the biographical notice of Dreyfus. Maurel discussed this, and then, feeling very ill, contented himself with passing round the other papers. The officers examined them and were convinced that they had before them an arch-spy. Although hitherto they had believed that only Germany was involved, now they saw that Italy too was in the game. They saw that the War Office believed in the prisoner's guilt, and they saw too that these documents could not have been shown in public. On the question of motive they were still bewildered; but Henry's evidence and the *canaille de D* letter seemed overwhelming in the light of the biography dating back four years. Each member voted Guilty. Neither president nor judges were required to support their verdict by a reasoned judgment. The death penalty for political crimes had been abolished by Article 5 of the Constitution of 1848. They therefore sentenced Dreyfus to deportation for life to a fortified place, to forfeiture of his rank and to degradation. It was the heaviest sentence they could give. According to military law, Dreyfus was not present at the delivery of the verdict and sentence. Demange when he heard it burst into tears. He at once went to the room where the prisoner was kept and still weeping embraced him, unable to speak. A few minutes later the prosecutor appeared and read the sentence, adding that the prisoner had twenty-four hours to lodge an appeal if he desired. On his return to his cell Dreyfus gave himself up to despair, and tried to beat his brains out against the wall. He begged Forzinetti to give him a revolver that he might commit suicide. Forzinetti, still believing in his prisoner's innocence, refused. That night he came to Dreyfus again and again, telling him that it was cowardice to accept defeat and that suicide would only confirm the verdict. His reward was a promise to survive and wait for justice to be done.

3

When the court rose, Picquart reported to Mercier and Boisdeffre. Mercier made no comment: Boisdeffre remarked that he would dine more peacefully. Before he left the court-room, Maurel had put the documents back in the envelope and handed it to Du Paty to take to Sandherr. On the next day, December 23, Sandherr brought the Secret File to Mercier, who destroyed the biographical notice and ordered that each document should go back to its original file. Sandherr did not obey his instructions. With Henry he went through the papers and apparently burned the false version of the Panizzardi telegram. Henry added the documents which Du Paty had used, but which had been discarded, and what was probably the original of the biographical notice. The whole he put into an envelope, wrote on it "*Dossier secret. D*" and added his own initials, J.H. He then, under the eyes of Gribelin, the filing clerk, put it in the office safe.

The press, whether for or against the trial *in camera*, welcomed the verdict. The unanimity of the judges swept away all doubts:

HENRY
with Picquart and Leblois at the Zola trial

DU PATY DE CLAM
at the Zola trial

DREYFUS AFTER DEGRADATION

no one imagined the possibility of the illegality of the proceedings. Liberal public opinion was reassured. The Socialists joined in the chorus of approval. Even the most bitter critics of Mercier were convinced: a volley of insult was fired at the traitor. The anti-semites shouted for the expulsion of the Jews. Mercier's reputa-tion was no longer in danger; he had saved France from betrayal. The single regret was that the traitor could not be shot.

On December 24 Mercier tabled a bill to re-establish the death penalty for treason and espionage; included in the text was an article which made it practically impossible for the press to discuss Army affairs. The restoration of the death penalty was at least equitable, since a mutinous, even an insubordinate, soldier could in certain circumstances be shot in peacetime: a conscript had recently suffered the penalty for throwing a button from his tunic at the president of a court-martial. The contrast between the two cases brought Jaurès to the tribune of the Chamber, but instead of con-tenting himself with the facts, he attacked the court-martial and the Government, which could have ordered Dreyfus's execution but had refrained merely because he was a rich bourgeois. The Chamber was indignant; even his own group forbore to applaud. Dupuy rebuked the orator, and Jaurès rushed back to the tribune roaring abuse at a Government which protected cosmopolitan speculators and liars masked as patriots. In the midst of the tumult, Brisson (since December 12 President of the Chamber in the place of Burdeau, who had died) suspended Jaurès. Mercier's bill was sent to the Army Commission. Later the Senate, in response to the criticisms of the press, considerably modified the text. Jaurès's speech won the applause of—the *Libre Parole*.

On December 31 the revising court rejected Dreyfus's appeal. Since they could not deal with matters of fact, only with matters of law, which so far as was known had not been mishandled, there was no case. By now Dreyfus had recovered his strength of mind: he wrote to his wife that he would face punishment with the dignity of a clear and calm conscience. He had other trials to endure. Mercier, knowing how near-run the verdict had been, sent Du Paty to offer him certain alleviations: a choice of prison, the presence of his wife and children, if he would confess, confess almost anything in confirmation of the verdict. The conversation between the two men was peculiar: Du Paty, shaken by Dreyfus's unfailing denials of guilt, but holding to what he had taken to be circumstantial evidence, appears to have tried to make the prisoner admit that he had handed over unimportant documents to Schwartzkoppen to get in return information useful to France. Dreyfus stubbornly maintained that the traitor was another man, and that it was the duty of the War Office to discover him. He wished he could put a knife to the throat of the foreign military attachés to force them to reveal who it was. At the end he told Du Paty that it was his duty to pursue the investigations. "If you are innocent," cried Du Paty, "you are the greatest martyr in history." "Yes, I am a martyr, and I hope the future will prove it. Search."

Du Paty regretfully reported to Mercier that the prisoner was adamant. His report was left in the Minister's private office: in due course it vanished, to be replaced by a more politic account written in September 1897. Dreyfus wrote a full account of the meeting for Demange. On the same day he wrote to Mercier that he did not ask for mercy, but that in the name of his honour he begged that investigations into the identity of the culprit should be pursued. Mercier was enraged. He persuaded the Cabinet that the hardened traitor should be sent, not to the Ducos peninsula in New Caledonia but to The Devil's Island, a leper settlement which was just being cleared to accommodate criminals, off the Guiana coast.

On January 2 Lucie Dreyfus was at last permitted to see her husband at the Cherche-Midi behind a double grill. The interview so harrowed Forzinetti that he persuaded Saussier to allow them to meet in his private office. They saw each other again two days later, and so far as they could comforted each other. "For you and the children," he said, "I shall submit to to-morrow's Calvary"— the public degradation.

4

Mercier had desired that the degradation should take place at Vincennes or Longchamps, in order to bring together as many people as possible: the Cabinet, not wishing a mob demonstration, decided for one of the courts of the Ecole Militaire. Though crowds gathered in the streets, only a few favoured journalists were given permission to watch the spectacle.

Dreyfus was brought from the Cherche-Midi, handcuffed, in the charge of Captain Charles Lebrun-Renaud of the Republican Guard. At the School he was put into a small room and kept waiting for an hour. Asked by Lebrun-Renaud why he had not committed suicide, he told the whole story so far as he knew it, and added that the Minister of War knew he was innocent; he had even sent Major Du Paty de Clam to him in prison to ask if he had not handed over an unimportant paper in order to obtain others in exchange. At length his escort came. The courtyard into which he was marched was filled with detachments from each of the regiments of the Paris garrison. The parade was brought to attention; the drums rolled. Dreyfus was led before General Darras, commanding the parade. The sentence was read. At its conclusion Darras shouted: "Alfred Dreyfus, you are unworthy to bear arms. In the name of the French people we degrade you!" Immediately in a loud voice Dreyfus shouted: "Soldiers! An innocent man is being degraded! Soldiers! An innocent is dishonoured! Long live France! Long live the Army!" The crowd beyond the walls hearing his voice broke into howls and whistles. A warrant-officer stripped him of his badges and buttons, and drawing Dreyfus's sabre from its scabbard, snapped it across his knee. The condemned man was then marched round the courtyard, still proclaiming his innocence. The soldiers were silent, but the pressmen and reserve-officers who had been admitted to the atrocious ceremony shouted abuse at him. Outside the walls the mob still howled "*A mort.*" When he had completed the circuit, his wrists were tied, he was thrust into a police-van and taken first to the Depot and then to the Santé.

5

Dreyfus had scarcely reached the Santé when rumours began to circulate that he had confessed. Their originator was Lebrun-Renaud, the dull heavy escort, who, in the few minutes between the time when he had handed Dreyfus over and the beginning of the parade, had joined a group of officers and given them a hurried garbled account of what the prisoner had said. As he was later to admit, there was nothing amounting to a confession, but he let fall apparently a version, omitting Du Paty's name, of Dreyfus's account of Mercier's offer of better treatment in return for a confession. This version ran: "The Minister knows that if I handed over documents, it was to get more important ones." At this moment he certainly had not taken Dreyfus's words as amounting to an admission, since he did not report them to General Darras, nor did he enter anything about his conversation with Dreyfus on the formal report he put in after the parade to Military Government Headquarters. Nevertheless, a story of a confession remained in the minds of those who had heard him and, from this, rumours began to circulate: by evening the newspapers were printing as a fact that Dreyfus had confessed.[1] The rumours reached the ears of Picquart, who had been present at the parade as the representative of the Minister of War. Believing that he had missed a matter which he should have reported, he sought confirmation of Military Government Headquarters. Colonel Guérin told him that he too had heard the rumours, but that nothing of the kind was stated on Lebrun-Renaud's report. Picquart brought this news to Boisdeffre, who took him to Mercier. The two generals, after a private word, dismissed Picquart, who, it being Saturday night, went off to his mother's house at Versailles.

At this point the complications foreseen by the now bedridden Hanotaux materialised. The diplomatic aspects of the case, which had hitherto scarcely impressed the public, but which had a little disturbed the Cabinet, began to assume threatening colours. Hanotaux's *démenti* of November 30 through Havas, that no foreign Embassy was involved, had not silenced Drumont or Rochefort. Mercier's *Figaro* interview of November 27 had clearly impeached Germany, while stories of documents filched from the German Embassy had wide currency. On December 26 Münster, once

[1] The statement appeared in *Le Temps* dated the 6th, in fact issued at 5 p.m. on the 5th.

more through *Figaro*, issued a denial: "The German Embassy has never had the slightest contact, direct or indirect, with Captain Dreyfus; no approach has been made for a trial *in camera*." Since Dreyfus had been convicted three days earlier, Drumont, Barrès and Rochefort replied with a volley of anti-German invective.

That day Hanotaux took himself and his troubles off to the south. He was perhaps really ill with anxiety over the crisis he had so signally failed to contain: it seems clear that he guessed Mercier had made an unforgivable error. In his absence, Dupuy took over the Foreign Office; but no more than Hanotaux did he dare withstand the press. On the day of Dreyfus's degradation, January 5, Münster visited Dupuy and presented an official note:—

> His Majesty the Emperor, with complete confidence in the honour of the President and Government of the Republic, requests your Excellency to tell M. Casimir-Perier that should it be proved that the German Embassy has never been implicated in the Dreyfus case, His Majesty hopes that the Government of the Republic will not hesitate to make the declaration.
>
> Without a formal declaration, the legends that the press continues to foster concerning the German Embassy may persist and compromise the Emperor's representative.
>
> Hohenlohe

The note was stiff. Dupuy, perturbed, hurried over to the Elysée and asked Casimir-Perier to see Münster. As has been seen, the President had been held at a distance by Hanotaux, and though he had been informed of earlier conversations between the Foreign Minister and the Ambassador, knew nothing of their substance. He agreed to talk to Münster, but before inviting him, required to know what had been said at the previous exchanges. He sent over to the Foreign and War Offices for the relevant files.

His request had just reached Mercier when Boisdeffre arrived with Picquart, bringing news of the rumoured confession of Dreyfus. Mercier was embarrassed. An avowal extracted by Du Paty could have been couched in suitably vague terms and officially made public, whereas if Dreyfus had talked freely to Lebrun-Renaud he might well have given away the fact that the Statistical Section had an agent in the German Embassy who had stolen the *bordereau*. Moreover, an avowal might show that Dreyfus was betraying both his masters, and since the German Embassy had denied all knowledge of the traitor, a confession broadcast through the press would convict the German Ambassador of either conscious or unconscious mendacity, from which all kinds of complications would arise. Mercier told Boisdeffre to bring Lebrun-Renaud, whose name neither had yet heard, to his office early the next morning. Considerable difficulty was met in running the officer down. Finding himself the centre of interest, he had spread his story round his mess, and now between 10 and 11 p.m. was doing the same at the Moulin-Rouge. About this hour, Boisdeffre, accompanied by Gonse, was seeking Picquart at his lodgings, only to find that he had gone to Versailles. Boisdeffre laid it on Gonse to discover the Republican Guard captain, and to bring him to the War Office early next day. Gonse rose early on the Sunday morning and with some trouble got hold of Lebrun-Renaud and took him to Mercier's room.

To Mercier and Gonse, Lebrun-Renaud denied that any confession had been made. His questioners, very impatient, were severe. He then told them, so far as he recalled, exactly what Dreyfus had said, including a version of the interview with Du Paty. Nothing, however, amounted to an avowal of guilt. Lebrun-Renaud was told very sharply to say nothing about Du Paty's visit to the prisoner, and nothing of any theft from the German Embassy; in short, to hold his tongue, hard.

None of the three men knew that this morning's *Figaro* carried a version of Lebrun-Renaud's talk at the Moulin-Rouge, picked up from his lips by an enterprising journalist. The story as printed said nothing about a confession, though it repeated Dreyfus's protests of innocence, but it stated that the main piece of evidence was a paper stolen from a wastepaper basket in the German Embassy. This item had already come to the eyes of Casimir-Perier and enraged him. He spoke to Dupuy, who in turn telephoned to Mercier.

Mercier at once sent the thoroughly scared Lebrun-Renaud to the Elysée.

After a long wait, he was taken by Dupuy to the President. Casimir-Perier questioned him closely as to what he had let fall about the paper stolen from the German Embassy: but Casimir-Perier apparently had not seen the note in the *Temps* and, since the *Figaro* had said nothing about a confession, asked him nothing more on this score. Finally the unhappy officer was sent off, having been told for the future to be silent. Dupuy then, with the aid of Mercier, concocted a message for Havas, to the effect that Lebrun-Renaud had certified that he had given no information to any newspaper or journalist. It was hoped that this would evade any fresh trouble with Münster.

For all his dislike of his office, Casimir-Perier was a cool and capable man. Now given the opportunity of action, which he had missed for the last six months, he did what Hanotaux had had neither the wit nor the firmness to do. He had only looked through the files on the previous evening. Out of the few pieces in the War Office file, which did not, of course, contain the Secret File, he concocted yet another version of what had happened. Although it was not in the file, he remembered the *canaille de D* letter and linked it with the *bordereau*. There was no reason why he should not believe Dreyfus guilty, no reason why he should not believe that the *bordereau* had reached the German Embassy and been read. He believed that Schwartzkoppen was deceiving Münster—as indeed he was, but not about Dreyfus. He invited Münster to visit him during the afternoon.

Münster and Casimir-Perier were old acquaintances. From the moment the Ambassador was seated, the President led the conversation. Pointing out that he was constitutionally without responsibility, he said he would have left the matter to the Prime Minister, but since he was mentioned in Hohenlohe's despatch, he took this to be in a way a private conversation between the heads of two sovereign states, the Emperor and the President; the matter was therefore personal and not diplomatic.

Having thus made his position clear, he took up the German

despatch. He stressed the word "implicated," and said that nothing of what he was about to say *implicated* the German Embassy. Dreyfus had been the object of suspicion for some time and had been watched. In course of time the Cabinet had been informed of an anonymous letter, coming, they were assured, from the German Embassy. Münster interrupted him by saying that he had made full enquiries: the Embassy received many letters, but it was impossible that an important document could be stolen. Casimir-Perier rejoined that it was possible that the letter from Dreyfus had been thought unimportant and thrown away. Whatever its value, it was enough to establish Dreyfus's guilt, but its receipt by the Embassy in no way made them responsible for it. All that was required was to have the traitor sentenced without involving the innocent Embassy staff. Hence the trial *in camera*. Münster naturally accepted Casimir-Perier's version. It remained to find a formula which would satisfy the Kaiser and not raise trouble in France. After some argument they agreed that a note through Havas clearing all the foreign Embassies of any connection with the traitor would be most sensible. On the Monday (January 7) Dupuy, with the agreement of the President and Münster, drafted a soothing communication, which, after it had been approved by Berlin, was sent out by Havas. The slight diplomatic tension, which was known only to a few highly-placed men, was at once relaxed.

The matter would be of no importance but for the fact that, on the basis of the intervention of the President, Mercier was to build up a legend of the night of January 5 (or 6—he was never sure of the date) when he and Boisdeffre stayed at the War Office, expecting each moment to be told that war was imminent and that mobilisation orders should be sent out. On the other hand, he had said nothing either to Dupuy or to Casimir-Perier of Dreyfus's alleged confession to Lebrun-Renaud, nor did he take any steps to go behind the message he and Dupuy had drafted together for Havas denying Lebrun-Renaud's story.

Gradually the fury of the gutter press over Dreyfus died away. The victim's protests of innocence were played down. But Demange said openly that while he submitted to the findings of the court, he remained at heart convinced of his client's innocence. The press told him to be silent; by talking he proclaimed himself an accomplice.

6

Casimir-Perier had had enough of the position of President. He had been considering resignation since early in October. He was tired of the threats and abuse of the press, of his treatment by his Ministers, of being no more than a rubber stamp. The death of his intimate friend Burdeau in December had deprived him of the moral support he needed. His suggestion of Félix Faure as President of the Chamber in succession to Burdeau had been vetoed by Dupuy; the Radical Brisson had been elected over the Republican Méline. In the New Year a further demonstration against him was staged, when Gérault-Richard, who in November had been sentenced to a year's imprisonment for insults to the President, was put up as the Socialist candidate at a by-election in the XIIIe arrondissement of Paris, and on January 6, the very day when Casimir-Perier was smoothing out the German difficulty, was elected. The Chamber, waiving an old privilege, rejected a motion from the Extreme Left to have Gérault-Richard's sentence suspended, but the motion was defeated only by 309 to 218: the Radicals joined with the extremists, their leaders—Léon Bourgeois, Sarrien, Doumer and Lockroy—voting with the Socialists.

Within the next week political uncertainty was brought to a crisis by a non-political imbroglio. The financial crash of the Union Générale in 1882 had made it impossible to carry out the provisions of the Government's share in the Freycinet scheme of railway development. The Government had been driven to negotiate with the companies and force them to accept a greater share of the financial burden. Among the terms was the State guarantee of interest on the railway stock. Owing to somewhat imprecise wording, the date on which the guarantee should terminate became a matter of controversy, the railway companies holding that the guarantee continued until the termination of the railway concessions in 1956; the Ministry of Public Works, that it ended in 1914. Barthou, the Minister, took the question to the Conseil d'État, which on January 12 found for the companies. Barthou, the youngest Deputy, as he was fond of proclaiming, who had ever held a ministerial portfolio—he was now thirty-two—and not yet broken of being clever, told Dupuy that, as the opponent of the companies, he could not carry out the Conseil's award: he resigned on January 13 and refused to relent. Whereupon his intimate friend Raymond Poincaré, Minister of Finance, with the budget for 1895 not yet voted, said he too would resign. Dupuy called the Cabinet for the next day and then handed in their collective resignation to Casimir-Perier. The President considered this resignation a trap, in so far as he would be bound to invite the Radical leader, Bourgeois, who had so recently shown his hostility, to form a Government. He told Dupuy that if the Cabinet resigned without being defeated, he too would resign. Dupuy therefore withdrew his resignation, but sought to escape from his difficulties by other means. He was at once given his chance. On January 15 the Socialist-Radical, Millerand—within a year he was to move over to the Socialists—attacked the Government for taking the railway case to the Conseil d'État instead of securing the support of Parliament for the interpretation it desired. He proposed the setting up of a committee to go into the original transaction carried through in 1883 by David Raynal, then Minister of Public Works, a Bordeaux Jew who on more than one occasion had had to defend his name against libellous attacks. Millerand suggested that Raynal had either been bribed by the companies, or else by negligence had shamefully surrendered the rights of the State. Raynal defended himself and welcomed the proposal of a committee, which he knew would clear him of calumny.

Dupuy asked for a vote of confidence. The Chamber, playing the old game of what it delightfully called "pure politics," refused him: many of his supporters abstained, and others, among them Méline, voted with the Opposition. The Cabinet at once went to the Elysée with their resignation, to which Casimir-Perier answered that he too would retire: in the accusation against his old friend

Raynal he saw yet another personal attack, and he was determined
not to have anything to do with the Radicals. The Ministers protested, but he sent them away. He spoke to a few individuals:
Félix Faure, to whom he explained his reasons; Challemel-Lacour,
President of the Senate, who upbraided him for his weakness; Poincaré, though what was said to that enigmatic neutral is not known.
Finally he wrote out his message of resignation and sent it to the
Presidents of the two Chambers. The message stated that he found
he was deprived of the means of action and control. In spite of
twenty years' service to the Republic, Republicans distrusted
him. He had been the victim of a campaign of obloquy against
the Army, the judicature and himself personally. He believed that
reform could be carried out only by a strong executive resolved to
secure respect for the laws and to command the obedience of its
subordinates. Hence he resigned.

The message and the action were received by Parliament and the
press with condemnation. Abroad the reaction to the message was
one of shocked amazement. Yet those who knew the President well
were not surprised. "Casimir adores clear-cut situations," wrote
his old friend Paul Cambon from Constantinople: "now, in politics
situations are never so. . . . And Casimir has never understood the
divine aspects of politics, as one talks of the divine 'aspects' of
war. . . . He has never looked on politics as the art of guiding men
. . . and forms of government as essentially transitory. . . . He
thumbed the Constitution instead of manipulating ministers" (19,
383 and 384).

The two Chambers were summoned to meet in National Assembly
at Versailles on January 17. The Left put up the inevitable Henri
Brisson: it was the fourth time he had stood. The Republicans
of the Chamber were for Félix Faure, but those of the Senate
wanted Waldeck-Rousseau, who had recently shown a reviving
interest in politics. The Monarchists had no candidate: but the
Duc d'Orléans, who, owing to the recent death of his father the
Comte de Paris, was now the Bourbon representative, remembered
that in 1886 Faure had spoken against the expulsion from France
of the claimants to the throne and their families, and told his

followers to support him. It is said (72, 17) that the Catholic Right asked both Faure and Waldeck whether they were Freemasons. Waldeck, who was not a Mason, disdained to reply: Faure, who had certainly been one, swore by all his gods that he was not. The Right backed Faure. Privately General Mercier allowed it to be known that he too was a candidate; he circulated an advertisement commending himself as the saviour of the Republic, and accusing Casimir-Perier of meditating a *coup d'état*.

At the first poll Brisson led by 338 to 244 for Faure, and 184 for Waldeck: Mercier secured 3. On this Waldeck withdrew, and at the second poll Faure was given an absolute majority over Brisson, 430 to 361. The declaration was greeted by the now usual hullabaloo from the Extreme Left, the Socialists and Socialist Radicals, in which accusations of bribery and threats to force the new President from office were mingled.

The career of Francis Félix Faure had been unspectacular but solid. The son of the owner of a tannery at Le Havre, he had, it was said, worked in it as a manual labourer in his youth. He had later turned to shipping and had some connection with the Turkey trade. In 1881 he was elected for one of the constituencies in this most republican and bourgeois city, whose interests he firmly defended in the Chamber. He had been Minister of Marine in Dupuy's Cabinet. He was tall and handsome. With his eyeglass, his well-cut coats, check trousers, gleaming waistcoats, four-in-hand ties and shining white spats, he was said to be "rotten smart." He was conservative, something of a snob, and though now on the edge of fifty-four, he liked it to be known that he had preserved all the vigour of his youth, in the saddle and in other less public activities. Naturally he leant towards the Army. His election produced caustic shafts from all sides. "Laid by Aynard, hatched by Léon Say," wrote Clemenceau. "The poor gentleman is not a president," said Millerand, "but a ballet-dancer." Jules Delahaye, the Nationalist, claimed: "He owes his election to the affability of his approach, his incontrovertible mediocrity and his tailor, much appreciated by the Parliamentary Right."

On his arrival at the Elysée, Faure at once called on Léon Bour-

geois, whose group had been the biggest in the majority against
Dupuy, to form a Government. To the general surprise Bourgeois,
who was believed to have a Cabinet ready to take office, failed to
secure enough support in the Chamber. After long negotiations
with the other group leaders, he abandoned the attempt. Ribot,
summoned in his place, had no difficulty. A conservative Republican, thoroughly hostile to the Left, Ribot had already twice
presided over the Cabinet, and had steered the Chamber through
the last months of the Panama scandals with some success. In his
team he retained Hanotaux at the Foreign Office, moved Leygues
from Public Instruction to the Interior, and Poincaré to Public
Instruction from Finance, which he took over himself. A Senator,
the worthy Trarieux, became Minister of Justice, André Lebon
Minister of Commerce, and a mild Radical, Alphonse Chautemps,
Minister of Colonies. Mercier was dropped: his administrative
errors had been too gross and his attempts to exploit the Dreyfus
case so indiscreet that he could no longer be borne. "Thus," wrote
the Nationalist Millevoye, "Dreyfus is avenged." Mercier's place
was taken by General Zurlinden. An admiral, Besnard, went to
the Marine. Ribot, in spite of the fact that he was five times Prime
Minister, remains a negative figure, liberal in professions, conservative in actions, a dialectician, a lawyer who would never commit himself in office. In opposition he was, in a mild way, a
knocker-down of ministries, as Clemenceau had been in the eighties.
A half-hearted Liberal, full of good will but incapable of action,
"the kind of mug," wrote Jacques Bainville, "who, when Jaurès
speaks, withdraws into himself and feels ashamed not to have done
more for progress and democracy." "The ministry's weakest
link," wrote Edouard Millaud in his diary, "is the Prime Minister."

7

Dreyfus was held in the Santé from January 5 to 18. During that
time he was allowed to see his wife twice. On the night of January
18 he was wakened and taken to a train for La Rochelle, in freez-
ing cold, with irons on his wrists and ankles. At La Rochelle his
presence was given away. A mob gathered and it was only with

difficulty that he was saved from its blood-lust. He was taken to the Ile de Ré, where he was treated with brutal savagery by the head of the prison. He was not allowed to speak to his jailers; his letters to his wife were deliberately delayed. He wrote one petition to the Minister of the Interior, begging him to continue investigations to establish his innocence. The letter was not answered. Yet he continued to believe that the truth would one day be known.

In February Lucie Dreyfus received permission to visit him: but her visits were limited to half an hour, during which she stood out of reach, with the chief warder between them. She saw him for the last time on February 21, but she was permitted neither to kiss him nor to take his hand. Though she had guessed from the sight of the ship lying in the harbour that this was their final meeting, she was told nothing. That evening he was once more stripped and searched—the daily routine since he had reached the island—by special order of the Ministers of Marine and Colonies. He was then taken on board the convict ship and put into his cell. A hammock was thrown to him. He was left without food. *La Ville de Saint-Nazaire* raised anchor and set sail for Cayenne.

CHAPTER SIX

Picquart

1

DREYFUS had been sentenced to deportation to a fortified area. By a special law passed on 9 February 1895, on the motion of Delcassé, without discussion, the Îles de Salut, off the coast of Guiana some thirty miles from Cayenne, were added to the usual Ducos peninsula in New Caledonia as places of detention for political prisoners. These were three islands, on one of which were already incarcerated the most desperate convicts, and on another the permanently sick, mostly criminal lunatics; the third, The Devil's Island, was a leper colony. It was now hurriedly cleared for Dreyfus. On this burning and desolate lump of rock, four hundred yards wide, two miles long, a small stone hut was built with a tiny yard in front, to accommodate him and the jailer on duty. The chief warder had received instructions to shoot the prisoner down at the slightest movement to escape. He was permitted to exercise only on a narrow path some two hundred yards in length. He was not allowed to communicate with the jailers. His food was scarcely adequate; he must prepare it himself; he was not allowed wine. A lamp burned all night in his room, in which clustered a myriad insects. He was eventually permitted to write and receive a limited number of letters, strictly censored at the Ministries of War and the Colonies. Always he hoped to have news that the real traitor had been found. He heard nothing, and his appeals to the President, to Boisdeffre, to Du Paty, went unanswered. Yet he refused to give in. On a number of occasions he was ill, either from the intolerable heat and the insects, or mentally. He suffered and he aged. Neglecting his appearance, he let his beard grow; it turned white. Except for his career and his family he had had no interests. Without them he had no resource. His existence

111

was death in life. Except by his jailers and his family, he was forgotten.

Why should he not be? His case had been a minor nuisance. The Cabinet had much on its hands. As some had foreseen, a law was passed on February 2, granting amnesty for crimes against the internal security of the State, for press crimes except libel, for electoral misdemeanours, etc. It was Parliament's revenge on the President it had thought strong and found weak: Gérault-Richard was released and took his seat among the Socialists; Rochefort and Drumont returned from exile.

In Paris Mathieu Dreyfus had begun his task. Conscious as he was that anti-semitism had grown fiercer with the trial, he moved very cautiously. Some men knew or guessed that his brother had been condemned on documents not shown to the defence; few of them, even Ministers, were aware that the communication to the court was illegal. Indeed, had they known, it would not have weighed with them: at the Zola trial, Trarieux, Ribot's Minister of Justice, now a leading Dreyfusist, admitted that, had Dreyfus really been a traitor, he himself would not have had the courage to raise any questions about illegality in the form of the trial. A few Alsatian friends, a few editors, encouraged Mathieu. Whatever scent he followed, it ended in air. He had copies of some of the trial documents, parts of Ormeschville's report: he kept them hidden lest the police-agents who watched him should raid his sister-in-law's house.

Lucie Dreyfus petitioned the Government to be allowed, as was her right under a law of 1873, to join her husband. Her petition was twice rejected without explanation. On the third occasion, Guieysse, Minister of Colonies, saw her and told her that it was, in the circumstances, impossible.

2

Ribot's Government did not have an easy life. There were difficulties with the Russians, who treated their French paymasters as a smart cocotte treats an elderly banker. They needed money. Hanotaux, faced by grumbles in the Chamber and the press that the treaty was one-sided, at length grew stiff, forced the Russian Government to agree to his alluding to the convention in Parliament, and to join a Russian squadron to that of the French at the formal opening of the Kiel Canal as a demonstration of solidarity.

Ribot, having in his policy speech to the Chamber stressed the need for pacification and understanding, almost at once showed he meant peace with a difference. To please the Radicals he proposed to fill the gap in the budget by squeezing the religious Orders. As it in fact worked out, the Orders were a match for the Treasury; little more than a third of the expected sum came in after five years of law-suits. Ribot had however exasperated the Ralliés, the bishops and the Vatican, who saw that the Pope's advance was not being met halfway by the Republicans. Leo XIII made no public protest, but he let it be known that he was deeply wounded by the Government's ingratitude. The clerical press rushed into action. *Croix, Vérité, Univers, Libre Parole*, Cassagnac's *Autorité*, abused Ribot with all the venom and disrespect at their command.

On top of all this, although they were not responsible, the Government had to meet bitter criticism of the casualness with which the expeditionary force for the conquest of Madagascar had been prepared by Mercier. No French transports had been available, and the Republic had had to hire ships from British companies; the sanitary and medical preparations had been abominable; five hundred men had died on the voyage, and three thousand more within a few months of landing.

Finally on October 28 Ribot was defeated on the question of the change of judges in the middle of a trial. "M. Ribot's Cabinet, say his adversaries, fell on a question of morality. The only morality which can possibly be extracted from the debate is the incoherence of Parliament," was the bitter comment of a political editor (82, November 1898).

Félix Faure summoned Léon Bourgeois as the leader of the main group in the hostile vote. Bourgeois produced the first wholly Radical Cabinet, with a civilian, Cavaignac, at the War Office. Hanotaux declined to serve, and the Foreign Office was taken over by Marcellin Berthelot, a distinguished chemist, who knew nothing about diplomacy.

The new Ministry was received with enthusiasm by the Left, with chilly courtesy by the Republicans, and with hostility by the Liberals and Conservatives. The Boulangists at this point tried to concentrate their forces by forming a parliamentary group under the name of Nationalists.

Léon Bourgeois had made his career up the ladder of the Ministry of the Interior, prefecture by prefecture. He was notorious for promoting his friends: "He is the leader not so much of a party as of a clientèle," someone had said. Naturally he himself took over the Interior. It was too late in the year to offer much of a programme, since the Budget of 1896 still had to be passed. On many of the reforms demanded in opposition he was silent, but the mention of a further discussion of income-tax, coupled with the presence of Doumer at the Ministry of Finance, augured a stormy existence, while the inclusion in the Cabinet of nine Freemasons, one of them Emile Combes, the renegade seminarist, at the Ministries of Public Instruction and Public Worship, warned the Catholic members that they would have to fight for their beliefs. In one direction Bourgeois was successful. Adopting the financial proposals of the Ribot Government, he pushed the Budget through both Chambers by the end of the year, a feat which had not been accomplished since 1890.

The year 1895 ended in a dust-storm of scandals, dying storms raised by the widespread activities of the late Baron Reinach. In January Doumer spoke of his intention to reduce indirect taxation and compensate the losses by a progressive income-tax: "a Republican Budget would replace a Monarchical one." The Senate became restive. In February a Senator accused the Minister of Justice of illegal interference in a case, and on the debate the Ministry was defeated. In the Chamber the Ministry maintained that the Senate were in error and secured a vote of confidence. The Senate riposted by confirming their original vote. Bourgeois refused to acknowledge the right of the Upper Chamber to press his resignation. Three of the four Republican groups in the Senate at once issued a declaration maintaining the Senate's equal rights with the Chamber in the matter of Cabinet responsibility. At the end of February the Chamber Finance Commission rejected Doumer's income-tax proposal by an overwhelming majority. In March Doumer brought the proposal before the Chamber. In a series of complex debates Bourgeois four times in five days had to request a vote of confidence. His majorities were tiny, between seven and sixteen. In the provinces over eighty per cent of the departmental councils declared their opposition to the tax proposals. Clearly the Bourgeois Cabinet was not going to survive long. The Senate felt strengthened. On April 22 a vote of credit for the Madagascar operations came to it from the Chamber. The Senate decided to adjourn the vote "until it finds before it a constitutional Ministry possessing the confidence of both Chambers." After some hesitation Bourgeois resigned. At once the Senate passed the vote of credit.

Félix Faure asked a Radical, Sarrien, to replace Bourgeois, but Sarrien could get no support. Faure then sent for Jules Méline. He was an old Republican, an old Gambettist from the days of the National Assembly, a frontiersman from the Vosges. He had once been Minister of Agriculture and had been the proponent of the tariff laws of 1891 with their heavy duties: "His heart," said an irreverent journalist, "beats only for cereals." But he was an old parliamentary hand. First he tried to get a Cabinet of concentration by the union of the Centres, that elusive dream which every Prime Minister had pursued in vain. His advances were repulsed by the Radicals. He fell back on the Government Republicans. On April 29 he met the Chambers, with Hanotaux once more at the Foreign Office, Barthou at the Interior, Cochery at Finance and General Billot at the War Office. The survival of his Ministry seemed problematical. Bourgeois, in defiance of tradition, attacked him, asserting that the crisis had arisen solely out of the conflict with the Senate, and that constitutional revision to eliminate the Upper Chamber was the only remedy. Méline got his vote of confidence by no more than thirty-four, not a strong majority. Yet the Cabinet was to live for more than two years.

Whatever conflicts of doctrine might exist between the Right and
the Republicans, they could always be relied on to unite to prevent
the return of a Ministry dedicated to the imposition of income-tax.
Méline's fall was eventually to come through unforeseen and mysterious events revolving round the case of the forgotten prisoner
on The Devil's Island.

3

In October 1895, among other letters, Dreyfus received one, as
usual passed by the Director of Prison Administration, Guégen,
signed "Your old cousin, L. Blenheim." The name was unknown to
him; the letter of no importance; he threw it into the drawer in
which he kept his papers. He did not discover until after his return to France in 1899 that between the lines, written in an invisible ink which would become opaque only by the application
of heat or by gradual discoloration, was a cryptic message. This
ran: "Thread broken. Try to re-knot. Our two attempts have
failed. We are forced to be very careful. Everything nearly discovered. Let me know where 2249 was. The Jura business 34 is
known."

It is evident that the writer counted on the message becoming
visible to the censor, and thus another nail would be firmly driven
into Dreyfus's coffin. Who was the writer? Only someone whose
interest it was *at this time* to produce further proofs of guilt. Since
Sandherr was already as good as dead, since Esterhazy as yet had
no knowledge that he was involved, since Du Paty was back in the
Third Bureau and was no longer in touch, the only probable author
is Henry, who knew that not only was the evidence of the prisoner's
guilt dubious, but that the Chief of Staff had desired that the case
should be strengthened by the discovery of a motive.

4

Neither Schwartzkoppen nor Esterhazy had an inkling that it
had been their relationship which had led to the arrest of Dreyfus.
During 1895 Esterhazy appears to have passed to the German
attaché, at ever-increasing intervals, papers of less and less value

to the Germans. He had in fact no serious knowledge of guns or gunnery, and, as came out later, he drew the attention of Captain Le Rond, the officer in charge of the visitors to the Châlons exercises in 1894 and 1895, by asking questions which demonstrated his basic ignorance (7, II, 114–15). By the beginning of 1896 Schwartzkoppen was considering dismissing this useless and despicable agent. In March he broke with him.

Before this time, changes had occurred in the Statistical Section. During the spring of 1895 Sandherr's disease had suddenly worsened and in June he was stricken with paralysis. His second-in-command, Cordier, had no desire to remain in the office he detested; he was posted to an infantry regiment. Sandherr's place was taken by Major Picquart of the Third Bureau, the War Office representative at Dreyfus's trial.

Marie-Georges Picquart was, like Sandherr, an Alsatian. Born in Strasbourg in 1854, he was sixteen when Alsace was annexed. At Colmar, under the eyes of the Germans, he studied for the French Army. He left Saint-Cyr fifth in his class, and joined the 4th Zouaves, with whom he fought in Algeria in 1878. He then entered the Ecole Supérieure de Guerre, from which he went as Intelligence Officer to Galliffet's staff. In 1893 he was seconded to the Third Bureau (Operations and Training) at the War Office. His chiefs throughout had had a high opinion of his abilities. As a Strasbourger he was bilingual in French and German, and he possessed a knowledge of other languages. He was good-looking, quiet, cultivated, thoughtful and reserved. He was unmarried and lived in very modest lodgings near the Etoile. Boisdeffre, as he said at the Rennes trial, thought that he had too good an opinion of himself; nevertheless he could not disregard the strong recommendations of Miribel, Galliffet and Millet, the Director of Infantry, under whom Picquart had served. Picquart, though not a violent anti-semite, had like other Alsatians prejudices against the Jews. At the trial he had been unmoved by Dreyfus's protestations of innocence.

He took over the Section on July 2, with the rank of Lieutenant-Colonel. Sandherr, whose mind had not yet wholly given way (he died in May 1897), saw him a couple of times and handed over the secret funds. He warned him that Boisdeffre was still worrying about the Dreyfus case, but that he himself thought the less it was looked into the better: Picquart would find the file which had been communicated to the judges, with its convincing proofs of guilt, in Henry's hands.

On taking over, Picquart was seen by Boisdeffre, whose uneasiness seems to have derived from a recognition that, even with the secret documents, the case against Dreyfus was inconclusive. He told Picquart to follow up the case: it was absolutely necessary to discover the motive for the crime.

Whether, as has been alleged, Henry was disappointed at being passed over for a younger man, even though his senior in rank, is impossible to verify. Picquart at least had no doubts about Henry's loyalty. For light on Dreyfus's private life, Henry recommended the ex-policeman, Guénée. Picquart soon found that Guénée was incompetent: he could fish up nothing better than gossip from door-porters of gambling-houses. At the same time Picquart had the correspondence of the Dreyfus family intercepted and read, as well as the letters to and from Dreyfus on The Devil's Island. Again nothing emerged: he read unmoved Dreyfus's continued protestations to his wife and brother of his innocence. Gradually he discovered that every seedy rogue of the underworld was ready to sell information about the prisoner and that all of it was worthless. Fragments brought by Bastian were either unintelligible or trivial. Moreover, it was certain that staff papers were still being filched. He was severely shaken at being offered by an Englishman at an enormous price a copy of the mobilisation positions opposite the German frontier, accompanied by a threat that if he did not pay, the document would go to Germany. Knowing that the seller would keep a copy anyhow, he refused, and, after enquiries of the Bureau from which it had come, found that it had been in so many hands that no hypothesis could be formed as to who had lost or sold it. Thus during eight months nothing came to light to stiffen the case against Dreyfus. Nevertheless, Picquart's work more than satisfied both the Chief of Staff and the successive

War Ministers, Zurlinden, Cavaignac and Billot. In April 1896 his temporary rank of Lieutenant-Colonel was confirmed. In March of that year Henry, still the recipient of Bastian's waste-paper, was much absent from Paris, partly employed on a treason trial at Nancy, partly visiting his mother, who was dying at Pogny. However, he succeeded in making a rendezvous with Bastian between two trains, about March 15. It was a big delivery, which he had just time to hand over to Picquart. Picquart locked the bags in his cupboard and next day gave them to Lauth to sort out and reconstitute. In a few days Lauth came to his chief with a reconstructed *petit bleu* (a special-delivery letter resembling a letter-card on thin blue paper, for local use in Paris), and laid it before him, saying: "It's frightening. Is this another of them?"

The *petit bleu* had been reconstituted from a great number of tiny fragments, none of them bigger than a little-fingernail. It ran:

> Sir, Before all I await a more detailed explanation than you gave me the other day on the question in suspense. Will you therefore be good enough to let me have it in writing to enable me to decide whether I can continue my relations with the firm of R—— or not. C.

It was addressed to Monsieur le Commandant Esterhazy, 27 Rue de la Bienfaisance, Paris.[1]

5

Marie-Charles-Ferdinand Walsin-Esterhazy was the son of a distinguished French general of an illegitimate branch of the Hungarian Esterhazys, who had died in 1857. Although later some stress was laid on Esterhazy's origin, with the implication that he was a foreigner, he was by blood almost wholly French (64, 39, f.n.). Stories that he entered Saint-Cyr but failed his examinations, that he later entered the Austrian Army and in 1866 fought at Custozza, appear to have no foundation. In 1869, at the age of twenty-two,

[1] See Appendix v, p. 367.

he joined Lamoricière's Roman Legion, and in 1870 secured a commission in the French Foreign Legion, from which, during the Franco-Prussian War, he had been transferred to the 2nd Zouaves. After various re-postings, among which he was, for a year or so, Orderly Officer to General Grenier, he was sent to the Statistical Section in 1878, where he stayed until 1881, thus getting to know Sandherr and Henry. By this time he had reached the rank of Captain. From July 1881 to 1884 he was in Tunis, during which time he claimed, quite falsely, to have been decorated. Returning to France in 1884, he married two years later Anne-Marie de Nettancourt, younger daughter of the Marquis de Nettancourt-Vaubecourt with a dowry of two hundred thousand francs, and a little later bought with his wife's money a country house at Dommartin-la-Planchette, near Sainte-Menehould. From 1889 he was stationed in or near Paris, running after women, speculating on the Bourse and losing. In 1892 he had been one of the seconds to Captain Mayer in his duel with Morès, and on this score was never backward in claiming help from the Jews.

By the close of 1893, perhaps earlier, he had reached the end of his resources. In 1892 he had been promoted to Major, but ordered to a regiment garrisoning Dunkirk. He had made such a fuss about this exile that in the end the War Office transferred him to the 74th Infantry Regiment at Rouen, at this date within two hours of Paris by train.

Esterhazy was an adventurer, but without purpose. He took little interest in his battalion, spent as much time as he could in Paris, leading a debauched but apparently unhappy existence, always short of money, in debt to his tradesmen and borrowing where he could. On the other hand, he was apparently far more widely read than the average army officer, and was possessed of a fantastic and sardonic humour. Moreover, he was an impressive figure. Corporal Benda, no respecter of persons, when he was doing his military service at Courbevoie in 1892, watched him one evening strolling to and fro in front of the officers' quarters: "tall, thin, a little bent, the face sallow, bony and lined . . . a careworn air. He might have been an elegant and treacherous gipsy, or, better, a

great wild beast, alert and master of itself. Charmed by his distinction, I could not take my eyes from him" (13, 181).

This was the man who had boldly offered himself to Schwartzkoppen on 20 July 1894, and to whom the *petit bleu* picked up in
the German Embassy was addressed.

6

The *petit bleu*, as Lauth pointed out to Picquart, had no postage
stamp: thus it had been torn up before despatch: it could therefore not be used to incriminate the intended recipient. The
writing was not that of Schwartzkoppen, but appeared to be the
partially disguised hand of a woman known to be the attaché's
mistress.

Picquart naturally jumped to the same conclusion as Lauth, that
here was possibly another traitor. However, remembering the
difficulties caused by leakages from the War Office in 1894 and the
consequent press campaign, he decided to make no report until
he had more solid information.

The 74th had been transferred from the Rouen area to Paris in
October 1894. Finding that among the officers of the regiment was
an old friend, Major Curé, he invited him to call and asked his
opinion of Esterhazy. Curé replied that Esterhazy was a thoroughly
bad officer, dissolute, a stock-market gambler; on the one hand paying little attention to his duties, on the other always trying to
obtain confidential information on guns and gunnery, adding that
he had twice gone to firing-practices, and a third time at his own
expense, and finally that he employed soldiers in his battalion to
copy documents. Curé, however, refused to help Picquart to procure an example of Esterhazy's writing.

Picquart consulted Henry, who admitted having known Esterhazy in the Statistical Section fifteen years earlier, but said he had
lost sight of him. They arranged to have him shadowed by one of
the special police attached to the War Office, Desvernine. He discovered Esterhazy's financial troubles, and also that, in the Rue
de Douai, he kept a woman, Marie, called Marguérite, Pays, a
registered prostitute, known as Four-Fingered Margaret, whom he

had picked up at the Moulin-Rouge. Desvernine twice saw his quarry visit the German Embassy in broad daylight, but Picquart was warned by Curé that Esterhazy had probably gone there on legitimate business. The shadowing continued during May, June and most of July without result, and in the meantime no further fragment of interest came from the German Embassy by the "ordinary route." The *petit bleu* was photographed by Lauth and Junck, still another Alsatian who had joined the Section late in 1895.

For much of this period Picquart was away from the Section, owing partly to the illness of his mother, partly to his accompanying Boisdeffre on a staff tour. During this tour Boisdeffre's Orderly Officer, Pauffin de Saint-Morel, told him that the French military attaché in Berlin, Colonel Foucault, had written to him saying that a renegade German agent, one Richard Cuers, had confided in Foucault information which Picquart ought to know. On his return to Paris Picquart saw Foucault and learned from him that the German War Office staff had never themselves employed Dreyfus, nor had they found a single military attaché in any capital who had ever heard of him before the trial. The only agent known to be a French officer was a battalion commander, aged about forty-five, who had given Schwartzkoppen information about artillery, much of it of little value, and had recently given notes on various technical details from the gunnery school at Châlons.

Picquart, knowing from Curé that Esterhazy had borrowed from the colonel of his regiment and had copied some of the Châlons papers, was roused. He arranged with Foucault to send Cuers to Bâle, where he would be interviewed. He told Lauth and Henry to meet and examine Cuers, and sent with them two agents from the Sûreté. On August 5 Cuers was met—Tomps, one of the Sûreté men, knew him by sight—but was interviewed by Henry, who knew no German, and Lauth; Cuers's French was poor. The interview was a failure. The only serious information was (*a*) that four documents had been received by Berlin, reports on a new rifle, on the quick-firing gun, on the entrenched camp at Toul, and on the

Nancy fortifications, but Cuers could give no date of delivery; and
(b) that the German General Staff suspected that the French
officer was a counter-spy and had told Schwartzkoppen to break
off relations. And he refused to name the man.

On the day that Lauth and Henry set out for Bâle, Picquart reported to Boisdeffre that he feared they had discovered another
traitor, Major Walsin-Esterhazy.

Boisdeffre commended the discretion with which Picquart had
acted, and approved his proposal that for the present the information should be given only to the War Minister, General Billot, and
not to Gonse, the Assistant Chief of Staff. Billot, after hearing
Picquart, also commended his prudence, but refused to allow him
to ask Esterhazy's colonel for a specimen of his writing. A little
later Boisdeffre, while showing no signs of a desire to shield Esterhazy, said: "I don't want another Dreyfus case. He'll be put on retired pay and sent about his business. He must be got rid of without any scandal."

In August Esterhazy, no longer on Schwartzkoppen's pay-roll,
conceived the audacious scheme of getting himself seconded to
the War Office. To further this, he applied to an old friend, who
had been with him in the Statistical Section about 1879, Weil.
Maurice Weil, an officer on the retired list, was now employed
as Orderly Officer to General Saussier, the Military Governor of
Paris. A pleasant little Jew, his main business in life was to run
errands for his elderly General and to have a wide circle of useful
connections. He had, however, had the misfortune as a Jew to
have been denounced as a traitor in the *Libre Parole* by Drumont's
bully, Morès. There was nothing tangible to support the accusation, but as always, the smell of the mud which had been thrown
remained. (Picquart, on the evening of Dreyfus's degradation, had
questioned Colonel Guérin, Saussier's Chief of Staff, about Weil,
whom he had heard of as possibly a traitor.) Weil wrote a personal
recommendation to Calmon, Billot's chief private secretary. Esterhazy also approached several Deputies, among them Adrien de
Montebello and Jules Roche, a former Minister. In spite of their
support nothing happened. He continued to press Roche, and also

secured the help of a couple of generals. He followed this up by writing, on August 25, directly to Calmon.[1]

A day or two later, when Picquart was reporting to Billot, Calmon told him of Weil's recommendation. Picquart told Boisdeffre, who laughed at the impudence, and Billot, who said he was being inundated with letters from Deputies and generals. Picquart spoke of his suspicions of Weil, to whose door Desvernine frequently tracked Esterhazy, whereupon Billot told Calmon to give the correspondence from Weil and Esterhazy to the head of the Statistical Section. On August 27 Picquart received two Esterhazy letters. As soon as he saw them, he perceived that the writing was already known to him. He compared it with one of the prints of the *bordereau*; the hands were identical.

Since his talk with Foucault, it had once or twice crossed his mind that Dreyfus might be innocent but, having been present at the court-martial, he had dismissed the idea. Now he was convinced. However, he took care. He covered up the dates, the signature and one or two revealing phrases in the Esterhazy letters, and had Lauth photograph them. He showed the prints to Du Paty, who had believed that the Dreyfus brothers had collaborated in the writing of the *bordereau*. Du Paty at once exclaimed: "Mathieu Dreyfus!" Bertillon, to whom he also showed the prints, said: "Ah, the handwriting of the *bordereau*. So the Jews have been training someone for a year to imitate the writing."

For the moment, bewildered, Picquart believed that Esterhazy

---

[1] Reinach's contention that Henry was already Esterhazy's accomplice breaks down completely at this point. Had they been in direct touch, Henry could scarcely have failed to tell Esterhazy about the *bordereau* and the *petit bleu*, of both of which Esterhazy was ignorant. And, although Esterhazy might not have told Henry that he was trying to get into the War Office, he probably would have done so. There is no indication that Henry knew of his advances, but it is highly improbable that he did not hear about them either from Picquart or Gonse. If Esterhazy had been his accomplice, to have him in the War Office would have been the last thing he wanted. Esterhazy's applications are therefore not as machiavellian as Reinach supposes.

Roche's reputation was damaged by his connection with Esterhazy. It is possible that he was one of the other unnamed "personalities" suspected by Billot as being a member of the Dreyfus–Esterhazy gang; he had been *rapporteur* of the Army estimates for 1894. One day in 1899 Combarieu, Loubet's secretary at the Presidency, noted these suspicions in his diary (24, 38).

and Dreyfus were accomplices: but since the writing of the *bordereau* was Esterhazy's, on what evidence had Dreyfus been found guilty? Henry was on leave, and Picquart told Gribelin to get him the Secret File which had been shown to the judges, and sought in it the crushing proofs of which Sandherr had talked. Not one of the few documents showed a trace of Dreyfus, though the Schwartzkoppen scribble, "*Zweifel, Beweise, Patent,*" might refer to Esterhazy. The only other piece was a commentary in what Picquart believed to be Du Paty's hand. To the Criminal Appeal Court Picquart said: "I broke off relations with him but without a row" (6, I, 213).

On September 1 Picquart set out a full written report, sustained by the documents, added a request for an enquiry, and submitted it to Boisdeffre. Boisdeffre heard him in silence until he produced the Secret File, when he exclaimed: "Why wasn't it burnt as was arranged?" Otherwise he made no comment, merely told him to see Gonse, then in the country, and take his opinion. Picquart visited Gonse two days later.

Gonse, but for his thirty years' friendship with Boisdeffre, seems to have had no qualities. He looked like a battered Napoleon III, and had the reputation of being a gasbag. He was without decision or moral courage. After Picquart had made his explanation, Gonse merely grimaced and said: "So it looks as if a mistake has been made." On being asked for instructions, he replied: "Separate the two cases, Dreyfus's and Esterhazy's." Picquart thought this absurd, since the *bordereau* belonged to both. At Rennes Gonse claimed that, being incompetent to judge handwriting, he had told Picquart that the *bordereau* was Dreyfus's, and the charge against Esterhazy should be based on the *petit bleu* and any other exhibit that could be found, which, if true, shows that he had no intention of looking back into the Dreyfus case.

Picquart saw Boisdeffre again: Boisdeffre showed only indifference, and told him to wait before reporting to Billot.

7

On the same day on which Picquart saw Gonse, the London *Daily Chronicle*, quoting the *South Wales Argus*, announced that Alfred Dreyfus had escaped. When the report reached Paris, André Lebon, the Colonial Minister, cabled to Cayenne and on the following day received a denial of the story. The false news had in fact been "placed" by Mathieu Dreyfus. All his efforts to find evidence to refute the accusation against his brother had failed. Realising that by now Alfred was nearly forgotten, he conceived the idea of reawakening interest by publicising news of his escape. It was a singularly unhappy stratagem, which was to add to his brother's sufferings. In spite of the wholly reassuring reports from Cayenne, André Lebon feared the attitude of the press. He cabled to the Governor to build round Dreyfus's hut a double palisade, and until that was completed, to put Dreyfus in irons each night. Thus for four and forty nights of insupportable heat the wretched prisoner was clamped immovably on his bed. The fetters cut into his shins, and although his warders tried to ease the pain by winding rags round his legs, his flesh was cut and bruised. Furthermore, he was no longer allowed to leave his cell. At first, since the warders were not allowed to speak to him, he could not understand this new torture: he thought he was going mad. But on the second day Bravard, the commandant of the islands, visited him and explained these new security measures. When at last he was freed, he found that one of his few consolations, the sea, was hidden from him by the eight-foot palisades within which alone he was permitted to take exercise. Lebon, both ashamed and afraid, did not disclose to his colleagues what he had ordered. Bravard appears to have protested to the Governor of Guiana, who tried to reassure the timorous Minister. Lebon replied by recalling Bravard and sending from France a prison officer, a pitiless sadist called Deniel.

Lebon's fears had also been increased by a further mystery. Within a day or so of the *Daily Chronicle* alarm, a letter was addressed to Dreyfus through the Colonial Ministry. It was ostensibly written by a Jew calling himself Weill or Weyler.

Commonplace in content, between the lines were written in bad
sympathetic ink words which, when the letter was treated, conveyed a cryptic message that implied a regular secret correspondence with the prisoner concerning documents. Lebon and
Picquart were bewildered. Picquart thought it genuine, that it
emanated from the Dreyfus clan, whose recent letters had indicated
a hope that they were approaching a solution of the judicial error.

Mathieu Dreyfus's aim had been achieved. The prisoner was
remembered by the journalists. The anti-semitic papers announced
that the vast Jewish international "Syndicate" was going to buy
off the warders. On the other hand, Gaston Calmette, one day to
perish at the hand of Mme Caillaux, published in *Figaro* a sympathetic article describing Dreyfus's existence and miseries on The
Devil's Island, while Cassagnac once more forcibly expressed his
doubts about the trial: military judges were "no more infallible,
no more enlightened and no more honourable than their brothers,
cousins and friends, the jurymen who are so often mistaken."

Picquart had already feared that the Dreyfus family would find
some clue to the truth and that the deplorable nature of the case
would be revealed to the humiliation of the officers concerned. He
learned from Guénée that the editor of the *Eclair* was a friend of the
Nationalist Deputy, Castelin, who was thought to be in touch with
Mathieu Dreyfus. On September 10, the *Eclair* printed a measured
article stating that Dreyfus had not been condemned on his writing
alone, and that he had made quasi-admissions both at his arrest and
after the trial.

Hence, when on September 11 Castelin, in an open letter to the
Prime Minister, announced that, on the reopening of Parliament,
he would raise the question of the nonchalance of the Government
towards the activities of Dreyfus and his friends, Picquart, deceived as to the Deputy's motives, came to the conclusion that
revelations damaging to the War Office were about to be made. If
this was so, it would be the wisest course to admit at once that an
honest error had been made, to prosecute Esterhazy and release
Dreyfus. He now, after several applications, obtained Boisdeffre's
permission to lay the whole case before Billot.

As to what was said at this interview, the testimonies of Billot and Picquart before the Cour de Cassation in 1898 conflict. Picquart said that at this moment Billot was persuaded of Dreyfus's innocence, but subsequently swung back to the opinion that both Dreyfus and Esterhazy were guilty. Billot replied that he warned Picquart that the guilt of Esterhazy did not in itself absolve Dreyfus, and that he inclined to think, since spies do not work alone, that other men were involved besides Dreyfus and Esterhazy: he had seen the writing of two who should be looked into. He did not name them, but one was certainly Maurice Weil.

He did, at the interview, direct that enquiries should be pursued and better evidence procured: above all, in view of the approaching visit of the Tsar in October, rumours must be prevented.

Billot, a tubby, white-moustached old gentleman nearing seventy, had been a political general for the last twenty-five years. He had been elected to the National Assembly in February 1871, one of the three soldiers who voted against the acceptance of the German peace terms, and one of the few Republican army officers. He had taken a big share in the reconstruction of the Army in 1875, and had been elected a life-senator. Once before, in the early eighties, he had been Minister of War. It is argued that had Billot been a strong man, had he at this point sent for Boisdeffre and taxed him with having left him, the Minister, in the dark for ten days over this judicial error, had he then faced the Cabinet and the Chambers, none of whose members knew more than did the general public about the original trial, he would have carried the revision through, to his own undying glory. It may be so, but it is doubtful, since even Picquart at this date had not really got to the bottom of the case.

On September 14 the *Eclair* published a second more detailed article in which its author claimed to tell the truth about the trial. In distorted form it gave items from the *bordereau* and, more important, stated that certain secret papers had been shown to the court. For the *canaille de D* phrase it substituted a sentence running, "*Décidement cet animal Dreyfus devient trop exigeant.*" It also gave a version of the arrest and trial. Travestied though they were, these details could have been derived only from someone familiar with the whole story. The article was written in a sober and judicious style.[1]

Picquart had been told by Boisdeffre to put himself for the future under the direction of Gonse. When he saw the *Eclair* article, he at once wrote to the Assistant-Chief: "I told you we were going to have heavy troubles on our shoulders if we did not take the initiative." He would try to discover who had so cleverly prepared this bombshell, but first action must be taken. "If we still hesitate, we shall be overrun, cornered in an inextricable position, and we shall no longer be in a position to defend ourselves or establish the truth." Seeing Gonse next day, he suggested that steps be taken against the *Eclair*. Gonse declined to move; it was outside his competence; they must wait for the return of Billot and Boisdeffre, now at the manœuvres in Charente. He went on: "Why do you make such a point of Dreyfus leaving The Devil's Island?" Picquart answered: "But General, he's innocent." Gonse returned: "The case can't be reopened. General Mercier, General Saussier, are involved in it." "But since he is innocent!" "That is unimportant; that is not a consideration which should be brought into the reckoning." Trying another line, Picquart said: "You are well aware that the Dreyfus family are at this very moment at work. . . . Well, if they succeed in finding the real culprit, what will our situation be?" To which Gonse: "If you say nothing, no one will know."

"I confess," said Picquart at Rennes, "that I was completely floored, and I said to him: 'It's abominable, General. I will not carry this secret to my grave,' and I left the room."

Boisdeffre waited to see whether any controversy would follow the *Eclair* article, and as none did, he left the paper alone. Picquart

---

[1] The author, or inspirer, of the *Eclair* article has never been identified. The matter was revived before the Cour de Cassation in 1899. Henry was then dead; Guénée, who died before the Rennes trial, took refuge behind "professional secrecy." It is probable that Henry supplied the material. Picquart believed Du Paty responsible, which was unlikely as he was on manœuvres. But Picquart throughout displayed a kindness for Henry and a loathing of Du Paty (7, I, 439–40).

perceived that he was not going to be allowed to follow up the Dreyfus side of the affair.

He had already been forbidden on the grounds of security and prudence to place the *bordereau* and Esterhazy's letters before the graphologists. Now on September 16 Gonse asked him how he proposed to deal with Esterhazy. Picquart suggested arrest. Gonse thought this too elementary : there was no evidence, he said, except the *petit bleu*, which, since it had not been through the post, was valueless. Picquart then proposed to send Esterhazy a telegram, ostensibly from Schwartzkoppen, inviting Esterhazy to call. Gonse said he would consult Boisdeffre. Boisdeffre sent Picquart on to Billot. Billot refused to have Esterhazy arrested. "I won't be a sub-Mercier." He tentatively approved the bogus telegram, but on Picquart asking for a written order, refused to give it. At Rennes Billot sketched a noble portrait of himself repulsing temptation. Yet he was probably wise to refuse. If Esterhazy had read the *Eclair* article, he might have recognised the *bordereau* and would have taken precautions. Yet Schwartzkoppen, who did not know the *bordereau*, never having received it, but had received some of the papers listed in it, failed to identify them from the article.

Immediately after the *Eclair* publication, Lucie Dreyfus, observing no *démenti* from the War Office as to the revelation of documents withheld from the defence, addressed a petition to the Chamber. A few journals noticed it, but for most it was obscured by the preparations for the reception of the Tsar.

Left by his chiefs with his hands half-bound, Picquart interviewed one of Esterhazy's former copyists and also Le Rond the officer in charge of the firing practice at Châlons in 1894. But since he had been warned to be prudent, he was unable to push his enquiries to more than superficial corroboration. Esterhazy was still being shadowed. At the end of September, when his regiment was sent back to the Rouen area, he left 27 Rue de la Bienfaisance. His repeated applications through Deputies and generals had become a nuisance to Billot. He told Picquart to search Esterhazy's recent lodgings. Nothing was found except a couple of cards with cordially worded messages from Drumont, which at least showed

Esterhazy to be linked with the *Libre Parole*. About the same time Picquart heard from Cavard of the Sûreté that the "Weyler" letter which had so much disturbed Lebon and himself was not, as they had supposed, from the Dreyfus family, but probably a forgery, designed to strengthen the evidence against the prisoner.

8

During the summer Henry had been on the best of terms with his chief, but he had been first irritated and then alarmed at Picquart's fixation on Esterhazy, his "*marotte*." There is no vestige of evidence, either direct or indirect, to show a connection between Henry and Esterhazy at this period. Henry was neither more nor less than an experienced professional soldier, loyal to his country, to the service and to his chiefs, though he knew enough about these not to trust them too absolutely. He seems to have had quite a high opinion of Picquart, but he was growing to look on him as a menace to the service. A reopening of the case of 1894 would be disastrous, to the senior officers, to the Statistical Section and to himself, who had made so vehement a declaration at the trial on no basis whatever. He was perfectly conscious of the weakness of the evidence: he probably knew, from either Sandherr or Picquart, that Boisdeffre was uneasy over the absence of motive in the crime. He had (no one else can have done it) concocted the Blenheim letter to Dreyfus in October 1895, and it is not less credible that he was the author of the Weyler letter: both designed, if read by the Director of Prison Administration, to create a presumption of the prisoner's guilt. Watching Picquart slowly weaving the case against Esterhazy, whom he knew to be totally unscrupulous, but whose arrest and trial must lead to the release of Dreyfus, he began a more constructive foundation of the case against the prisoner, and since solid materials were not available, he turned to manufacturing them.

He had for a long time had connections with the reporters of the popular press. That he provided the writer in the *Eclair* with the materials for the articles of September 10 and 14 cannot be proved; but though a dozen officers could have given the information to the *Eclair*, only Du Paty, who was on manœuvres, had an equal interest in preventing the reopening of the court-martial, and Du Paty knew nothing about Esterhazy. That Henry was the source of the articles is supported by the fact that in this same month of September he began his career of falsification and forgery, an undertaking in which he more and more deeply entangled Bois-deffre, Gonse, Picquart, and Du Paty, tying a net from which they could not free themselves, while he himself, cunning but neither subtle nor far-seeing, was driven to strengthen his earliest experiments with further fabrications, until the day when the truth burst through the web he had created.

The first act of tampering with a document which can be definitely assigned to him appears to have occurred this month, September 1896. It was an old note of March 1894, from Panizzardi to Schwartzkoppen, which had reached the Section by the "ordinary route." It ran: "In the end, yesterday evening, I had to send for the doctor, who has forbidden me to go out. Since I cannot come to you, will you please come to me to-morrow morning, for P has brought me a number of interesting things and the work must be shared as we have only ten days left." Henry rubbed out the P and substituted a D, while, since the letter, in accordance with the usual negligence of the office, bore no date of receipt, he added "March 1894" in his own hand, a date which, as was discovered later, happened to be correct. This he carried to Gonse, without informing Picquart. Gonse, as he had been with Picquart, was hesitating and indecisive. Failing to make an impression here, Henry then approached Boisdeffre, who roughly told him that he was uninterested and threw him out. Henry then went back to Gonse, a far more malleable subject, and confidentially suggested that while Picquart was an upright and intelligent man, he was distracted, and neglecting the work of the Section in favour of the Dreyfus–Esterhazy problem.

It was untrue. Picquart, left without orders either to drop the case or to continue, had turned back to his ordinary work, the study of foreign armies. But when talked to by the two Generals about the case, he invariably showed that he could not be dissuaded from his belief that Dreyfus was wrongly convicted. In consequence, Boisdeffre and Gonse came to think that Henry was wholly right in his criticism of Picquart, and decided that he must be removed from the head of the Section. Boisdeffre proposed to Billot that he should be posted to Indo-China, but Billot considered that this would be a bad mark against a good officer. He thought of sending him on a special mission to organise the intelligence section along the frontier, while, to avoid comment, Gonse should take provisional charge of the Statistical Section. Picquart was told of the decision, which was to take effect at the end of October.

Picquart in evidence said that he had never yet spoken to any member of his staff about the connection between the Dreyfus and Esterhazy cases, though they must have guessed it after the interview with Cuers at Bâle. Now for the first time Picquart took Henry into his confidence and laid the matter before him. The ex-ranker replied: "When I was in the Zouaves, some fellow, son of a colonel, got involved in theft. His officer wanted him charged. The seniors thought differently. The officer was broken and the culprit set free." Henry knew his army on a different level from Picquart's: he knew that one doesn't make oneself a nuisance to one's superiors. "Your words are golden," answered Picquart, "but this is a case of conscience. I can't say the opposite of what I think." This exchange no doubt wiped away whatever hesitations Henry may have had: Picquart was becoming a serious danger. He began planning the decisive stroke.

The autumn extraordinary session of Parliament opened on October 27, with the Castelin interpellation still pending. Billot and his staff had been perplexed. They had believed that Castelin, in spite of being a Nationalist, was in the pay of the Dreyfus family, and that a highly compromising situation might arise. Billot, on the point of sending Picquart off, postponed his tour. At the same time Gonse took the Secret File into his own keeping.

On All Saints' Day, a holiday, Henry set to work, with the aid of papers removed from various files, and at his side a former agent, who at present passed under the name of Lemercier-Picard —his real name was Leeman, but he had had many aliases—an accomplished forger. They had before them recent but unimportant letters to Schwartzkoppen from Panizzardi, signed with the usual "Alexandrine." Both were written on paper with squared feint lines in blue. From each Henry removed the bottom of the page which had not been written on. On these pieces Lemercier-Picard wrote in pencil, in Panizzardi's hand, the body of two letters. One ran:

> I have read that a Deputy is going to interpellate about Dreyfus. If new explanations are required at Rome, I shall say I have never had relations with this Jew. You understand. If you are asked, say the same thing, for no one must ever know what happened with him.[1]

The second letter was as follows:

> Here is the manual; I have paid as arranged (180) on your account. It is agreed for Wednesday, 8 p.m. at Laurent's. I have invited three from the Embassy, but only one is a Jew. Don't fail.

To each of these Henry attached one of the headings and one of the signatures with the usual gummed paper. To the first he added in his own hand "Sept. 1896"; to the second "14 June 1894." The second trivial letter was put in to show that the handwriting of both pieces was the same. The first, if accepted, would blow Picquart's circumstantial evidence into thin air: it was the ace of trumps.

But, although he knew it not, there were two fatal flaws. In the first place, while in 1896 there were indeed three Italians of Jewish descent at the Italian Embassy, in 1894 there was none. In the second place, the papers on which the two original letters had been written, although to a casual eye identical, were in fact different. On one, the feint lines were blue-grey, on the other grey-claret. Not observing this, Henry stuck the blue-grey head and tail on to

---

[1] Henry indulged in a number of forgeries and improvements of documents, but this one is the central piece, and is known throughout the subsequent proceedings as the "*faux Henry.*" In order to distinguish it from the other fakes, I shall refer to it in future by that name.

the grey-claret body, and the grey-claret head and tail on to the blue-grey body.

On November 2 Henry showed these documents to Gonse. Gonse, whose various appearances before courts of law demonstrated his ability to credit anything he would like at the moment to believe, took them to Boisdeffre. Much later Boisdeffre was to say that he had found the similarity of the handwriting in the two letters a little too perfect, but at the time he expressed no doubts, and seems never to have reflected that Panizzardi, well aware that papers drifted from his Embassy to the War Office, was not such a fool as to commit a compromising statement to paper when he could easily have spoken to Schwartzkoppen. But perhaps he thought the improbability of no great importance, since the letter need never to be shown except to a War Minister in order to fortify him against the Chamber. He carried it to Billot, who was delighted that Picquart's suspicions could no longer be justified, and decided that the young officer had acted too precipitately and indiscreetly. He agreed to his departure from Paris as soon as the Castelin interpellation was out of the way.

Meanwhile Mathieu Dreyfus believed that he had prepared the ground for the revision of the case. Some time earlier he had been approached by a young Zionist Jew, Bernard Lazare—something of a saint—who believed that an error had been made by the court-martial. Lazare had prepared and had printed in Brussels a pamphlet which showed the contradictions between such facts as had leaked out. The *Eclair* divulgations gave him a great deal more matter. On November 6 *La Vérité sur l'Affaire Dreyfus* was published, and copies sent to Members of Parliament and other prominent men. It made little stir. Jaurès was cold. Clemenceau would not read it. Rochefort, curiously enough, welcomed the author, but since the circulation of *L'Intransigeant* was failing, he refused, on the advice of his manager, Vaughan, to undertake a crusade. Rodays of *Figaro*, though he believed in Dreyfus's innocence, shrank from action. Zévaès of the Socialist *Petite République* was insulting.

On November 10 the *Matin* published a reproduction of the

bordereau. Although the photographs distributed to the various individuals working on the case had been called back by the Statistical Section, no check had been carried out. Teysonnières, one of the graphologists of 1894, had kept his print, and had now sold it to the newspaper. The publication excited a good deal of comment. Schwartzkoppen, though he had never seen the document, recognised the traitor's hand, and at once informed Panizzardi, from whom he had been concealing Esterhazy's identity. Two other men (one abroad) also recognised the hand, but for private reasons held their tongue. No one came forward to name the writer.

On November 12 Billot told Picquart that he now had in his hands a document completely establishing Dreyfus's guilt and read out to him Henry's forgery. Surprised that such a paper should not have passed through his Section, Picquart expressed some doubt as to its authenticity, but Billot would not discuss it, and dismissed him.

On the following morning Maurice Weil found among his letters an anonymous note in a hand he did not recognise, to the effect that he and Esterhazy would be accused by Castelin of complicity with Dreyfus. Much alarmed, he sent for Esterhazy, and after discussing what to do, Weil asked Adrien de Montebello, one of his friends in the Chamber, to hand the letter to Billot.

It would seem that the information contained in this letter must already have been given by someone to Boisdeffre: for, accidentally meeting Picquart that morning, the Chief of Staff, visibly in a state of irritation, cried: "Ah, Lieutenant-Colonel Picquart, they're regular wrong 'uns, your Weil and your Esterhazy, and this looks like the moment to catch them red-handed." He swept on, leaving Picquart speechless.

Henry had now been working on the pliable Gonse for some time. He had told him that Picquart was responsible for the article in the *Eclair* and for the facsimile *bordereau* in the *Matin*, and that he was no doubt also the prompter of Castelin, the confidant of the Dreyfus family. Only some such intervention can account for the fact that the normally deferential and hesitant Assistant-Chief went that afternoon to the Minister himself, and in the presence of Boisdeffre told him that either Picquart must go or he would resign. Billot at once agreed.

In consequence, on November 14 the three generals had Picquart before them. Billot reproached him with lack of discretion in handling Esterhazy's case and read out the letter which Weil had received. He asked how another letter from Weil to Esterhazy had reached Picquart's hands. Picquart said that it had been seized in the post, the normal practice of the Section over years. Billot played the noble Roman over these police practices, and declared that Picquart would not only find himself in jail, but would compromise his Minister. He would not, however, punish him for indiscipline, but he must leave the Section for the time being. He was to set off at once on the mission they had already discussed. Realising that he was being got rid of without being allowed to defend himself, the disciplined and obedient soldier made no protest. Next day he handed over the Section to Gonse, and to Henry confided the *petit bleu*. "You'll see us again at Christmas," said Gonse. On November 16 Picquart reported to Corps Headquarters at Châlons-sur-Marne.

9

Superficially it would appear that Picquart had been sent away because he wished to reopen the case of Alfred Dreyfus, and this superficial aspect has passed into legend. But there is a case for Picquart's superiors, and their problem deserves examination. Dreyfus had been condemned, if not legally, at least in their minds justly. That the condemnation was based on error seemed to them improbable. As regards Esterhazy, he might well be a traitor, but there was no evidence against him that would carry conviction to a court-martial. He might be a loose fish, but that was not enough. The *petit bleu* in fact contained no more than the fact that he might be in correspondence with some unidentified member of the German Embassy, not necessarily the military attaché. Therefore, real evidence must be found before steps against him could be taken. Picquart had found none—nor, as is known to-day, was he likely to, since Schwartzkoppen had broken with Esterhazy before the *petit bleu* was written. Six fruitless months had passed, and his persistence was becoming a nuisance: Alsatians had the reputation of being obstinate. His obvious preoccupation with the case meant that he was becoming less useful as head of the Section, and, worse, his conduct was bordering on indiscipline. Hence, he must be removed. There is not a shred of evidence to suggest that they were swayed by other motives than the efficiency of the service.

It is said that they ought to have suspected the *faux Henry*, as Picquart had. But only those who had examined the documents in full and over many months read the interchanges between Schwartz-koppen and Panizzardi could have done so. The senior officers re-lied, as all senior officers do, on the technical skill of their sub-ordinates. They had no reason to consider Henry other than honest. They were in fact grossly misled.

CHAPTER SEVEN

The Beginning of the Crisis

1

ON November 18 Castelin's dreaded interpellation came before the Chamber. The Deputies were uninterested; few had read Lazare's pamphlet, many disliked Castelin. Billot, sustained by Henry's forgery, took the wind out of Castelin's sails by mounting the tribune at the opening of the session. In grave tones he told the members that both justice and State security were involved, and that everything from the preliminary investigation to the final rejection of Dreyfus's appeal had been carried out in conformity with the rules of military procedure. "The case is therefore *res judicata* and no one has the right to reopen it." He added that the higher considerations which had necessitated the hearing *in camera* in 1894 had lost none of their validity, and he appealed to the patriotism of the Chamber to cut short a dangerous debate. Since not even his colleagues knew what lay behind his words, he was applauded. Castelin could do no more than take up the crimes of the Syndicate, make charges of attempts to bribe officers, etc., and leave the stand, shouting, "*Vive la France! Vive la République!*" As usual with these frivolous interpellations, there was much confusion as to what motion should be put forward. Méline, bored with the whole thing, accepted Castelin's motion of confidence which enjoined the Government to investigate the Dreyfusists: it was passed after a show of hands. Experienced political commentators regarded the whole thing as one more example of the incurable levity and lack of discipline of the Deputies. Méline, with no reason to doubt Dreyfus's guilt, and preferring to let sleeping dogs lie, prevented the Minister of Justice, Darlan, from ordering the prosecution of Lazare.

On December 3 the Chamber Commission of Petitions rejected Mme Dreyfus's appeal on the grounds of *res judicata*.

2

Henry recognised that by the forgery of the letter from Paniz-zardi he had put himself in jeopardy, if Picquart should bring about the unmasking of Esterhazy, and Picquart might well be brought back. Therefore his best security was to blacken irremediably his late chief's reputation. Picquart's correspondence was still coming to the War Office. Henry proceeded to open it and take copies. Picquart had a small circle of friends, who met at the house of the Comtesse Blanche de Comminges, a middle-aged cousin of his. They often wrote to each other using a slang of their own and imaginary names. From these letters Henry began to forge others in the same style, which implied that Picquart was involved in a conspiracy, and for the first of these he chose a code signature, *Speranza*. Beyond this he opened a file on Picquart for future use, into which he put the *Speranza* letter.

During 1895–96 Picquart had on several occasions consulted a lawyer friend of his, Louis Leblois, on legal points connected with the registration of carrier-pigeons and with the case of a minor German agent. Henry persuaded Gribelin that Picquart had shown secret documents to Leblois, including letters in the Dreyfus file. Further, he attempted to make Commissioner Tomps of the Sûreté produce a report indicating that Picquart had given the photograph of the *bordereau* to the *Matin*. Tomps refused, and thereby earned the distrust and enmity of the Section. Next, tak-ing the *petit bleu*, Henry first scratched out Esterhazy's name on the outside, then rewrote it, with the intention of making it appear that another name had originally been there, thus suggesting that Picquart had attempted to fix another man's crime on to Ester-hazy (but he forgot to look for and destroy the plate and prints of the *petit bleu* made by Lauth in April 1896). In addition, seeing in a newspaper in January 1897 an announcement of the death of Esterhazy's father-in-law, the Marquis de Nettancourt, he cut it out and dated it January 1896, intending by this to show that Picquart had already decided to fasten the *bordereau* on to Ester-hazy four months before the arrival of the *petit bleu*. Finally, he took a letter from Panizzardi, dated 28 March 1895, in which the attaché said that he was on the point of receiving the French railway mobilisation plan, and dated it 1894: again he omitted to find out whether copies of the letter had been made, as indeed they had. All this ingenious work could succeed only if the Dreyfus file never left the War Office, never came before a civil court or went to the Sûreté. And this depended on his ability to persuade his chiefs to hold to the *res judicata*, and on the unlikelihood of the Dreyfus family finding a new fact which might lead to the reopening of the case. These conditions were precarious.

In the meantime Gonse had thoroughly entered into the spirit of the game of making intolerable the life of an officer rash enough to become a nuisance to his superiors. He sent Picquart from corps to corps, writing to him continually, requiring daily reports of his activities. Finally, having driven him from Châlons to Marseilles, he despatched him to organise the intelligence service in Tunisia, attaching him to the 4th Tirailleurs (December 29). All his letters were friendly; Picquart's pay and allowances were handsomely raised; he was given to understand that his somewhat fatuous mission was highly secret and demanded the utmost prudence. Picquart was not deceived and felt that his career was finished. He asked for a transfer to a regiment; he was told to wait. In between times he exchanged friendly letters with Henry, and admitted to him his depression, to which the astute soldier answered: "I should tell you frankly, and as man to man, that you should have listened to me on the day you said my words were golden. . . . Now I can do nothing and I am profoundly sorry for it" (December 4). Indeed Picquart's situation was unbearable. He had lost the confidence of his seniors, he had perhaps ruined his career, and he had not quietened his conscience. In April he wrote out a long statement of the case, saying where the documents were to be found, and addressed it to the President of the Republic, to be handed to him in the event of his, Picquart's, death.

During the spring, since they had not been informed of his absence, agents continued to write to him at the War Office. At length, on May 1, he wrote a sharp personal note to Henry, asking him to tell the agents something of the truth—he was tired of "the lies and mysteries" raised by his mission. Henry, on Gonse's counsel, drafted a bold answer, which with Gonse's quasi-approval he despatched on June 3, but dated May 31. He wrote that, as a result of Picquart's reference to "lies and mysteries," an enquiry had been held in the War Office into the fact that he had suggested to two members of the Section that they should testify that a paper filed in the office had been seized in the post and had come from an identified individual, and that he had opened a Secret File and examined its documents, which had led to indiscretions. He added that there were material proofs of these actions, while as for the word "lies," the enquiry had not discerned when, how and to whom this word should be applied.

It was not the letter a junior officer writes to his senior unless he has powerful backing. Picquart saw that Henry too had turned against him: what was worse, he knew from the Dreyfus trial what "material proofs" could mean. He replied on June 10 in a brief note protesting against the insinuations. He applied for leave to go to Paris. Arriving on June 20, he at once saw Leblois and gave him a general sketch of his situation, without, however, mentioning the *petit bleu*; but he showed him fourteen letters from Gonse. To all the courts before which he was to appear in the future, he claimed that he was merely taking steps to defend his personal honour. Leblois, however, saw that the fate of Picquart was now inextricably bound up with that of Dreyfus, and urged him to pursue both ends. Picquart hesitated. He was still a soldier subject to military discipline, which he respected. The argument lasted a week. Then, while giving Leblois general powers for his defence and leaving with him the Gonse letters, he forbade him to communicate with either Mathieu Dreyfus or Demange. On June 29 he went back to Sousse. There can be no doubt that he was watched during his visit and that Henry knew he had seen Leblois frequently.

3

Although Mathieu Dreyfus had found sympathy among some unprejudiced men, he was no nearer the truth. Among the poli-

ticians and journalists the only champions he had found were
Arthur Ranc and Joseph Reinach. Ranc had had a stormy career.
A Republican journalist, he had been Gambetta's director of
Sûreté at Tours in 1870–71. Later he had been the victim of Right-
wing hatred, had been condemned as a Communard and had spent
several years in exile. He had been one of the most formidable
opponents of Boulanger and had thus earned the hatred of the
Nationalists. He was now one of the Senators for Seine and a power
on the *Radical.* Joseph Reinach, the nephew of the luckless crook,
the Baron de Reinach of Panama notoriety, had also been a Gambettist, one of the "tribune's" secretaries, and for a time owner and
director of the Gambettist *République Française,* which had now
been acquired by Méline. "He was a blatant, domineering, loud-
voiced French Jew," writes one who knew him, "yet with the
accent on the French. . . . The Reinachs, though very Jewish,
were even more French; and Frenchmen, notwithstanding their
dislike of Jewishness *per se,* recognised in Joseph Reinach a devotion to France equal to their own. This was the secret of his
personal influence. For him the Affair was not solely or even primarily a Jewish concern: it was a fight for principles he believed to
be essential to save Republican, Revolutionary, Democratic
France from the clutches of Reaction" (Private Information).
Reinach had a deep interest in military matters; as a reserve officer
he had served on the staff of Galliffet, perhaps the best senior
officer in the Army in the nineties, and a thorough Republican.

Both Ranc and Reinach had been convinced early in the affair
that there was something fishy about it. They had met the Dreyfus
family and been moved by the letters which the prisoner wrote
from his ghastly cell. They realised that they needed powerful
support. They therefore approached the much-respected Alsatian
patriot, Scheurer-Kestner, vice-president of the Senate.

Scheurer-Kestner had been a manufacturer of explosives in
Thann. After 1871 he had crossed the new frontier into France,
and in the National Assembly was the embodiment of the lost
provinces. A founding father of the Republic, he had been a close
friend and associate of Gambetta and had succeeded him as the

editor of the *République Française*. Early in 1895 he had met
Mathieu Dreyfus and been, if not convinced, shaken by what he
had to say. He took up the matter with various prominent politicians, among them Billot. Billot warned him in veiled terms not
to meddle in the case. Freycinet and Berthelot also cautioned him
in vague phrases. Dissatisfied, he began his own enquiries, but
except for the unsupported opinions of his friends in Mulhouse, he
made no progress. In the spring of 1897, again adjured by his
Alsatian friends, he once more embarked on an examination of the
case. He found little. He read Lazare's memoir, but he confessed
he was not capable of judging between the handwritings. Among
the Senators he found one sympathetic ear, that of Trarieux,
Minister of Justice in Ribot's Government, who also thought an
error had been made. Nor could Demange help him. Yet again
Scheurer-Kestner approached Billot, but, now armed with Henry's
forgery, Billot affirmed that the evidence was overwhelming. He
went so far as to give his interlocutor a brief version of the *faux
Henry*. Scheurer at once suspected a forgery and said as much,
but Billot was not to be persuaded.

Scheurer was on the point of giving up, when he happened to
meet Leblois at a dinner of Alsatians. Leblois asked for an appointment with Scheurer, and on July 13 told him in confidence
Picquart's story. Scheurer-Kestner, who, like many others,
romantically believed Army officers to be the pattern of honour,
was horrified on reading Gonse's letters: but he perceived that if he
approached Billot the ruin of Picquart would follow. Nevertheless, on the following day, at the Longchamps review, he told a
number of Senators that he was now convinced of Dreyfus's innocence. Waldeck-Rousseau, having picked up some of Scheurer's
remarks and himself having private suspicions of the conduct of
the case, begged Méline to look into it, as the matter might have
serious consequences; but Méline, after a talk with Billot, refused
to move. Scheurer's difficulty remained: how to bring up the case
without uncovering Picquart. Leblois suggested securing some of
Esterhazy's handwriting; but though he obtained several letters
and convinced himself that Esterhazy was the author of the

bordereau, Scheurer realised it was only his word against that of Bertillon and the other experts. Further proof was needed.

4

When nothing followed the *Matin* publication of the *bordereau*, Esterhazy's fears gradually faded. He appears once more to have applied to Schwartzkoppen, but the attaché refused him. He set about a further siege of his political acquaintances to procure him a staff appointment. No one in the War Office would touch him. Henry promised one of his friends to help him, but in fact did nothing: Esterhazy wrote a scathing letter about Henry to Jules Roche, in which he claimed that Henry was his debtor since 1876 —an improbable statement. On a direct approach, Billot told Jules Roche that Esterhazy was a rogue and a bandit and that he lay under the worst suspicion that a Frenchman could lie under. Esterhazy's friends dropped him; he turned to the gutter press. In March 1897 he dashed off a series of letters for the *Libre Parole* and the *Intransigeant*, attacking Billot and drawing attention to the fact that the head of the Intelligence Section, Henry, did not know a word of German. As for Boisdeffre, he was "lazy and ignorant as a carp, glib, self-assured and full of effrontery" (50, 3 March 1897).

During the spring, however, he found temporary relief. He had got into touch with a young cousin, Christian Esterhazy, who had a recently widowed mother. These Esterhazys, though not wealthy, had in the Gironde some property which had recently been sold. Esterhazy, saying that he was a friend of the Rothschilds, offered to re-invest the money, and managed to get hold of some thirty-three thousand francs. In June Billot, tired of this vagabond parasite and possible traitor, told Boisdeffre to get rid of him. Boisdeffre had him put on half-pay for "temporary infirmities," and Esterhazy, perhaps realising that he had done himself harm, submitted and retired to Dommartin.

5

Scheurer-Kestner's confident statements on July 14 had disturbed Billot. Although the War Office possessed Henry's forgery, in the genuineness of which he believed, his doubts of Esterhazy were still not allayed; he was almost persuaded that the ruffian was Dreyfus's accomplice. Moreover, in replying to Castelin's motion of the previous November he had committed himself to the treatment of the Dreyfus verdict as *res judicata*. Even if, in defiance of Hanotaux's refusal to involve the foreign Embassies, he should dare to produce the *faux Henry*, he would be retreating from the impregnable position of the *res judicata*, and this would lead to a reopening of the Dreyfus case. Since Mercier, his predecessor, must be sheltered (there is, by the way, no indication of how much Billot knew of the proceedings of 1894), the reopening of the case was out of the question. But Scheurer-Kestner might become a nuisance. In September Billot sent Bertin-Mourot, now his orderly officer, to find out from the Senator what evidence he had. Scheurer refused to say. Therefore, on Bertin's report, Billot sent a message to Scheurer begging him to do nothing until they had met. Scheurer consented, but Billot, not satisfied, tried through other emissaries to discover what lay behind Scheurer's confidence in Dreyfus's innocence. He failed, and in October spoke to Boisdeffre of his uneasiness as to what was being prepared. Boisdeffre passed this on to Gonse.

Gonse, somewhat alarmed, at once got to work. For some time he had intended to move Du Paty de Clam from the Third Bureau to command of the Second. He now took him as his own personal assistant, and brought him and Henry together. Du Paty had had nothing whatever to do with the case since 1894. He had heard nothing about Esterhazy, whom he had met twice in Tunisia seventeen years earlier, and nothing of the *petit bleu*. Gonse and Henry now revealed to him the existence of a campaign to substitute Esterhazy for Dreyfus; Esterhazy's wild life, his debts, his *bizarrerie*, were obvious weaknesses for the "Syndicate" to seize on, though he was in truth merely a sick and embittered man: they feared that if he were denounced by Scheurer-Kestner he would either commit suicide or jump the frontier, which would be taken as tantamount to a confession. There would follow terrible complications, in which the generals (not to mention Du Paty himself) would be involved; there might even be an international incident. The romantic Du Paty swallowed every word of it.

At this point Henry, deeply involved in apparently successful forgery, took a new course. It is said that he was a great reader of newspaper serials. Whatever the reason, he undoubtedly became inspired by the same imp that inspired Tom Sawyer: only the rescue of the negro Jim in the last chapter of *Huckleberry Finn* is comparable to his activities during the next three months. First he appears to have despatched to Esterhazy at Dommartin a letter [1] written in capital letters and signed "Espérance," a reminiscence of the forgery signed *Speranza* placed earlier in the year in Picquart's dossier. In this it was stated that the Dreffus (sic) family had procured through Picart (sic) letters from Esterhazy and were about to denounce him as the author of the *bordereau*.

Henry had already made a serious blunder in his fabrication of the Panizzardi letter (the *faux Henry*), but so long as the forgery remained invisible in the War Office, it could not harm him. His new move—the drawing into his web of Esterhazy—was infinitely graver, an error of tactics. For, by indicating the existence of Picquart to Esterhazy, he was ensuring the reopening of the Dreyfus trial. From the moment Esterhazy revealed Picquart's name, Picquart must be called in evidence, and thus the documents could no longer remain hidden in the Rue Saint-Dominique. Boisdeffre and Gonse had in fact seen far deeper than Henry when, in 1896, they had ordered Picquart to separate the Dreyfus case from that of Esterhazy. If Picquart could have secured the conviction of Esterhazy on other evidence than that of the identity of his writing with that of the *bordereau*, then there would never have been any need to re-examine that fatal document, or recall the court-martial of 1894. Henry, clumsy and with short views, was now, by his very audacity, to become the author of the revision he was so actively trying to prevent. At the same time, it is another proof

---

[1] It is assumed that Henry was the writer. Esterhazy at this date had never heard of Picquart. Du Paty knew nothing relevant about Esterhazy at this time.

of Gonse's stupidity that he allowed himself under the persuasion
of Henry to fall into the error he had so carefully avoided a year
earlier. True, Henry had acted without his knowledge, but there
was still time to suppress Esterhazy.

On October 19 Billot received a letter written in a form much
akin to that of the "Weyler" letter, summoning him to take action
against Scheurer-Kestner and Picquart, who were trying to substitute Esterhazy for Dreyfus. The letter was passed to Gonse,
who on October 20 again consulted with Du Paty and Henry.
Various methods of warning Esterhazy were mooted, for one an
anonymous letter. Drafted by Du Paty, it was shown by Gonse to
Billot, who forbade its transmission. On his return to the Section,
Henry added the initials "P.D.C." (Paty de Clam) and filed it,
thus beginning to enmesh Du Paty. On the same day Gonse sent
for Lebrun-Renaud, Dreyfus's unwise escort on the morning of the
degradation, and under his and Henry's eye got him to write out
and sign a declaration that Dreyfus had then said: "I am innocent;
in three years my innocence will be proved: the Minister knows that
if I handed over unimportant documents, it was to obtain serious
ones from the Germans," thus once again travestying Dreyfus's
account of what had passed between him and Du Paty on 31
December 1894.

According to Reinach (47, I, 347 et seq., II, 579–82), on this same
day Henry produced to Gonse an ultra-secret file, which he said
had been put together by Sandherr in 1894 and had been shown to
nobody since that date. It contained (a) photographs of seven
letters alleged to have been written by Dreyfus to the German Emperor, and one from the Emperor to Münster, in which occurred
the phrase that the Schurke (i.e. canaille) was becoming too exigent;
(b) a photograph of the bordereau with prices added to each item,
and annotated by the Kaiser: "The rogue is asking too much—
nevertheless the delivery of the documents must be hastened. W."
Henry said that the originals had been stolen from the German Embassy, and in the face of Münster's threats had been handed back,
but only after having been photographed.

That such letters had existed and that this was their history is ridiculous. If there were such photographs (which nobody ever saw, or found, in spite of a thorough search of the War Office in 1904), they must have been manufactured by Henry, helped by Lemercier-Picard or Guénée. Since all the Section photography was now done by Lauth or Junck, the work must have been done outside. Probably if they ever were made, Henry, on further reflection, realised their absurdity and destroyed them. Nevertheless he succeeded in floating the absurd tale, gave hints of the file at the Zola trial, and the legend of the Kaiser's letters persisted up to the final stages of the case.[1]

Still in his vein of *roman policier*, Henry now suggested to Du Paty that Esterhazy should be warned that he would be protected. By telling Du Paty that there were some things that an officer should do on no more than a hint from his superiors, Henry persuaded him to act as the intermediary for the General Staff. Henry sent Gribelin with a note for Esterhazy, making a rendezvous at Montsouris Park on October 23. Gribelin thought the scheme silly. If Esterhazy was to be protected, why not tell him to report to the War Office? Nevertheless, after some trouble in finding the adventurer, he got the message to him at the address of his mistress Marguérite Pays on the morning of the rendezvous. That afternoon, shadowed by Desvernine, Esterhazy, in civilian clothes,

---

[1] The first hint of the letters and the annotated *bordereau* was published by the *Libre Parole* on 8 December 1894 and in the *France* of December 10, but then let drop. Gonse at the various enquiries denied all knowledge of the letters. Reinach picked up and printed a secondhand story that Boisdeffre had talked of them to Princesse Mathilde, which Boisdeffre denied. (This was repeated by Münster to Princess Radziwill in May 1898 (46, II, 133).) Reinach produces no evidence whatever that Henry in fact showed them to Gonse. However, on November 2 or 3 Henry made a covert reference to them to Maurice Paléologue of the Foreign Office, who scouted the idea. But Henry must have given the tale to Drumont, who on November 4 printed a garbled note about an "overwhelming" document, while on December 12 Rochefort gave a full version, which was greeted with general scepticism. Further, the foolish Nationalist, Millevoye, rashly gave to an audience at Suresnes, on 15 February 1898, the text of the Kaiser's letter to Münster and was overwhelmed by a howl of laughter from the audience. On 14 August 1899, during the Rennes trial, an open letter was printed in the *Gaulois*, and repeated by the *Libre Parole* and *Intransigeant*, calling on Mercier to produce the documents. The appeal naturally met with no response. In 1904 Mercier denied the whole story.

drove to the German Embassy and saw Schwartzkoppen. Apparently he behaved with extreme violence, told the military attaché that he was about to be denounced and that Schwartzkoppen would be involved. He urged him to threaten Mme Dreyfus. Schwartzkoppen very naturally refused, and after a stormy scene Esterhazy left and Desvernine lost sight of him.

He went to Montsouris Park, where he was accosted by Du Paty and Gribelin in civilian clothes, Gribelin wearing blue spectacles and Du Paty a false beard. Henry remained hidden in the cab which had brought them: he had told Gribelin that as Du Paty talked too much he was to keep an eye on him. Du Paty told Esterhazy that the guilt of Dreyfus was certain, and that he himself would have resolute defenders if he obeyed orders: these orders would be sent to him every evening at the Cercle Militaire. Esterhazy pretended that he had not pierced their disguises, showed them the "Espérance" letter, and played up to them. After half an hour's conversation they parted. Esterhazy seems thereon to have returned to Schwartzkoppen and told him that he was now under the protection of the French Government.

That evening Schwartzkoppen made a clean breast of the whole business to Münster. The Ambassador was relieved that his statements to Casimir-Perier and Hanotaux regarding Dreyfus had been correct. He at once reported to General Schlieffen at the Kriegsamt in Berlin. Nine days later Schwartzkoppen was gazetted to the command of the 2nd Kaiser Franz Guard Grenadier Regiment.

On October 24 Du Paty saw Esterhazy twice. At one meeting he told him to apply for aid to the Minister of War and dictated to him a letter which Esterhazy delivered in person at the Rue Saint-Dominique. Billot, in ignorance of what was going on, angrily refused to see him but, on reflection, told General Millet, the Director of Infantry, to hear what he had to say. So, on the 25th, Esterhazy was interviewed. He showed Millet the "Espérance" letter and poured out his wrongs, while justifying such actions as he thought might be traced. Millet told him to put it down on paper and send it in. This he did, adding that, if driven, he would appeal to the Kaiser, who would no doubt authorise "his aide-de-camp" to protest against the accusations. The letter came to Billot, who delayed several days before showing it to Boisdeffre. It is impossible to elucidate the contacts between Henry and Esterhazy from October 1897 onwards. Esterhazy claimed later that they were intimate and continuous, but no reliance can be placed on his statement and there is no evidence for this one, save that he was undoubtedly put in possession of most of the facts of the Dreyfus case and of what was known against Dreyfus. Henry told Gonse in July 1898 that he had seen Esterhazy only twice, just before his duel with Picquart, and it is clear that he sought to avoid meeting him: had he done so, he could scarcely have escaped the notice of the Sûreté agents who seem to have shadowed Esterhazy over a long period.

On the other hand, as has been said, Esterhazy was somehow kept fully informed. Du Paty admitted that he had given him a résumé of the preliminaries of the case. What Du Paty would call a résumé was probably an extremely full account. For the rest, no doubt Esterhazy received his information from Henry through some agent such as Guénée. Of the papers seized when Esterhazy was arrested in July 1898, two, and only two, letters were apparently from Henry, and their contents were of no significance.

6

Scheurer-Kestner had returned to Paris on the evening of October 22. He had now perceived that without Picquart's testimony he was not sufficiently equipped, but Leblois felt that he had already gone too far; he had told Picquart nothing of what he had done and for two months had not written to him. He refused to do so. Scheurer thought of appealing to Félix Faure, but held back. He refused to lunch with Billot. But he continued to tell his friends that he was convinced of the truth of his earlier statement and would move for revision. Among these friends was Ranc, who passed it on to the Socialist Deputy, Paschal Grousset. Grousset gossiped at the Palais Bourbon, and the rumour spread. Journalists of all colours invaded Scheurer's house. He detested journalists;

beyond confirming his original statement, he would tell them nothing and showed them out. Getting nothing from this source, they went off to the War Office, where they were made welcome and primed with material against the Senator; among other items they were told that although Billot had offered to show him the proofs, he would not listen.

Scheurer-Kestner persisted. He obtained an appointment with Félix Faure for October 29. In the meantime Esterhazy, having received no official word from the War Office, had, on his own initiative, written in his usual high style a petition to the President, and attached a copy of the "Espérance" letter. This Faure had received before he saw Scheurer. Irritated and perhaps alarmed, he was very short with him, refused to hear what he had to say and declared he was powerless.

On the following day Scheurer at last agreed to see Billot. They fenced for four hours. Scheurer asked for some proof of Dreyfus's guilt. Billot produced none, but admitted that Dreyfus had been condemned on other documents than the *bordereau*. Scheurer begged him to make a personal investigation of the case; he would allow him a fortnight to complete it. Billot promised.

From October 31 the press campaign against the Dreyfusists rose rapidly in temperature. Drumont (*Libre Parole*), Rochefort (*Intransigeant*), Millevoye (*Patrie*), Vervoort (*Jour*), Humbert (*Eclair*), Judet (*Petit Journal*) and Arthur Meyer (*Gaulois*) heaped abuse on Scheurer-Kestner and Reinach, sold to the Jews, sold to Germany: Méline, Billot, and Darlan, the Minister of Justice, were their accomplices. New anecdotes of Dreyfus's dealings were invented; the old tale of the confession was refurbished.

At this juncture Vaughan, who had been Rochefort's manager but had broken with him, founded a paper of his own, *l'Aurore*. Its contributors were almost entirely Dreyfusists, and among them was Clemenceau. He, since his defeat in 1893, had been slowly and painfully learning the trade of journalism. He was now fifty-seven and he had not found it easy to learn. The mere labour of writing was something he had never practised. He had always thought on his feet. Nor was his style that of a literary man. He wrote as he spoke—in short, incisive sentences, often brutal in expression. He had not been very successful. But he had not attempted to get back into politics. His own party feared him; the younger members did not want him back. He was filled with hatred for those who had had any hand in his downfall, for the Nationalists naturally, with their vociferous and dubious patriotism, and for the younger Republicans—Poincaré, Barthou, Cavaignac and Deschanel—whose interference in 1892 had resulted in the Panama enquiry. Hitherto he had not been a Dreyfusist. After the trial of 1894 he was furious that the crime of treason had been relegated to political crimes. "We were not even capable of shooting Bazaine." Ranc, however, persuaded him to see Scheurer-Kestner, whom he had known for thirty years and trusted.

Although Clemenceau was not persuaded that Dreyfus was innocent, he saw the illegality of the court-martial. His first articles appeared early in November, and from then onwards for over four years he wrote almost daily. Within three months he was to become the most formidable and indefatigable denouncer of the General Staff, the Government, the Radicals, the Church. He had been thought politically dead. Within ten years he would be not only reinstated in Parliament but would for the first time preside over his own Cabinet.

On October 31, having received no acknowledgment from the Elysée, Esterhazy wrote a second letter to Faure. Once more he demanded justice, but this time he threatened. Unlike Du Paty and Henry, Esterhazy had a sense of humour, and now entered heart and soul into the mad conspiracy. He invented a veiled lady who communicated with him by letters in a disguised hand— they were in fact written to his dictation by his young cousin Christian—and gave him information at night in odd quarters of the city. This high-souled woman he now produced for the edification of the President. She had given him a photograph of a document which she had secured from Picquart. It came to be known as the "liberating document." "This document," he wrote in his letter to Faure, "stolen from a foreign legation by Colonel Picquart, is most compromising for certain diplomatic personages. If I am given neither support nor justice, and if my name is made public, this photograph, which is to-day in a safe place abroad, will at once be published." Perhaps nothing better reveals the confused and credulous minds of the President, the War Minister and the War Office than that this rodomontade was taken seriously. On November 1 Billot telegraphed through Boisdeffre to Picquart's General in Tunisia to question him about a photograph stolen by a woman. At the same time Gonse ordered the seizure of Picquart's correspondence in the post. On November 5, Esterhazy yet once more wrote to Faure, stressing the fact that the publication of the document would mean either war or the country's humiliation.[1]

This third and last letter to the President was handed to Billot, who told General Saussier to have the writer interviewed. The next day, November 7, Saussier received Esterhazy personally and with his habitual courtesy. Although he believed Dreyfus to be innocent, he was old—he retired two months later—and far too prudent to mix himself up in public brawls. So he heard Esterhazy's tale without comment, and after considering it for three days ordered him to stop writing letters and to send the photograph of the "liberating document" to the War Office.

On the day of the Saussier–Esterhazy interview, Scheurer made his final appeal to Méline. He had at last wrung from Leblois his consent to the mention of Picquart. He offered to show the Prime Minister Gonse's letters to Picquart. Méline declined: "I do not wish to read them." "Ah," exclaimed Scheurer, "neither Gambetta nor Ferry would have refused to listen to me." Méline shrugged his shoulders and told him to make formal application to the Minister of Justice. That evening Barthou issued a press note to the effect that Scheurer had given no documents to the Prime Minister,

---

[1] Whether, as Picquart said at the Zola trial (cf. p. 190) and as others believed, the "liberating document" was a photograph of the *canaille de D* letter is a question not worth pursuing, since no answer can be given. Its only interest lies in its influence on Faure and Billot. In any case Esterhazy does not appear to have relied on it, since, according to Marguérite Pays, he had a weightier document, which he called "the Imperial Guard," and which he had hidden in the lining of his service cap when Bertulus arrested him in the following July. Nobody ever saw the document, Esterhazy never revealed it, and it may never have existed (cf. p. 219).

and therefore the Government could only adhere to the verdict of 1894.

Scheurer was left with his dilemma. To make a formal appeal to the Minister of Justice he must offer new evidence: except for Esterhazy's handwriting he had none, and the experts who had already identified that of the *bordereau* with Dreyfus's were unlikely to modify their opinions. Demange wanted Scheurer to reveal the communication of secret documents to the 1894 court and to denounce the real traitor, whose identity he did not yet know. Leblois rejected this scheme, since Billot would simply believe that Scheurer had been primed by Picquart.

The hesitations were not to be prolonged. Lazare had already issued the second, and public, edition of his pamphlet, with a discussion of the writing of the *bordereau*, and on November 9 Mathieu Dreyfus, who, be it remembered, knew nothing of Esterhazy or Picquart, put out for sale on the streets facsimiles of the *bordereau*. Three days later a member of a financial house named Castro bought a copy and at once recognised the writing of Esterhazy, with whom he had done business. This information was passed to Mathieu, who consulted Scheurer, and was now introduced to Leblois. On the latter's advice, Mathieu prepared a denunciation of Esterhazy to the Minister of War.

On November 9, at a formal Cabinet meeting with Félix Faure in the chair, there was a brief discussion of the Dreyfus case. Méline, after the press note of November 7, had been asked to clarify the position to the Chamber. Neither Esterhazy nor Picquart was mentioned. It was decided to stand by the policy of *res judicata*. Darlan, the Minister of Justice, asked to see the file of the 1894 court-martial, since, in the event of an appeal being lodged, he would have to know whether Dreyfus had been condemned legally, and further, since he might be interpellated, he must have the information necessary for his reply. Darlan was in fact by no means sure that the judgment of 1894 had been regular. Billot consented, but a few days later, supported by Méline, withdrew his consent on the ground that it was better that Ministers should not know the roots of the case. This was enough to add to Darlan's suspicions. On November 30 Méline dropped him after he had received an adverse vote in the Senate on a minor administrative error. He was replaced by an obscure senator named Milliard.

Thus all the Cabinet, save Faure, Méline and Billot, remained in the dark.

During the next few days Scheurer decided to apply to the Minister of Justice. To prepare the way, he wrote to Ranc an open letter, which was published in the *Temps* on November 15. Unluckily he was anticipated; for on Sunday, November 14, the Corsican Deputy Emmanuel Arène published in the *Figaro*, over the signature *Vidi*, an article in which, without naming anyone, was set out the whole Dreyfusist story: the question of the handwritings, the communication of the Secret File to the judges, the existence at large of the real traitor, who was not a member of the War Office but a titled officer in garrison not far from Paris, well known in the capital. It also referred to the *faux Henry* as a forgery.[1]

On the Monday *Vidi* was answered in the *Libre Parole* by an article signed *Dixi*. This article was brought to Drumont by Esterhazy, but whether he or Henry was the author cannot be verified, although only someone in the Statistical Section could have provided the material. It claimed that a plot had been devised by a high officer, XY, at the War Office, who had worked out a scheme of correspondence with Dreyfus. Dreyfus from The Devil's Island had been able to show how he had forged the handwriting of an innocent, if somewhat wild, officer. *Dixi* accused XY of being in the pay of the Syndicate, and of suborning junior officers to procure the handwriting of the victim. The plot was ready when XY was suddenly, for unknown reasons, transferred from Paris. But he had come back in June, and, with his accomplice, a lawyer, he

[1] From whom did Arène get his information? The article was headed "Scheurer-Kestner's File." Arène, so far as I know, was not one of the, at present, few Dreyfusists. Reinach is silent on the point. It is odd that Arène made the tactical error of forestalling Scheurer-Kestner's open letter. Whatever the explanation, this error in tactics emphasises the fact that the Dreyfusists were by no means the great Syndicate that their enemies denounced.

had met the Syndicate again. In any case, the *bordereau* was only one of a hundred documents on which Dreyfus had been condemned. In short, the article exposed the line the Statistical Section was about to follow.

That evening Esterhazy walked into the War Office and handed to the officer on duty a packet containing the famous compromising photograph. At the same time Mathieu Dreyfus was addressing a letter to Billot denouncing Esterhazy as the author of the *bordereau*. The public was at last seized of the case.

The Cabinet agreed to Billot's proposal for an enquiry into Esterhazy, whose name most of them now heard for the first time. In the Chamber on November 16, in answer to the Prince d'Hénin, a Vosges Deputy, Billot was non-committal. He did not say that Dreyfus was guilty, merely that further research had not shaken his faith in the principle of *res judicata*; but that he had invited Scheurer-Kestner to make a formal application to the Minister of Justice, and that, since the Dreyfus family had made public accusations, they had been asked to justify them. For the rest, he uttered a few platitudes about the honour of the Army and the security of the State. The Deputies thought he had been weak. A Nationalist Senator tried to raise the matter at the Luxemburg. The Senate rejected his motion, while Scheurer sat silent, but with an air of confidence.

From the War Office a note informed Esterhazy that an enquiry would be opened, while another acknowledged receipt of the famous document. He was not even put under open arrest, and he now hurried from editor to editor relating a number of fables which he did not trouble to make consistent. The press embroidered his story to their own taste. The usual lunatics, by the dozen, wrote to editors offering to give evidence. Scheurer-Kestner, in his unwise spurning of the journalists, had done nothing to enlist them in the cause. The better papers, such as the *Temps*, held to a strict neutrality. Only a few editors dared to protest—Rodays of the *Figaro*, Yves Guyot of the *Siècle*, and the contributors to the new *Aurore*. Scheurer was bespattered with obscene abuse by Drumont, Rochefort, Alphonse Humbert and "The Monk" of *La Croix*.

Méline's attempt to keep the case out of politics was already
futile, but he did not recognise the fact. Under his very eyes the
Chamber was adopting the colours of the newspapers. On the
Right the clericals were beginning to enjoy the intoxication of
anti-semitism. So too were the Ralliés. On the Left the Socialists
were unable to reach a coherent policy; many, ex-Radicals of the
Jacobin tradition, preferred the patriotic rôle; others felt that the
case was none of their business, while some, Viviani and Rouanet
for two, were even anti-semite. Among the Radicals, Bourgeois
flinched from a pronouncement, while maintaining his anti-
clericalism; but his colleague, Cavaignac, Billot's predecessor and
friend of Boisdeffre, became one of the mouthpieces of the War
Office and the most intractable anti-revisionist of the Left. Méline's
own supporters, the Progressists, havered and hesitated: no less
than Méline, they wanted the whole affair hushed up, and for the
time being they supported the policy of *res judicata*.

It was too late to stifle the case. Everywhere Deputies found
themselves spied on by journalists: a smile or a cordial word exchanged with Scheurer brought a deluge of vituperation from
Drumont. Billot found himself pilloried daily for his hesitations
and accused of pilfering the secret funds. The abuse was always
vulgar and never witty. Drumont was far too much in earnest, and
Rochefort had lost his former verve.

Nevertheless a few thoughtful, sober and older politicians and
editors were coming round to Scheurer's point of view—old
Royalists, old Republicans, who knew the world of government
offices, men in the Foreign Office, at the Ministry of the Interior
and at the Police Préfecture, who knew that the Intelligence
Service was one of the worst in the whole French administration
(J. Develle, 6, I, 334). Now it was the turn of the German and
Italian Ambassadors to protest yet again. Their protests were received with polite grimaces. No publicity was given to their statements, nor to confirmations by the French Ambassadors in Berlin
and Rome.

7

Picquart had been kept in the dark by Leblois as to his revelations to Scheurer-Kestner, and he appears to have remained wholly in ignorance of Scheurer-Kestner's activities. In October he was due for his annual leave. Orders were sent to General Leclerc in Tunisia, first to keep him at Sousse, then to send him to Bizerta to organise the surveillance of foreigners. As soon as it was known that Scheurer was about to see Félix Faure, it was guessed that he would mention Picquart, who would then be summoned from Africa. Therefore on October 29, on the excuse that Arab bands were collecting on the Tripoli border, orders were telegraphed once more to Leclerc to send Picquart there. Did they hope he would be killed? Gonse and Billot indignantly denied it. General Leclerc, puzzled by the eccentricities of the War Office, sent for Picquart and from him learned what had happened to him. Leclerc forbade him to go farther south than Gabes.

About a week later, on November 7, Esterhazy wrote an insulting letter to Picquart, accusing him of bribing non-commissioned officers to hand him samples of Esterhazy's writing, and of having stolen War Office papers to hand over to the friends of a traitor. A copy of this he audaciously sent to the War Office. On November 10 he went further: he sent Picquart an anonymous note written in capital letters, of which part ran: "Take care; whole work discovered; withdraw quietly; write nothing." On the same day he telegraphed to Picquart: "Stop the demigod; all is discovered; case very grave. *Speranza*," while on the same evening he sent a still further telegram: "Proved that the *bleu* was manufactured by Georges. *Blanche*" (the Christian name of Picquart's cousin Mlle de Comminges). The telegrams were of course seized in transit and passed to the War Office. Photographs were taken and prints sent to the Sûreté, whose chief Cavard jumped to the conclusion that Picquart was associated in some plot.

Picquart received the two telegrams on November 11 and 12. The first to reach him was that signed *Blanche*. Not understanding it, he tore it up: but the *Speranza* one shook him; he saw that some friend of Esterhazy was pursuing him, and asked to have the *Blanche* telegram repeated. On November 15 he applied directly to the War Office by letter for the matter to be investigated. The anonymous letter he did not receive until November 17. Realising that it might be compromising if a search of his quarters was ordered, he destroyed it. He did, however, see that the writers could only come from the narrow circle of those who knew of the *petit bleu*. Of what was happening in Paris he still had not the faintest idea. He telegraphed to the War Office for leave to come to Paris. The telegram crossed one from the War Office ordering him to report there.

MATHIEU DREYFUS

PICQUART

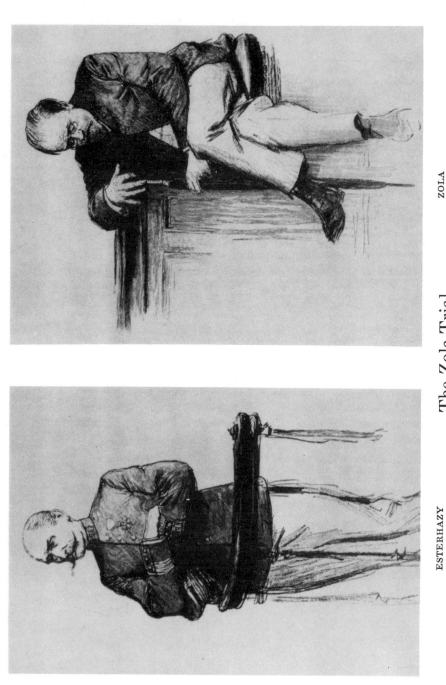

ESTERHAZY

ZOLA

The Zola Trial

CHAPTER EIGHT

The Esterhazy Court-Martial

1

THE enquiry into Esterhazy had been entrusted to the General in charge of recruiting in the Paris district, Brigadier-General Gabriel de Pellieux, a man of forty-five, young for his rank, tall, well set up, pleasant in face and speech. Yet another Alsatian, he had brains, courage and energy; his fault was impetuousness.

He opened his enquiry on November 17, on which day he saw Mathieu Dreyfus and Esterhazy. To Mathieu he was courteous, but said little. Mathieu had little to give except a facsimile of the *bordereau* and specimens of Esterhazy's handwriting. Pellieux heard Esterhazy's rodomontade without expression. On the next day he heard Scheurer-Kestner and asked whether he had any documents. Scheurer replied that he had none, but that Leblois would explain, and now for the first time he mentioned Picquart, with whom he admitted he had had no contact, but whose evidence he regarded as indispensable. Leblois, when he appeared, told the General more than he should have done, more than he had told Scheurer. He showed Pellieux Gonse's letters to Picquart and talked freely. Pellieux, who had seen some of the War Office papers, believed that Picquart had disclosed the *petit bleu* to his lawyer, who had then communicated it to Scheurer. Pellieux handed in his report on November 20, to the effect that there were no serious proofs against Esterhazy, as neither Scheurer nor Leblois had anything but his handwriting, and that since the *bordereau* had been attributed to Dreyfus in 1894, nothing should be done. At the same time he indicated grave faults against Picquart, who appeared to have disclosed confidential documents to an unauthorised person, Leblois.

Already Billot had telegraphed to Leclerc to interrogate Picquart

161

as to whether he had made such communications. The reply had been: only to Leblois. Pellieux now asked that Picquart should be heard. Summoned by telegram, he left Tunis on November 23.

Billot ordered Pellieux to reopen his enquiry, and on this occasion to make it an official one. Pellieux very naturally had no hesitation in consulting the head of the Statistical Section—Henry. And Henry had no trouble in putting forward the story he had concocted, that Picquart often had Leblois with him in his room at the War Office. He had, Henry said, seen the Secret File with the *canaille de D* letter on the table between them, as well as other files. But he seems not to have revealed the existence of the *faux Henry*. It was Gribelin who, unknown it appears to Henry, mentioned it to Pellieux. Pellieux went to Gonse, who was now keeping the file and showed him the forgery. Pellieux was of course at once convinced of Dreyfus's guilt, and in consequence of Esterhazy's innocence.

At the same time Pellieux gave Henry permission to carry out a search of Picquart's lodgings in the Rue Yvon-Villarceau. Nothing of any interest was found among his papers, but it made a news story and cast early suspicions on Picquart. There was no search of Esterhazy's rooms.

The second enquiry opened on November 23, and differed from the first. Mathieu was harshly treated; Esterhazy was ordered to hand over the letters of the veiled lady. Henry, Lauth and Gribelin were heard on the subject of Picquart's dealings with Leblois.

On his arrival in Paris, Picquart was met by his friend Lt-Col. Mercier-Milon, who brought him an order from Boisdeffre that he was to see nobody before appearing at the enquiry. He therefore did not see Leblois, and when he came before Pellieux knew nothing of what Leblois had revealed. Pellieux allowed him to depose everything he knew about Esterhazy. Shown the *petit bleu*, Picquart said that he thought the writing on the outside had been clearer: he did not perceive that it had been tampered with. Pellieux was severe with him and told him he had committed a grave misdemeanour. When dismissing him, he forbade him to make contact with Leblois, an instruction which Picquart so scrupulously obeyed that he burned unopened a letter from the lawyer. On the following day, when Picquart wished to discuss the *bordereau*, Pellieux refused on the usual grounds that the Dreyfus case was closed. He then showed him the *Speranza* letter (the letter forged by Henry in the spring to place in Picquart's file), which Picquart had never seen, and questioned him on a number of minor matters in his private life. Throughout he treated him as an accused man. Picquart was given no hint of the accusations made by his late colleagues, except that he had one day been seen showing the Secret File to Leblois. He was able to prove that on that day Leblois was not in Paris. There was no confrontation. At the end he was granted permission to talk to Leblois.

Almost at the same time as Picquart was being examined, a packet of letters written by Esterhazy between 1881 and 1884 to a Mme de Boulancy was passed by her lawyer to Scheurer. In these Esterhazy told his correspondent exactly what he thought of the French and the French Army: "Our great leaders, ignorant poltroons, who will once more go to populate the German prisons"; "the people are not worth a cartridge to kill them, and all these little beastlinesses of drunken women to whom men surrender confirm my opinion wholly"; "if this evening I were told that I should be killed to-morrow as a captain of Uhlans, sabring the French, I should certainly be perfectly happy." He looked forward to "a red sun of battle in Paris taken by assault and handed over to pillage by a hundred thousand drunken soldiers; that is the feast I dream of. May it come to pass." Scheurer took the letters to Pellieux, who tried to laugh them off, but under Scheurer's anger arranged that Bertulus, an examining magistrate who had been lent to him by the Minister of Justice, should make a legal seizure of the letters for the Esterhazy file. Mme de Boulancy was summoned by Pellieux, who bullied her but failed to shake her testimony.

On November 29 the *Figaro* published the letters, with one in facsimile facing the *bordereau*. Esterhazy was shaken to the roots. He thought all was over and talked wildly of running for it. One of the police agents shadowing him warned the Préfet of Police, who passed it to the War Office. Billot was thoroughly alarmed. If Esterhazy fled, it was as good as a confession, and he, Billot, would have to explain why the "Uhlan," as he had now come to be called, had been left at large. Somehow Esterhazy was warned what flight would imply, and stayed. He insisted that the letters were forgeries, and the anti-Dreyfusist press took up the cry: there was nothing of which the Jews were not capable.

Meanwhile Pellieux was completing his report. He had one sultry interview with Scheurer, to whom he said that Esterhazy's writing could not be compared with a mere facsimile of the *bordereau*. When Scheurer pointed out that the original was in the War Office, he answered calmly that to ask for it would throw doubt on the authority of the *res judicata*. At the same time he admitted that he had been shown a conclusive proof of Dreyfus's guilt, though he did not identify this conclusive proof as the *faux Henry*.

As was guessed from what he had let fall, his report, while severe against Picquart, exonerated Esterhazy. For the War Office, what the world thought of Esterhazy was no matter for consideration; he was a crook, a liar, a low-living ruffian, whom they would willingly dispose of. Their sole aim was to prevent a revision of the 1894 court-martial, and a report clearing Esterhazy of the authorship of the *bordereau* was enough. On the other hand, if Esterhazy, as he had threatened far and wide, were to sue Matthieu Dreyfus and Scheurer for libel, the case would go before a civil jury, and no one could tell what might then come to light. Esterhazy's lawyer, Maître Tézenas, observing the harm the Boulancy letters were doing to his client's cause, recommended him to ask for a court-martial. If he were acquitted of the charge of treason, as in view of Pellieux's report he certainly would be, he would be not only rehabilitated but safe. This plan appealed to the War Office, since it would avoid the unreliable jury and at the same time confirm the verdict on Dreyfus. They agreed, and Esterhazy in an eloquent letter to Billot, to which Pellieux rashly lent an editorial hand, applied to appear before a military court. It was the ratification of a bargain. Should the War Office desert him, he could always expose their support of him at this point.

On December 4 Saussier, on Billot's recommendation, rejected Pellieux's finding of "No Case," and signed the order to proceed against Esterhazy.

It is clear that from December 1897 all the leading actors in this obscure drama were so involved with each other that not one could break away. For Billot and Boisdeffre, as well as for Mercier, still commanding his corps at Le Mans, any reopening of the Dreyfus trial, any bringing of documents before the eyes of civilian judges, experienced in the handling of evidence, would entail disaster, perhaps even criminal proceedings. Du Paty de Clam had to fear not only his conduct of the case in 1894, but now his commerce with Esterhazy. Gonse, who had allowed so many unjustifiable activities, was in no less danger, and moreover he had given hostages to Henry. Henry, although he had kept himself in the background, could be betrayed by some unpredictable speech or action of Esterhazy, while his own agents, Lemercier-Picard and Guénée, knew far too much. As for Esterhazy, his peril was perpetual, but he had a grip on both Henry and Du Paty, not to speak of his new supporter, Pellieux, and could use them against their superiors.

If one asks how this could happen, the answer is that it goes back to the whole conception of the duties of the Statistical Section, a secret department working on obscure and often sordid tasks, whose officers and agents knew they would be disavowed by their superiors if they made a false step. Their superiors on the other hand shrank from knowing too much of the Section's activities, though they were ready enough to take the kudos for any successful coup. Henry's advice to Picquart not to worry his chiefs, and his counsel to Du Paty that there were things which an officer does on no more than a hint, expose the whole structure of distrust. It is probable that Billot, Boisdeffre and Gonse were, either through shame or diffidence with each other, failing to talk the case over frankly. Indeed it becomes clearer, as the series of enquiries and trials proceeds, that, far from there being a concerted plan or even any serious knowledge of the evidence, they had in fact avoided discussion. Gonse almost certainly never revealed much of his own or Henry's proceedings to Boisdeffre. Billot, on the other hand, partly deceived—he certainly seems not to have suspected the *faux Henry*—partly flinching from coming to grips with the Chief of Staff, technically so much more versed in the business of the Army than he was, failed to work out a policy of his own to lay before the Cabinet. And an inherent loyalty to the uniform forbade him to enquire too deeply into Mercier's delinquency of 1894. Thus each man said as little as possible to the others and allowed matters to drift on a course laid for them by their subordinates and by the maleficent fanatics of the press and parliament.

2

Du Paty had seen Esterhazy several times since their original interview. From mid-November he ceased to have direct contact, either, as he alleged, on orders from Gonse—Gonse denied that he knew anything about the Du Paty–Esterhazy connection until the following July—or from fear that he was taking too great a risk. But he continued to communicate through the agency of Marguérite Pays and the cousin Christian. He had removed his false beard after the interview at the Montsouris Park, but he met Christian in dark corners of the city, on bridges or in public lavatories, where messages were read and answers written by match-light.

Christian had swallowed his cousin's stories whole. He believed that the rogue was what he said he was, the victim of a plot, and that everything must be done to save him. In spite of the fact that Esterhazy was now living in open concubinage with a common prostitute, he was shocked when Esterhazy's wife threatened to divorce him. He put himself completely at Esterhazy's disposal and, apart from writing the letters his cousin dictated, in August he had handed over to him another seventeen thousand francs, bringing the total up to fifty thousand: he had not yet seen a penny of the profits Rothschilds were to make for him.

As for Du Paty, it was not until the end of November that Gonse revealed to him the whole matter by showing him both the file Picquart had compiled on Esterhazy and the file Henry had concocted against Picquart, as well as the Dreyfus file as it now was. Du Paty later admitted having misgivings. He did not believe that Picquart was in any way dishonourable, and said so. He was only half-deceived by the *faux Henry*: he said that Panizzardi had never written a capital D like the initial to "Dreyfus," and he told Gonse he believed it to be a trap. Lastly, Du Paty was surprised to perceive, from a comparatively rapid glance through the commentary shown to the judges of 1894, that it in no way resembled the one he had made. He had no opportunity to examine it more thoroughly, for a week or so later, when Mercier happened to be in Paris, Gonse, on Boisdeffre's orders, handed it to Mercier, who promptly destroyed it.[1]

On December 4, when the Deputies entered the Palais Bourbon, they read on the notice-boards the order to charge Esterhazy. At the opening of the session Castelin requested Méline to make a statement which would reassure the Army, public opinion and the Chamber. Méline at once replied: "I shall say at once the decisive words in this debate: there is no Dreyfus case." After a burst of applause he went on: "At this moment, there is not and cannot be a Dreyfus case." (A Socialist: "At this moment!") "An accusation of treason has been made against an army officer; this particular question bears no relation to the other. The examining judge can propose either an appearance before a court, or an ordinance stating that no case lies." He then launched out into a disquisition on constitutional principles and legal procedure. "This case cannot be handled with unrestrained publicity without serious imprudence, which might lay the country open to unforeseen difficulties. The campaign, of course, in no way touches the honour of the Army, which is above polemics of this nature; but it has caused much pain, already far too much." He went on to accuse the Left of trying to bring the case into the political sphere. "If politics bear no relation to it, why do you interrupt me so noisily, instead of listening to what I have to say? I should like to see you with a responsibility as heavy as mine. . . . If you think we should have acted otherwise, come here and say it! I appeal to all impartial men, to all good Frenchmen, who put love of France above everything. In the interests of the country and of the Army, I beg you

[1] See Appendix iv, p. 366.

to support a Government at grips with difficulties of this kind, at grips with furious passions."

Castelin asked Méline to stress the absence of connection between the cases of Dreyfus and Esterhazy. Méline said he would accept a motion. At this point Count Albert de Mun rose.

Albert de Mun was a retired cavalry officer, handsome, devout, humourless, eloquent and philoprogenitive. He formed, with the two priests in the Chamber, Gayraud and Lemire, the tiny group of Christian Democrats, but he was the Jaurès of the Right. As a soldier he had been horrified at the excesses of both sides during the Commune of 1871; he had resigned from the Army and flung himself into social work, becoming one of the founders of the Catholic working-men's clubs, long before the Republicans had recognised there was such a thing as a social problem. "He resigned from the cuirassiers to enlist in the gendarmerie," said Drumont caustically. Throughout his parliamentary career he had represented the Church far more than the Monarchy. The anti-clericals had so feared his influence in Brittany that again and again they had unseated him on the ground of clerical pressure, and each time he had been re-elected. He had more than once made his position clear as the champion of the Church against the Revolution and the principles of 1789. Up to 1889 he had been a supporter of the Monarchist cause, but the alliance of the Comte de Paris with Boulanger, whom he regarded as an undisciplined soldier, had shaken his faith in it. Thus he had welcomed the Ralliement and placed his hopes in the advent of a Catholic Republic, of which the Méline Government seemed to be the harbinger. Like many honourable men, like Scheurer-Kestner, he had implicit faith in the honour of the army officer. Attacks on the Army, whether from Drumont or from Ranc, disgusted him; he looked on them as treasonable. And, like many others on both sides, he made the crude error of confusing the honour of the Army with the honour of half a dozen officers. The fact that he himself was the pattern of honour, the fact that he was liked as a man by all sides in the Chamber, and the fact that he was eloquent, caused him to be heard with respect.

From this time, December 1897, de Mun, the representative of Catholicism—had not a bishop proclaimed that he had received "*le mandat impératif de Dieu*"?—became the champion of the General Staff.

De Mun summoned Billot, who was not present in the Chamber, to avenge the Army and to defend Boisdeffre against the charge that he had told Esterhazy he would cover him. Simple-minded, he raised the question of the occult power which was undermining the confidence of the soldier in his leaders; he looked across at Reinach. He received an ovation, not only from his friends but also from the Left and Extreme Left.

Billot was fetched, and after a short adjournment mounted the tribune. He had already spoken twice on this infernal question. Now he staked his all on giving the answer which would end the clamour for ever. "Dreyfus," he said, "has been rightly judged and unanimously condemned by seven of his peers on the evidence of twenty-seven officers. The case has been regularly tried. On my soul and conscience, as a soldier and the head of the Army, I hold that verdict truly delivered and Dreyfus guilty." He went on to pay a tribute to Boisdeffre, "with whom for eighteen months I have worked in silence to put France in a position to meet every contingency."

Millerand, Socialist and anti-Dreyfusist, followed up de Mun's attack by accusing the Government of weak complacence towards the Dreyfusists, whose underground activities they had never troubled to prevent. Why had not the Government rejected the case for revision? Because their friends had begun the campaign! And he too looked significantly across at Reinach.

Seven motions were put forward by the various groups. One from de Mun, asking the Government to put a stop to the attacks on the "Army," was defeated by the narrow margin of eighteen; another, that the Chamber should not interfere in purely judicial questions, found only ninety supporters. The comparative peace of the past eighteen months was breaking up like icicles in a thaw. The Chamber was not dividing on party lines, and, as so often happened, chaos followed. At length a composite motion was put together, with Méline insisting on a vote of confidence. "The Chamber, acknowledging the *res judicata*, associating itself with the tributes paid to the Army by the Minister of War, approving the declarations of the Government, and blaming the leaders of the odious campaign undertaken to disturb the public conscience, passes to the order of the day." The whole was carried by a majority of nearly two hundred and fifty, but the clause approving the Government was too much for the Radicals; they voted against it. Throughout, the uncompromising opponents were seventeen Socialists, ready to vote against anything and anybody; several of them were, in fact, anti-Dreyfusists: Méline was confirmed in his confidence that he now could and would keep the case out of politics. Billot and Boisdeffre could congratulate him and themselves. They had not realised that de Mun, the supporter of the Army as well as of the Government, had in fact taken the case out of the Army's hands and thrown it into the political dogfight.

Scheurer had as yet made no move. He was disgusted with Billot's evasions. He put down a notice to interpellate Méline and Billot in the Senate. The case was now exciting other countries than France, and on December 7 the Luxemburg Palace was thronged with foreign journalists, while half the Deputies had come over from the Palais Bourbon. Scheurer went into action at a complete disadvantage. Picquart had refused to allow Leblois to give Scheurer Gonse's letters, and had forbidden the mention of his name to the Senate: he wished to remain the good soldier, and he had not yet perceived that his seniors, as well as his late colleagues of the Statistical Section, intended to destroy him. Nevertheless Scheurer spoke well, declaring that he had begged Méline to undertake the revision himself: moreover, it was not true that Dreyfus had been well and truly condemned: documents had been shown to the judges but not to the defence. Billot retorted that Scheurer had no evidence that the *bordereau* was the only basis of accusation against Dreyfus. Of the Secret File he did not breathe a word. The Senators lapped up his statement. Méline added that the "Government had acted with perfect correctness; its sole guide was

the Law." Scheurer, and Trarieux who supported him, were heard
in dead silence; the Senators thought that their hearts were better
than their heads, and they gave the Government a unanimous vote
of approval. In neither Chamber was the matter reopened before
Parliament rose on December 23.

3

In the criss-cross of charges and counter-charges of espionage,
bribery, falsification, mendacity and illegality, with the anti-
Dreyfusists at one moment crying for action, at another for silent
respect for the *res judicata*, with Rochefort boldly stating that the
German Emperor was himself involved, with Ministers sometimes
professing the regularity of the 1894 trial, at others admitting
further unspecified charges against the traitor, at others again
holding tenaciously to the sanctity of the judgment and never very
sure whether they were lying or merely telling half-truths, it is
little wonder that in Paris—for the case hardly as yet interested the
provinces—Parliament and society, inflamed by a reckless press,
began to take sides. None except the handful of Dreyfusists in
part, and the War Office staff again in part, had any evidence on
which to base an opinion. Hence rumour pursued rumour, fantasy
fantasy. Yet as Christmas passed and Twelfth Night approached,
it became clearer that the case or cases could not remain sealed
up in the judicial circle, and that they must in the end involve the
Government, the Chambers, the Judiciary, the Army and even the
Church. The old conflicts of doctrine were reappearing; Jacobinism
was once more stripping for battle against the Ancien Régime. And
only five months ahead lay the general election. Could Méline hold
out until the crucial month of May was passed? The politicians of
the Centre and the Radicals were resolved to prevent the Dreyfus
case from becoming a question for the electorate. None the less,
the Radicals had no intention of permitting Méline an easy passage.
Now that de Mun, representing Church and Army, had thrown
down the challenge from the Right, they would not shrink from
attacking them both, not on the particular issue, but on general
principles of doctrine.

At this hour the Church in France had not yet spoken. The French ecclesiastical hierarchy was far too experienced, and far too cautious, to intervene. Cardinal Richard, Archbishop of Paris, invited by some University professors to lend his prestige to the cause, said that it was not the duty of the Church to interfere or to call in question the uprightness of Republican justice (72, 184). Cardinal Lecot of Bordeaux, when pressed by Canon Chaîne, recommended silence and neutrality (20, 8). Some priests protested against the demagogic pretensions of the Assumptionists and their anti-semitism. "For the observer," wrote the Abbé Pichot, "there are scarcely any Jews favourable to Dreyfus. And of those who should be blamed, it is the rich and powerful Jews, the great Jewish newspapers, for not siding with their co-religionists (43, 28)." "I have thought," he added, "of possible reprisals, and I have asked myself with anguish if the attitude of *La Croix* would not bring reprisals" (43, 30). Several—Archbishop Sueur, Bishops Fuzet and Mignot—regretted that they could not control the Assumptionists. They were helpless. The Dreyfusists, rebuffed, began to look elsewhere, to the University.

It must be emphasised that in January 1898 there was as yet no movement in favour of Dreyfus, because, except for the few who had been the recipients through Leblois of Picquart's opinions, there was no evidence that Dreyfus had not been justly, even if not legally, found guilty. It was the irregularity of the proceedings, and not the presumed innocence of Dreyfus, that alarmed and angered men like Trarieux and Waldeck-Rousseau in the Senate, and a few journalists such as Cassagnac, Yves Guyot and Clemenceau.

It must also again be stressed that in itself the Affair was of minor importance from a governmental point of view: it merely gave an opportunity for the Opposition to sow the wind. Each Minister had his own important tasks to fulfil. The Budget for 1898 was not yet near completion, and the Government must obtain provisional credits to carry on. Hanotaux, moreover, had been embarrassed by the rumours of the *faux Henry* and the name of Panizzardi. The Italian Ambassador, Tornielli, had warned him that any letters believed to emanate from his military attaché, in which Dreyfus was mentioned, were forgeries. He had wrung from Hanotaux a promise that no paper claimed by a friendly Power to be false should be made public. To the Cabinet Hanotaux said that he believed Panizzardi to be lying, but prudence was imperative. In any case, the Cabinet could hardly disbelieve Billot, and they had all seen previous newspaper tumults pass away. Moreover they bore no particular love to either Reinach or Ranc. The policy of silence was accepted.

4

Méline has never been called a great statesman, but he possessed some of the statesman's qualities. He knew why he was head of the Government: his business was to guard and preserve the existing structure of society against those who would break it down in favour of one of their own systems. In particular he was there to resist the Radical proposal, considered dangerously revolutionary, to substitute income-tax for a large part of the indirect taxes. For eighteen months he had successfully resisted all attacks. His passage had not been altogether easy, but the Ralliés and some of the Conservatives had supported him without fail. These, added to the two hundred and fifty Progressists and Liberals of his own following, had assured him the necessary majorities. He had made no bargain with the Right, but he had refrained from hostility to the Church and the Orders. The Radicals of course accused him of betraying the Republic, and in May, Delcassé, a Progressist, had moved that the Government should rely only on a majority of Republicans, but he had failed to carry the Chamber. Méline's single danger lay in the appearance of some unexpected, eccentric controversy, some question of principle, which might split his own group.

Now, for the first time, he was faced by a problem turning on that awkward word, justice, a word calculated to excite demagogues and preachers to violence. Worse, it involved one of the great institutions of state, the Army, which, whatever its faults, was popular. Even more disturbing was the fact that its defenders were drawn from both wings of the Opposition; on the one side De

Mun, the acknowledged representative of the Church, on the other Cavaignac, the Radical proponent of income-tax, while the Dreyfusists, although few in numbers, were drawn from his own party. And the elections would take place in less than five months. If his Government were defeated by a combination of Conservatives and Radicals, it would almost certainly be succeeded by a Radical Government, which in May would have in its hands, through the Ministry of the Interior, all the levers to exercise political pressure on the voters. For these reasons he chose what appeared to him the course of wisdom: to entrench himself behind the judgment of 1894, the *res judicata*, and to refuse to hear anything which might weaken that resolve. He undoubtedly knew of the *faux Henry*, but the question of Dreyfus's guilt or innocence was irrelevant; it was a question of the conduct of his trial. Hence he must, as Hanotaux put it, on principle refuse to hear anything about the materials of the case, either from Scheurer-Kestner or from Billot. He had probably never read Goethe, but he would have approved the poet's preference for order above justice.[1] And in pursuit of this policy of neutrality he must ignore the accusations of the Dreyfusists and yet refuse to oblige the anti-Dreyfusists by attacking them.

5

The summary of evidence for Esterhazy's court-martial was entrusted to a retired army major called Ravary, who opened his examination at the Cherche-Midi on December 8 and continued it up to December 30. Gonse and the officers of the Statistical Section gave evidence, largely against Picquart and Leblois. Esterhazy, having been stiffened by the information that Ravary had been primed—he said later by Du Paty—told his customary story and proliferated accusations. Marguérite Pays, Scheurer, Reinach, Mathieu Dreyfus, were all heard. The weak spot was the *bordereau*. None of the available professional experts wished to be mixed up in the Dreyfus case. But they were assured that the examination of

---

[1] "Es liegt nun einmal in meiner Natur: ich will lieber einer Ungerechtigkeit begehen, als Unordnung ertragen" (*Belagerung von Mainz*, 1795).

the *bordereau* was only to decide whether it was in the hand-writing of Esterhazy. On this they got to work, dealing simultaneously with the Boulancy letters. Then an incautious note from Du Paty raised the suspicion in Esterhazy's mind that the verdict on the Boulancy letters would not be given until after his court-martial, and he guessed that the perfidious War Office, while securing his acquittal on the *bordereau*, would get rid of him through the other correspondence. From drafts of it seized in his room in the following July, it appears that he wrote a letter to some general threatening that he would demand a full examination of Dreyfus's handwriting and the *bordereau*—that is, he would reopen the Dreyfus case.

The experts, under pressure, concluded that the *bordereau* was a poor copy of Esterhazy's writing, and went on to say that the Boulancy letters might equally be the work of a forger. Ravary's summary cleared Esterhazy, but, on Henry's testimony, accused Picquart of showing the *canaille de D* letter to Leblois, and stated that the *petit bleu* was a fraudulent document. Nevertheless, in order to allay public opinion, Saussier was persuaded to order a court-martial on Esterhazy. But was the hearing to be held *in camera* or in public? The War Office insisted that defence secrets required a closed hearing. After much argument a compromise was reached, that only Esterhazy and the civilian witnesses, though not the handwriting experts, should give their evidence in public. Scheurer-Kestner and Trarieux were both outraged at the news and published letters of protest in the *Temps*, but without avail.

Mathieu Dreyfus was naturally represented by his brother's counsel, Demange, who now knew much more than in 1894. For Mme Dreyfus, Demange recommended a rising young advocate, Fernand Labori, ambitious, vigorous, handsome and noisy. "Labori," said Barrès, "is not an intellect—he is a temperament." The court of seven officers, presided over by General Luxer, assembled on January 10 in the same room in which Dreyfus had been tried. Since the Minister of War had publicly declared on three occasions that Dreyfus was a traitor, their minds were already made up: moreover, in view of the Pellieux and Ravary conclusions, they had no alternative to acquitting Esterhazy. Demange and Labori were refused leave to plead, on the ground that the case did not concern Alfred Dreyfus.

By five votes to two the court decided to hear the military witnesses and the experts *in camera*. Esterhazy made charges right and left, and became confused in his own evidence, but nobody pressed him. He refused to identify "the liberating document." During Picquart's examination, Pellieux intervened to prevent the mention of Billot or Boisdeffre. The court was rough with Picquart until one of the junior judges remarked: "I see that Colonel Picquart is the real accused. I request that he be allowed to offer all the explanations necessary for his defence." Picquart then completed his evidence. He did not know, and would not know until the following day, the accusations made against him by his late subordinates, Henry and Lauth. Faced by Henry, he rebutted the charge of communicating the Secret File to Leblois, and Leblois supported him. The court believed both to be lying. There was a curious exchange between Tézenas, Esterhazy's lawyer, and Mathieu Dreyfus. The former said that Paris had been inundated for some days with foul pamphlets, a manœuvre against justice, and that three hundred thousand francs had been spent. "Not a word of truth in it," replied Mathieu. "Then, sir, how much?" asked Tézenas. "That's my business," retorted Mathieu. "I defend my brother as I intend. It is my right" (2, 145).[1]

After hearing Tézenas's speech for Esterhazy, the court found him not guilty. The audience broke into applause, and outside the prison the court gave "the martyr of the Jews" an ovation with shouts of "Long live France! Down with the Syndicate!" Trarieux

---

[1] The part played by money in the Affair remains and will remain obscure. It is certain that a great deal changed hands on both sides. Reinach is very discreet, but Mr Wickham Steed tells me that when, as correspondent of *The Times*, he was transferred from Rome to Vienna, the Viennese Jews openly said that Reinach had bled them for the cause. On the side of the anti-revisionists, it is certain that Mme de Loynes financed in part the Ligue de la Patrie Française, just as by will she left money for the benefit of Maurras's *Action Française*. The enquiry made by Méline of the Préfets of three frontier departments can have been merely to satisfy trouble-makers in the Chamber. Did anyone believe that money would arrive in notes or specie? And if so, why not ask the Préfets of the other frontier departments?

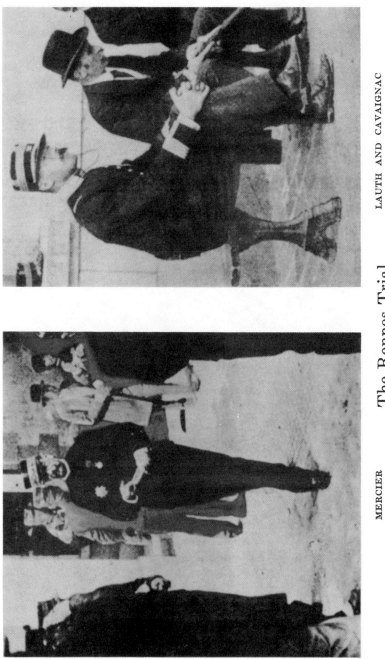

MERCIER   The Rennes Trial   LAUTH AND CAVAIGNAC

DÉROULÈDE AND THE LIGUE DES PATRIOTES

at the Rennes trial said: "Esterhazy has been acquitted: he has not been judged."

On the following day Pellieux permitted Esterhazy to publish the findings of the experts on the Boulancy letters. On this day too—January 13—Billot ordered Picquart under fortress arrest to Mont-Valérien.

The partisans of revision had not coalesced. Some knew one part of the case, some another. Picquart had the greater number of threads, though by no means all, in his hand. He had shown them only to Leblois and had talked with none of the revisionists. Only now did the basic material factors begin to be known. On January 7 Reinach dared to publish the Ormeschville report of 1894, which gave the lie to Billot's declaration of December 7 that the *bordereau* was not the only evidence against Dreyfus. On January 12, with the Ravary summary of evidence for the Esterhazy trial, the *petit bleu* came to public knowledge. Enough was now known for the revisionists to become a coherent body and work out a plan of campaign. The precipitating element of this cohesion was at hand.

CHAPTER NINE

The Intervention of Zola

1

THE most widely read and most heartily detested novelist of the day was Emile Zola. The list of his novels, of which sin was the obsessive theme, had been extending since 1868. His writing was both violent and tedious: he held for precise documentation, but he was a deplorable psychologist. He was regarded with horror by the Catholic conservatives, with contempt by other writers. "Zola," wrote Anatole France, "has no taste, and I end by thinking that lack of taste is that mysterious sin of which the Scriptures speak, the greatest of sins, the only one which will not be forgiven." He had recently completed his trilogy *Lourdes, Rome, Paris* and was casting about for a theme when the Dreyfus case re-emerged in November 1897. He had written two articles on Dreyfus for *Figaro*; then de Rodays, the editor, thought by the owners to be too Dreyfusist, was replaced.[1] After this Zola published a couple of pamphlets which fell flat. The acquittal of Esterhazy roused him, and he set feverishly to work. It is possible that his self-esteem, which had never been low, led him to believe that he had but to speak. Probably he did not foresee the furies that "*J'Accuse*" would raise. As Sorel said, he was always throwing bombs and was surprised when people were hurt. It is also possible he had not realised that, if he were taken at his word and prosecuted, he would not be the centre of the trial, that the real drama would be played by other actors, and that his words would seem fustian against the exchanges of the confronted witnesses. A recent critic has said: "Whatever he may have done for the Dreyfus family, it was noth-

---

[1] It was being rumoured that the Dreyfusists had given the *Figaro* four hundred thousand francs to support Dreyfus, but that the Government had paid the paper five hundred thousand francs to counter this (46, II, 106).

ing to what the Dreyfus family did for him." In so far as his support of Dreyfus made him acceptable to many writers who had hitherto shrunk from him, it is true. Yet his action must not be underestimated. His trial forced into the light much that had been hidden, and removed many of the barriers to revision.

During two nights and a day after Esterhazy's acquittal he composed a long open letter to Félix Faure. In it he arraigned the War Office, Mercier, Billot, Boisdeffre, Gonse and chiefly poor romantic Du Paty de Clam; he attacked Pellieux and Ravary and the handwriting experts at the Esterhazy trial. He accused the War Office of running a campaign in the *Eclair* and *Echo de Paris* to cover their tracks. He accused the first court-martial of violating the rights of the defence, and Esterhazy's court-martial of acquitting him on orders from the War Office. "As for the people I accuse, I do not know them; I have never seen them. I bear them neither ill-will nor hatred. For me they are no more than entities, spirits of social evil. . . . My fiery protest is only the cry of my soul. Let them dare to bring me to the Assize Court and may the examination be made in the light of day. I wait!" He took it to the office of the *Aurore* on the evening of January 12. Vaughan, on Clemenceau's suggestion, ran the headline "J'ACCUSE" and placed it on the front page. It was on sale at eight next morning, and by evening two hundred thousand copies had been sold.

Méline was taken completely by surprise. Since he had refused to look into the case, he was angered at the accusations against the various officers. But he was careful. At first he thought the sensible line was to do nothing, as in the past. But on reflection, and after talking to his ministerial colleagues, he realised that it was impossible to ignore the article, with the patriot press in eruption and the Chamber warming up to overthrow the Government. De Mun had at once given notice to interpellate Billot, and Billot and Boisdeffre knew they must act.

The Chamber resumed its sittings on January 14. Brisson, once again re-elected President, in his address made a few comments on the perils of dictatorship, and announced that he had received notice of an interpellation from the Comte de Mun. The Government bench was empty except for Cochery, the Minister of Finance, who was expecting to deal with the urgent matter of the overdue Budget. The Right noisily backed de Mun in his demand for Méline and Billot. "The Army," roared De Mun, "will not be kept waiting." Méline, when he appeared, said that he well understood the indignation of the Chamber: Zola would be prosecuted, in spite of the fact that what Zola actually wanted was to prolong the agitation. De Mun insisted on summoning Billot, who added nothing save a few platitudes to Méline's declaration. Jaurès, amid hostile murmurs, remarked that the Government was handing the Republic over to the generals.

It was the turn of Cavaignac, who hoped to overthrow Billot. He asked why the Government had not published Lebrun-Renaud's account of Dreyfus's confession: it escaped him that this confession, if it existed, should have appeared in January 1895. In reply Méline, while not denying the existence of Lebrun-Renaud's report, said that to follow Cavaignac on to this ground would lead to the reopening of the case, and in Parliament. All he need do was to hand Zola over to public justice. The man who had been Prime Minister in 1895, Dupuy, held his tongue. Although Cavaignac's reference to a confession had reassured a number of members, his motion of censure on Billot was defeated. Méline got a vote of confidence, but well over a hundred members abstained from voting.

On the same day, in the Senate, Scheurer, vice-president for as long as anyone could remember, was defeated at the annual re-election.

On January 18 Billot, after a full meeting of the Cabinet, requested the Minister of Justice to lay an information against Zola and the manager of the *Aurore*, Perrenx. The charge was skilfully drawn. It was confined to the passages which accused the judges at Esterhazy's court-martial of acquitting by order a criminal whom they knew to be guilty: "the first court-martial may have been unintelligent, the second is criminal." Thus the trial would be restricted to matters on which the defence could produce no evidence, and by eliminating the accusations against Du Paty and Mercier would keep the Dreyfus case remote from the proceedings.

2

The excitement caused by Zola's letter was not confined to the Chamber. It was a signal to the anti-semites. From January 17 onwards Jules Guérin, who had succeeded to the leadership of Morès's butcher-boys, and the professional patriots of the press and the political lobbies, set on foot a series of anti-Jewish riots in the provinces, beginning with Nantes. Nancy, Rennes, Bordeaux, Tournon, Moulins, Marseilles, Montpellier, Angoulême, Privas, Toulouse, Angers, Châlons-sur-Marne, Saint-Malo, Lunéville, Epinal, Bar-le-Duc, Grenoble, Niort, Le Havre and Orléans were in turn the scene of riots by students, ne'er-do-wells, and hirelings, in which the shops of the few Jews were smashed and pillaged.

In Paris there was little but demonstrations. The only serious outbreak occurred, as might be expected, in Algeria, where the trouble began on January 18 in Algiers. After four days' looting of shops, the mob, inflamed by agitators, swept down on the Jewish quarter and sacked it. Lépine, the Governor, who had been sent from the Préfecture of the Police in the previous October with the mission of discouraging trouble of this kind, was powerless to keep order, as were the Préfet and the Maire; the police were overwhelmed. These scenes were repeated on a lesser scale at Constantine and Oran as well as in smaller towns. The inspirers of the violence, Morinaud and an Italian named Max Régis, were neither restrained nor arrested.

On the revisionist side, the article in the *Aurore* had been followed by a petition against the violation of procedure in the trial of 1894 and the manifest incapacity of the court-martial on Esterhazy. It called for a revision of the Dreyfus case. It was signed by many men, savants, writers, philosophers, painters, teachers and students—by Grimaux, Anatole France, Monet, Reclus, Emile Bourgeois, Lucien Herr, Renan's son-in-law Psichari, the two young Halévys, Élie and Daniel, Marcel Proust; in all some three thousand names. There would have been many others but for fear of reprisals. "Yesterday," wrote Clemenceau in the *Aurore* of January 18, "one of our most distinguished secondary schoolmasters said to me: 'You'll get no one from the schools. If I gave you my name, that ass Rambaud [Minister of Public Instruction] would send me to rot in the depths of Brittany.'" Nevertheless the so-called intellectuals were far from unanimous. A great number were hostile, among them Brunetière, Lemaître, Barrès, Degas (almost blind, revelling in hearing the *Libre Parole* read to him each morning), Coppée, Forain. "The Dreyfus case," said Albert Thibaudet, "was a tumult of the intellectuals."

Except for Guérin's bands of ruffians, the case had roused no interest among the workers of Paris. The Socialist leaders were both cautious and far from unanimous. Guesde and Chauvin suggested to Jaurès that he should take up the case as the spokesman of the party. Either because he knew Guesde to be jealous of him and feared desertion after he had committed himself, or possibly from reluctance to break with his right-hand man, Millerand, Jaurès refused, on the ground that he was not yet convinced. Certainly the Socialist Union was not of one mind. Vaillant and his Blanquists, whose constituents were the small Paris shopkeepers, would not come out in a Jewish cause. Others were themselves anti-semites. The Allemane group was for revision. Jaurès's group was split; Millerand, its most powerful member, was for the Army and against revision. Those Socialists who were closest to the Radicals followed their patriotic line. In the end the policy which Guesde, dropping his first advice to Jaurès, recommended, was adopted: since Dreyfus belonged to the capitalist class, the enemy class, let the rival factions of the bourgeoisie, the opportunists and the clericals, fight it out. "Between Reinach and De Mun, maintain your full liberty" (Manifesto of January 19). After the event the Socialists were to claim that they were the first in the field for revision, but their votes during the next six months betray them.

In the Chamber the Finance Minister was still struggling to get his Budget passed. In view of the elections, Deputy after Deputy was presenting amendments to confer benefits on interests in his

constituency. In the course of the next three months, against the
resistance of the Ministers, additional credits to the tune of 117
million francs were added to the expenditure. On the side of
economy, the Public Worship estimate, taken on January 21, led
to two traditional Radical proposals, the denunciation of the Concordat and the suppression of the Public Worship budget. Both
were handsomely defeated.

January 22, according to a political correspondent, "will remain
without precedent in our parliamentary annals since the Convention." Cavaignac had once again pressed for the publication of
Lebrun-Renaud's report, and also one by Gonse which he alleged
bore the date 6 January 1895—a letter from Gonse did exist, but
Gonse had only just written it. Méline once more perceived the
shadow of a Right-and-Left coalition against him. He admitted
that on the evening of Dreyfus's degradation Lebrun-Renaud had
made a report such as Cavaignac indicated, but he refused to read
it; the judgment had been legal and could not be questioned: and
he swept into an attack on those who slandered the generals.

He had admitted the existence of a confession, which probably
he had never seen. That was enough for the Chamber. Amid
immense applause, Cavaignac withdrew his motion. At that
moment Jaurès dashed to the tribune and broke into a violent
harangue against Méline, against the "Jesuit generals protected by
the Republic." "We are dying of equivocation and cowardice, in
the lies and cowardice of the incomplete charges against Zola."
Rebuked by Brisson, he returned to the attack, scarlet in the face,
thundering against the Ministers and the generals. A noisy,
truculent member of the Right, the Comte de Bernis, called him a
member of the Syndicate. Jaurès returned that Bernis was a
miserable coward. Bernis moved to the centre of the Chamber,
on which twenty Socialists flung themselves at him and the Right
rushed to the rescue. Gérault-Richard slapped the Comte's face.
The ushers vainly tried to part the shouting combatants. Bernis
freed himself and, running up the tribune steps, hit Jaurès on
the back of the head. Brisson, after frenziedly and impotently ring-
ing the presidential bell, clapped on his hat and closed the sitting.

The Palais Bourbon military guard marched in and swept out the struggling and vituperating members.

At the next session the shame-faced Deputies sat in silence. Jaurès put a series of questions to Méline: had the first court-martial been given documents not shown to the defence? Why was there systematic use of *in camera* procedure? What was he afraid of? Méline refused to answer questions, and justified his attitude by saying: "The Government will not substitute itself for the justice of the country." Once again he fell back on his impregnable entrenchments, the separation of the powers and the *res judicata.* Later, a few members said to Jaurès: "What a pity this business broke out just before the election."

On this same day, January 24, von Bülow, the German Foreign Minister, told the Budget Committee of the Reichstag that he did not desire to enter into French domestic affairs: he would limit himself to a formal and categorical denial that there had ever been relations of any kind between Captain Dreyfus and any German agent. In Rome an analogous statement was made by the Foreign Under-Secretary to the Deputies, and a few days later William II called on the Marquis de Noailles, the French Ambassador in Berlin, and repeated Bülow's declaration. Hanotaux passed these on to Méline and Billot. Even if they believed the statements, they were now far too deeply involved to be able to act.

Billot and Boisdeffre decided to deal with Picquart before the Dreyfus case came on. Although he should properly have gone before a court called by his own commander in Tunis, he was described for these purposes as an officer on the staff, temporarily detached. The Court of Enquiry was presided over by General de Saint-Germain, a squat, ill-tempered dwarf, intimate friend of Mercier, while the junior member, Captain Anthoine, was to give some evidence against Dreyfus at Rennes eighteen months later. Picquart was accused of all the old crimes, of showing the Dreyfus and the two other files to Leblois, of having handed him Gonse's letters. Leblois, called, successfully destroyed one of the accusations, but the President refused to allow him to confront Henry, Lauth and Gribelin. Gonse, very hostile, said that Picquart should have been relieved of his duties instead of being sent to Tunis. Alone General Galliffet spoke boldly and warmly for Picquart. Picquart addressed the court in his own defence, rebutting the charges one by one, and ended: "If it is desired to thrust me out of the Army, I bow to the wish, fortified by my own conscience. The court will weigh whether Lt-Col. Picquart should be hunted from the Army while Major Esterhazy still walks the streets with his rank and his decorations."

The court, by four to one, found that there were grounds for dismissing Picquart from the service for grave infractions of discipline. He should at once have been released. Instead he was sent back to Mont-Valérien. Billot, who should immediately have accepted or rejected the findings, delayed in the hope that Picquart would show discretion at the Zola trial.

The trial of Zola and Perrenx was called for February 7.[1] Zola's counsel was Maître Labori, profuse as usual. Perrenx, the manager of the *Aurore*, was represented by Albert Clemenceau, younger brother of Georges, but Georges Clemenceau himself, although not a member of the Bar, was authorised to appear on behalf of the newspaper. As has been seen, the policy of the defence was to justify *all* the charges made in *J'Accuse*, whereas that of the

[1] French legal procedure differs from English in a number of ways. As regards evidence, a witness makes his statement in full, and without examination by counsel. Article 319 lays down: "The witness cannot be interrupted. The accused or his counsel may through the presiding judge question him after his deposition, and say, as much against him as against his evidence, everything which may be of use to the defence of the accused." In cross-examination, questions to witnesses are thus put through the judge, who can refuse to put them, or worse, put them in a form different from that put by counsel, though in practice it seems that frequently he does not intervene. But the most remote contacts with the case are admitted. To blacken Du Paty, Labori produced a witness to say that Du Paty many years earlier had got him ten days' C.B. for writing an essay to show that brains, not force, ruled the world. But the witness was found to have identified the wrong officer.

Possibly the least satisfactory practice is that hearsay evidence, what some third person has told the witness of the acts or conduct of the accused touching his guilt, is admitted and given probative effect. This was particularly bad at the second trial of Dreyfus in August–September 1899, where the statements of at least twenty out of the hundred witnesses were of this character; sometimes they had no factual basis whatever, sometimes they were contradicted by the person they were quoting.

See Lord Russell's comments on the Rennes trial (40).

Minister of War was to confine the case to the Esterhazy court-martial. Thus the defence wished to call almost two hundred witnesses, not only Mercier, Billot, Boisdeffre, Gonse, Du Paty and the officers of the Statistical Section, but the Cabinet Ministers of 1894, the judges of 1894, Casimir-Perier, Pellieux and Ravary, Picquart, Leblois, Esterhazy, Lebrun-Renaud, many journalists, philosophers and savants, Panizzardi and Schwartzkoppen: in short, anyone who could throw light on the 1894 trial.

Billot did not want to appear, and as a Minister he need not. Boisdeffre wished to prevent the officers from attending. Billot showed him that they must, but that Boisdeffre, by refusing to release them from "professional secrecy," could close their mouths.

The Dreyfusard writers charge that the Judge, Delegorgue, a round and rosy man, took his orders from the Minister. It may be so, but he was wholly correct in preventing the evidence, as far as he could, from straying away from the specific accusation of Zola.

February 7 saw the Assize Court invaded by an excited crowd of journalists, lawyers, army officers, society women—the fashionable first-night audience. Guérin had patrols of his anti-semite roughs outside the Palace of Justice, ready to cheer or hiss any recognised face. The witnesses waiting in the corridors divided into two opposing groups: between them the lean and sinister Esterhazy, in civilian clothes, stalked to and fro, cut by both sides. The jury consisted almost entirely of tradesmen. As soon as they were empanelled, the Advocate-General, Van Cassel, asked that the trial be limited to the single charge on the indictment, the insult to Esterhazy's judges. "There is no right to question even indirectly the *res judicata*. Behind that lies the wish to provoke a revolutionary revision." Counsel for the defence protested, but not strongly, their chief object being to get the military witnesses into the box. In this they were aided by the Judge, who rejected Billot's attempt through the Minister of Justice to prevent the appearance of witnesses other than those concerned in the Esterhazy trial— Lauth, Gonse, Pellieux and Gribelin. Delegorgue ruled that the military witnesses should appear. Esterhazy tried to avoid going into the box, but the Judge enforced his appearance.

Esterhazy had been enraged by the cool attitude of the officers towards him. He spoke about it to someone, possibly Pellieux, and on the third morning Boisdeffre came up and shook him by the hand. Others followed his example. None the less they did not like it, and as soon as they could, left him alone. He felt the slight, became irritated, and suddenly burst out to a group of civilians, who were talking to him: "They bore me with their *bordereau*. All right, yes! I wrote it! But it was not I who invented it; I did it by order!" (Evidence of Chincholle, reporter on *Figaro*, 6, I, 267.) [1]

On February 8, when Labori called Lucie Dreyfus, Delegorgue, since she had nothing to say concerning the Esterhazy case, refused to question her. On this, Zola, his moment come, demanded the freedom "granted to murderers and robbers; they can defend themselves, they can call witnesses." Delegorgue interrupted him: "You are aware of Article 52 of the law of 1881," to which Zola returned angrily, "I don't know the law and I don't want to know it." There was at once an uproar, in the midst of which he explained that he rebelled against the sophistries of a hypocritical procedure. It took some time to restore silence and then Lucie Dreyfus was asked to leave the box. She was followed in it by Leblois, who told what he knew about the *Blanche* and *Speranza* telegrams, about Du Paty and the "veiled lady." Scheurer, the next witness, wanted to read the correspondence between Gonse and Picquart, but was forbidden.

Boisdeffre was heard the following morning: he claimed, for reasons of State, the right to answer only those questions he could answer without endangering security. He whitewashed everyone except Picquart, who had been blameworthy in accusing Esterhazy without being able to discover any serious proofs. As for Dreyfus, he said that while the 1894 case was outside the discussion, "later facts had confirmed his own certainty." In allowing this statement, Delegorgue had accepted evidence on a matter on which Lucie Dreyfus had been silenced. Gonse, who followed,

[1] According to Charpentier (60, 318), Esterhazy, shortly after the publication of the Boulancy letters, told his wife that he had written the *bordereau* on Sandherr's instructions. Reinach (47, II, 111, f.n. 1) thinks Esterhazy took the hint from articles in the *Intransigeant* and the *Libre Parole* of 19 November 1897.

sheltered behind the plea of professional secrecy: the exchange of letters with Picquart had nothing to do with Dreyfus, to whose case he would not think of referring. (Reinach that morning had published several of these letters in the revisionist papers.) Lauth and Gribelin took up against Picquart the accusation that he had shown secret War Office papers to Leblois. Confronted with Leblois, Gribelin stuck to his story that he had seen them together in October 1896: Leblois proved that he was in Germany at that time. Then came Mercier.

Shortly before the trial, Mercier at Le Mans had had several conversations of considerable frankness with his artillery commandant, General André, a firm Republican and anti-clerical (9, 229–33). Mercier had no doubt about the existence of the "Jewish syndicate," since some years earlier he had been prevented from prosecuting a well-known army contractor who had cheated the Government. Now, called on to give evidence in the Zola case, he told André that in 1894 he had had in his hands crushing proofs of Dreyfus's guilt, but these proofs, if produced in open court, would infallibly have led to war with Germany at the moment when the new guns were not ready and the Germans were in possession of the French plans. In view of the risk, his only solution was to give the judges the evidence in secret. "It was serious for me; it was an abuse of authority, I knew. Between the safety of my country and judicial crime, I chose the crime." But now that the war plans had been redrafted, and France was once again on equal terms, the case could be reviewed and judged in open court. The court can "say if I am blameworthy for having, even at the price of my peace of mind, wanted to assure the security of France."

Possibly he intended, if driven to the wall, to admit what had been done in 1894. But Labori botched his cross-examination. By misquoting the *canaille de D* letter and suggesting that it was a postscript, he gave Mercier a loophole. He disclaimed all knowledge of what Labori was talking about, and then withdrew behind the verdict of 1894.

On February 10 four of the judges of 1894, and Ormeschville, were called, but Delegorgue refused to allow them to give evidence. The main witness of the day was Henry. He had not wanted to appear, but the defence succeeded in their request. On reaching the box, he said he was ill: "I have eighteen campaigns behind me and I have every right to have a touch of fever!" He took his time over answering questions. Asked about the Secret File, he replied that he had had it from Sandherr, but refused to state its contents. "It was the file of the Dreyfus case?" "No, the Dreyfus file had been sealed up since 1895." Confronted with Leblois as to the alleged conferences with Picquart, he got muddled and contradicted himself, until Gonse, saying that he was a very sick man, secured his withdrawal.

Pellieux, convinced as he was by the *faux Henry*, could not do otherwise than insist on Esterhazy's innocence: Picquart himself, he said, had been deceived by a combination of forgeries. Since he was speaking of the marrow of the case, he was listened to attentively, and his decisive bearing was convincing. He pointed out that the court-martial which tried Esterhazy could, after they had seen his own and Ravary's reports, do nothing except acquit him. He stated emphatically that Esterhazy's judges had been honourable, and that he was proud to have been "their leader." Zola, who had been silent since his outburst on the second day, broke out: "France can be served by both the sword and the pen. General de Pellieux has doubtless won great victories. I have won mine. By my works the French language has been spread through the whole world. I have my victories. I bequeath to posterity the name of General de Pellieux and the name of Emile Zola. Posterity will make its choice." The demonstration was alas! irrelevant, and Pellieux remained master of the field.

One other witness appeared that day, but was not heard. This was an elderly lawyer named Salles, who had heard from one of the judges in 1894 that Dreyfus had been convicted on documents not shown to the defence. Delegorgue, having elicited that his evidence did not touch the Esterhazy trial, refused to hear him. Every attempt by Labori and Albert Clemenceau was cut short with: "The question will not be put." Salles left the box.

On February 11 it was the turn of Picquart, still held, pending
Billot's decision, at Mont-Valérien. Here he had been sent two
officers to advise him that his future depended on what he said to
the court. The first, Colonel Maurice Bailloud (who—by then "a
rosy old Punch of a man"—was to command the French Expeditionary Force at the Dardanelles), was shamed by Picquart's
friendly manner and did not deliver the message. To the other
Picquart simply answered that he would tell the truth. Furthermore, Bertulus, the lawyer seconded to advise Pellieux, was asked
by Gonse to let Picquart know that if he, so to speak, remained in
the military family, as everyone desired, and held his tongue, his
career would not be ruined. Picquart coldly replied that he would
do his best to reconcile his duty as a soldier with his duty as a
witness.

He was wearing uniform. Tall, thin, with an impassive face, he
told an enthralled audience of his discovery of the *petit bleu* and his
first horrified examination of the Dreyfus Secret File, which contained no proofs. Of his conversations with Gonse, Boisdeffre and
Billot, of Henry's betrayal, of the *faux Henry* and the Weyler
letter, he said not a word. In examination by Labori, he pointed
out that no one had ever told him that Esterhazy could not be the
author of the *bordereau*; no one had ever told him to stop his
investigations. He hinted, no more, that Esterhazy had been protected. Pellieux had shown him the so-called "liberating document": it was the same as that alleged to have been shown by him
to Leblois, the *canaille de D.*

Picquart had burned his boats and could expect no mercy.
From this moment the centre of the case swung away from Zola,
away from Dreyfus, to Picquart. As Pellieux said: "Without
Picquart the case would not exist." From this moment the members of the Statistical Section set about him. Gribelin asserted that
he had seen Picquart and Leblois with the Secret File open between them. Lauth swore that Picquart had tried to force him to
say that the *petit bleu* was in the hand of a military attaché, and
further had tried to persuade him to fake the photographs to show
that the *bleu* had passed through the post: he said he believed, but

would not swear, that Picquart had himself planted the letter in Bastian's bags. Clemenceau tore most of this to pieces, but Lauth resolutely maintained his statements.

On the following day Henry was confronted with Picquart. Once more he repeated that he had seen the file with his initial on the cover lying on the table between Picquart and Leblois. Cross-examined, he was led on to say that the *canaille de D* letter was sticking out and that he recognised it. Picquart replied that it was impossible to know it at a distance. "I could recognise it at ten paces," said Henry. Picquart said that he formally challenged the statement, whereupon Henry exclaimed: "There's no arguing about it, particularly if one is accustomed to seeing a document, and I've seen this more than once. I maintain formally what I said, and I say again, Colonel Picquart has lied." For one moment Picquart nearly lost control of himself; he raised his fist to strike but let it fall again, merely remarking: "You have no right to say that." The Judge blandly interrupted: "So you two disagree."

Clemenceau angrily protested at Delegorgue's remark, before turning to Henry. Going back to the witness's evidence of two days earlier, he showed that Henry then denied that the file with the "*canaille*" letter had anything to do with the Dreyfus case, and had said that the Dreyfus file had been under seal since 1895 and had never to his knowledge been opened. How did he reconcile that with his current statement that the letter he saw between Leblois and Picquart was the "*canaille*" letter, and part of the Dreyfus file? Henry replied that it had nothing to do with the Dreyfus case. "However, I will explain this file. It is a long time since I took responsibility for it. *Allons-y*. Here goes." He went on to say that Sandherr in 1894 had told him to collect in one file all documents relating to espionage. "I found eight or nine pieces, of which one was highly important, very confidential, ultra-secret. Sandherr kept it from November until the 15th or 16th of December, when he gave it back to me: in the interval he had had a few photographs taken of it. I then put all the documents of the file into an envelope, marked it '*Dossier secret*' with the letter D and my

initials on the back. This lay in my cupboard until Gribelin got it
out for Picquart. When Sandherr gave me back the file I asked
him why he no longer needed it. He showed me a letter, making me
swear never to talk about it and added: 'I have several pieces besides this one; I keep them beside me, and if need be I shall use
them.' I have never heard anything more about this [ultra-secret]
file; the Colonel never handed it over to me. He spoke of it only
the once, on 16 December 1894."

Henry had successfully blurred the traces. Neither Labori nor
Clemenceau appears to have done any serious work on the case.
They do not seem to have understood what Henry was saying;
they did not pursue the line of the *"canaille"* letter. They let
Henry go.

On the same day Demange in the witness-box uncovered a little
more. Delegorgue was momentarily caught napping. To Labori,
Demange admitted that had he believed the Dreyfus judgment to
be legal, he would not have applied for an annulment. "What
makes you think it illegal?" asked Labori.

"Because M. Salles learned from a member of the court that the
judgment was null and void."

Albert Clemenceau quickly put in: "Is that because a secret
document was shown to the judges?" And before Delegorgue
could stop him, Demange whipped out: *"Mais oui, parbleu!"*
Later Stock, the publisher, stated on oath that a member of the
court had told him that four documents had been communicated.
Delegorgue cut him short.

By the end of the fourth day the revisionists, seeing that some
light was gradually filtering through to the original case, were
inclined to congratulate themselves: they even began to believe
that Zola would be acquitted, though, considering the body of the
indictment, it is difficult to see the grounds for their optimism.
In any case they had reckoned without the power of the anti-
revisionist press. In all the popular newspapers the reports
were, as usual, abridged, and concentrated on the more dramatic
aspects. According to the views of the editors, awkward statements were omitted, favourable ones enlarged: there was no hesita-

tion about falsification when required. Beyond this, the unhappy jury received veiled threats: one unlucky juryman, having been discovered to be one of the Rothschilds' tradesmen, was denounced by Drumont as being in the pay of the Jews, and judiciously went sick.

During the trial the anti-revisionists invited Déroulède to return to the field of patriotic action. The leader of the now defunct Ligue des Patriotes accepted, and during the rest of the case appeared in court as the leader of the anti-Zola claque. In the corridors the Nationalist advocate Auffray worked up tumults of his fellow-barristers and army officers. Each day outside the precincts the crowd increased to watch Guérin's ruffians jeer, pelt or even assault the witnesses on Zola's side.

Meanwhile the case dragged on. From February 12 to 17 were heard those who wished to testify to Zola's virtues—Jaurès and his friends. The evidence of the handwriting experts was taken: on one side were ranged Bertillon, "the stubborn defender of the unintelligible," and his overawed or venal fellows: on the other, brought in by the defence, the expert palæographers of the Ecole des Chartes and the Institut, who demolished the prosecution's witnesses and, as one man, swore that Esterhazy was the writer of the *bordereau*.[1] The dreary case seemed scarcely to move. By February 15 *The Times* correspondent, Fullerton, was writing: "This affair is even beginning to affect business. The shops are suffering, timorous foreigners hasten their departure and postpone their arrival . . . foreign orders are falling off from a supposed uncertainty of punctual execution."

On the afternoon of February 17 Picquart was recalled. He gave it as his constant opinion that Esterhazy could, from many sources, including the firing-practices he had attended, have procured all the information described in the *bordereau*. Pellieux and Gonse in confrontation asserted that the information about Madagascar could not have been obtained by Esterhazy, since at the time when the Madagascar expedition was being planned—August 1894—he was at the artillery ranges. Picquart remarked that surely

---

[1] On the other hand, Locard (63, 33) insists that the experts from the Ecole de Chartes were not graphological experts.

the *bordereau* was of April, whereon Pellieux sharply replied that it was not, and appealed to Gonse to confirm him. Picquart was shaken; he could merely tell Delegorgue what he had always heard, that the document had been written in April, and had always accepted it as of that date. On this Labori asked Gonse why Ormeschville in his indictment had accused Dreyfus of procuring a document on Madagascar in February (before any confidential work on Madagascar had been done): Gonse stammered that he could not explain, but he stuck to his statement. Labori—it shows how little he understood—failed to take up the point, which could then and there have destroyed the prosecution's case of 1894.

Throughout the trial Pellieux had been becoming more and more irritated. In complete honesty he had accepted the *faux Henry* as genuine. He could not understand why his chiefs—Billot, Bois-deffre, Gonse—with such a weapon at hand, were reluctant to produce it and preferred to shelter behind the *res judicata*. It does not appear that he at any time took up the point with Gonse. Now, however, having seen the handwriting experts covered with ridicule by the palæographers, having seen Gonse contradicting himself in the box, he determined to play the *coup de maître*. On the plea that the defence had read a passage from the Ormeschville indictment of Dreyfus, he claimed to speak not of the case itself, but to adduce further evidence. He then related that at the moment of the Castelin interpellation of 1896 the War Office had received a posi-tive proof of Dreyfus's guilt. So far as he recalled it, it ran: "There is going to be an interpellation on the Dreyfus case. Never say anything about the relations we were in with this Jew." He went on: "The revision of the trial has been sought by a roundabout way; I give you this fact; I affirm it on my honour, and I call for the support of General de Boisdeffre." There was a howl of joy from the anti-revisionists. Zola and Clemenceau at once demanded the production of this document. Pellieux was furious that his mere word was not accepted. Gonse asked to speak, and confirmed Pellieux's statement, but insisted that this proof, which was real and absolute, could not be brought into the public court.

Pellieux, abashed and angry at Gonse's covert reproof, tried to regain control of the situation. When Delegorgue said that Boisdeffre's evidence could be taken next morning, he shouted to his orderly officer to fetch Boisdeffre at once. Then, turning back to Zola's counsel and the audience, he roared that he would not be interrupted, that he would be believed. "No proof has been brought of secret communication to the judges ... The newspapers [i.e. *Figaro*] have abridged Ormeschville's indictment." Clemenceau expressed surprise that, in all his speeches, Billot had never mentioned this decisive letter. Pellieux shouted: "General Billot does what he likes; it's none of my business. But there are other pieces, as General Boisdeffre will tell you."

Delegorgue hastily closed the hearing. That evening the noise outside the court was worse than ever. An attempt was made to get hold of Leblois, who escaped with difficulty. Zola and his counsel left by a side door.

On the following morning Boisdeffre, having approved Gonse's refusal to produce the document, made a brief and dignified appearance in the box. "I confirm the deposition of General de Pellieux in all its points as exact and authentic. I have nothing more to say. I have not the right. You, gentlemen, are the jury; you are the nation. If the nation has no confidence in its Army's leaders, in those responsible for the national defence, they are ready to leave the heavy task to others. You have only to speak. I will say nothing more. I ask leave to withdraw." It was, of course, a threat, and the wretched jurymen knew they could not resist. How could they ask for the resignation of the Chief of Staff? Delegorgue refused Labori permission to cross-examine.

Picquart, recalled later in the day, said it would be well to verify the authenticity of some of the documents, notably the one which had reached the War Office at the moment when it became necessary to show serious proof that another than Esterhazy had written the *bordereau*: for "the moment at which it appeared, the absolutely improbable terms in which it was conceived, gave every reason to think it a forgery. This is the piece of which General de Pellieux spoke yesterday." It will be remembered that Picquart had had from Billot's lips a version of Henry's fabrication.

This concluded the material body of the evidence, though not the trial. After Boisdeffre, Esterhazy was called. He had been thoroughly coached by Pellieux. His orders were to refuse to speak. Gaunt and yellow, he stood in the box and faced Albert Clemenceau. Clemenceau had prepared a list of questions covering his career, his letters about the French, their Army and their generals, about the *bordereau*. To none did Esterhazy reply. Implacably and remorselessly his adversary questioned him. The spectators grew restive as through forty minutes the ordeal went on. After the last question they gave Esterhazy an ovation, which was loudly renewed as he left the court. Prince Henri d'Orléans congratulated him on his courage, and Guérin's boys carried him shoulder-high to his cab.

On February 21 the final speeches began. That of the Advocate-General was cold, dull and flat. Zola replied. Egotistical and romantic, although claiming to speak for Dreyfus, he spoke of himself. "He began," wrote Fullerton of *The Times*, "with an insult to the Prime Minister and at the same time to the jury; and such glorification of himself must have displeased the unpretentious men who form the jury." Even Reinach, his admirer, admits that the "I" was superabundant. Labori followed, and continued on the next day. He spoke quietly, tracing the whole history of the case from the arrest of Dreyfus: he implied that the generals had been mistaken, and that someone, not in the War Office, but a friend of Esterhazy, had forged the evidence. Finally, on the evening of the 22nd, Clemenceau rose on behalf of Perrenx. Throughout their speeches the counsel had been interrupted by Déroulède and his claque. Clemenceau pursued his way unmoved; he had faced Déroulède before. He stuck to his theme that he did not know whether Dreyfus was guilty or innocent, but that it was invincibly evident that he had been condemned by violation of the law: and "illegality is a form of iniquity, since the law is a guarantee of justice." This did not answer the charge against Zola and Perrenx, but it brought out the higher issues. The jury retired. That morning each had received an anonymous offer of ten thousand francs if Zola were acquitted.

They returned to the court forty minutes later and gave their verdict. By a majority they found both the accused guilty, while on the question of extenuating circumstances they were equally divided. In face of the indictment, they could not have found otherwise; no evidence had been offered against Esterhazy's judges.

The verdict was greeted with a howl of joy, echoed in the corridors and taken up by the street: "Up the Army! Down with the Jews!" Zola was condemned to the maximum sentence under Article 31 of the Press Law of 1881: imprisonment for twelve months.[1] Perrenx got four; both were fined the maximum, three thousand francs.

"Yesterday," wrote the *Berliner Tageblatt* on the following morning, "the French Army won its first victory since its defeat in 1870–71."

---

[1] Zola appealed, and on technical grounds the appeal was allowed. He stood his trial again at Versailles on July 18, and was again condemned to the maximum penalties. On the night of July 19 he set out for London, where he remained for eighteen months. He went much against his will and only under the heavy pressure of his friends.

CHAPTER TEN

The Death of Henry

1

AT this point it is well to consider how far the facts about the trial of Dreyfus were known to the general public. Readers of the press had seen very poor facsimiles of the *bordereau* and of Esterhazy's writing. They could have read Ormeschville's summary of evidence, an unconvincing document. From the reports of the Zola trial they could conjecture that at the court-martial of 1894 documents not available to the defence had been shown to the judges, but the evidence of this divulgation was far from clear, and in any case the contents of the documents were unknown. They may have read some of Esterhazy's letters to Mme Boulancy, but these were irrelevant except as to Esterhazy's character. As for the *petit bleu*, its existence was unknown to all save some of the War Office staff and to Picquart: even the leading revisionists never heard of it until Picquart was dismissed the service.

On the other side, there was Picquart's not very illuminating evidence at the Zola trial, which had been stoutly challenged by a number of officers. As to the Secret File, the story given by Henry had completely obscured the matter. There was Pellieux's deposition as to subsequent irrefutable evidence against Dreyfus, confirmed by Gonse and Boisdeffre. Furthermore, Schwartzkoppen had been transferred to Germany, a significant removal.

On top of all this confused evidence there were the rumours that letters from Dreyfus to the Kaiser and one from the Kaiser to Münster were, either as originals or photographs, in the possession of the War Office, that vast sums of money were being sent to France by foreign Jews, and so forth. And there was always the fear of war with Germany.

"Fanaticism begins at the point where evidence stops short."

In Society everyone had his opinion and everyone clung to it tenaciously, coloured as it was with his own political and social prejudices. In these circles the case from being a subject of conversation swelled into furious discussion, and from discussion to open quarrels. Families were torn apart; engagements broken off by partisan parents; old friendships were ruptured; partnerships dissolved. "Whatever you may say or do," wrote Paul Cambon, then on leave from Constantinople, "you are classed as a friend or enemy of the Jews and the Army" (19, 436). Loisy in his memoirs relates that he had scarcely been aware of the case before his society split and foundered. Agitated hostesses wrote on their cards of invitation requests that the Affair should be treated as taboo.

Outside these circles the effects of the trial were small. "I am bound to admit," wrote Clemenceau on the morrow, "that the working classes appear to take no interest whatever in the question." *The Times* correspondent had already noted that, amid all the appeals to violence by the anti-semites, "there prevails a sort of indifference. . . . Anti-semitism has not penetrated the masses. . . . The shopkeeper fights a very easy battle with them [the Jews], and does not really fear them."

Apart from Paris the country was little interested. As yet the provincial bourgeoisie were immune; they did not catch the infection until the appearance of the Waldeck-Rousseau Ministry in June 1899, and the Rennes court-martial. The provincial artisans and the peasants were never roused. Many of them did not read newspapers. In the provinces, it is true, there were the whipped-up anti-semitic riots in Nantes, Rennes, Lyon, Rouen, Marseilles, Clermont-Ferrand and other towns, chiefly of students and ne'er-do-wells intent on plunder: the only serious trouble was in Algeria, where the outbreak of mid-January had hardly died down, and where, in spite of the urgings of Barthou and Méline, the authorities found themselves impotent to quell the anti-semites.

In Parliament indifference reigned. On February 18, after hearing Boisdeffre's evidence with its threat of resignation, Jaurès tried to raise the scare of a military *coup d'état*: "the Republic has never run so great a danger." His fellow-Socialists were cool.

Did the Left at any time believe that the danger existed? It is difficult to be definite. Undoubtedly cooler men of great political experience entertained the idea. Paul Cambon, looking at the attitude of the soldiers to revision, thought that a revival of Boulangism might occur: "It may be a general will be found to take up a spectacular defence of the honour of the Army. But," he added, "it is true, I don't see the general." In fact there was none. All the soldiers desired was to be master in their own house, without interference from the politicians, to whip their own dogs, and for that they were ready to go to lengths, but not to extremes, not to revolt. As isolated as monks from the main currents of civilian society, the generals did not know enough to decline the help of political charlatans who hoped to use them for their own purposes.

Thus there was mutual misunderstanding. The civilians, the Senators and Deputies, were no less ignorant of the Army. They did not attack them on the score of incompetence: they accused them of the one thing from which every general would have drawn back in horror, rebellion. The members of the Army committees in the Chamber and Senate did not know their business, and they permitted freedom to their fellows to attack, on political grounds and for electoral purposes, the institution they should have protected.

There were even weaker foundations for the attacks on the Church. Anti-clerical writers presented the Church as a reactionary body allied to the Army in conspiracy against the Republic. The evidence is thin. In every organisation there are those who cannot be silent. The utterances of a few priests and laymen were identified as the attitude of the whole Church. A sermon of Father Didon, an article by Drumont, would be publicised: the protests of the Abbés Fremont and Brugerette or the Catholic *Salut Public* of Lyon would not be quoted by the anti-clerical press. The Society of Jesus with its romantic reputation for conspiracy was naturally singled out for special treatment, and the confessor of Boisdeffre and de Mun, Father Du Lac, at worst a minor intriguer, pointed to as the centre of the conspiracy. But the Society at this date was far from belligerent. One foolish anti-semitic article in the *Civiltà Cattolica* in January 1898 does not make a campaign. Father Lecanuet (72, 179) believed it to be an unwise opening shot. Sorel, the anti-clerical, thought it a counter-attack. It may have been either, but what Reinach, for whom it is the basis of his charge of Jesuit anti-semitism, ignored, is a no less violent polemic against the Church in the *Univers Israélite* published a few days earlier.

The single body which justifies the charges of anti-clerical writers was the Assumptionist Order, plebeian and violent, which did much harm to Vatican policy; which was deplored by many bishops; and over which they had no control. For the Vatican, Dreyfus was a minor matter, of the smallest importance in comparison with the doctrinal warfare which raged during these years throughout the whole Catholic Church. It may well be that, as Monsignor d'Hulst, Rector of the Catholic Institute in Paris and deputy for Brest, said, Rome was blind: but in fact the Biblical controversy was shaking the very foundations of belief, and in such a situation the Dreyfus question agitating Parisian society was of little moment.

2

In the French Parliament the disposition to damp down the Zola and Dreyfus cases remained. On the day after the verdict two Deputies put forward a somewhat academic motion on the predominance of civil power over the military. Méline, while admitting that the generals had been drawn on to say too much, maintained they had been provoked to exasperation by Zola's counsel. He claimed that the incessant accusations made by the Dreyfusards were responsible, and that the Jews who had so rashly undertaken the campaign were themselves the provokers of anti-semitism—they and "this intellectual élite which seems to take pleasure in adding venom to raw hatred." While he rejected the idea of reprisals, he said that, where circumstances demanded, disciplinary measures would be taken. The speech was greeted with immense applause from all sides. The Deputies, with the elections so near, were not likely to respond to the jeers of Clemenceau, who in his daily column was lashing the hypocrisy of those who professed liberal ideas while failing to put them into practice. "The prize for the most consummate hypocrisy seems to me to go incontestably to those who in the press and the Chamber denounce clerical danger and military dictatorship, while they simultaneously give free play to those powers against the wretched Semite whom aristocratic Aryanism will not touch. Alone, with a small group of friends, Jaurès has appealed to generosity, advanced arguments of reason. Since he is a leader, shoulders are shrugged and the *politicians* have shown their indulgence by preventing the Party from compromising itself in this 'sentimentality'" (22, 260–61).

Naturally the anti-revisionists made no bones about their victory; they triumphed noisily. They believed that revision was dead. They were wrong. In spite of the verdict, the Zola trial had demonstrated to those who read the full report of the proceedings that much was being concealed. If the politicians ignored the omens, the despised "intellectuals" read them aright. Immediately after the trial there came into being the League for the Defence of the Rights of Man and the Citizen. Its earliest members were found among professors from the Ecole des Chartes, who had heard from the palæographers at the Zola trial of the fatuity of Bertillon and company; from the Collège de France; from the Ecole Normale Supérieure, brought in by its Socialist librarian, Lucien Herr, there were serious publicists, such as Yves Guyot, former Minister, economist and editor of *Le Siècle*, and François de Pressensé, and a few Senators, Ranc, Trarieux. Particularly notable is the large proportion of Protestants among the leading members. The Protestants knew well that they were as odious as the Jews to militant Catholicism. The League's growth was not rapid, but it had excellent speakers, who began to carry their mission beyond the boundaries of the Seine. Slowly its influence began to be felt.

The League's statutes had been drafted by Trarieux and the eminent Catholic savant, Paul Viollet, who became its first secretary. Viollet suggested that a master-stroke against the Right would be for the League to put forward the readmission of members of the teaching Orders to the State schools. The League committee rejected the proposal unanimously, and Viollet sadly resigned. This early manifestation of anti-clericalism by the committee set the future course. Within five years the League was to become as fanatic and as treacherous as its enemies.

Meanwhile Méline's disciplinary measures were being taken. On February 16 Picquart was dismissed from the service for grave professional faults; his pension was commuted to rather less than £100 and, being no longer liable to recall to the Army, he would wear uniform no more. He was released from Mont-Valérien. Leblois was relieved of his duties as assistant Maire of the VIIth arrondissement: he was also suspended for six months by the Paris Bar Council on the grounds of professional misconduct in communicating to Scheurer-Kestner the confidences of his client, Picquart. Even Demange escaped censure only by the vote of a majority. Grimaux, senior professor of chemistry at the Polytechnic and the Agricultural Institute, was removed from his chairs, at the Polytechnic by Billot, at the Institute by Méline: he had rashly testified on Zola's behalf.

In the world of journalism, where no holds were barred, interprofessional abuse led to frequent duels, of which the most prominent was that between Clemenceau and Drumont. Both were ageing; they fired three times, and three times they missed. It is fair to say that in all these encounters there were no deaths and very few wounds. One duel had some importance. For his insult at the Zola trial, Picquart challenged Henry. Henry refused to meet him, on the ground that Picquart was a dishonourable person. Pellieux told Esterhazy to challenge Picquart. Picquart, in turn, refused to cross swords with Esterhazy. During the negotiations between seconds, Henry called openly at Marguérite Pays's apartment to discuss matters with Esterhazy, with whom he had hitherto had no acknowledged contact. In the end Henry accepted Picquart's challenge. They met on March 4, when Henry received a slight wound in the arm.

On the day before the duel, another possible source of light was extinguished. Henry's chief forger, Lemercier-Picard, was found hanged in his shabby lodgings. Was it suicide? Or was it, as some hinted, an operation of the Paris police? During the past three months the forger had been making approaches to the revisionists, but they, grown wary, had fought shy of him.

3

As has been seen, Picquart, since his arrival in Paris, had had little contact with the revisionists. He had seen Leblois only once before the Esterhazy trial. He did not meet Scheurer, Mathieu or Mme Dreyfus until the first day of the Esterhazy trial. To Mathieu he said: "You need not thank me; I obeyed my conscience." Forty-eight hours later he was in Mont-Valérien. Now he was free from the bonds of discipline, and as a free man he could openly join those who were working on behalf of Alfred Dreyfus.

During the Zola trial he had three times seen Bertulus, the examining magistrate who had been lent to Pellieux. Bertulus had been requested by the War Office to look into the telegrams sent to Picquart in Tunisia, *Blanche* and *Speranza*. Further, Picquart himself had laid an information against a person unknown for forging these telegrams. On several occasions in the past Bertulus had helped Sandherr and Henry on legal points. When Picquart took over the Statistical Section, Bertulus had thought of making his acquaintance, but was warned off by Henry, who told him Picquart was difficult to get on with, a hair-splitter who made trouble, a type the magistrate had no love for. Now, beneath a free-and-easy manner Bertulus was extremely acute. After talking to Picquart, he found that the man against whom he had been warned was clear-headed, intelligent, and so far as he could judge reliable.

Picquart, admittedly, had never seriously examined the Dreyfus file. With his eyes firmly fixed on Esterhazy, he had failed to discover the false dating of the *bordereau*. Knowing the part Du Paty had played in the original examination of Dreyfus, he now jumped to the conclusion that this was the person whose interest it was to save Esterhazy, that he was the author of the telegrams and the mainspring of the accusations against himself. He conceived a violent hatred for the man who was in fact about to become his fellow-victim. He imparted his suspicions to Bertulus. Bertulus saw Du Paty, who assured him he knew nothing about the telegrams or the veiled lady. His statement on the telegrams was confirmed by the experts who compared his handwriting with that on the originals in the Post Office. Nevertheless, Du Paty's lack of common sense and his inability to hold his tongue were again to betray him. Since Esterhazy's acquittal, he had begun to suspect him of being, if not a traitor, at least a rogue and a blackmailer, and he regretted having involved himself in his defence. Furthermore, he had an inkling that Henry, secretly, was also trafficking with the ruffian. Unable to be silent, a few days after the condemnation of Zola he had told Henry of his suspicions of the *faux Henry*, which he had already given to Gonse.

Henry had intended that this famous document should never be seen except by those to whom he had shown it. He had cursed Gribelin for telling Pellieux of its existence (8, II, 99). Now that the light-headed Du Paty was on the right track, the whole of his great construction might crumble. From the moment that Du Paty came to him with his suspicions, Henry decided to deal with him as he had dealt with Picquart. Du Paty's unwise confidence was made a couple of days before Henry's first open contact with Esterhazy. At that meeting Marguérite Pays let slip that the only mistake they had made had been the *Blanche* and *Speranza* telegrams. Henry, who had not known their origin, and had believed them to be part of the Esterhazy–Du Paty collaboration of November, took the story to Gonse. Gonse demanded an explanation from Du Paty, who denied all knowledge of the matter, and said that Esterhazy's mistress was a *drôlesse*. Not content with sowing suspicion of Du Paty in Gonse's mind, Henry went on to complain to his subordinates, Lauth and Junck, that by his clumsiness and arrogance Du Paty was responsible for all the recent trouble, and thus he created round him an atmosphere of distrust. At the same time, knowing the unreliability of the fantastic Esterhazy, and afraid that in a wild moment he would divulge to Du Paty the truth about the telegrams, he warned Esterhazy that Du Paty was speaking ill of him. Thus, of those who were playing some part in the affair of Alfred Dreyfus, Henry remained the only one not to be suspected either by his seniors or by his juniors. Du Paty slowly discovered that he was being cold-shouldered and avoided. Proud as he was, he suffered, and his sufferings were visible. "He looks as if he was crucified," said one. This was in April.

Bertulus not only failed to discover anything about the telegrams, but he began to grow suspicious of the people to whom he was attached. Gonse had filled him with false information. He had told him that Mathieu Dreyfus had tried to bribe Sandherr, and at the same time he gave him a bunch of papers which included Sandherr's accurate account of the interview, with its testimony to Mathieu's innocence. Pellieux had involved him with a married woman, Picquart's mistress, by pretending that she was the famous veiled lady. He suspected that he was being given deliberately false scents, and guessed that he was thought a nuisance. Being an intelligent and persistent man, he decided to lie low for the time being, while showing all his accustomed affability to those who were trying to mislead him. At this point an incident wholly foreign to his business opened up a new line of enquiry.

Christian Esterhazy had gone back home to the Bordelais. He had received none of the profits promised him by his cousin, and, from all he could hear, Esterhazy was in very low water. Esterhazy had told him that as soon as he was clear of the great conspiracy against him all would be well, but his letters offered little more than vague promises. Christian's mother was well aware that Mme Esterhazy had refused to live with her husband and had begun divorce proceedings. She and Christian asked for the repayment of the fifty thousand francs they had handed over.

Esterhazy returned a threatening letter, and to Christian's mother he sent one accusing her son of frequenting prostitutes. Christian at once came to Paris, and on April 23 called on Esterhazy at his mistress's flat. Esterhazy bluntly told him the money had flown, and threatened to denounce the young man as an unregistered moneylender: in addition he spoke of committing suicide. Christian had witnessed this scene before and was not alarmed. Receiving confirmation from Rothschilds that they had never had a penny of his money, he went, on the advice of an acquaintance, to see Labori, to whom he related the whole story of his collaboration with Esterhazy, as well as that of Pellieux and Du Paty; at the same time he agreed that Labori should pass the information on to Mathieu Dreyfus. Christian also sought out Trarieux, who was one of the Senators for his own department. Trarieux, not, as was Labori, bound to professional secrecy, repeated the story to Picquart, Leblois and Reinach. But the revisionists could not be sure that Christian would not retract what he had retailed to Labori and Trarieux in an hour of agitation. They decided that Picquart should pass the story to Bertulus, who as an examining magistrate could subpoena Christian to testify. There for the moment the matter rested.

4

Parliament rose on April 7. In the Chamber, Brisson, in his farewell presidential address, ignored the question which had been agitating society: instead, he made a fierce attack on clericalism, stressing his distrust of the perfidious Ralliés.

The month preceding the opening of the elections was quiet. Only in those constituencies where active Dreyfusards or anti-Dreyfusards were standing was the case mentioned. One unhappy Radical who was rash enough to announce himself in favour of revision was at once disavowed by Léon Bourgeois and Cavaignac, who both won the praises of the anti-semite press for their patriotism. The Radicals remained unyieldingly anti-revisionist; their chief newspaper in the South, the *Dépêche de Toulouse*, owned by the Sarraut family, jeered at Zola and supported the Army, while remaining doctrinally sound on anti-clericalism.

Brisson's attack on the clericals had certain justification. Two years earlier, Leo XIII had confided to Etienne Lamy, a Catholic Republican, who had been one of the famous "363" Republicans to defy Broglie's Sixteenth of May Government in 1877, the task of federating and leading the various Catholic groups with a view to the elections of 1898. Unhappily, of the dozen or so organisations, the strongest in numbers, wealth and influence was the

"Justice-Egalité," founded and controlled by the Assumptionists. This organisation rejected the recommendation to pool the Catholic resources. They came to the election in the spirit of no compromise with the Republic and refused Lamy's policy of negotiation with Republican candidates. They not merely preferred Royalists, but even Radicals, to Ralliés. Their action is reckoned to have given as many as sixty seats to the Radicals (72, 122–29 and 70, 253–59).

It is said that Méline wanted to use the government machinery to support the candidates of the Right against the Radicals, but that Barthou refused. None the less, Barthou himself was believed by the Radicals to have used administrative pressure against them. The electors polled on May 8 and 22. The results showed no great change in the groups in the Chamber. The Republicans lost a few seats, the Radicals a few more. Lebon, Minister of Colonies, was beaten by a combination of Dreyfusards and Conservatives, while Reinach was defeated at Digne. Guesde lost his seat at Lille, and Jaurès his at Carmaux. Jaurès's failure was due to his mishandling of a strike situation two years earlier, which cost him the support of the glass-workers. Of the 581 Deputies in the Chamber, 205 were new. Among them was Lafferre, Grand Master of the militant anti-clerical Freemasons, the Grand Orient of the Rue Cadet, whom Méline had transferred as dangerous from his teaching post at Narbonne to Privas. There were Drumont, Morinaud, instigator of the Algerian riots, and two other proclaimed anti-semites, who had been elected for four of the six Algerian seats. They advertised their arrival at the Palais Bourbon by shouting "Down with the Jews" and moving ostentatiously to the Extreme Right of the semi-circle, where they were joined by the group of Nationalists who had hitherto sat with the Socialists at the Extreme Left.

In spite of this superficial appearance of identity with the previous Chamber, the position of the Government was uncertain. The changes had indicated a slight movement towards the extremes: there were fewer Radicals and more Socialist Radicals. Much depended on intangibles, and although no one wanted to revive the Affair, it lay like a small cloud on the horizon of the Chamber. The Government Republicans, who had now adopted the title of

Progressists, felt that it was the moment when they should assert their predominance. Their demonstration at the opening on June 1 took the form of proposing against Brisson, for the presidency of the Chamber, Paul Deschanel, a youngish Progressist Deputy from Eure-et-Loir, a Republican of unimpeachable republicanism, whose ambitions had led him to steer a dexterous course between conservatism and radicalism, and between the Dreyfusists and their enemies. Deschanel defeated Brisson by a single vote, and his victory was confirmed by two subsequent ballots, each with an increased majority. Brisson, President for the last four years, the scourge of the clericals, was now up in arms, ready to seize the first chance to overthrow Méline. On June 14 the usual motion requiring an outline of Government policy was put down. The Opposition attacked the Prime Minister for relying on the Right for his majorities. Méline replied that he had never sought or bargained for Right support, and on a motion of confidence carried the House by a majority of twenty-three. Here was Brisson's opportunity. He put up two Radicals to add a rider that the Government should rely on a purely Republican majority, a motion which Delcassé had proposed in May 1897 and lost. Méline resisted the amendment, but a number of his followers, who no doubt had posed to their constituents as unyielding Republicans, dared not vote against the motion. Twenty-six, having voted their confidence in Méline, now voted against him, while a further twenty took refuge in abstention. The Government was beaten by forty-nine, and Méline went with his resignation to Félix Faure.

Méline had been a far from unsuccessful Prime Minister. He had been in office for more than two years; in the last twenty-three years only two other Cabinets had lasted as long. Some useful work had been done: some reforming Acts added to the Statute Book. But for the Case his reputation would be higher than it is. Yet it is difficult to see how, by any other policy than that of entrenching himself in the *res judicata*, he could have survived the last six months. Had he let the Radicals in on the eve of the elections, he would have lost the confidence of his party and earned the anathema of all conservative Frenchmen.

His successor was not easy to discover. Félix Faure, who had recently spoken publicly about the success of "my" policy, naturally wanted a conservative Republican, but the contradictions of the votes of June 13 and 14 demonstrated, if anything, a swing to the Left. He called on Ribot. Ribot, privately more than persuaded that Dreyfus was innocent, declined the dangerous office. Faure then invited Sarrien, a lobby-politician, Radical in no more than name, to form a Centre Cabinet of Right-wing Radicals and Left-wing Republicans. Sarrien could get no support. Peytral, the next choice, a Radical but a Senator, which implies that the strong waters of doctrine were considerably diluted in him, almost succeeded, but his combination broke down. The Radicals invariably demanded the key Ministry, the Interior, and, on the nomination of a Radical to the post, Charles Dupuy's group deserted Peytral.

In the end, much against his will, Faure had to send for the author of the crisis, Brisson, whom he should have summoned in the first place. Brisson quickly got together a Cabinet in which, except for Delcassé at the Foreign Office, the main portfolios were in the hands of Radicals, Brisson himself taking the Ministry of the Interior. He came before the Chamber on June 30, and after a studiously careful declaration, from which all Radical policies except the supremacy of the lay State were omitted, he received a vote of confidence by a majority of a hundred and ten.

The transfer of current business from the old to the incoming Cabinet appears to have been as superficial as was usual in these circumstances. Méline said nothing to Brisson about the Affair. Hanotaux, infuriated at having to make way for Delcassé, whom he considered in every way his inferior, passed on none of the representations and warnings of the German and Italian Ambassadors.

Superficially it appeared odd that the Chamber which had rejected Brisson for its President a month earlier should now give him a handsome vote of confidence. The reason was that Cavaignac had accepted the Ministry of War. Godefroy Cavaignac, son of the general who had put down with much bloodshed the revolt of the unemployed workers in June 1848, had been brought up from childhood to regard himself as the future Cromwell of the Republic, the reincarnation of the purest pures of 1793. He prided himself on his honesty and inflexibility, along with other appropriate virtues, including impenetrable solemnity. He had the long, lean head of a greyhound, a touch of whisker, and sad, staring eyes: an impish journalist had nicknamed him "Corporal Werther." He had been one of the four junior Deputies who in 1892 had forced the Panama enquiry and had won much praise for his virtuous speech, as well as the detestation of Clemenceau. In January 1898 he had spoken in the debate on Zola, when he had told the Chamber that there existed "contemporary evidence" of Dreyfus's admissions. Since Dupuy, who should have known of these admissions, sat silent, Cavaignac believed that what he had said was true. Known as the adversary of revision, he was now acceptable to both the Right and the Radicals, the former believing that he would run the Brisson Cabinet. "Brisson," wrote Drumont, "is a dummy on which Cavaignac will sit."

Indeed Brisson seemed bulliable. In addition to the normal transfer of Préfets on demands from his Radical followers, he was weak enough to yield to Drumont and his anti-semites, and withdrew Lépine from the governorship of Algeria.

From his assumption of office Cavaignac decided that he himself would have done with the shilly-shally methods of Billot and Méline. He would clear up the Affair by a personal examination of the Dreyfus dossier. Credulous and obstinate, and having already convinced himself of Dreyfus's guilt, he took the papers at their face value. He ignored the fact that Lebrun-Renaud had not reported the alleged confession after the degradation of 1895, and accepted as a genuine report the note that the Republican Guardsman had written at Gonse's dictation in November 1897. He was not, however, convinced that the *bordereau* was in the handwriting of Dreyfus; it resembled Esterhazy's; but, since Esterhazy was not a gunner, the information must have come from Dreyfus. Therefore he assumed that the two had collaborated.

This theory absolved him from having to support Esterhazy as the alternative to Dreyfus; he had no love for Esterhazy, whom

he looked on, quite rightly, as a bad soldier. As for the other documents, he accepted the application of the *canaille de D* letter to
Dreyfus, and swallowed the *faux Henry* without a second thought.
Last of all he seized on another of Henry's manipulations, the letter
of 1896 in which Henry had changed the letter "P" to "D," "who
has brought me a number of interesting things," re-dated by Henry
"March 1894." He had informed the Cabinet of his intentions.
Brisson was dubious: like Méline, he believed that the *res judicata*
would suffice; to fall back on a document subsequent to date was
to undermine the principle, to question "the majesty of judgment." Cavaignac was obstinate. He invited Brisson and Sarrien
to the War Office, and laid before them some sixty or so pieces from
the Dreyfus file. They let him have his way.

Armed with his three documents, he came before the Chamber
on July 7, to answer yet another interpellation by Castelin. "I
am completely certain of Dreyfus's guilt," he announced, to the
applause of the Radicals and Socialists. Without uttering Esterhazy's name, he went on to say that this officer had been acquitted
in error; he was, in fact, the writer of the *bordereau*; he would be
dealt with. But this in no way exonerated Dreyfus, who had been
justly condemned. He then read to the silent Deputies the three
documents he had selected from the file, suppressing only the
phrases which would identify the foreign military attaché. It is
said that Méline turned paler than his wont; from the wording of
the *faux Henry* he recognised the piece which Tornielli had assured
Hanotaux was a forgery of Panizzardi's handwriting. Then Cavaignac went on to give a version of Dreyfus's confession. Once again
Dupuy made no comment. At the end the Chamber rose spon-
taneously and cheered the War Minister to the echo, Radicals
vying with Nationalists in patriotism. Brisson declared that Cavaignac had spoken in the name of the Government, and invited the
Chamber to vote on the *affichage* of his speech.[1] On the demand for
a vote on the proposal, the motion was carried by 545 to 0: three

[1] *Affichage* means the printing of a member's speech and its distribution to
each of the thirty-five-thousand-odd communes in France, to be pasted up outside each Mairie.

Radicals abstained. So did Méline: to vote for the motion would have been the denial of his past judicious policy. So too did fifteen of the fifty-odd Socialists. No one had remarked that the most striking document, the *faux Henry*, had been known ever since Pellieux gave it at Zola's trial, and that even then many had qualified it as suspect. But the Deputies wanted to be convinced, to be quit of this menacing case, and they accepted Cavaignac's insistent statement with the enthusiasm born of relief. That evening Cavaignac signed the order for an official enquiry into the conduct of Esterhazy.

Two days later Picquart, after consultation with Reinach, Labori, Demange and Trarieux, sent to Brisson an open letter, communicated to the press, in which he wrote that he felt it his duty to say that two of the letters quoted by Cavaignac did not refer to Dreyfus, and that the third displayed all the marks of a forgery. This thesis he was prepared to defend before any competent tribunal. The undoubted good faith of the War Minister had, he said, been taken advantage of.

Before Billot left the War Office he had set Gonse to put together in one file all the documents relevant to the Affair. Gonse had naturally called in Henry, who supplied him with everything, including all the papers he had forged or tampered with. One document was missing: the deciphering of Panizzardi's telegram to Rome of 2 November 1894. Gonse told Henry to obtain a copy from the Foreign Office. Henry casually dropped in on Paléologue and asked him for a copy. Paléologue said shortly that he could supply it only after application through the usual channels, but he dictated to Henry a version from memory. Henry, putting the dictation in his pocket, returned to Gonse and told him that the Foreign Office would not supply the copy. After Billot had also failed to get it from Hanotaux, Gonse, instead of making a formal approach, sent for Du Paty and asked him to recollect it. Du Paty, foolishly, allowed himself once more to become the tool of Gonse and Henry, and produced some vague recollection of the first erroneous deciphering which the Foreign Office had later discarded. He refused, however, to admit the phrase about the messenger being warned. On this, Gonse concocted a version which ran: "Captain Dreyfus arrested. War Office has proof of his relations with Germany. All precautions taken." He showed it to Billot and Boisdeffre, and then added it to the file, with a note that it had been reconstituted by Du Paty from memory: no mention was made of the final Foreign Office text.

All these documents, amounting now to nearly four hundred, had been handed over to Cavaignac, together with a numbered list of the contents, when he took office. He had taken as the chief of his military secretariat a temporarily unemployed Brigadier-General, attached to the War Office, Gaudérique Roget, a meridional with all the temperamental garrulousness of the Provençal, who had reported unfavourably on Dreyfus in 1893. He also included among his aides Captain Louis Cuignet, a member of the Fourth Bureau, who had been employed by Gonse to copy the *catalogue raisonné* of the documents. These two officers had both come to the War Office within a few weeks of Henry's arrival; they knew him well and liked him. To Roget, who, like others, could not resist the fascination of the case, and had already received many confidences from Henry, Cavaignac gave the duty of reconstructing the whole case from its beginning. Roget, looking at the *petit bleu* in the course of his examination, discovered a hitherto unnoticed fact: in the superscription Esterhazy's name had been tampered with. (It will be recalled that Picquart, when shown the *petit bleu* by Pellieux, had observed a peculiarity in the writing of the name.) Roget thought that something else had been there before, and that Esterhazy's name had been written over it. He had no reason to know that Henry had been at work. He showed his discovery to Gonse, who saw no significance in the fact. Roget, however, jumped to the conclusion that Picquart had deliberately written in Esterhazy's name over another.

5

Two days after the appearance of Picquart's letter, on July 11, Bertulus at last secured the appearance of Christian Esterhazy before him. The young man was reluctant to give evidence: all he would say was that he had heard that Marguérite Pays was responsible for the two false telegrams. Bertulus at length persuaded him to produce the file of letters which had been handed to Labori. From these Bertulus found that he had sufficient to warrant the arrest of Esterhazy.

For the moment he was held back. Cavaignac, furious at Picquart's open letter of July 9, determined to have done with this tiresome gadfly. He ordered the prosecution of both Picquart and Leblois on the almost forgotten charge of showing and examining confidential military documents, and with the agreement of the Cabinet ordered Picquart's arrest. He permitted Bertulus to proceed to a search of Esterhazy's dwelling, hoping that the documents with which the rogue had threatened the Ministers and the Staff would be found; but he would allow no matters to be dealt with other than the false telegrams. Finally he ordered Captain Cuignet to make a thorough examination, in the light of Picquart's public statement, of the documents handed over by Billot.

Bertulus guessed that, if he were not to be stopped, he must act at once. That evening, July 12, he went to 45 Rue de Douai and under the eyes of Marguérite Pays proceeded to a seizure of Esterhazy's papers. There were many, and before he and his men had finished, Esterhazy arrived. Bertulus at once told him he was arrested and ordered him to be searched. Esterhazy tried to bluff it out, but did not intimidate the magistrate. The search went on until towards midnight, when Esterhazy was committed to the Santé and Marguérite Pays to Saint-Lazare.

Picquart only heard by chance of the order to prosecute him during the afternoon, and nothing of that to arrest him until he was told by Trarieux, on whom he happened to call. Trarieux kept him for the night. In the meanwhile the law officers called at his lodgings and searched them—in his absence an illegal action. On the afternoon of July 13 he went to the Palais de Justice and surrendered to the police. He too was conducted to the Santé.

The mass of papers which Bertulus seized and put under seal threw little light on the telegrams or the heart of the Dreyfus case, but they demonstrated that some members of the Staff had collaborated in Esterhazy's defence; there were notes from Pellieux, Du Paty, and Boisdeffre's orderly officer, Pauffin de Saint-Morel, while one obscure note in which occurred the words "Bâle" and "Cuers" postulated that Esterhazy had received information from a source in the Statistical Section. But many notes were unsigned, and there was nothing to connect Esterhazy or Pays firmly with the *Blanche* and *Speranza* telegrams.[1]

The arrest of Esterhazy, as well as that of Picquart, gave many members of 4 Rue Saint-Dominique food for thought. Boisdeffre conveniently went sick. Gonse was to follow his example at the end of the month. Neither had as much cause as Henry. He had seen the folly of Pellieux's evidence in February, but he had hoped that the blunder had been forgotten. Now it had been disinterred by this infernal ass Cavaignac. "The Minister would have done better not to read those letters," he murmured in Gonse's hearing. He had Gonse and Roget well in hand, but Cuignet was working through the Dreyfus file. And now, worst of all, Esterhazy was in jail, subject to the keen intelligence of Bertulus; and Esterhazy was capable of betraying anyone, either to save his skin or from sheer malicious humour. Henry made one attempt to cover himself when, at the beginning of May, as part of his scheme to discredit Du Paty, he had disclosed to Roget the meeting with Esterhazy at the Montsouris Park, underlining the fact that he himself had not then spoken to Esterhazy, and that he had met him in the flesh only at the time of his duel with Picquart.

Cavaignac also was in an ill humour. Bertulus, by his rapid action, had snatched away his prey. He sent a sharp note to the Minister of Justice, Sarrien, who passed it on to the examining magistrate. Bertulus calmly replied: "I have arrested a criminal

---

[1] Reinach (47, IV, 71) says bluntly that there were notes from Henry, implying a good deal more. In fact, the *procès-verbal* of Esterhazy's examination (6, II, 234–37) lists no more than two unimportant letters from "a colonel," who may be taken to be Henry, but whom Esterhazy refused to identify. The content is not transcribed, merely referred to—e.g. "Seal No. 4, No. 19." Henry had been very careful. There were, however, cardboard stencils (*grilles*) for composing cypher letters.

without other domicile than the bed of a prostitute." The military
Court of Enquiry on Esterhazy was adjourned *sine die*.

Cavaignac sent for Du Paty, who was a distant relative, and
asked him about his connection with Esterhazy. Du Paty confessed
to the Montsouris Park and other meetings, claiming that his
superiors knew about them; but he denied all knowledge of the false
telegrams and of the "liberating document," save that he knew
that another officer had also had dealings with Esterhazy. This
officer he refused to name, but it seems that he had Boisdeffre's
orderly officer, Pauffin, in mind. Gribelin, also questioned by
Cavaignac, simply referred him to Du Paty. Gonse said that he
had only just heard of the Esterhazy interview from Henry, whom
he had told off; as for Du Paty, he must have been out of his
mind: neither Boisdeffre nor himself had ever suggested so fantastic
a scheme. Cavaignac would have sent Du Paty, too, before a
Court of Enquiry, but he knew that if he did so, Bertulus would at
once join Du Paty with Esterhazy and Marguérite Pays in the
charges of forgery. The one action he might have taken he did not.
He did not ask Sarrien to remove Bertulus and substitute a more
pliable examining magistrate. It may be that it went against his
principles; it may be that he recalled similar substitutions which had
led to the resignation of Ministers.

On July 15 Bertulus had Pays brought to the Santé to be present
at the opening of the sealed packets of papers in Esterhazy's presence. She impudently asked him why at their previous meeting
he had not questioned her; she would have told him that she was
the writer of the *Speranza* telegram. Later she retracted the statement. Next day, in the presence of Esterhazy, Pays and their
lawyer Tézenas, the papers were examined.[1] Esterhazy admitted
that one draft was that of a letter he had written to Boisdeffre, but
he refused to sign the summary of evidence unless the General's name
was omitted. It was a threat to the War Office, should they not

[1] Esterhazy was lucky. Had the examination taken place eight months
earlier, he would have had no legal adviser. The law of 8 December 1897 made
the presence of the prisoner's counsel obligatory at the preliminary examination.
The law had taken nearly four years to reach the Statute Book. Further, he
would have had no lawyer if his case had been before a military court.

protect him, and he knew that Tézenas would report it. Further, he gave no names, but merely indicated the writers or addressees by their rank.

Cavaignac had bethought himself that the Esterhazy papers might contain matters of interest to the War Office. He allowed Henry, designated by Gonse and Roget, to call on Bertulus as the War Office representative. On July 18 Henry went to Bertulus's chambers. The magistrate, who had begun to see that some, as yet mysterious, link existed between Esterhazy and his visitor, could only show him the papers already examined; among others, the rough note with the words "Bâle" and "Cuers." Henry was taken aback. Bertulus saw his change of face, and in a flash of intuition said: "You'll never make me believe that Esterhazy could know the story of Cuers and the Bâle interview from his own sources. Who but you, or someone close to you, can have told him?" He went on to deal with the charges against Esterhazy and Du Paty, spoke of the forged telegrams, on which Henry stammered out that they had been despatched by those two officers. Pressed, he begged Bertulus before going any further to help him save the honour of the Army, to do nothing before talking to General Roget. Bertulus replied that he would gladly talk with Roget, but insisted that the officers who were compromised must be sacrificed.

On Henry rising to leave, Bertulus pushed his advantage: "Let Du Paty blow his brains out, and let justice follow its course against Esterhazy. He has once been acquitted irrevocably as a traitor, but he is a forger! And that's not all. There is still you. I have read one letter in which Esterhazy draws a terrible portrait of you. If that letter falls into the hands of your enemies, it will be seen that everything you have said is a lie, that for long you have had contacts with Esterhazy. Some minds could easily go so far as to hold that the man who documented Esterhazy was none other, Henry, than you!"

Henry was overwhelmed: bursting into tears, he flung his arms round the magistrate, crying, "Save us! save us!" The astonished Bertulus pushed him back into his chair. After a silence, Henry groaned: "Esterhazy is a bandit." Quickly Bertulus retorted: "Is he the author of the *bordereau*?" Henry only replied: "Don't ask any more (*N'insistez pas*). Before all, the honour of the Army."

Bertulus had only half-penetrated Henry's secret. Believing that he had him in his power, he let the soldier go: it was a bad error. Henry quickly recovered from the shock, and made a mendacious report to Gonse and Roget. When, now quite jaunty, he reappeared at the examination of Esterhazy and Pays on July 26 he brought Junck with him from the Section. As the seals were broken, they coolly examined the documents and took away no more than two as of security interest. Again reporting to Gonse, who by now had taken refuge in a nursing-home, they said that Esterhazy had made a good impression, and that Bertulus had said that though he was a rogue, he was not a traitor—words that Bertulus later denied. Esterhazy went through his examination with skilful bravado. To Bertulus, who remarked that he could not think what Henry was looking for, he said impudently that it was the Imperial Guard, but he did not explain what he meant. Both he and Pays denied all knowledge of the telegrams. Christian, who was present, he insulted.

As a result, Bertulus felt that he needed further weight to the indictment. He advised Picquart to prefer a charge against Du Paty of complicity with Esterhazy and Pays in forgery, while at the same time he at length persuaded Christian to bring an action for malversation of funds against Esterhazy. Esterhazy breathed again: the linking of Du Paty with himself made him believe that he could rely on War Office support.

Meanwhile the anti-Dreyfusard journals, fully alive to Bertulus's hunt, were fulminating against him and demanding his withdrawal from the case. Cavaignac tried to have the case against Du Paty brought before a military and not a civil court. The Public Prosecutor, following him, applied to the courts to dismiss Bertulus from the case, on the ground that he had no *locus standi*. The judges could find no good reason for this, but since, if they desired, they could examine the evidence themselves, they adopted this

procedure against Esterhazy and Pays. They reached the conclusion that the evidence was too flimsy, and on August 12 found
for the accused. Whether pressure had been applied by Cavaignac
is unknown, though it seems probable: Tézenas, on the day before
the judgment, had told Esterhazy that he would be free, and
advised him to get out of the country at once, since he still had to
face the War Office enquiry as well as Christian's suit. But Esterhazy, strong in the feeling that he had Henry in his grip, refused. The Dreyfusists had once more met defeat: they had not
yet found their way to the centre of the maze.

While Esterhazy was being examined, Picquart and Leblois had
been undergoing (July 13–August 20) a similar experience in the
matter of communicating and receiving security matter. Their
examining magistrate, Fabre, was honest but a stickler. He
picked on the fact that, at the time Picquart had put his interests
and his defence in the hands of Leblois, he was accused of nothing,
and was an officer on duty. Moreover, Fabre heard all the War
Office witnesses and was shown all Picquart's correspondence
which had been stopped and copied. At one meeting, Henry, confronted with Picquart, made an effort to come to terms. "What a
pity," he said, "that we haven't been able to reach an arrangement." Fabre cut him short. Later, Picquart, who still believed
that Du Paty was the sole villain of the piece, said to Henry: "You
have been a tool; perhaps you don't think so?"

Fabre, no more than any other outsider in the case, understood
the significance of the prosecution; he was shown none of the
documents or files which, according to the witnesses, were so
dangerous that war with Germany would follow their publication.
After consultation with his chief, Fabre found against both men on
the connected charge. In consequence Picquart would automatic-
ally accompany Leblois before a civil tribunal: if, as Cavaignac had
hoped, the charges had been separated, Picquart could have been
sent before a court-martial, which would have faithfully dealt with
him. Refusing temporary release, Picquart returned to the Santé.

Cavaignac had long reached the pitch of exasperation. He had
been publicly given the lie: the Dreyfusards were more and more

active, and it was not in his nature to think that he could be mistaken. He believed that the Army, for which he was responsible, was being gradually undermined by the remorseless sapping of the Syndicate. On August 11 he appeared at a dinner given by Brisson to the Cabinet, with a note he had prepared. It was his intention to bring the whole revisionist group before the High Court of the Senate under the Constitutional Law of 2 August 1875, on the charge of attempts against the security of the State. The accused would be not only Picquart and Leblois, but also Scheurer-Kestner, Trarieux, Mathieu Dreyfus, Bernard Lazare, Christian Esterhazy, Zola, and all the Dreyfusard journalists—Clemenceau, Ranc, Reinach, Guyot and the rest. On a joking enquiry from Vallé as to why he had not included the lawyers, he added: "Of course, and Labori and Demange." The Cabinet was staggered. Brisson exclaimed: "It's mad, preposterous," and said he would refuse to look at such a proposal even if it were brought to him officially.

Two days later Captain Cuignet, who for a month had been going through the Dreyfus file piece by piece, reached Henry's masterpiece. It was evening and he had a lamp. When he came to look closely at the document, he was surprised to perceive that while at the head and tail of the letter the feint lines were blue-grey, those in the body were grey-claret. He took up the letter prepared by Henry for comparison, the letter assuring Schwartz-koppen there would be only one Jew at a dinner-party, dated in Henry's hand 14 June 1894. He saw that here the feint lines at the head and tail were wine-tinted, while those in the body were blue-grey. Cuignet was a friend of Henry; but at the same time he was a disciplined soldier. Next morning he reported his discovery to Roget. Roget, who himself had had some doubts about the letter, led Cuignet to Cavaignac, and Cavaignac suffered the exquisite horror of seeing that the document which was placarded outside every one of the thirty-five thousand Mairies, and which he had guaranteed, was false.

6

Henry was on leave. Cavaignac wanted the truth: as he said later, an official examination carried out by a judicial officer would have led to a superficial enquiry, where the accused would have been so protected by procedure that the truth would not have emerged. He decided to wait for the time being until he could carry out the examination himself. He confided in nobody, not even in Brisson, not even in Boisdeffre. He had a number of political engagements in the provinces, but before he left Paris he ordered Esterhazy to appear before a military court on August 24.

Before the court Esterhazy took a strong line. He admitted all the faults of his private life. He stood on the ground that he had obeyed the orders of the Cabinet and the General Staff. The Jews had offered him six hundred thousand francs to betray his Army chiefs, but he would not. He called Du Paty. Du Paty owned to helping him in the confection of the letters to the President and to correcting the article by "Dixi." On many points he was hesitant, and moreover he refused to uncover Gonse, Henry and even Gribelin. Esterhazy had no such scruples; in his defence he named Henry as one of the party at Montsouris Park. He went on to a farrago of truth and lies: everything he had done, every line he had written, had been at the direction of the War Office. After confusing the judges, he succeeded in holding up the case until he could produce a letter of Du Paty's with the damning line: "General Boisdeffre is not uninformed that I have had indirect relations with Major Esterhazy." The bewildered and browbeaten court at last delivered its verdict. By three to two they found that Esterhazy should be dismissed for habitual private misconduct. On the charges of failure in respect of honour and discipline, they acquitted him by four to one.

Cavaignac, who received the findings through Zurlinden, Military Governor of Paris, had no intention of sparing the culprit, in spite of the fact that he was condemned on no more than one charge and that by a majority of one—the so-called "majority of favour"—which normally led to the defendant's receiving the benefit of the doubt. He ordered Esterhazy's dismissal from the service.

During the court of enquiry Esterhazy must have come to the conclusion that his life-lines were becoming frayed and precarious. He began to prepare his retreat. One evening he went to the Paris correspondent of the London *Observer*, Rowland Strong, and in the course of the conversation told him that he had written the *bordereau* at the request of Sandherr for the purpose of providing evidence against the traitor Dreyfus, against whom Sandherr could find nothing but "moral proofs."

Meanwhile Cuignet had made a further test of the two forged letters and had verified his previous opinion. Finding that Henry was to pass through Paris on August 30, Cavaignac ordered him to report to the War Office on that day, and telegraphed for Boisdeffre, who was still on sick leave. When the latter was shown the documents, he felt that they were susceptible of a reasonable explanation; but neither he nor Gonse thought of warning Henry.

On August 30, at 2.30 p.m., Gonse brought Henry to Cavaignac's room. Boisdeffre was present, and Roget, who took a note of the examination (8, I, 420–29). Cavaignac alone interrogated. Told that the two exhibits showed signs of being mixed and altered, Henry said that he had received them on the dates he had inscribed, June 1894 and September 1896. Cavaignac offered him a chance by suggesting that he had in fact reconstituted both letters at the same moment in 1896. Henry missed the hint, and affirmed that he never kept any paper longer than ten days without reconstructing it: he had, he said, mislaid the 1894 exhibit and found it again some days after he had given that of 1896 to Gonse. Having thus lost the chance of clearing himself of no worse than an error he might easily have made if he had in fact been dealing with the torn fragments of both letters at the same moment, he could only stammer when Cavaignac, implacably, pressed him on the question of facts: "What do you want me to say?"

"What you have done."

"I did not manufacture the papers."

"You put the fragments of one onto the other?"

Henry then went so far as to say that he had cut bits out of one to insert in the other: nothing more.

"What you say is belied by the material facts."

Failing to understand the tenor of Cavaignac's questions, Henry embroiled himself more and more deeply. At last Cavaignac gave him the clue: "The squares on the fragments of paper are of different shades."

Lost, Henry could only offer denials, first of tampering, then of fabricating. "I acted for the good of the country."

"That is not the question I asked you . . . you had better tell everything."

"I received the heading and a few words."

"What words?"

"Words which had nothing to do with the case."

"So this is what happened. You received in 1896 an envelope with a letter of no significance in it; you destroyed the letter and you fabricated the other."

"Yes."

The interrogation had taken nearly an hour. Cavaignac told Roget to keep Henry under his eye in the next room. Boisdeffre sat down and wrote out his resignation as Chief of Staff. "I have just received proof that my trust in Colonel Henry, head of the Intelligence Service, has not been justified. This trust, which was absolute, has led to my deception, and to my declaring to be genuine a piece which was not so, and to my handing it to you as such. In the circumstances, I have the honour to ask to be relieved of my duties." Cavaignac in vain tried to dissuade him. Boisdeffre rejoined that no one but he had had the misfortune to swear to a jury that a forgery was genuine and to claim that he was ready to resign if he were not believed. He insisted. His brilliant career, of which the peak was the Franco-Russian alliance, was ended. He retired to his family house in Maine. Except for his appearances, tired and disillusioned, at the subsequent trials, he was seen no more. He survived until 1919.[1]

[1] Boisdeffre's place was temporarily filled by Sub-chief General Renouard. No permanent appointment was made until Freycinet became Minister of War

The imperious Cavaignac had already broken every rule of procedure. He should now have rung up the Military Governor and ordered Henry's removal to the Cherche-Midi prison. He could himself have ordered his arrest. Instead, he agreed with Zurlinden to put the man merely under fortress arrest at Mont-Valérien, with no charge offered. An officer was summoned and Henry despatched under escort by cab, first to his home, where he packed a bag and made a hurried explanation to his wife, then to Mont-Valérien.

While they had waited for Cavaignac's orders, Roget had asked Henry a few questions. Henry repeated firmly that he had had no accomplice. Asked whether Esterhazy had ever had relations with Sandherr, he replied that he had only once seen him at the Section, when he had come to Sandherr with some documents he had picked up by chance, a fact which he had never revealed to Picquart.

Cavaignac at length informed Brisson, who was overwhelmed. That evening those of the Cabinet who were in Paris dined with Delcassé. Cavaignac told his story. Then, after a silence, Vallé broke out: "Come, this means revision." "Less than ever," came back swiftly from Cavaignac.

Cavaignac, it will be recalled, was the Deputy who had brought up the alleged confession of Dreyfus in the Chamber in January. His statement had never been denied by Dupuy or Boisdeffre, or, of course, by Mercier. Thus he remained convinced of the existence of the confession, exactly as he had already convinced himself of the complicity of Dreyfus with Esterhazy. Even now he was unable to explain Henry's work to his own satisfaction. With no insight into the motives of common men, he began to think that Henry had forged the Panizzardi letter to conceal something that could not be shown, perhaps the famous letter from the Kaiser. No doubt, had he had the opportunity, he would have renewed his examination of Henry. He was not to have it.

---

in October, when General Brault, a soldier of high reputation, was appointed. Gonse was replaced by General Delanne. Henry's place at the Statistical Section was taken by Major, later Lt-Col. Rollin, who had been in the Section some years earlier. Lauth, his tour of staff duty terminated, went back to the Dragoons in November.

On the following day, August 31, Henry in his cell asked for some notepaper. He then wrote and had despatched to Gonse a letter: "I have the honour to request you to be good enough to come to see me here. It is essential that I talk to you." Then during the afternoon he wrote a letter to his wife. "I see that, except you, everyone is going to desert me, and yet you know the interest for which I acted. My letter is a copy and there is absolutely no touch of forgery. It only confirms information given me a few days before. I am absolutely innocent; it is known, and everyone will know it later, but at the moment I cannot speak." Later he scrawled: "My beloved Berthe, I feel quite mad, a terrible pain is pressing my skull, I am going to take a bathe in the Seine. . . ." It was three o'clock on a burning afternoon. He took off his jacket, lay down on his bed, and with his razor cut his throat. The orderly bringing his supper at six o'clock found his dead body, drained of its blood.[1]

That day the Cabinet had met four times (17, 64–65). A note had been issued through Havas on the previous evening, stating that Henry had admitted forging the letter of 1896 and that he was confined to Mont-Valérien. Now the Ministers argued over Bois-deffre's resignation. Brisson, scandalised at what had occurred, demanded a complete change of the senior War Office staff. Cavaignac refused. They decided to wait for the return of Léon Bourgeois, who was in Switzerland. Revision was not discussed. At one meeting Félix Faure signed the order dismissing Esterhazy from the service. On leaving the last of these meetings, Brisson went to glance over the latest telegrams. He found one from the commandant of Mont-Valérien reporting Henry's suicide. He tele-phoned to Zurlinden, who confirmed the report. On returning to his room, he found Cavaignac, who had come back to agree to the resignation of Boisdeffre. Cavaignac had not yet heard of the

---

[1] Later a rumour was picked up and printed that a senior officer had visited Henry and taken away a number of papers. Another story involved his friend Junck, whom the Dreyfusard papers (e.g. Le Siècle) did not flinch from saying had murdered him. Junck had in fact been with Mme Henry at the time. As a result of the rumour, Jules Cambon, Ambassador in Washington, advised that Junck's appointment as military attaché there should be cancelled.

suicide, but the news made no impact on his mind. Ignoring the information, he spent an hour with Brisson arguing the terms in which Boisdeffre should resign.

On September 2 Henry's body was taken to his native village of Pogny. The burial took place two days later. Monsignor Latty, Bishop of Châlons, forbade a religious service, and instead the Maire made a patriotic and moving speech.

On September 1 the world had the news. All those papers which had hitherto maintained neutrality came out for revision, and even the Nationalist and other hostile journals accepted it as inevitable, except those of Drumont and Rochefort. One of the judges of 1894, Gallet, announced publicly that his eyes were opened.

Pellieux, when he read the Havas message, was seized with fury, and poured out his wrath in a letter of resignation from the Army. "Sir, The dupe of men without honour, with no hope of keeping the confidence of my subordinates, without which command is impossible, while on my own side I have lost faith in those of my superiors who set me to work on forgeries, I have the honour to request you to allow me to retire on the ground of length of service." Zurlinden, upset by the tone and terms of the letter, sent for him, tried to calm the agitated man, and told him he would keep the letter for two or three days to allow him to think it over. Eventually Pellieux withdrew the letter, but not before giving a version of it to a Monarchist newspaper. Many Army officers now saw the light and desired a reopening of the case. Galliffet related that, having entered a railway carriage with some junior officers, he had said: "We won't talk about the Case," on which an officer replied: "No, General, we are not as anti-revisionist as you think. We want the truth and the punishment of the wrongdoers."

It is said that when Mercier heard the news, he uttered one word: "*Foutu!*" and tore up the telegram.

For one person Henry's suicide was the end: Esterhazy. Hearing the news on the evening of August 31, he walked out to Saint-Dénis early next morning, took a train to Maubeuge, where he shaved off his huge moustache and slipped over the

Belgian frontier on foot. He went on to Brussels and thence to London.

Yet in spite of the quasi-unanimity of the press, nothing happened. Brisson seems to have been paralysed with indecision and inertia. Did he shrink, as he had already done, from challenging his formidable War Minister? It is said that, being a practising Freemason, perhaps the only one of the old Gambettists who had not resigned from that peculiar institution, he hated to move before consulting the brethren at 16 Rue Cadet, who in turn needed to consult the provincial lodges. In any case no move was made. Sarrien, Minister of Justice, was favourable to revision, but wanted the request to come from Cavaignac. Cavaignac, obstinately clinging to his opinion that the discovery of the forgery made no difference to Dreyfus's guilt, resolutely refused to make any application. Since both Ministers were immovable, Brisson sent a message to Mathieu Dreyfus, telling him to present through Lucie Dreyfus a petition for the reopening of her husband's case. Further, he sent Léon Bourgeois, who had now come home, to soften Cavaignac's resistance. Bourgeois, most persuasive of men and an old friend of Cavaignac, failed. Cavaignac argued dourly, and ended by saying he would resign. He then called on Brisson, who himself offered to resign in favour of Cavaignac if he would consent to revision. Cavaignac rejected the offer, and a few hours later sent in his letter of resignation, which he also communicated to the press. It ended, "I remain convinced of Dreyfus's guilt." The anti-revisionists, reading it, raised their heads.

An as yet little-known journalist, Charles Maurras, set forth in the Royalist *Gazette de France* the thesis that Henry's forgery was in fact an act of intellectual and moral nobility. He was the heroic servitor of the great interests of the State. Maurras promised that Henry should be avenged. "Your unlucky forgery will be acclaimed as one of your finest deeds of war." This initiative, though it did little for Henry, sent Maurras along the path he was to follow with success for more than forty years.

CHAPTER ELEVEN

Lucie Dreyfus's Appeal

1

WITH the death of Henry, the period of what might be called the "detective novel" side of the Affair ends, although the discussion and interpretation of the documents continue in an atmosphere of misunderstanding and mendacity. From September 1898 the leading figures are the politicians and the judges. Sometimes it is the judges in contention with the politicians, sometimes part of the judiciary in alliance with the Dreyfusards against their fellow judges supporting the anti-revisionists. The ten months following the death of Henry are months of confusion.

During the nineties the eminent critic Emile Faguet published two small books, entitled respectively *La Culte de l'Incompétence* and . . . *Et l'Horreur des Responsabilités*. Faguet pointed out that under a centralised administration, with each Ministry the jealous guardian of its own prerogatives, the tendency was for officials to avoid acting, on the ground that the action did not lie within the sphere of their competence; behind this they were able to shelter from responsibility. It was from this shirking of responsibility rather than from ill-will that the successive delays in dealing with the cases of Dreyfus and Picquart proceeded. Through month after month, lest they compromise themselves, Ministers shrank from using their powers and threw the onus of decision on to the members of the Courts of Appeal. It was, of course, cowardice, in which the majority in both Chambers followed them. Yet it is arguable that the consequences of political action, in what was essentially judicial business, might have done serious injury to the Army. That a great number of the senior Army officers were deceived is a fact; that of these perhaps the greater number wished to be deceived is probable. The men who misled them were in two groups: in one, those who expected to make their reputations out of the case; in the other, those who put loyalty to their superiors above every other consideration. As Du Paty was to say before the Court of Appeal at the final revision on 22 March 1904, the opposition of the second group to revision arose from the fact that the disclosure of the communication of secret documents to the judges of 1894 would lead to the accusation of Mercier, and his former subordinates were obliged to cover him until such time as he accused himself.

Henry's mortal remains were buried, but his works lived on, and he had heirs. He had owned to nothing beyond the forgery of the two Panizzardi letters. No one had asked what else he had done, and there still lay, with others in the file, two key papers, the *petit bleu* with the name Esterhazy erased and written in again, and the letter quoted by Cavaignac in which the initial "P" had been changed to "D." His heirs, who perhaps hoped to profit from the case, were Captain Cuignet and General Roget; they assumed the role of leading advocate of the Staff thesis and determined enemy of Picquart. Gonse, who by his frivolity and stupidity had contrived the fall of his friend and patron Boisdeffre, and who had not resigned, was put on half-pay in October, and remained unemployed until his retirement in 1903.

2

Brisson, in spite of his recent conviction that the Dreyfus case must be reopened, remained in an agony of indecision. The Cabinet wanted him to take the War Office himself and promote Vallé, the under-secretary, to the Ministry of the Interior. But Brisson considered, probably rightly, that if revision was to take place, it must be supported by the head of the War Office, and that only a soldier could undertake the task without stirring up trouble in the Army. He invited old Saussier, who declined; that wasted four days. In the meantime he had invited Félix Faure to return from his holiday at Le Havre. The President recommended the Military Governor of Paris, Zurlinden, who had shown signs of treating the case on its merits, and who, though he had once for a few months been Minister of War, was not a politician. On Brisson's invitation, Zurlinden accepted, but with the proviso that he should be given time to study the Dreyfus file himself before recommending revision.

Zurlinden, naturally enough, consulted those members of the Staff who were versed in the peculiarities of the file—Roget and Cuignet, whom he took over from Cavaignac's secretariat. Roget, proud of his earlier perspicacity, showed Zurlinden the *petit bleu* with the erased and rewritten name. Like Roget, Zurlinden jumped to the conclusion that it was the work of Picquart in his desire to hunt down Esterhazy. Neither man seems to have thought that Henry might have been responsible. Hence within a fortnight Zurlinden was convinced that the charge of treason against Esterhazy was, in spite of his flight, baseless. Further, he believed, wrongly but with some justice, that if a revising court recondemned Dreyfus, he himself would be made the scapegoat by the civilian Ministers. On September 17 he resigned.

Soon after he reached the War Office, Zurlinden had ordered an enquiry into Du Paty's relations with Esterhazy. It was taken on September 9 and 10 by General Renouard, acting Chief of Staff. Du Paty admitted that he had acted on his own initiative, under Henry's influence. "Henry has a broad back," returned Renouard. He implied that the influence had been reciprocal, a suggestion resented by Du Paty, since "it leads to the idea that I suggested Henry's forgeries." He insisted that his superiors knew what he was up to, because on 18 November 1897 they had forbidden him to make personal contact with Esterhazy.

Gonse in evidence said that he knew nothing about Du Paty's connection with Esterhazy until informed in July 1898. As in all his evidence at the many enquiries and trials at which he appeared, he had no other motive than to protect himself: again and again he lied, without perceiving that each lie contradicted an earlier one.

Renouard reported that Du Paty deserved to be reprimanded severely, but that account should be taken of his past and his devotion to his superiors. Zurlinden thought that Du Paty was a liar. He put him on half-pay and informed Brisson that he intended to order the Governor of Paris to open an enquiry into the "origin and sophistication of the *petit bleu*," against Picquart. Brisson forbade him to do so until the Cabinet had discussed the matter.

On the same day Brisson pitched on a General Chanoine, recommended to him as a revisionist, as Zurlinden's successor. According to an English journalist who saw him at Rennes, Chanoine "looked like a Nonconformist Member of Parliament who had accidentally strayed into a Covent Garden ball." He was told that revision was already decided on by the Cabinet, and he accepted the decision.

Nevertheless, within a few hours of his arrival at the Rue Saint-Dominique, without informing the Prime Minister, he signed the order to lay an information against Picquart which Zurlinden had drafted before he returned to the Military Governorship of Paris. Zurlinden, now back at the Invalides, promptly acted on the order which Brisson had forbidden him to give, and put in motion the prosecution of Picquart. He also refrained from telling Brisson when he called on him. When Brisson heard of it, he was outraged, but once more flinched from accusing the generals of disobedience and bad faith. Nor did he revoke the order.

Chanoine had given the order with such speed because Leblois and Picquart were to appear on September 21 on the charges following the Fabre examination. When the criminal court sat on that day, the prosecution asked for an adjournment, partly on the ground that the "door was now open to revision," partly on the ground that Picquart was now charged with forgery. Labori opposed, pleading that the new charges were part of a plot by the War Office staff. Picquart, having been permitted to speak, looked straight across the court at Gonse and Pellieux, and said: "It is possible that this evening I shall go to the Cherche-Midi. It is probable that this is the last time, before being accused in secret, that I shall be able to speak in public. I wish it to be known that should there be found in my cell either Lemercier-Picard's rope or Henry's razor, it will be murder; for a man such as I am could never for one instant think of suicide."

The court adjourned the case. Picquart returned to the Santé, whence in due course he was transferred to the Cherche-Midi and put in solitary confinement to await court-martial.

The Dreyfusard papers broke out in fury at Brisson's latest capitulation to the War Office. Clemenceau whipped the Cabinet with his tongue, denouncing the whole gang of the *Radicaille* as more jesuitic than the Jesuits. Even Zurlinden, disturbed at the outburst of rage, and anxious to cover his treachery, said publicly that the Cabinet could have adjourned the prosecution of one who would be an important witness in the imminent revision. Brisson, sunk in his habitual inertia, took no steps. Sarrien, however, called together the committee on revision, three Appeal Court judges and three civil servants from the Ministry of Justice, to consider Mme Dreyfus's application. They split evenly, the judges opposing revision, the civil servants favouring it. Sarrien, not the man to take a decision when his chief hung back, told the Cabinet that this amounted to a rejection. For once Brisson refused to listen. He insisted that the committee was purely consultative, and that the initiative in revision was the business of the Cabinet. The argument went on all day and the next. On September 26 the Cabinet members present voted: Brisson, Bourgeois, Delcassé and three others for; Sarrien, Lockroy, Peytral, Viger against; Chanoine abstained.

Brisson had won. Sarrien forwarded Lucie Dreyfus's application for a revision of her husband's case to the Court of Criminal Appeal.

During this week, Rowland Strong published in the *Observer* (September 19) an article giving the gist of his conversations with Esterhazy, in which the officer had asserted his responsibility for the *bordereau* (under Sandherr's orders) and for the *Blanche* and *Speranza* telegrams. These revelations were printed in the *Temps* of September 23 and 27, and in the *Figaro* of October 4. Esterhazy at once played his old game of denying everything, and through Arthur Newton—it was inevitable that he would fall into the hands of this shady solicitor—threatened the *Observer* with an action for libel and succeeded in getting five hundred pounds. The revelations do not appear to have had the slightest influence on public opinion. In November he published, through Fayard, his version of what had happened, *Les Dessous de l'Affaire Dreyfus* (30), in which he attempted to portray himself as the counter-espionage agent of Sandherr, passing false documents to Schwartzkoppen. He was lavish in abuse of all the senior officers, but now warm in praise of Henry.

2

While Brisson pondered and procrastinated, tempers were rising. Not only was the Paris press abounding in abuse and counter-abuse: the press of foreign nations was now taking a hand. Having seen the conduct of the Zola case, having heard the accounts of Henry's confession and suicide, and now hearing from Esterhazy in London that he had indeed written the *bordereau*, inevitably the foreign journalists and their editors took the Dreyfusard side. But instead of confining their criticisms to discussion of the known facts and to reports of day-to-day information, they attacked the French nation as a whole. Naturally Frenchmen, whether Dreyfusard or anti, Left or Right, resented these impertinences and hardened in their own attitude to the case. The anti-revisionists accused their opponents of being sold to the foreign enemy, of being *sans-patrie*; the revisionists accused the Army of putting itself above the country's laws.

At the same time the political sky was darkened by disturbances wholly foreign to the Affair. From early September, for more than two months, Delcassé was involved in serious controversy with the British over the appearance of the Marchand expedition at Fashoda on the Upper Nile. Since he had no cards in his hands, he could only hope to save his face in the negotiations, but his task was not eased by the noisy support of the French press.

To this diplomatic trouble were added labour conflicts, a strike of the building hands working on the site for the Paris Exhibition planned for 1900, which was joined by other workers in the building trades to the number of twenty thousand. The leader of the Anti-Semitic League, Guérin, had recently got onto the pay-roll of the Duc d'Orléans. Hoping to create anarchy from which the Royalists might profit, he infiltrated his own men into the strikers with

orders to incite attacks on blacklegs. Simultaneously the secretary
of a railway union, Guérard, who had been one of the adherents of
the general strike, called out his whole union. Brisson drafted
sixty thousand troops into the capital and occupied the railway
stations.

There was thus enough explosive opinion in Paris, in the last
two weeks of September, to make nervous people foresee some outbreak, some new "*Grande Peur,*" a prelude, if not to another 1789,
at least to riots. The Duc d'Orléans's followers, watched by the
Sûreté, were known to be rather more active than usual in their
amateur plotting, as if they expected an opportunity for trouble.
Then, on September 25, Déroulède, now Nationalist Deputy for
Angoulême, who had recently begun the reconstitution of his
Ligues des Patriotes, dissolved after the Boulanger fiasco, began
calling public meetings in which he poured out threats against
Clemenceau, Jaurès and Reinach, and claimed that if Dreyfus were
brought back he would be lynched. On October 2 there was a
street-fight between his followers and some Dreyfusards and the
police had to interfere. Wild rumours of a military plot passed
from mouth to mouth. The Socialist leaders took alarm. Momentarily sinking their differences and jealousies, Guesde, Jaurès,
Millerand, Fournière, Allemane, Viviani, Briand, met together on
October 16. There was no representative of the Blanquists. With
the conventional romantic belief in the Revolution, they decided
that, should the Nationalists demonstrate outside the Palais
Bourbon on the day the Chamber reopened, they would call out
"the people" and form a committee of vigilance. Within a few
days manifestos appeared from the Socialists, the Ligue des
Patriotes and the Anti-Semitic League, all promising a bloody riot
outside the Chamber on October 25. The Ligue des Droits de
l'Homme, perturbed at the prospect, hastily collected the more
reasonable Socialists, who, aided by the cold sense of Guesde and
Millerand, threw cold water on the bellicose enthusiasm of Jaurès.

3

The Court of Criminal Appeal[1] got to work on Lucie Dreyfus's appeal immediately after receiving the order from Sarrien. Its president was an Alsatian named Loew, a man of integrity who had long foreseen that the case might come to his court, and had refused to hear private confidences from friends. The Procureur-Général, Manau, having read the documents submitted to the court of 1894, and seeing the emptiness of the case, asked to see the secret dossier. Chanoine refused, and on a more formal application from Sarrien refused again, on the grounds of security; the refusal was an insult, but Brisson weakly submitted to it. Loew, having read Manau's preliminary agreement to the appeal, appointed the junior member of the court, Bard, to be the *rapporteur*. The anti-revisionist press broke into a volume of threats against the judges, obviously sold to the Germans. Unmoved, the judges went on with their work, and the full meeting of the court to consider the case for revision was set down for October 27.

Brisson had summoned the Chambers for October 25, before the Criminal Appeal Court had reached its conclusion as to whether there were grounds for revision. The Cabinet was in a bad situation. Its acceptance in June by the Republicans had been solely due to their trust in Cavaignac. Cavaignac had first deceived them, along with the whole Chamber, and during the vacation had resigned. The *raison d'être* for Brisson's Cabinet had gone. Furthermore, since Henry's death and Cavaignac's resignation, Brisson had displayed the most woeful vacillation and lack of determination, while quite recently he had dismissed three senior Préfets with the utmost brutality—it was said, to soothe his own Radical party.[2] Peytral,

[1] The Appeal Court (*Cour de Cassation*) consisted of three Chambers, the Court of Criminal Appeal, the Court of Civil Appeal, and the Court of Petitions (*Requêtes*), today defunct. They all sat in the Palais de Justice.

[2] The dismissals are somewhat mysterious. One of the Préfets was Alapetite, who was subsequently reappointed and became a most successful government servant, ending as Governor-General of Algeria. Laurenceau and Rivaud, Préfets of Nord and Rhône, had recently been asked to enquire into the introduction of foreign subsidies for the Dreyfusards through Lille and Lyon: both had reported that they could discover no traces. Anti-Dreyfusism rather than Radicalism therefore lies behind the dismissals.

the Finance Minister, had put forward a bill for the institution of income-tax, an action guaranteed to rouse the opposition of the Republicans.

On the morning of the reopening of the Chamber the groups held their private meetings. The Radicals were torn between their dislike of revision and their need to support a Radical Cabinet. At the Republican meeting Barthou proposed that the group should vote against the Government, which had sought through Cavaignac the support of the Nationalists and anti-semites and now, since Henry's suicide, had made a *volte-face* and was asking for the Republicans' support against its earlier allies: he had no confidence in its ability to meet the crisis.

The Chamber opened in the afternoon. A noisy mob had already gathered round the Palais Bourbon and in the Place de la Concorde, while the Tuileries Gardens were occupied by cavalry, and the approaches to the Chamber guarded by a strong police force. Drumont, according to the Socialist Clovis Hugues, was listening for "the drums of Augereau."

Brisson was faced by five interpellations. He said he was ready to discuss them, and claimed the honour of lifting the Affair out of the political field into the judicial. He was at once attacked by Déroulède, who accused him of having outlived a mandate which had been accorded him only because of the presence of Cavaignac. It was time to turn him out, even if in doing so, and in spite of its respect for the Army, the Chamber included General Chanoine in their condemnation of the Ministry.

Chanoine at once asked to speak, and from the tribune announced that he held exactly the same opinions as his predecessors in the Government, and would here and now resign his office. Then, hurriedly leaving the stand, he fled from the building.

His action, which had obviously been concerted with Déroulède, was unpardonable. Chanoine had given no warning to Brisson of his intention, and had outraged parliamentary convention. In spite of the frantic applause of the Right, the Republicans for the moment rallied to the Prime Minister. Brisson spoke angrily of Chanoine's treachery and demanded that the Chamber uphold him in his determination to sustain the civil power. After an interval for consultation, the united Republican groups, Republicans, Radicals and Socialists, brought forward a resolution in which, having stressed the supremacy of the civil power and their confidence in the loyal obedience of the Army to the laws of the Republic, they agreed to adjourn for two days. Had this been voted without discussion, it would have been passed: but one Deputy after another rose to argue and add riders. Barthou listened for some time, and then intervened to say that neither he nor his group could give their confidence to the Government. After a confusion of motions, one of confidence was defeated. The Chamber adjourned for a week and the Cabinet resigned.

Outside the building Guérin had tried to bring his gangs into action. The police would have no nonsense. Guérin and some five hundred demonstrators were arrested.

Chanoine, the cause of the crisis, was forgotten: he was left "at the disposition" of the next Minister of War. No job was found for him. He had already taken care of his friends—it shows how little spontaneous was his resignation. General Roget was given command of the 17th Infantry Brigade of the Paris garrison.

Four days later the Court of Criminal Appeal gave its judgment on Lucie Dreyfus's appeal. By ten votes to four it declared that the appeal was well founded, and that the Court would now proceed to a further investigation of the Dreyfus case. But it refused to follow the request of the Procureur-Général that the sentence on Dreyfus should be suspended.

4

Félix Faure consulted the Presidents and Vice-Presidents of the two chambers as to Brisson's successor. The primary need was a Prime Minister strong enough to prevent attacks on the Army. Ribot would not do: he was already known as a quasi-revisionist, and his wife was reported to look on Picquart as a hero. On the other hand, the Republican groups of both Chamber and Senate put out a manifesto that they would only give their support to a Cabinet which maintained the authority of civil government, the separation of the powers and the free exercise of the judicial authority. Therefore the revision could not be postponed. Félix Faure invited Dupuy, who, whatever his behaviour in 1895 against Casimir-Perier, could, with the right Cabinet, manipulate parliamentary opinion. To lend him strength he must have a Minister at the War Office capable of soothing both civil and military susceptibilities. Thus Freycinet, who had been largely effaced since the Panama scandal, was pressed to return to the office he loved.

Dupuy, on November 4, promised to rely on Republican support alone, and to introduce no *ad hoc* laws of circumstance. More than four-fifths of the Chamber voted approval; but at once his troubles began. A motion was put forward to transfer the Dreyfus appeal from the Court of Criminal Appeal to a united Court of the three Chambers, Civil, Criminal and Petitions. Dupuy said that, having declared that justice should be respected, he would not give an example of disrespect. The declaration sounded well, but in fact Dupuy had resolved to place all future responsibility on the Criminal Appeal Court. He refused to allow Dreyfus to be informed that his appeal had been before a court and had been admitted. The Criminal Appeal Court, hearing of this, ordered that Dreyfus should be informed by telegraph, and further that he should be invited to prepare his defence. The order caused something of a sensation. Who were these bold men? The anti-Dreyfusard press informed their readers that Reinach had but to command and the judges obeyed, and began a new campaign of vilification.

The Court proceeded to take the statements of the witnesses, first the five War Ministers, Mercier, Billot, Cavaignac, Zurlinden and Chanoine. Billot was evasive, Cavaignac full of argument, Zurlinden and Chanoine negligible. Mercier alone fought. He admitted that he had secured no confession from Dreyfus through Du Paty, but he accepted Lebrun-Renaud's statement. Asked why, in that case, he had not made a report, he coolly answered that, since the case was finished, it was unnecessary: "It could not be foreseen that a whole race would later line up behind Dreyfus." Asked about the communication of the secret dossier at the trial, he claimed that since Mme Dreyfus's application had not mentioned this, the matter was irrelevant, and refused to say yes or no. Yet he was driven to deny that any of the papers read by Cavaignac in July had figured in the trial of 1894. Since the *canaille de D* was one of these papers, he lied. He, and several of the others, held to the opinion that Esterhazy could not have obtained the information given by the documents listed in the *bordereau*. One new item of evidence against Esterhazy was suddenly produced—a letter written by him from Châlons gunnery range on 11 August 1894, on paper which, when examined by three paper experts, proved to be of exactly the same make as that of the *bordereau*.

While the Appeal Court was beginning its examination of witnesses, the War Office had already got far in the proceedings against Picquart for forgery of the *petit bleu*. Before an officer named Tavernier, the same witnesses from the Statistical Section made the same imputations. But on this occasion the handwriting experts refused to follow the line dictated to them: unanimously they reported that the name "Esterhazy" had been scratched out and written in again, and they refused to connect the rest of the *petit bleu* with either Schwartzkoppen or Picquart. Picquart had been heard by Tavernier nine times between September 23 and October 22, but he had been confronted with no witnesses and had not been allowed to consult his lawyer, Labori. For seven weeks he was in solitary confinement, permitted to receive no visits save from a few close relatives. From October 22 to November 5 he heard nothing more of the case against him. Labori at length applied to Freycinet for permission to consult.

Freycinet is perhaps the most ambiguous character in the history of the Third Republic. Of a distinguished southern family, he had done good work as an officer in the Ponts-et-Chaussées under the Second Empire. In 1870–71 he had been Gambetta's organiser at Tours, when he had produced some order in the wild chaos of the last months of war. Unlike Gambetta or Ferry, he had never been a doctrinaire politician, never a preacher of crusades. As a private member of the Senate, he abstained more often than he voted. He had been Prime Minister on four occasions and, more relevant to the situation in 1898, he had been the first civilian Minister of War, a portfolio he had held from 1888 to 1892. He was properly speaking a technician, an executive who had strayed into politics. His misfortune was that he was weak, and that he disliked violent controversy. He looked timid, and on every occasion when he found himself in a seriously difficult position, he resigned and disappeared. Yet in many ways he was valued. He had a great gift of persuasion, and his passion for Army matters was quite genuine. But during his four years at the War Office, in order to secure his ends he had to all intents bribed his military collaborators. Certainly he surrendered ministerial control over the senior appointments. According to Galliffet and Casimir-Perier, his activities at the War Office had resulted in serious damage to the Army. Now he had come back at perhaps the most difficult moment since 1871, the indispensable man, who, it was hoped, would restore harmony between the service and the politicians.

At once he found himself in difficulties. Urged by the soldiers to press on with the court-martial of Picquart, urged no less strongly by the Dreyfusists to release him, knowing that there was almost certainly no case, calumniated by the Drumonts and Rocheforts on one side, upbraided on the other by Clemenceau, who loathed and despised him, he temporised. He sheltered behind the fact that the Law of December 1897, which made it obligatory for a prisoner to be advised by his lawyer, had not been extended to the code of military law. At once Antide Boyer, a Socialist, in the Chamber and Constans in the Senate tabled bills and asked for their urgent consideration. They were too late. Tavernier immediately closed his examination of Picquart's case, and on November 19 Zurlinden sent the summary of evidence, which pronounced for a court-martial, to the government commissioner. He then permitted Labori to see Picquart. Freycinet once more submitted. Zurlinden set down the court-martial for December 12.

The fact that Picquart was now a civilian made it arguable that he could no longer be tried by a military court, but his friends, mistrusting the power of argument on the military mind, appealed to public opinion: a public protest was organised. A vast roll of signatories was inscribed, including members of the Institute, professors and savants, painters, sculptors, musicians, distinguished writers, ambassadors, famous actresses. The Ligue des Droits de l'Homme sent its best speakers out to whip up adherents. Students from the Sorbonne and the Ecole Normale stood outside the Cherche-Midi shouting "*Vive Picquart!*"

The intention of the War Office to discredit Picquart, even to destroy him as Dreyfus had been destroyed, was too obvious. If, as was alleged, he was a forger attempting to fasten a crime on an innocent man, his guilt would undoubtedly be made plain in the Criminal Appeal Court. By attempting to forestall the Court's action, by attempting to produce yet another *res judicata*, they outraged a whole new body of opinion which hitherto had displayed no particular bias in the Affair.

Far worse, however, were the wider consequences. Up to now the early revisionists—Reinach, Ranc, Scheurer-Kestner, Trarieux —had done their best to limit the case to that of justice for Dreyfus. Failing to secure redress, they had been forced to find other allies. With the increase in their forces, the original case became generalised. The point at issue was no longer the rehabilitation of one man, but the cause of all men subject to military justice; from that it became swollen by propaganda to the case of the nation against the Army. A dozen officers in the War Office and the Military Government of Paris, aided by a group of demagogic politicians and journalists, had brought the Army to the situation where it had assumed the appearance of an autonomous body within the State, and had thereby marshalled against it all the elements of anti-militarism, anti-clericalism and anti-capitalism. Zurlinden, in no way a politician, but "pig-headed as all Alsatians," trying, as he believed, to save the Army, had in fact put it in a position where it could not, short of revolution, defend itself.

Zurlinden's action shocked in particular the one body which looked on itself as the guardian of the constitution, the Senate. The four Republican groups delegated their presidents to protest to Dupuy. The Prime Minister, recognising the need for immediate decision, brought the matter up in the Chamber on November 28. The thesis put forward by the Left was that a court-martial on

Picquart, whose prosecution in company with Leblois in the civil criminal court had been adjourned until the judgment on Lucie Dreyfus's appeal had been delivered by the Appeal Court, would be acting *ultra vires*. Millerand put the case with his usual clarity; the Government had an absolute authority to vary the order convoking the court-martial; the members of the court-martial themselves could adjourn it, and if they did not use this power, then it was the responsibility of the Government to do so. The Opposition tried to shift the debate on to the villainy of the Syndicate and Jewish finance. Suddenly Poincaré, Minister of Finance in Dupuy's Cabinet at the time of the Dreyfus court-martial, was heard to exclaim: "Really, enough of this!" and rose to speak. Poincaré, it has been said, had "the mind of a chartered accountant." It is true that in many ways he was narrow, but he was an upright and completely honest man, though possibly too balanced: like Freycinet, he had the reputation of abstaining from voting. Since 1895 he had returned to legal practice and had taken little part in politics. He had, however, watched, and had gradually reached the conclusion that there had been something very wrong with the court-martial of 1894, and that it behoved him to say what he knew.

"At the present moment," he said, "silence on the part of some of us would be undisguised cowardice." Everyone could see that a supreme attempt was being made to prevent light from being thrown on the abusive conduct of some War Office departments, while each attack on Picquart had been made at a moment when it had all the appearance of being a reprisal. If a judicial error had been made in 1894, it was the imperious duty of the members of the Cabinet of that time to do nothing to prevent the error from being brought into the open. He called on his former colleagues by name—Dupuy, Barthou, Leygues, Delcassé. He said that none of them had ever heard of any charge against Dreyfus other than the *bordereau*, had never been told of a Secret File, had never been informed of Dreyfus's confession to Lebrun-Renaud. Cavaignac shouted that the avowals had been given to Mercier. Poincaré replied that Mercier had never spoken of them to any of his colleagues, and he appealed to Dupuy. Dupuy sat silent. Poincaré ended by saying that he knew that in breaking his silence he was exposing himself to attack. "I do not care. I am glad to have taken this opportunity, for which I have waited too long, to unburden my conscience." The speech was so completely honest that a great part of the Chamber, many members almost against their will, broke into applause.

Cavaignac, harassed by the jeers of the Extreme Left, now attacked Brisson for deciding on revision without consulting Parliament, and for removing the case from the political to the judicial field. Dupuy interrupted sharply: "It should be left there now." Later, from the tribune, he developed the theme crystallised in his exclamation. He admitted that the Government had the right to adjourn Picquart's case; but would the Chamber order him to use that right? In any case he would not accept such an order, because he would be trespassing into the forbidden field. Constitutionally the Court ruled; it could adjourn the case. It had already asked for the documents relative to Picquart, which would be given to it. Thus he thrust the responsibility on to the Court of Criminal Appeal, and though he was upbraided by Ribot for refusing to take responsibility, he secured a huge majority.

On the following day in the Senate, Waldeck-Rousseau, who had played little part in politics for the last five years, proposed that a simple law granting the Appeal Court permission to adjourn all prosecutions connected with the revision would absolve Dupuy. The proposal was narrowly defeated.

For another week the legal and constitutional arguments continued, until the solution of the problem was found. Since Leblois and Picquart still had to appear before the civil criminal court for communication of the secret dossier, it was impossible that one of them should appear before a civil and the other before a military tribunal: there might be a conflict of judgment on the same set of facts. Picquart lodged an appeal to have all charges against him transferred back to the civil criminal court. On December 8 the Criminal Appeal Court granted what was tantamount to a stay of proceedings. Temporarily saved, he remained in prison.

5

During the controversy over his court-martial, Picquart, under the guard of an officer of the gendarmerie, had appeared as a witness before the Criminal Appeal Court on four days between November 22 and 29. He was spied on by his guard, by the clerk of the court and by other parasites, and all civilities shown to the prisoner by members of the court were reported in exaggerated form to Zurlinden and the anti-revisionist journalists. On one occasion, while Roget finished his deposition, he was kept waiting in the room of the President of the Court of Petitions. Bard, the *rapporteur*, having been asked by the President of the Criminal Appeal Court to tell the prisoner that his deposition must be postponed until the following day, went by mistake into the room of the President of the Civil Appeal Court, Quesnay de Beaurepaire, who said that the man Bard was looking for was perhaps in the room of the President of the Court of Petitions.

Quesnay de Beaurepaire must surely be the most eminent oddity among the high officials of the Third Republic. He had been an imperial legal officer before 1870, when he resigned his post, and had great difficulty in getting back on to the *parquet* under the Republic. However he had worked his passage, and after various minor posts was appointed Avocat-Général in Paris. As a side-line he wrote novels, which are said to have been "of the most revolting sentimentality." His prosecutions appear to have been conducted with the maximum of dramatic fire. He had been in charge of the case against Boulanger, in which his abuse of that unsuccessful dictator revolted even the anti-Boulangists. At the trial of the Anarchist Ravachol, having asked for a sentence of death, he said to the jury: "If you find extenuating circumstances—it would insult you to suppose that you will—you can only be impelled by the lowest and vilest of emotions: fear. Who is afraid? This evening you will be escorted to your homes by bodies of the police. But I shall proceed alone; I have need of no man's aid. You must send Ravachol to the scaffold!" Needless to say, the jury added a rider of extenuating circumstances. During the Panama scandals he again sought advertisement by resigning noisily at the moment when Carnot and Loubet, then Prime Minister, were doing their utmost to bring measure into the proceedings. He was, however, promoted by Léon Bourgeois to the presidency of the Civil Appeal Court. In the winter of 1897–98 he had been attacked by a combination of Socialists, Radicals and Nationalists, and, weakly defended by Méline, had suffered a vote of censure by the Chamber. Although he was purged by a legal committee set up by the Minister of Justice, he was raw with resentment. Further, he could not bear a public case as exciting as that of Alfred Dreyfus to proceed without his intervention. He began to talk to anti-revisionists and to soldiers, such as General Roget; he entered on a course of calumniation of his colleagues of the Criminal Appeal Court. And he invented the story that when Bard came to his room to find Picquart he had said as he came in, before noticing that it was not Picquart but he, Quesnay, who was in the room: "My dear Picquart, give me your opinion on this deposition of . . ." He invented further imaginary crimes of the Criminal Appeal Court judges. When now the Nationalists, his former enemies, sought his aid, he expected to be called on to lead the crusade to save the Army. On January 8 he resigned uproariously from the presidency of the Civil Court of Appeal.

6

In the tangled wood of truth, half-truth, insinuation, misinterpretation and falsehood, all investigators had at one time or another become hopelessly misled. By October Reinach had convinced himself that Henry had been Esterhazy's accomplice since the beginning. From scraps of evidence and gossip, from the fact that the War Office had been losing documents during 1893, from the fact that Henry had known Esterhazy in the late seventies, from the fact that by manipulation of the Section's accounts Henry had been able to build up a *caisse noire* of twenty-nine thousand francs, from the now partly established fact that much of Esterhazy's information about the case must have come from the Statistical Section, Reinach reached the conclusion that Henry was

the major traitor, the man who supplied the information to
Schwartzkoppen. His reasons he published at intervals in the
Siècle between October 25 and December 6. (They were re-
published in volume form, *Tout le Crime* (48).) He had failed
entirely to guess the truth about Henry: that before all he was
a serving officer, with the narrow loyalties of a not very intelligent
soldier.

On the day after the last article appeared, Mme Henry wrote
protesting against these calumnies on her husband. She was taken
to see Drumont, who urged her to prosecute Reinach and at once
opened a public subscription, placing a streamer on the balcony
of the office of the *Libre Parole*: "For the widow and orphan of
Colonel Henry against the Jew, Reinach." In a month some fifteen
thousand persons subscribed a hundred and thirty thousand francs,
say six thousand pounds, among them both active and reserve
officers, including Mercier; a number of members of the aristocracy;
various politicians, including the ex-Communard and present
Socialist, Cluseret; journalists and writers, Barrès, Paul Valéry and
Léautaud among them, and three hundred priests. Much was made
later by the anti-clericals of the priests who subscribed; but three
hundred out of fifty thousand is not overwhelming evidence of
clerical anti-semitism.[1]

The incident is unimportant but for the fact that it demonstrates
the strength of the anti-Dreyfusard and pro-Army sentiment which
still flourished in spite of the unmasking of Henry. The revisionists
complained that the anti-revisionists exploited Mme Henry's
sorrows: but they had exploited Dreyfus's.

7

During these interludes the Criminal Appeal Court had been
quietly taking depositions from all and sundry. They had turned
Lebrun-Renaud upside-down, faced him with his empty report
after Dreyfus's degradation, his silence to Dupuy and Casimir-
Perier, the contradiction between the first sentence of Dreyfus's

---

[1] For various reasons Mme Henry's case against Reinach was not disposed
of until 1902, when the plaintiff was awarded five hundred francs.

alleged confession: "I am innocent" and the rest, and his destruction of the leaf in his notebook after rewriting his statement under
the eyes of Gonse and Henry. They called various Ministers of
1894, who could say little more than that the only evidence they
knew of against Dreyfus was the *bordereau*. Hanotaux preserved
a discreet silence on his share in the diplomatic difficulties started
by Mercier's impetuousness. Gonse and Boisdeffre added nothing
to their earlier testimonies. Roget, who had taken on himself the
part of mouthpiece for the War Office, was voluble at great length,
chiefly to the effect that Dreyfus *could* have had access to information of value to foreign staffs and Esterhazy could not, while Picquart was of course the villain: a judge shrugged his shoulders and
Roget took offence. By mid-November the court decided it could
go no further without seeing the Secret File. For some six weeks
the question was at intervals debated in the Chamber. Freycinet,
having seen the file, knew its emptiness. The Nationalists fought
hard to have it withheld. Eventually, at the end of December,
under stringent safeguards, it was agreed that Captain Cuignet
should show it to the court and at the same time explain it to
them.

Like practically every other man who had once got involved in
the web of documents—Picquart, Roget, and much later Major
Targe—Cuignet was by now obsessed. The Secret File had acted
on him like a witch's philtre, and with more violence than on any
of the others who became involved. At the same time the dis-
coverer of Henry's forgery and a friend of the forger, he was both
immensely proud of his perspicacity and resolute to cover the dead
man. Before the court he produced the invention that Henry, both
because he was honourable and because he was a rough uneducated
man, could not have imagined the *faux Henry*: the villain was Du
Paty, who had been the author of the forgery and had made Henry
his cat's-paw. Du Paty was responsible for all the errors in tactics
and for all the forgeries: it was he who had revealed the name of
Dreyfus in 1894; it was he who had written the *Eclair* article in
1896; it was he who had sent the *faux Weyler*, had written the
letters of the "veiled lady," had sent the *Blanche* and *Speranza*

telegrams—all from a desire to defend his work of 1894 and from hatred of Picquart.

His demonstration of the documents in the file was equally personal and eccentric. He disregarded entirely the three documents that Cavaignac had read to the Chamber on July 7, including the *canaille de D* letter. But because Dreyfus had been through the railway sub-section at the War Office, he brought forward as genuine Panizzardi's letter of March 1895 saying that he would shortly have the railway organisation, the letter from which Henry had torn the date and substituted April 1894. He insisted that the version of the Panizzardi telegram of 2 November 1894, which Gonse had concocted from Du Paty's memory, was authentic and that the version given by the Foreign Office was false, going so far as to contest the good faith of the gentlemen at the Quai d'Orsay. There were many other original interpretations, which it would be otiose to detail.

The judges listened to this fantastic travesty with stupefaction. Cuignet, who, if the press photographs do him justice, looked like a comic mongrel terrier, was taken aback by their attitude to his triumphant exposition. He did not perceive that he had in fact broken the case against Dreyfus.

Quesnay de Beaurepaire's posturings and lies gave the anti-revisionists a new idea. Perhaps they believed that Quesnay's attitude represented the feeling in the Civil Appeal Court; perhaps they relied on the information that the Minister of Justice, Lebret, had sounded the members of the Civil and Petitions Appeal Courts and discovered that, if the three courts sat together, the Criminal Appeal judges would be out-voted. Certainly they became convinced that if they could force the Government to remove the case from these hostile judges to a combined assembly of all three courts, they would secure by a majority a judgment against revision. To work for this, there came into existence yet another league, the Ligue de la Patrie Française (which should not be confused with Déroulède's Ligue des Patriotes), dedicated to the dismissal from the case of the Court of Criminal Appeal and the creation of a special body of the three courts. Its public sponsors were three professors, Dausset, Vaugeois and Syveton, but the true founder was Charles Maurras. It soon collected some fifteen thousand members, a figure which demonstrates the extent of anti-Dreyfusard sentiment. Among these were almost as many "intellectuals" as had joined the Ligue des Droits de l'Homme, though perhaps of lesser calibre: the historians Houssaye, Vandal and Rambaud; the artists Detaille, Gérôme, Forain, besides Barrès, Mistral, Heredia, Theuriet, Lavedan, Coppée, Melchior de Vogüe, Emile Faguet, and the Comtesse de Martel, otherwise Gyp. On the committee sat Cavaignac. The League's spokesman was the well-known critic Jules Lemaître, the lion of the Comtesse de Loynes's salon. Strong in the confidences which had been imparted to him, Lemaître boldly asserted that the League would loyally submit to any judgment delivered by the combined courts.

Beset by their propaganda, Dupuy saw that the responsibility for the conduct of the Affair was once more being passed back to him. And once more he and Lebret evaded the issue. They forced Mazeau, First President of the united Courts of Appeal, and a Senator, to form a committee to enquire into the charges made against the Criminal Appeal judges, and to advise. The committee spent ten days listening to the fables of Quesnay, the slanders of the underlings of the courts, and to Roget's and Cuignet's fury against the obvious disbelief in their evidence shown by the judges. At the end, while clearing the Criminal Appeal Court, the committee recommended that the judges should be protected from assuming full responsibility for the judgment they had not yet delivered, and that the other two courts should be joined to that of Criminal Appeal from now onward.

Dupuy decided to carry the destitution of the Criminal Appeal Court with a high hand. He met with an unexpected opposition within the Cabinet. Georges Leygues, the Minister of Public Instruction, stuck in his heels against this insult to some of the highest judges in the country. He was followed by the Minister of Commerce, Delombre, and by Delcassé. Their protest was in vain. The rest of the Cabinet backed Dupuy.

The bill to remove the appeal for revision to the united Courts was brought to the Chamber by Lebret on January 30, and thence sent to a committee. The committee, having found Mazeau's report full of gaps, insisted on having further evidence.

But before the committee had reported, the Court of Criminal Appeal had nearly finished the hearing of the evidence. Among the new witnesses were four artillery experts, two retired, two active, who all declared that the terms employed in the *bordereau* could have been written only by someone who knew nothing about artillery, and that so far as they could judge from the wording, the subjects had been dealt with time and again in the press. One of these experts, Ducros, said that on two occasions he had invited Dreyfus to visit the artillery shops at Puteaux where the most secret gun-parts were manufactured, and that he had not come. Finally Esterhazy appeared. He had bargained for and received a safe-conduct. He lodged at a religious house. All his former backers deserted him except Drumont and a few Nationalists. Through these he asked Freycinet to relieve him of the duty of "professional secrecy." Freycinet, seeing the threat, sent him a letter engaging him to refer compromising questions to himself. To the court Esterhazy said nothing, except that he had been supported by the General Staff until Cavaignac resolved to have his head, whereupon he had been deserted by cowardly and ungrateful superiors. He refused to say anything about his alleged relations with Sandherr, and as to the *bordereau*, he replied that since the first court-martial attributed it to Dreyfus, and the second had found the document was not his work, he had nothing more to say. As soon as his evidence was completed, he left the country.

At the end of December the Appeal Court had directed the legal authority at Cayenne to send a commission to The Devil's Island to examine Dreyfus as to his alleged confession to Lebrun-Renaud. The commission's report with the prisoner's indignant denials was received before the Chamber had discussed the removal of the case from the Criminal Appeal Court.

The commission on Lebret's bill was presided over by a Deputy of long legal and political experience, Renault-Morlière. Of the eleven members, eight and the chairman looked on it as an outrage.

Either the judges were innocent of the charges brought against them, or they should be subjected to legal proceedings. According to Lebret's plan, all tribunals would be at the mercy of any journalists whom they displeased. "Principles are not violated with impunity." In the Chamber Renault-Morlière fought hard for rejection. "You are killing the very idea of justice in the country." A few followed him. Dupuy defended the extraordinary bill on the ground that the case was extraordinary, while Lebret uttered a sentence which became notorious in French parliamentary history: "Gentlemen, think of your constituencies." Few others spoke, and none of the leaders. The Right, the Progressists and most of the Radicals voted for the bill, and it was passed by over a hundred majority. There still remained the Senate.

CHAPTER TWELVE

The Death and Funeral
of Félix Faure

ON the evening of February 16 Félix Faure, his labours for the day finished, was entertaining a certain handsome Mme Steinheil in his private office. About 6.45 p.m. the chief of his civil secretariat, Le Gall, heard screams coming from the President's room. Entering, he found that the President had suffered a cerebral hæmorrhage and was unconscious. The lady was patched up and sent off by a private side-door. Doctors were called, but the case was hopeless. Félix Faure expired shortly before ten o'clock, without having regained consciousness.

It was all very awkward. The discreet recitals of Le Gall and other members of his staff were discounted by the gossip of the Palace servants. Editors gave versions of what had happened according to their taste and political colouring. Drumont attributed the unhappy man's death to a Delilah in the pay of the Jews. Looking to the future, Clemenceau, with more than usual brutality, wrote: "Félix Faure has just died. It means not a man less in France. All the same, there is a good situation vacant. . . . It will be put up to auction, the succession to the throne, the continuation, the achievement of the abominable work. . . . I vote for Loubet."

This was the fourth President in succession who had terminated his period of office prematurely. The Members of Parliament were by now inured to the hurried election prescribed by the Constitution. It had not needed Clemenceau's finger to point to the obvious candidate, Emile Loubet, President of the Senate, sixty-one years of age, from peasant stock in the region of Montelimar, of which he had been Maire for nearly thirty years, thoroughly Republican, calm, simple and experienced. The only charge that had ever been made against him was that in 1892, when Prime Minister, he had done his best to circumscribe the scandals surrounding the death of Baron Reinach, and earned thereby the hatred of the followers of the dead Boulanger, the Nationalists. Without seeking the office, he became the candidate of the Senate, and then of the main body of Republicans. Méline refused to stand, but did not discourage his supporters from putting him forward.

Since Loubet was known to be in favour of revision, there were the usual libellous and insulting articles in the *Libre Parole* and the *Echo de Paris*, by Drumont, Lemaître, Quesnay. On February 19, at Versailles, Loubet was elected by 483 out of 812 votes cast. Méline was given 279, while Cavaignac, Deschanel, Dupuy, Colonel Monteil, Rochefort, and a few more together received fifty. On his drive from the Saint-Lazare station to the Elysée the new President was hooted by Déroulède's leaguers, Guérin's anti-semites and the followers of the Duc d'Orléans. Bicyclists followed the state carriage yelling "Panama" and, since he was supposed to be pro-English, "Oh, yes." Loubet, however, was full of courage and confidence. "The Republic will not founder in my hands," he said that evening. "They know it, and it maddens them" (38, 18 February 1899).

Dupuy offered Loubet his formal resignation, which the President refused. The Chambers voted to give Félix Faure a State funeral on February 23, to be attended by representatives of all the State institutions: after a service at Notre Dame, the funeral cortège would march to Père-Lachaise for the interment.

If Félix Faure's term of office was something of a vulgar comedy, his final curtain belongs to farce. There were now two revolutionary groups contending for the right to take charge of a parliamentary system they abhorred and had no prospect of overturning; Déroulède's Ligue des Patriotes and the Royalist followers of the Duc d'Orléans—the followers of the Bonapartist candidate, Prince Victor, preserved the greatest discretion. Between these, waiting to join whichever was successful, hovered Guérin and his anti-semites. Déroulède had perhaps talked himself into believing that a *coup de force*, the one Boulanger had failed to make, might sweep away the whole of the parliamentary racket. This *coup* would receive its impulse from the populace backed by the Army. For some time he had been sounding generals to lend themselves to his schemes, should the occasion appear. The only one who appears to have taken him seriously was the embittered Georges-Gabriel de Pellieux, who was to command a column of troops in the funeral procession.[1]

Déroulède hoped that, at his signal, Pellieux would march his brigade to the Elysée Palace, thrust Loubet forth amid popular acclamation and allow the Ligue des Patriotes to form a provisional and dictatorial Government, in which no doubt would sit his own friends Marcel Habert, Deputy for Rambouillet, Lasies, Deputy for Condom—both Nationalists—Maurice Barrès, ex-Deputy for Nancy, and Thiébaud, the journalist who practically invented Boulanger.

André Buffet, the chief agent of the Duc d'Orléans, had made scarcely any preparations. His assistants were young aristocrats, wholly inexperienced in affairs, who took to conspiracy as light-heartedly as they went racing. They hoped that, as soon as the situation in Paris had turned to anarchy, they would only have to bring on the claimant for the monarchy to be restored. They expected assistance from Guérin, now in the Duke's pay, and that the Army, of which they knew nothing, its reality obscured for them by the traditional myth, would do the rest. One of them had sounded Déroulède to find out if he would join them; but Déroulède, as Republican as any Socialist, replied that if the Duke appeared he would himself arrest him. Further, Déroulède had no use for Guérin, and looked jealously on his anti-semite leaguers as desirable recruits to the Patriots.

On February 23 Déroulède and his fellow-conspirators were all ready. Their intention was to meet the troops as they marched back from Père-Lachaise to their barracks in the Rue de Reuilly,

[1] It is said on the authority of Vaughan of the *Aurore* that in August 1898 Pellieux had had several interviews at Brussels with Prince Victor Napoleon and that the Government was warned by Viviani and Vaughan himself. It appears strange, if this is true, that Pellieux was not transferred from Paris, and also that the Sûreté, whose men were in constant attendance on the pretenders, had apparently not notified the Minister of the Interior of Pellieux's movements.

at the Place de la Nation; then, taking their General, Pellieux, by the hand, to march on to the Elysée Palace. Pellieux, who had not been taken into Déroulède's confidence, seems to have heard of the scheme only on the morning of the parade, and realised that he would be involved in an adventure not at all to his taste, with the prospect of being lodged in the Cherche-Midi before nightfall. He recoiled with horror. At Notre Dame he quietly told Zurlinden that there might be trouble. Zurlinden supposed he had the wind up, but eventually agreed to let him break off from the main column, with the battalion he was leading, before he reached the place of rendezvous. Hence Pellieux led his men to Vincennes and, avoiding the centre of Paris, betook himself quietly home.[1]

Déroulède had taken up his position with Habert, Barrès, Guérin and some two hundred followers in a side-street at the entrance to the Place de la Nation. There was not a policeman to be seen; Dupuy, in spite of warnings, had massed the police at the Elysée, the Préfecture and the Ministry of the Interior. As the column of troops approached the Place de la Nation, Déroulède perceived that the General at the head was not the expected Pellieux, but Roget. It was too late to turn back. With his friends he rushed at Roget and shouted wildly: "Follow us, General, have pity on the country. Save France, save the Republic. Follow us to the Bastille, to the Hôtel de Ville. To the Elysée, General!" His followers tried to fall in behind Roget, cutting him off from the leading troops. The crowd, who had not the faintest idea what it was all about, shouted *"Vive l'Armée, Vive la République."* The band of the leading regiment struck up the Marseillaise and with immense gusto hundreds of cheerful, well-liquored citizens joined in. Roget's horse took fright and he had some trouble in keeping his seat; besides, he was slightly deaf and in the pandemonium could not hear what the gesticulating Déroulède was shouting. He devoted his energies to staying in the saddle and getting the regiment back to barracks. He led them down the Boulevard Diderot, and at the gates of the Reuilly barracks beckoned to the regimental

---

[1] It is fair to Pellieux to say that this version of his behaviour was given after his death by Déroulède.

sappers to clear the crowd out of the way. Still at his side, Déroulède was screaming; "Save France, General. Not that way; you must take the road into Paris." Roget spurred his horse and swept into the courtyard with Déroulède struggling to get hold of the bridle. They were followed by some dozen of his adherents who were carried in by the weight of the leading battalion. The gates were closed on the crowd, leaving Lasies, Barrès and Guérin outside. Roget, when he at last gathered the meaning of this extraordinary exhibition, requested Déroulède and his friends to go home. Déroulède refused for himself and Habert (both of whom now displayed their Deputy's scarves, which they wore under their overcoats), but sent away the others, saying grandiloquently: "Go, tell Paris that I am a prisoner of the Army, under arrest among the soldiers for whom I have sacrificed myself." He knew only too well that if he was shown out into the street, he would be the laughing stock of Paris.

Roget was in considerable perplexity; he knew only too well the touchiness of the Chamber in defence of its members. Eventually, after consulting his immediate senior, he reported to Zurlinden, who passed the news on to Dupuy. Dupuy took his time to think out the easiest course. At last, at one o'clock in the morning, Cochefert of the Sûreté took delivery of the two unsuccessful but loquacious conspirators, charging them merely with "trespassing into a barracks at the head of a crowd of demonstrators and refusing to depart, in spite of the orders of the military authorities." It was an insult. Déroulède insisted that it should be inserted on the record that "he had gone to the Place de la Nation to seduce the troops to an insurrectionary movement and overturn the parliamentary Republic." Then he and Habert went off to the police-station.

The Royalist conspirators, who had been hanging about all the evening waiting for Déroulède and the troops, went home to bed, and André Buffet telegraphed the expectant Duc d'Orléans that it was useless for him to cross the border.

CHAPTER THIRTEEN

United Appeal Courts

THE police-court proceedings against the infatuated revolutionaries saw the examining magistrate attenuating the offence and
the prisoners struggling to swell their crime. Déroulède wanted
his case to be treated as treason and to be taken before the High
Court of the Senate. He was unsuccessful: the prosecutor and
examining magistrate calmly ignored his insults to the President
of the Republic and the Government. The prisoners were remanded
for the Assize Court.

Simultaneously Dupuy moved against the Leagues under the
Law of 1834, as unauthorised associations of more than twenty
persons, and in order to demonstrate his impartiality ordered the
prosecution not only of the Ligue des Patriotes, the Anti-Semitic
League and the Jeunesse Royaliste, but also that of the Ligue des
Droits de l'Homme. The courts merely fined each sixteen francs.
They continued to exist.

The bill to dismiss Lucie Dreyfus's appeal from the Criminal
Appeal Court and to transfer the case to the three courts came
before the Senate on February 27. The debate lasted three days,
and the proposal was fought hotly by the most respected Republicans. They repudiated the Government's suggestion that the
transfer was dictated by reason of State; they claimed that it was a
violation of elementary principles. On the last day, March 1,
Waldeck-Rousseau said that the Government talked of pacification, but that this was not the time to diminish the authority of
justice. "We Frenchmen were once hungry for justice. Now it has
been possible to declare, and without a shudder running through
the whole country, that *raison d'état* can outweigh justice to the
individual. You talk of opinion. I answer; let us talk of justice."
Nevertheless the bill was passed by a majority of twenty.

Two days later the Criminal Appeal Court, in defiance as it seemed of Parliament, finally put the charges against Picquart—save for two minor charges unconnected with the Affair—back to the civil court of first instance. Picquart was re-transferred from the Cherche-Midi to the Santé.

Meanwhile the First President of the united Courts, Mazeau, had selected as *rapporteur* Ballot-Beaupré, the successor of Quesnay to the presidency of the Civil Appeal Court and a man of integrity and balanced judgment. The records of the proceedings of the Criminal Appeal Court were printed, in an extremely limited edition, and given to the judges. However, the Criminal Appeal Court had ordered the communication to the defence of the evidence it had heard, and Lucie Dreyfus's counsel, Mornard, had legitimately shown this to Mathieu Dreyfus. He in turn showed it to Rodays, now back at the *Figaro*. By devious means the whole was copied and printed in the *Figaro* day after day during April. A great number of people, hitherto dependent on rumour and false reports, were suddenly enlightened. Paul Painlevé, lecturer in mathematics at the Ecole Normale Supérieure, later Prime Minister, discovered that evidence he had given to Gonse, of a conversation tending to show Dreyfus's innocence, had been completely falsified by that officer.

On March 27 the new judges demanded the delivery of the Secret File. It was brought to them by Colonel Chamoin, head of Freycinet's secretariat. Having examined it and found, as had the Criminal Appeal judges, that it contained nothing incriminating Dreyfus, one of the judges asked Chamoin whether they had received the whole dossier, whether there were not some other document inculpating Dreyfus directly: he appears to have had in mind the rumoured letter of the German Emperor. Chamoin replied that the file contained everything.

During April and May the courts heard other witnesses who had now come forward. Among these was one of the experts of 1894, Charavay, who had then, somewhat against his better judgment, allowed himself to be persuaded by Bertillon that Dreyfus was the writer of the *bordereau*. He now volunteered that had he seen Esterhazy's writing he would not have failed to say that he was the writer. Lépine, Préfet of Police in 1894 (now returned from Algeria), testified that the police evidence that Dreyfus was not a frequenter of gambling-houses or brothels had been given to the War Office, but not presented to the court-martial. Delcassé informed the court in writing that the German Ambassador had come to him to tell him that Schwartzkoppen admitted corresponding with Esterhazy by *petit bleu*. And Du Paty, shown Cuignet's accusation against him, was allowed to rebut it.

But the most important witness was Captain Freystaetter, the junior member of the 1894 court-martial. For a long time Freystaetter had been convinced that Dreyfus was guilty. He had gone on active service to Madagascar soon after the trial. It was not until early in 1898 that he began to have misgivings. Cavaignac's declaration in July had puzzled him. Henry's confession and suicide opened his eyes. He had returned to France in January 1899, determined to say what he knew. The usual delays between government offices prevented his being heard before mid-April, and by that time another judge of 1894, Gallet, had told what he knew. One difficulty lay in the way of hearing Freystaetter. The court had decided by a majority that it had no right to ask the judges of the 1894 trial what, in the privacy of the judges' room, had motivated their finding. During Freystaetter's evidence efforts were made by individual members of the Appeal Court judges to discover if other evidence than that given in the public hearing had been communicated to Maurel, Gallet and the others; each attempt was cut short by Mazeau. Then one of the judges asked whether in evidence Henry had spoken of the *canaille de D* letter. Freystaetter replied: "Only the *bordereau* was discussed at the [open] hearing." It was a vital admission.

By the time they had heard all the witnesses and had read all the evidence, the new Appeal Court judges had in the majority reached the same conclusions as their brothers of the Criminal Appeal Court. The latter sat through the proceedings in dignified silence, trusting to the professional integrity of the newcomers to support them. They were to be justified.

During the proceedings a new quarrel blew up between Delcassé and Freycinet, over Cuignet's impudence in contesting the Foreign Office version of the Panizzardi telegram and his charges of bad faith. Delcassé took the matter up with Freycinet, who had blandly accepted Cuignet's interpretation. A small, energetic quick-tempered southerner, already convinced of Dreyfus's innocence, Delcassé was not going to permit his department to be insulted by a creature of the War Office. He was very sharp with Freycinet, and sent Maurice Paléologue to the Appeal Court with the full record of the deciphering. Paléologue ended his demonstration of the documents by saying: "The version in the War Office file is not merely erroneous, it is false." Freycinet twisted and turned, assisted by Cuignet, for a couple of months before the matter was straightened out.

But Cuignet was not to escape the consequences of his vaporous intelligence. Early in May, Georges Duruy, a professor at the Polytechnic, had been hissed by his students for having written articles in which he begged the Army not to support so obvious a rascal as Esterhazy. Freycinet, frightened by Drumont, had suspended Duruy. Attacked for his weakness in the Chamber on May 5, he had no serious defence and was violently heckled by the Radicals, formerly his supporters. He promptly repeated his usual disappearing trick; he resigned, on the ground that he felt he no longer had the necessary authority to remain in office.

Then, during the debate on his resignation, the Nationalist Deputy Lasies produced in the Chamber copies of the correspondence between Freycinet and Delcassé during March and April. Krantz, who had taken Freycinet's place, recognised that the only person to have read the correspondence was Cuignet, who promptly confessed that he had taken the copies and shown them to the Deputy. Krantz at once relieved him of his appointment and left him "at disposition," roughly the equivalent of half-pay.

On Monday May 29 Déroulède and Habert appeared at the Assize Court. The charge had been watered down to simple provocation against the security of the State. As before in the police court, both judge and prosecutor deflated the claims of the defendants. They allowed Déroulède to parade his extravagances in the box; they heard his witnesses—Barrès, Lasies, Syveton and Quesnay—extol Déroulède's "symbolic action" and their own association with him. They permitted the denunciation of the President of the Republic. But there was no cross-examination of either defendants or witnesses, and in due course the jury acquitted the prisoners.

On the same day the united Courts began the hearing of counsel. They heard Manau the Procureur-Général, Ballot-Beaupré the *rapporteur*, and Mornard for Lucie Dreyfus. All three men were agreed that there had been a miscarriage of justice, all three were equally convinced of Dreyfus's innocence. But there were difficulties as to the line to be adopted. It was open to the court to reverse the finding of the court-martial and order the liberation of Dreyfus without retrial, "if the annulment of the verdict leaves nothing in existence which could be qualified as a crime or delict." This was the course recommended by Mornard. On the other hand, Ballot-Beaupré and Manau, on a detail of legal technicality, considered that the judges should send the case back for retrial. This course was approved also by Clemenceau, since a verdict of "not guilty" by a court-martial would make the victory all the more resounding. Further, Lucie Dreyfus wanted this, as it had always been her husband's desire to be cleared by his peers (he had in 1894 refused to allow Demange to plead an erroneous wording in the indictment). Mornard bowed to her wishes.

The Appeal Court was crowded with journalists and sightseers. The forty-six judges in their scarlet and ermine heard in silence Ballot-Beaupré's long exposition of the case, the whole story of the four years since the arrest of Dreyfus, with the evidence marshalled and discussed. His great difficulty lay in the fact that, to secure a retrial of Dreyfus by his peers, he must produce a new fact which threw doubt on the verdict of 1894. He could not bring forward the illegal communication of documents to the judges, since that would force the court simply to annul the judgment without retrial. In his attempt to find this new fact he had other difficulties. He could not claim that Henry's oral testimony in 1894 was false, since that could not be proved without a trial of Henry, and Henry was dead. The evidence of the handwriting experts was still too conflicting to shake the authority of the *res judicata.* He laid these considerations before the court. (Perhaps it is well to remember that before both Courts, except for questions asked by the judges for the purpose of elucidation, there had been no cross-examination of witnesses, and no confrontation of contradictory witnesses.)

He turned to the "new facts" on which he was calling for the case to be sent back for retrial. First, there was the distortion of what were claimed to be admissions. The documents listed in the *bordereau* were purely hypothetical. The only fact established was that there were other spies and that the leakage had gone on after Dreyfus's arrest. The only remaining question was still the principal one, asked at the beginning and now almost forgotten. "The *bordereau,* the principal basis of both accusation and condemnation, is it, yes or no, in the hand of Dreyfus? Gentlemen, after profound consideration, for my part I have reached the conviction that the *bordereau* was written, not by Dreyfus, but by Esterhazy." A great sigh went up from the audience, and several of the judges wept.

Ballot-Beaupré went on to examine Esterhazy's evidence before Ravary, and showed that he had lied. Before concluding, he spoke of the dangerous defenders of both Dreyfus and the Army, which, "thank God, is above these discussions . . . its honour surely does not require that a man innocently condemned should be incarcerated on The Devil's Island." He did not ask the court to find Dreyfus innocent, but to find that a new fact of a character to establish innocence had arisen. The audience could not restrain their applause, and Mazeau did not attempt to check it.

After Mornard had spoken, the court adjourned for two days to consider its judgment. This evening, as a result of the accusations made by Cuignet before the Court of Criminal Appeal, Zurlinden, on orders from Krantz, had Du Paty arrested and sent to the

Cherche-Midi. It is said that when Picquart had been transferred back to the Santé two months earlier, he had remarked: "It's to make room that I'm being taken from here: it won't be long before Du Paty fills it."

No one knew that, during this crucial hearing of the appeal, Esterhazy in London was being interviewed by a bright correspondent of the *Matin.* On the morning of June 3 there appeared a report of the interview, in which Esterhazy announced: "I am about to tell all the truth; it was I who made the *bordereau.* Yes, I who wrote it at the request of Colonel Sandherr, my superior and my friend. . . . Billot, Boisdeffre, Gonse, knew that I was the writer of the *bordereau.*"

Mazeau considered that the united Courts must return a unanimous verdict if public opinion was to be pacified. The majority of the judges could not simply impute the *bordereau* to Esterhazy, since this would destroy the basis of accusation against Dreyfus and would be the equivalent of a reversal of the original verdict: there would then be no grounds for a retrial. A small minority— six of the forty-six judges—allowed reluctantly that revision could not be withstood but fought over the wording of the judgment. They attempted what was little less than blackmail. They insisted on the insertion of the reason for a retrial, the secret communication of the *canaille de D* letter. This would inculpate Mercier and embarrass the military judges at the second court-martial. The majority conceded the point.

As was to become clear later, this left the new court-martial free to hold Dreyfus the writer of the *bordereau,* or alternatively to decide that Esterhazy was the writer, but that the documents had been furnished by Dreyfus. Almost at the head of the long judgment, appeared:

> Whereas the communication [of the *canaille de D* secret piece] is proved, at once by the deposition of President Casimir-Perier and those of Generals Mercier and Boisdeffre.
>
> Since, in the first place, President Casimir-Perier has stated that he had it from General Mercier that the exhibit contain-

ing the words "*ce canaille de D*," then regarded as referring to
Dreyfus, had been laid before the court-martial.

Since, in the second place, Generals Mercier and Boisdeffre,
invited to say whether they knew that the communication
had been made, refused to answer, and thereby have implicitly
admitted it. . . .

The disappointment of the anti-revisionists, who had believed
that the united Courts of Appeal would reject Mme Dreyfus's
application, caused an explosion of rage. Denounce as they might,
the anti-revisionists could scarcely be taken seriously in their
claim that all forty-six judges had been paid by the Jews. Drumont wrote more shrewdly: "An army which cannot defend its
honour against a gang of Jews will not be able to defend the
country against a foreign invasion. If we could have found a
shadow of manhood in a pair of red trousers, we should have won
the battle. We found nothing, nothing, nothing, only congratula-
tions and handshakes." But Drumont was becoming a bore. For the
rest, the stock of Déroulède was waning, and though a few generals,
most of them on the retired list, made martial noises, no anti-
Republican could seriously rely on any one of them. The only
thing the young Monarchists could think of was to make a scene.
The day after the delivery of the judgment was a Sunday, when the
President of the Republic would appear at the races at Auteuil.
A number of young gentlemen proposed to hoot him when he
appeared. Since they were indiscretion itself, their intentions were
soon known to the ubiquitous Célestin Hennion of the Sûreté.
As before at the funeral of Félix Faure, the Minister of the Interior,
otherwise the Prime Minister, made the mistake of putting the
police anywhere except where they were needed. Loubet, on his
arrival at the racecourse, was greeted with shouts of "Down with
Loubet! Resign!" and shortly afterwards a gentleman rushed up
the steps of the presidential box and knocked Loubet's top-hat
over his eyes with a walking-stick. The assailant was thrown from
the stand by two generals and fell into the hands of the police. He
was identified as the Baron de Christiani. "The good Trublion,"

wrote Mme de Clermont-Tonnerre, "having lunched well and spurred on by a bellicose lady, had betted he would dot President Loubet one and shout 'Down with Panama.' " The well-dressed mob cheered their champion and joined battle with the rapidly mobilised police. Some hundred were arrested. All that Loubet said was: "I'm not hurt; all the same, it's a lesson."

Dupuy and the Préfet of Police had failed to protect the President. Some believed that Dupuy's laxness was deliberate, that he intended to sicken Loubet of office as he had sickened Casimir-Perier. On the other hand Combarieu, Loubet's chief civil secretary and an ex-Préfet (24, 36), believed that it was due to ignorance: that Dupuy was ambitious and calculating but did not know the administrative ropes. It is possibly the wisest comment. In fact Dupuy had failed to bring about the pacification he had worked for, and the policy of treating as childish exhibitionism demonstrations against public officials was now looked on as un-forgivable weakness in a man hitherto regarded as both tough and hard-headed.

The Chamber met on the day after the attack on Loubet, and Dupuy was faced with an interpellation on the scene at Auteuil. For the moment he succeeded in turning the wrath of the Republicans from himself to the Royalists; then the debate veered.

The judgment delivered two days earlier had to all intents accused Mercier of illegality in the Dreyfus court-martial. The Minister of Justice had no alternative to taking action against the former Minister of War. Lebret had therefore addressed to the President of the Chamber of Deputies a letter in which, after quoting the passages from the judgment, he stated that Mercier's action appeared to fall under a section of the Criminal Code, and that under the Constitutional Law of 16 July 1875 it was open to the Chamber to direct the opening of proceedings against him before a court instituted by the Senate. The Chamber should therefore be seized of the matter and required to decide as to the steps to be taken.

Early knowledge of this letter permitted the Right to switch the debate away from the Auteuil incident and to attack Dupuy.

Cassagnac asked whether Dupuy, head of the Ministry in which Mercier had sat, was about to hand his late Minister of War over to the law. Another member of the Right suggested that Dupuy, under the theory of collective Cabinet responsibility, himself stood in danger. In any event the Appeal Court's judgment was not the end of the case; there was the retrial, and until that was concluded no proceedings could be taken. The Chamber passed a vote rebuking the "hateful machinations of the Royalist and clerical reaction," and at the same time one of confidence in Dupuy: only a handful of the extreme Right opposed the first part. The assembly then passed to the discussion of Lebret's letter.

There was considerable perplexity regarding the interpretation of the Constitutional law: should the accusation proceed from the Government or from the Chamber? Ribot raised the point and then sat down. Dupuy, Lebret, Brisson, Poincaré and Barthou remained silent. A private member moved the adjournment until the conclusion of the second court-martial. The Socialists offered an amendment in favour of charging Mercier. The adjournment was accepted by the Chamber. Lastly, in an attempt to wipe out Cavaignac's (and its own) blunder, it voted the *affichage* of the Appeal Court's judgment. At the end of the debate the press of both Right and Left were at one in the opinion that Dupuy must go.

As for the Auteuil scandal, Christiani was sentenced to four years' imprisonment, and seven other demonstrators got a few weeks and minor fines.

The real danger, of which some were aware, was not discussed, at least openly. The Appeal Court in its desire for unanimity had included the damning passage on Mercier. At the retrial of Dreyfus the unhappy officers nominated as judges would in fact have to decide between Dreyfus and Mercier: in freeing the Jew they would condemn the General. Behind this lay the question, for the Government and for the Republicans, what would be the reaction of the Army if Mercier were sent for trial? Short-sighted Dreyfusards expected the triumphant acquittal of Dreyfus; the longer-headed were disturbed. Monod sent on to Reinach a letter from an officer which ran: "Since the law does not require the military judges to state how they arrive at their conclusion, Dreyfus will be condemned . . . he will suffer the revenge of the Army for the insults of the press." The great fault, which the early Dreyfusists had avoided, the identification of the Army with a dozen army officers, became all too apparent. The transfer of the case from the particular matter to the general plane had robbed the case of its precision and had brought in allies interested less in freeing Dreyfus than in forwarding their own political aims.

This might have been less serious had the Government been strong. It was not. Reinach attributes its weakness to the activities of the Radicals over twenty years, and to those of the more recently arrived Socialists, both of whom now asked for strong government, meaning thereby a Government supported by themselves and dependent on them. But he forgets that since the foundation of the Republic it had been a cardinal point that it was the Chambers, particularly the Chamber of Deputies, which ruled. Once only had the Republic seen a strong Government— Ferry's of 1883–85—which had been bowled over in a few hours on an unconfirmed telegraphic despatch. As has been seen (cf. Chapter One), the condition for the survival of a Government was fear, real or imagined, of what would result from its fall, a panic such as occurred in October 1885, in January 1889 and was about to reoccur. As soon as the danger passed, the antipathy to a strong Government returned.

Fear had arisen now as a consequence of the somewhat plebeian demonstration of the young Royalists on June 4. Dupuy had not reacted vigorously, and on June 5 had evaded the issue. Cassagnac on that day asserted the manifestation to have been that of the "People" against the Republic itself. No reply to this grotesque claim came from Parliament: the challenge was taken up, not by Deputies, but by the small Socialist groups of Paris. It was rumoured that the Royalists intended to repeat their behaviour at Longchamps on the following Sunday. The *canaille* prepared to meet them, and prudently they stayed away. Dupuy, however, this time took precautions: large bodies of police and soldiers, the gendarmes and the Republican Guard, were all on hand. From early morning a vast crowd surged towards the racecourse. When Loubet arrived he was greeted with a mighty roar. Otherwise the day passed without disorder, save for a few scuffles with the police on the way home. On the morrow, June 12, the Chamber passed a motion implying no confidence in Dupuy. He resigned.

In this account of the major movements during the months of May and June two lesser but important incidents remain to be recorded. On June 9 the case of Leblois and Picquart came before the ordinary criminal court. Before passing to judgment the court ordered Picquart's release from the Santé: in all he had spent 348 days in detention. On June 13 the court found no case against the two accused. Picquart thus had nothing more to fear from the military on the matter of Leblois, the Secret File and the connected charges. All that remained were the two minor affairs. Zurlinden moreover assured him that he would not be once more arrested and confined in the Cherche-Midi.

Immediately after the delivery of the judgment of the Court of Appeal, a cruiser was despatched to Cayenne to bring back the man who had been in solitary confinement on The Devil's Island for more than four years.

CHAPTER FOURTEEN

Waldeck-Rousseau

DUPUY's defeat tore down the façade which had marked the progressive dilapidation of the political structure since the fall of Brisson in October. The uncertain opportunism of the more prominent leaders of opinion in the Chamber had shaken the groups; they were now without cohesion, without leaders, without policies, without even beliefs. Ribot was seen to be no more than an elegant Frondeur, Méline to have done nothing to refresh his policy of twelve months back, Dupuy to have been an evader: "He was too clever," wrote Lemaître, "with a cleverness that stank too much of his own Auvergne." The Progressists were split. In February, on the occasion of the tabling of Lebret's bill to remove the case to the three Appeal Courts, Poincaré, Barthou and Jonnart had joined the Radical leaders in a note of protest to the Government. Thereafter Poincaré had broken openly with Méline and had founded his own group, the Républicains de Gauche. His friend Barthou at once resigned from the chairmanship of the Progressists and joined him. Thus within the Progressists there were, apart from the Liberals, three sub-groups: those of Méline, Dupuy and Poincaré.

The Radicals were equally disconcerted. Brisson had lost influence. Léon Bourgeois, appointed to represent France at the Hague Disarmament Conference, had joyfully fled there. The Radicals were without direction. Like the Scottish peers at the time of the impeachment of Dundas, "they knew not whither to turn; perhaps it might yet more truly be said, they knew not *when*." They had deserved the ceaseless mockery dealt out to them in the *Aurore* by their one-time leader Clemenceau, who, whatever his political vices, had never lacked courage. Similarly the Socialists were, as always, a prey to warring theories and jealousies. Vaillant and his Blanquists, whose supporters were the small Paris shop-keepers, were patriotic and anti-semitic; they were opposed by the followers of Allemane, Dreyfusists from the first, who cursed Guesde for his coldness. Jaurès, since his defeat in the previous May, had flung himself into the case; his articles, *Les Preuves*, were appearing regularly in the *Petite République*. "His speeches and his interminable articles have not brought him the halo of the author of *Nana*; he came too late. But . . . he has succeeded in grouping, according to himself against a rising neo-Boulangism, all the sects in a Committee of Vigilance. He has changed his note. He no longer works for the social revolution . . . it is all for 'the bourgeois civilisation which the bourgeiosie itself can no longer defend' " (82. xviii. 445).

On Deschanel's advice, Loubet invited Poincaré to form a Government. "With more scruples and less will," wrote Clemenceau, "Poincaré is another Dupuy." For all his honesty and his strict-ness, Poincaré was not a man of bold imagination. Instead of dis-carding the men who had failed, he sought them. Brisson and Bourgeois both refused. Ribot promised his help. For the key post, the Ministry of War, he thought of Casimir-Perier, who had resigned his seat. Casimir, knowing that the Chamber would not accept him unless he were a member, declined. Poincaré began bargaining with the Radicals and some members of Dupuy's Ministry. The Radicals told him clearly that they would not combine with Ribot nor, above all, with his friend Barthou, on whom Poincaré insisted and whom they distrusted. Millerand suggested that he invite the Socialist Viviani, whose talents Poincaré esteemed. Poincaré re-fused to include a Socialist, and then, tiring of bargaining office against office with the Radicals, threw in his hand. His indecision in negotiation had wasted time and increased the tension. He advised Loubet to ask Waldeck-Rousseau, the only figure he could see with the integrity, authority and energy to draw together the fragments of the Republican groups.

Since 1885, when the defeat of the Ferry Ministry, in which he had been Minister of the Interior, drove Waldeck-Rousseau from office, he had taken little part in politics. As a Senator he had hardly spoken, except for his speech against Lebret's bill in February, and had devoted himself to his legal practice, though outside Parliament he had in 1897 played some part in founding the Progressist party. He might be called an enlightened conservative. On one side he was a moderate but unimpeachable laïcist, on another he had been the promoter of the legitimation of trade unions. Moreover he was a revisionist. At no time had he ever shown himself a doctrinaire, far less a fanatic. A cropped head, a short moustache, calm and immobile features, gave the impression of great self-containment and perhaps capacity. "He has a horror of politics," wrote Galliffet to the Princess Radziwill; "he prefers water-colours, in which he is very talented, fishing, shooting, and the position of being the leading barrister in Paris" (46 337). Undoubtedly a sense of duty—he had no need of ambition—led him to answer Loubet's appeal.

His intention was a Cabinet which should embrace all good Republicans. In this he would take the place of danger, the War Office, and to strengthen himself he proposed to appoint as the chief of his military secretariat a soldier against whom the Army could utter no reproach: General the Marquis de Galliffet, Prince de Martigues.

Galliffet was now sixty-nine and retired. Slim and upright though limping from old wounds, he had a bronzed red face, the features and impassivity of a battle-axe. His fame was widespread as the leader of the last forlorn charge of the remnants of Margueritte's cavalry division at Sedan, with his cheerful reply to General Ducrot: "As often as you like, sir, as long as one of us is left." His caustic and ribald tongue was equally well known; he spared neither himself nor the aristocratic society from which he came. His single passion was the efficiency of the Army. It was Gambetta's care of this that had made Galliffet a Republican from the seventies, and he had never wavered in his loyalty. He had quarrelled with Boulanger, whom he despised, and at the enquiry on Picquart he had spoken warmly on his behalf: both actions had earned him the hatred of the Nationalists. One other thing damned him. During the bloody week of May 1871 he had been the

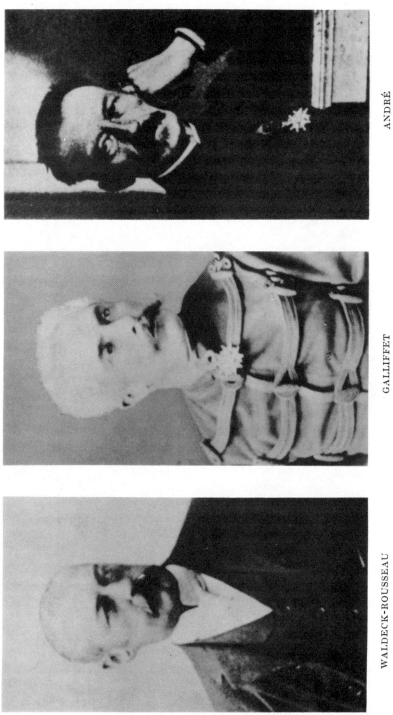

WALDECK-ROUSSEAU

GALLIFFET

ANDRÉ

ROGET

BOISDEFFRE

The Rennes Trial

GONSE

GRIBELIN

executioner of many Communards. Possibly the story was exaggerated, but it remained as a legend in Paris. He had never troubled to deny it.[1]

At some point—the date is uncertain—Waldeck-Rousseau invited Arthur Ranc to become Minister of the Interior. Ranc refused. As always, he preferred to work behind the scenes.

Then, on Reinach's and perhaps Ranc's advice, Waldeck invited Millerand. Millerand at this time was Jaurès's right hand. Originally a follower of Clemenceau, he had joined the Socialists in 1893. Unlike his leader Jaurès, he was not an eloquent speaker. His speeches were invariably appeals to reason—he was a member of the Paris Bar—and contained no fanciful flights. Until Henry's suicide he had been an anti-Dreyfusard: since then he had been a strong partisan of revision. He was at this time a convinced Socialist: his speech at Saint-Mandé in 1895 in favour of Collectivism had given him the reputation of a dangerous man. But he was in fact without prejudices. Alone perhaps of the Socialists, he was evolving from intransigent opposition towards statesmanship. A broad, heavy-shouldered man, with the head of a bull and a thick mat of dark hair: "He looks like a docker," said Caillaux. Millerand accepted the invitation.

Having secured what he considered two key men, Waldeck then invited the three members of the Dupuy Cabinet who had opposed Lebret's bill—Delcassé, Delombre and Leygues—and at the same time offered Poincaré the Ministry of the Interior. But these asked for more portfolios for their friends, including that of War for Krantz, an anti-revisionist. Waldeck gave up hope and retired.

Loubet hastily summoned Léon Bourgeois from the Hague, but Bourgeois, having failed to secure Galliffet, refused. Loubet thereupon once more pressed Waldeck, who received some vague promises of Radical support from Bourgeois, and at the same time was being urged on by his fellow-Senators. Beginning again, he

[1] At one of the Bixio dinners in November 1899 he said that his A.D.C. told him it was said that he had had thirty-five thousand federals shot. "That's a lot. How many do you think I had shot?" "Perhaps two hundred." "Well, it's useless to say two hundred; that will need explaining. Thirty-five thousand needs no explanation" (21, 123).

took both Millerand and Galliffet, now making the latter War Minister, and transferring himself to the other danger-point, the Interior.

The Socialist groups, when Millerand told them of the offer to himself, were on the whole in favour. But Vaillant, while not objecting to Millerand's acceptance, refused to give him the blessing of his group. None, not even Millerand, as yet knew of the inclusion of Galliffet.

This time Waldeck had no difficulties over his team. He included Delcassé and Leygues from Dupuy's old Ministry, both of whom were members of Poincaré's group. The rest were men who had never held office, but they included one retired ambassador, Decrais, and one ex-governor-general, de Lanessan. Two—Caillaux at Finance, and Baudin at Public Works—had been members of the Chamber for only a year, and both were under forty. Millerand was given the Ministry of Commerce. It was a Ministry of talents, but it was inexperienced. From Waldeck's point of view this was a merit; in his own house he would be master. To head his secretariat he appointed Demagny, a tough, hard-headed Préfet, trained by Constans.

As soon as the names of the Cabinet were announced there was a scream of horror from all sides. Méline's Progressists declared that the admission of a revolutionary, Millerand, was the surrender of the citadel and that they would at once attack. Many leading Radicals went up in flames at the prospect of Galliffet, but the Socialist Radicals decided to back the Government. Vaillant and his twelve Blanquists broke away from the other Socialists when these proposed to support a Cabinet containing the executioner of the Communards.[1] The Right, of course, called it a Dreyfus Cabinet sold to Reinach.

The great question for Waldeck was how far the rank and file of the Chamber would be swayed by these pronouncements, how blind they would be to the consequences of his immediate fall, to

[1] The evidence on the Socialists' debate is conflicting. It can be found in *Mouvement Socialiste*, February 15 (Vaillant), April 15 (Jaurès), May 1 (Vaillant) and June 1 (Lagardelle) 1901.

the anarchy which would follow, and again, how much part would be played by personal egotism and ambition.

On his return home on the evening of the day he took over the Ministry of War, Galliffet found Boisdeffre there, and immediately told him that while he and Gonse could never again be employed, they would not be touched. "No reprisals, I have made it a condition." Boisdeffre thankfully accepted the reprieve. Recently he had asked Father Du Lac for his blessing on one who was awaiting the firing-squad.

The Cabinet came before a threatening Chamber on June 26. Poincaré, Barthou and Aynard,[1] a strong Catholic but a Dreyfusist, had worked, and were still working, among the Progressists to secure deserters from Méline. The entrance of the new Ministry was greeted with a howl. As they walked to the Government seats, the Nationalists, the Extreme Left and part of the Radicals welcomed the hobbling Galliffet with shouts of "Murderer." (Later he said: "Pourquéry de Boisserin called me 'assassin' for three-quarters of an hour. I answered: 'Assassin? Present.'") In his declaration of policy Waldeck said very little. He asked for nothing but for justice to be permitted to fulfil its task in entire independence. He was at once attacked by interpellations. Mirman, the ambitious Radical professor, dragged up all the gutter slanders of the past against individual Ministers. As a Government supporter, Viviani answered: "These men came when the others fled. There are not three policies before us: there is defence of the Republic; there is treason. Choose." And he complimented Millerand on having understood the meaning of responsibility.

The report of Waldeck-Rousseau's reply in the Official Journal transcript is little better than fragments, such was the tumult that beset him. A few phrases were caught at intervals in the pandemonium. He stood for an hour attempting to say some eight hundred words, and at last left the tribune.

Pelletan had declared that between Galliffet and the Right he would not vote. Brisson—a haggard, sick man—climbed to the

[1] Aynard had consulted Lépine, once more Préfet of Police, as to how he should vote.

stand. "And I will tell you why I shall not abstain! The Government proposes to defend the Republic. I give it my vote. I ask all
those on whom I may have any influence to vote, I do not say for
the Government, but for the Republic." It is said that he raised
his arms and made the Freemasons' sign of distress.

The Chamber voted. More than sixty members abstained, but
the Ministry got home by the narrow majority of twenty-five. A
week later, on July 4, Parliament rose. For three months—the
months during which Dreyfus was to stand his second trial—the
Cabinet was safe.[1]

[1] In the Senate the Government declaration was read by Monis, Minister of
Justice, and accepted by an overwhelming majority.

CHAPTER FIFTEEN

Up to Rennes

1

WHEN on June 9 Dreyfus was taken on board the *Sfax*, although no longer a convict he was still in custody. He was placed in a cell but was allowed to exercise twice a day on deck. He had no communication with the ship's officers, though one lent him books and at the Cape Verde Islands gave him a newspaper in which he read of the arrest of Du Paty.

The Government (still Dupuy's pending the formation of its successor) had originally ordered the *Sfax* to Brest, but fearing demonstrations diverted the cruiser to Quiberon. It was a judicious action; Syveton of the Ligue de la Patrie Française had hastened to Brest with the intention of working up a riot. The *Sfax* was off Quiberon on the evening of June 30. At midnight, in drenching rain and a strong wind, Dreyfus was transferred by pilot-boat to the shore, where he was taken over by the director of the Sûreté, Viguié, and brought in the utmost secrecy by train and carriage to Rennes. He arrived while the city was still sleeping and was taken to the prison. A few hours later Lucie Dreyfus was shown into his cell. It was the first touch of humanity he had received for nearly five years. Thereafter she saw him daily, and a little later Mathieu Dreyfus and his other brothers were admitted.

He had borne his fifty-odd months of confinement on the grim rock with immense fortitude, but they had taken their toll of him. Solitary confinement and the silence of his jailers had robbed him of the faculty of ready speech; he could not easily recall words, and after listening for ten or fifteen minutes he was unable to follow what was being said. Furthermore, he knew next to nothing of his own story. The censorship had forbidden all mention of his case in the letters from his family. He knew only of Henry's suicide and the arrest of Du Paty. He had never heard of Picquart, or Scheurer-Kestner, or Zola. All the confusing detail of the past four years had to be explained and made familiar to him before the opening of the court-martial. He appears to have recovered fairly rapidly, although he suffered from the northern climate. It is doubtful whether he was really fit to stand his trial in August.

On July 3 he had his first interview with Demange. He had brought with him Labori, who had begged to be allowed to support Demange in the defence. Mathieu Dreyfus believed that the younger lawyer would be an admirable complement to the prudent and circumspect Demange. It was an error of judgment. It soon became apparent that the differences in temper and temperament between the two lawyers extended to differences over the strategy and conduct of the case. Demange had learned something of courts-martial; he advised circumscribing the case within the question left open by the Appeal Courts' judgment, the exact discussion of the material evidence and no hostility to the witnesses. Labori itched for a dramatic thundering battle. The two counsel were soon at cross-purposes.

2

While the advocates were discussing the documents with Dreyfus, the anti-revisionist world was busily engaged in the spreading of rumour. Quesnay de Beaurepaire had a seemingly inexhaustible store of inventions, none of value and many ridiculous: any rogue with a story, plausible or implausible, was able to gain his ear, frequently also his purse: by the end of July he had a list of witnesses prepared to offer the most damning testimony against Dreyfus. In contrast to Quesnay's publicity, Mercier according to the Dreyfusards was quietly circulating the story that he had in his possession one of the photographs of the invincible document: the *bordereau* annotated by the Emperor William. No one admitted having seen it; many professed to know someone who had. It was widely rumoured that Mercier intended to produce it: he did not deny this.

The two members of the Government officially involved in the case—the Prime Minister and the Minister of War, Waldeck and Galliffet—were agreed that no governmental pressure must be exercised on the court, and that no directions as to the conduct of the case, other than adherence to the questions left by the Appeal Courts, must be given to the military prosecutor, Major Carrière. "We are agreed," wrote Galliffet, "in wishing the Dreyfus trial to be judged in perfect freedom. As Minister of military justice, I could have sent general directions to the *parquet* of the court-martial. I renounced my right. The more they fling themselves at Dreyfus, the better his chance of acquittal, if he is innocent." And again: "Even before the court has been constituted, the president is committing irregularities, which would permit all annulments if Dreyfus is condemned. At other times I would easily intervene, but in the present circumstances I must act carefully lest the Government be suspected of partiality" (46, 338). Though it was within the rights of the Government to order Carrière to drop the charges against Dreyfus from the indictment, he could take them up again in his opening address to the court. His orders, in fact, were to avoid touching on any point on which the combined Appeal Courts had given a decision: on these he was to call no witnesses, "under penalty of excess of powers and [consequent] annulment."

This scrupulous prudence was perhaps unwise. Furthermore, Galliffet would not even appoint a civil legal adviser to guide Carrière. The anti-Dreyfusards filled the gap by sending him the notorious lawyer Jules Auffray.

The Dreyfusards had persuaded themselves that the trial would be a mere formality, leading to a triumphal acquittal. Many of the more violent were looking forward to the reprisals they would exact. Galliffet warned Reinach of the clumsiness of his allies, "too susceptible, too much in a hurry." And the more experienced Waldeck was far from sure. On July 16 he wrote that "the accused had only a few chances" (46, 338). Even these would be reduced if the Dreyfusard journalists continued to abuse the Army, and if the lawyers did not confine themselves to the matters left open by the

Appeal Courts. Galliffet believed that the military judges, "with not a single ill thought, would incline to give their preference to the soldiers' evidence."

The anti-revisionists jeered at the Dreyfusards, who had always called for full light on the case, for accepting the Government's directions to the commissioner not to wander outside the questions left by the Appeal Courts. Clemenceau, in touch with the ardent Labori, was foolish enough to accept the challenge and to claim that all questions relevant to the case should be reviewed. Nothing could have been more rash. For example, the combined Courts had rejected the testimony of Lebrun-Renaud and held that the story of Dreyfus's confession was without foundation. The question therefore should not be touched, and Carrière had subpœnaed no witnesses. The defence committed the colossal blunder of calling Lebrun-Renaud, and thus reopened the question.

At the same time Carrière made his own intentions clear by summoning all the witnesses hostile to Dreyfus, but not those, such as Freystaetter and Hartmann, who before the Appeal Courts had testified in his favour. By the time the court-martial sat, the judgment of the Appeal Courts was as good as forgotten.

3

Outside the narrow field of the legal proceedings, the Government had acted promptly from the hour the Cabinet was formed. The leading government counsel, who had behaved so weakly, as it seemed, at the trial of Déroulède and Habert, were transferred to places of less influence. Lépine was reappointed Préfet of Police in place of Charles Blanc, who had signally failed to protect Loubet. Galliffet dismissed Zurlinden from the military governorship of Paris, and Brugère, who had been attached to the military secretariats of Presidents Grévy and Carnot, was given the post. Roget was transferred from his brigade to another at remote Belfort. Several senior generals who were rash enough to make speeches implying that it was the duty of officers to be hostile to the Government were either removed from their appointments, reprimanded or told to hold their tongues.

Before the fall of Dupuy, Zurlinden had given instructions to proceed against Du Paty. This unhappy man had now become the scapegoat for all the sins of the War Office. He was charged with the forgery not only of the *Blanche* and *Speranza* telegrams and of the *Blanche* letter, but also even of the *faux Weyler* and the *faux Henry*; the last on the accusation of the now quite cracked Cuignet. In addition, he was accused of communicating the *canaille de D* letter to the *Eclair* in 1896, of giving the still unidentified "liberating document" to Esterhazy, and finally of anything else "that might be discovered." All the charges were found baseless in a couple of days. He was freed, and wisely retired to a sickbed, from which, such was his foolishness, he wrote privately to Mercier insisting that the version he had given to Gonse a year earlier from memory of the deciphering of the Panizzardi telegram was correct.

Almost simultaneously a War Office enquiry into the activities of the deceived Pellieux in the Esterhazy case led to his transfer from Paris to Quimper.

By this time the personnel of the Statistical Section had changed completely from the days when Picquart first saw the *petit bleu*. Henry was dead, Picquart a civilian. Lauth had returned to his dragoon regiment in November 1898, Junck was awaiting the court-martial before being sent to Madagascar. Gribelin had been transferred to the less exciting climate of Dunkirk. But the new members were no less resolute to defend the Section. It was now headed by Major Rollin, who had served on it six years earlier, with Captain Mareschal—he too had fallen under Henry's spell: he had accompanied the body of the suicide to Pogny churchyard—and Captains François and Fritsch. Against Picquart to a man, they were filled with the tradition of the Section and rancorous against their enemies.

4

"Defence of the Republic" had been the theme of the Prime Minister's speech on June 26, and of those who supported him. The words had been eagerly seized on by his opponents, who had tried to show that, by the inclusion of a Socialist as Minister of

Commerce, Waldeck-Rousseau was in fact compromising, indeed betraying, the Republic he pretended to defend. On both sides the speeches were like Captain Boldwig's estate—all very high and mighty and noble. But had they any validity? Was the Republic in any danger, and if so from whom?

As has been seen, in dealing with Déroulède, Dupuy had refused to take him seriously, and Dupuy's contemptuous attitude had been adopted by the more serious press. The patriotic agitator had taken the slight very ill: he would show them that he was not a man to be trifled with. The adjurations of his friends made him all the keener to start again. He believed that there was mass discontent. That there was discontent is possible, but its remedy was not to be had through Déroulède. In the Army there was anger at the abuse from such men as Gohier. Marchand, now back from Africa, was touring France making speeches against the weakness which had led to the evacuation of Fashoda. Mercier was becoming the pillar of the Ligue de la Patrie Française. In June Déroulède was approached by an agent of the Assumptionists, who offered him the help of their Catholic electoral committees, "Justice-Egalité." In the same month he received from the friends and agents of the Duc d'Orléans offers of support, collaboration and cash. It went against the grain that he, a Republican, should accept help from the Royalists; nevertheless he hardly repulsed them, and they decided to put all they could at his disposal, and to leave the disentangling of the alliance to the future. The Bonapartists followed them. It was a repetition of the Boulanger episode of 1888–89, but Déroulède was not "*un brav' général,*" but merely a battered minor poet with an uncontrollable tongue and a weak voice.

During the spring Jules Guérin of the Anti-Semitic League had purchased—with, it is said, money supplied by the Duchesse d'Orléans—a house in the Rue Chabrol, near the Gare du Nord, which he had fortified. It was here that during May and June the Royalist committees and a number of Deputies of various political shades met. So inept were they that they were quite unaware that among the conspirators were several police spies. Déroulède himself was a fountain of indiscretion. Moving from platform to platform, calling on his audiences, many of which seem to have been rigged, to recognise the auspicious hour, to come down into the street and revolt, he was convinced that he had a national following. The cheers he was given by happy holiday-makers at the Longchamps review on July 14 persuaded him that he had the people behind him. He assumed that the Army was with him, although he had not secured the support of a single general; for that matter, no general could be sure that he would be followed by either his officers or his men. Déroulède went on noisily preparing his stroke.

On August 4 he appears to have warned his friends and the Royalists that he would "march" either on the day when Mercier gave his evidence at Rennes or on the day of the verdict. He himself remained in Paris and saw to the mobilisation of brigades of patriots about the city, but he seems to have given no warning to a single one of the men he expected to appoint to high office when his *coup d'état* was accomplished. The trial at Rennes began on August 7, a Monday; Mercier was to testify on August 12.

Warned by Lépine of what was on foot, on August 10 Waldeck summoned a nervous Cabinet and rapidly obtained their approval of the steps he intended to take. That evening he and Lépine compiled the list of those to be arrested. At dawn on August 11 the majority, some hundred in number, were taken in their beds, Déroulède at the top of the list. Thiébaud, the Bonapartist, got away over the roof. Habert, who was not sleeping at home, went into hiding. Guérin, also not at home, fled to "Fort Chabrol" and barricaded himself inside with a group of his leaguers. André Buffet, the pretender's chief agent, was recognised trying to cross the frontier and arrested. The single Royalist Deputy involved, Ramel, was left at liberty.

So concentrated was public attention on what was happening at Rennes that this police operation caused not a tremor of excitement. Few believed in the existence of a plot. Indeed, with all the Royalist and Nationalist Deputies still at large, with no move from any army officer, it was a little difficult to believe in it. The sole sign of trouble was Guérin and his fourteen braves in the Rue de Chabrol. For several days they were left alone, it being believed that they would surrender to the police: they spent the time marketing. When summoned on August 15, Guérin made a bombastic refusal. Waldeck rejected a suggestion that the house should be stormed. On August 20 two groups—one of Anarchists who had no contact with Guérin, the other of anti-semites—rioted in the neighbourhood, and the police had a rough ride before breaking up the mobs. From that date the Fort became a sight for idlers and tourists. Nationalist papers tried to work up sympathy for the garrison; but no one was roused save Cardinal Richard, who foolishly and unavailingly visited the building on September 1. On September 20, eleven days after the Rennes verdict, Guérin surrendered, his hungry garrison being on the point of rebellion.

The satisfactory aspect of the business was that, by forestalling Déroulède, Waldeck had ensured tranquillity during the trial. Did he seriously believe that the Republic was in danger? Probably not; the whole thing was too fatuous; but very properly he was taking no chances. The greatest sufferer appears to have been Galliffet. Several members of his club—the Union—had been arrested. "Although nothing more than a soldier Minister, I am obliged to share the responsibility for all actions of the Ministry to which I belong. It isn't possible to belong to a club whose members are arrested—it's not clubbable. That seems to me so obvious that I've sent in my resignation, from a club of which I've been a member for thirty-three years" (46, 340).

CHAPTER SIXTEEN

Rennes

1

It has been said that the choice of Rennes as the place for Dreyfus's retrial was made by Dupuy from a malevolent desire to make it difficult for Dreyfusards to attend in strength, and thus proportionately increase the weight of the Nationalists present. The accusation is probably without foundation. Rennes was within reach of Paris, but not too easy reach; it was within range of a number of ports, which would allow the rapid transfer of the prisoner from shipboard to jail: it was not likely to offer opportunities for rioting. The headquarters of an army corps, the seat of an archbishopric, of a university and of the main Court of Appeal for Brittany, with a population of some seventy thousand, it was a quiet, stately eighteenth-century city—it had been burned in 1720 and rebuilt in uniform style. Some think its aspect severe, but in summer the creamy stucco of the walls catches and throws back the sun, making it a city of light. "In this antique city," wrote André Siegfried about 1910 (77, 101), "the nobility of Upper Brittany . . . find the aristocratic atmosphere they enjoy. Their sons attend the law schools; army officers discover a fashionable garrison. The Boulevard de Sevigné, the Rue de Paris, constitute a small-scale Faubourg Saint-Germain, in which the nobility lives apart and isolated. The upper-middle-classes of tradition, another aristocracy to-day almost extinct, scarcely mix more in the life of the town. . . . And the religious atmosphere of the West, the penetrating sound of bells morning and evening, the preoccupation with the affairs of the Church, haunting even to its enemies . . . invade the whole encircling air." Rennes was reactionary, and thus anti-Dreyfusard. Life had been made very difficult for two professors at the University who had taken the wrong side. Scandal was cried

when Lucie Dreyfus took rooms in a hotel: she was forced to remove herself, and at last was taken in by a humane woman, who
later was made to suffer for her charity. Mercier, now on the retired
list, was the guest of another retired general, the Comte de Saint-
Germain, the same who presided over the enquiry which had condemned Picquart in February 1898.

<h2 style="text-align:center">2</h2>

The commander of the Tenth Army Corps, General Lucas, had
wisely ordered the court-martial to be held in a room in the
ordnance stores, which would have limited the audience to the
shorthand-writers. Under the violent protests of Labori and the
journalists, he was compelled to move the court to the Lycée, to a
room large enough to accommodate several hundred. By August
1899 there was scarcely one foreign country that was not passionately absorbed in the Affair. Distinguished journalists from
all corners of the world descended on Rennes. There were MM.
Jules Claretie, Jaurès, Viviani, Maurice Sarraut and Varennes.
There was M. Maurice Barrès, who so recently had declared that the
case was beneath his notice, now quivering with bilious hatred and
ready to believe the worst of anybody. There was Mme Marguérite
Durand of the *Fronde*, accompanied by the beautiful revolutionary,
Mme Séverine. The *Daily Mail* sent G. W. Steevens, sometime
Fellow of Balliol and brilliant war-correspondent, *The Times*
W. R. Fullerton, and representing a Vienna paper was Karl
Liebknecht, the revolutionary German Socialist. Several crowned
heads had sent their private observers, and towards the end of the
trial there came from England, on behalf of Queen Victoria, the
Lord Chief Justice, Lord Russell of Killowen. But alas! above the
medley of passionate partisans, officers, Socialists, Nationalists, reporters, politicians and crooks, hovered the impish spirits of
Messieurs Bergeret and Dooley, who were to make the French the
laughing-stock of the civilised world.

The officers appointed as judges were, with the exception of the
president, all gunners, capable of understanding the technical
evidence—a contrast to the trial of 1894. The president, Colonel

Jouast, was on the point of retiring from the Engineers, a brisk old soldier with an enormous flowing white moustache and an eyeglass, who beneath a peremptory manner concealed a balanced mind. The rest—Lt-Col. Brongniart, Majors Merle, de Bréon, Profilet, Captains Parfait and Beauvais—were, so far as was known, little interested in politics or religion, except de Bréon, a believing and practising Catholic whose brother was a priest and a Dreyfusist. Only Beauvais, a dark, round-headed man with black protruding eyes, appeared to be seriously interested in the case; later he said that he alone had studied the dossier, sitting up until two or three in the morning and rising again at five to refresh his memory. None the less, they had all read much about the case and had discussed it. Being officers, they naturally took the side of the Army, and knowing little of civilians distrusted them. From the beginning their minds were loaded with suspicion and to a great extent with doubts as to the good faith of the Courts of Appeal.[1]

The prosecuting officer, Major Carrière, a dull and obtuse man, being about to retire, had begun a new career by becoming a law-student: he was somewhat in the state of a first-year undergraduate, but outside the court he was enthusiastically coached by the violent Nationalist lawyer Jules Auffray, who, like Labori, saw himself as a dynamic politician, a view shared by the electorate only once in thirty years. The War Office representative, Galliffet's liaison officer, was Colonel Chamoin, perfectly upright, but completely lost in the maze of procedure and the wilderness of documents.

The disagreement between Demange and Labori as to the conduct of the case had already become acute before the opening of the trial. Demange, from his experience of the first court-martial, well aware of the contrast between High Court judges trained in the weighing of evidence and untrained officers with their rough justice, perhaps also sharing Waldeck-Rousseau's opinion as to the unlikelihood of an acquittal, believed that the wisest course was to keep the case rigidly within the circle of Alfred Dreyfus and the *bordereau*; it was better to fill the minds of the judges with doubts

---

[1] De Bréon was probably more suspicious than the others. He had been the victim of the forger in the La Boussinière case, referred to on p. 75.

than to rouse their hostility by irrelevant appeals to public opinion, or great abstract principles. Labori, on the other hand, apart from his desire to repeat the personal success he had enjoyed at Zola's trial, thought that the strategy should be to dramatise the case, to shake and excite the audience, to appeal to the world and over-whelm the judges with the force of public opinion—in short, not to seek justice for one individual but to challenge the Army system. In spite of the efforts of Mathieu Dreyfus to harmonise their re-spective strategies, their differences were in the end to weaken the defence.

3

The August heat in Rennes is not conducive to prolonged clear thinking. Only the mornings were to be devoted to the trial, from 6.30 to noon. In the bare classroom of the Lycée the judges sat behind a table on a raised dais, while, for some unexplained reason, General the Comte de Saint-Germain, Mercier's host, sat behind them, squat, apoplectic and objurgatory. To the left of the judges was the seat for the defendant, and behind his chair sat his counsel, Demange, plumply benevolent, and Labori, an excited greyhound. Facing the judges were the shorthand-writers and the audience, chiefly journalists virulently hostile to each other.

At seven o'clock on the morning of Monday, August 7, Alfred Dreyfus, wearing the uniform of an artillery officer, was led in. The moment was dramatic. Here was the man over whom many had quarrelled for long months, over whom families were split, over whom friends and lovers had parted, but whom few had ever seen in the flesh. "There came in," wrote Steevens (56, 65), "a little old man—an old, old man of thirty-nine, a small-statured, thick-set old man in the black uniform of the artillery. Over the red collar his hair was gone white as silver, and on the temples and back of the head he was bald—a rather broad large-featured face, with a thrusting jaw and chin. It was not Jewish until you saw it in pro-file. The eyes under the glasses were set a trifle close together." It was a hard face until the sweetness of his smile changed it com-pletely. This description of a neutral may be put beside that of an

PALÉOLOGUE AND DEMANGE

LABORI AND PICQUART

The Rennes Trial

BERTIN-MOUROT
AND BILLOT

CAVAIGNAC
AND DE SAINT-GERMAIN

DREYFUS GIVING EVIDENCE AT RENNES

On left is Captain Beauvais and on right Demange and his junior counsel

enemy, Barrès (11, 143). "Dreyfus seems to me to-day completely
inoffensive. Either because he has suffered much sunstroke, or
because he is progressing towards general paralysis, or again, he
may possibly have some creeping affliction; he is done for. Certainly his defenders, the Laboris and Picquarts, are much more
dangerous. He no longer has the slightest intelligence; he is a
puppet."

After the clerk of the court had read the formal documents the
witnesses were told to retire. Colonel Jouast then asked the
accused a number of questions as to his guilt, the *bordereau* and the
documents mentioned in it, of which naturally he knew nothing,
and about the details of his private life. Jouast pressed him closely
on the matters he might have known and the information he might
have had. Dreyfus answered briefly and clearly with his habitual
military courtesy. He denied at some length his alleged confession
to Lebrun-Renaud and recalled his refusal, to Du Paty, of Mercier's
overtures.

The court rose soon after ten o'clock and went into secret
session for the examination of the now gigantic Secret File. This
occupied the next four days. It was not until Saturday, August 12,
that the hearing of the long list of witnesses, more than a hundred,
began.

The Rennes court-martial was not a trial: it was a spectacle,
sometimes a farce. All the important evidence had already been
heard by the Appeal Courts. That which was added was of little
moment. Several witnesses had volunteered or been pressed by
Quesnay de Beaurepaire. The earlier witnesses once more repeated their old stories with variations. Casimir-Perier came first,
followed by the War Ministers and the generals; Cavaignac in a
grey frock-coat and a Muller cut-down, "a tiresome prig with his
eternal protestations of Roman virtue," still clinging to the
alleged confession (56, 96); Billot struggling to prove that Picquart wasted the secret service-funds on frivolous investigations.
There was Roget, "this white Mephistopheles," with his waxed
moustaches, his jaunty air and his inexhaustible loquacity; "he
obviously intends to make his career by getting Dreyfus condemned,

and since he alone is not defending his actions, it looks the worse" (56, 111). There was Freycinet with his little fluting voice, talking vaguely of the thirty-five millions which the Syndicate had brought into France, but totally unable to provide the slightest evidence: "As we all know," wrote Fullerton, "he is incapable of giving an honest yes or no." There was Boisdeffre, still dignified and courteous in spite of his disaster. There was Gonse, now on half-pay, refusing responsibility for anything, lying and lying again to cover his errors, giving his friends away generously, driven to admit that he had falsified testimony, but claiming that it had no importance, driven again to admit that so little had he thought of Dreyfus's confession that he had never mentioned it to Picquart. There was Cuignet, bursting with crack-brained theories. There was Picquart "slouching up to the bar in an ill-fitting morning-coat. . . . Without hesitation or confusion he explained the case for seven hours and a half" (56, 123–25). There was Bertulus, vividly recounting his interviews with Henry, and suddenly checked by Mme Henry's cry of "Judas!" There were Lauth and Junck, both tall and athletic, giving their evidence for the fifth or sixth time without hesitation, doing their utmost to discredit Picquart. Lauth, remarked Steevens, was cool, ready and resolute: "If he was lying, he was the master liar of the world" (56, 146). But by this time none of these men who had so often told their tale was consciously lying; they had written and learned their parts, and their rôles had become second nature to them.

Beyond these there was a confusion of minor characters. A number of officers embroidered to their taste chance conversations with Dreyfus. A colonel appeared who had once got mixed up with a spy: after some time it was discovered his story had nothing to do with the case. A gentleman testified that he was shown round Potsdam Palace and in the Kaiser's private room he saw a newspaper with the words written on it in large letters, "Captain Dreyfus is a prisoner." Does he know any German? He does not. An officer told how, meeting Dreyfus accidentally on a station platform, Dreyfus asked, "Any news?"; it was highly suspicious. Another man stated that he had told Cavaignac of meeting Dreyfus in Brussels, that sinister city of spies, and that Cavaignac had pressed him to testify. Dreyfus readily agreed that they had met, at the time of the Exhibition. When was that? In 1886!

A retired officer insisted that he, Dreyfus, and all the staff learners of 1894 had known as early as May 17 in that year that they were not going on manœuvres. He and Roget quarrelled openly, but he made a deep impression on the audience. There was a group from Mulhouse come to assert and to deny that Dreyfus attended German army manœuvres. There were now ten hand-writing experts, each with his own system, all contradicting each other. There were the commissioners from the Sûreté, Tomps and Cochefert. Cochefert owned that, had he seen Esterhazy's hand-writing, he would have warned the Minister of War to be very careful. Tomps related how Henry prevented him from talking to the spy Cuers at Basle and how later, in order to discredit Picquart, he tried to make Tomps say that the copy of the *bordereau* printed in the *Matin* had not come from Teysonnières. Tomps also de-molished the Statistical Section's story that Picquart, in order to help Dreyfus, had put in hand the shadowing of another man; the order had come from Sandherr. Out of the testimony of these two men was to grow an underground quarrel between the Section and the Sûreté, with political consequences.

Once more the artillery experts Deloye and Hartmann met, and Hartmann had the better of the controversy. Colonel Cordier, now retired, cheerful and irreverent, told the court what he and Sand-herr really thought of Henry, and explained the methods of the Section, to the dismay of the audience. At the end a half-witted cunning Austrian adventurer named Cernusky was introduced by the efforts of Quesnay. After a good deal of argument he was heard *in camera*, when it was found that all he could offer was a rag-bag of lies.

Two well-known personages did not appear, Esterhazy and Du Paty. From London Esterhazy first said he would come, then said he would not, since the court-martial was resolved to acquit Dreyfus: besides, he had no money. During the trial he sent letter after letter from the National Liberal Club, or from 40 Upper

Gloucester Place, to Roget, who, after the first, handed them unopened to Jouast. Eventually he addressed Jouast directly, in a
letter full of threats and abuse. Hence, in place of his oral testimony, his empty deposition before the Court of Criminal Appeal
was read.

Du Paty, armed with medical certificates, stuck to his sickbed,
and there submitted to an examination by a representative of the
War Office. He merely repeated his earlier statements, and since
he was neither examined nor cross-examined, his deposition contributed nothing.

One figure dominated the trial—that of Mercier. He gave his
main evidence on August 12, and thereafter he remained in court,
ready to protest, ready to intervene, ready to confront. By August
1899 he had lived with the case for nearly five years. He had long
convinced himself that Dreyfus was guilty and that he, Mercier,
had, by his action in 1894, saved the country. "He has become
hallucinated," wrote Galliffet on the evening of August 12. "He
thinks France is incarnated in his person . . . but all the same he is
an honourable man (46, 339)." To Labori, who had carelessly used
a term implying that he was being examined as an accused person,
he haughtily took up the word: he was an accuser. Until the Courts
of Appeal stripped him of the weapon of silence, he had never
admitted the truth about the communication of documents to the
judges of 1894. Now, although he cunningly tried to imply that
Sandherr was the artisan of the scheme, he did not hesitate to
justify what was done. He led up to his dramatic moment carefully. While dealing with the documents, he mentioned here and
there pieces of gossip which tended to show that the Kaiser took a
personal and active interest in espionage. Then came his major
declaration. Casimir-Perier, he said, had referred to the "somewhat
unusual" approach of the German Ambassador: "but he did not
say that he, the President of the Republic, the Prime Minister and
I, waited from eight in the evening until half an hour after midnight
in his office at the Elysée, to know if peace or war were to issue from
the exchange of notes. I had ordered the Chief of Staff, General
Boisdeffre, to wait for me at the War Office with the officers re-

quired, should need be, for the despatch of the telegrams ordering the preparatory measures for mobilisation to be put in hand. You see that we were within measurable distance of war" (7, 1, 97).

Casimir-Perier insisted on being heard and indignantly tore the story into fragments. Mercier had seen him on the evening of Dreyfus's degradation, the night of January 5, but his interview with Münster had taken place on January 6. And on January 6 Boisdeffre was not in Paris. In any case there had been no controversy likely to lead to war. Moreover Dreyfus had by now been condemned. Unabashed, Mercier merely said that if it was not on January 5 or 6, then it was some other date. He hit on December 12, but on that date Casimir-Perier had not yet been told anything about Münster's remonstrations with Hanotaux. Mercier refused to give way. The "historic night" had certainly occurred, and he called on Boisdeffre to support him, which in due course Boisdeffre did. Few seriously believed the story, and yet some residue of it remained to perplex.

On other matters Mercier was equally reckless. Having at last been driven to admit the illegal communication of documents in 1894, he denied that the Panizzardi telegram was among them, but included Panizzardi's letter about the French railway organisation written three months after Dreyfus's degradation. And he suddenly produced a new document: a copy of a letter alleged to have been written by the Austrian military attaché, Schneider, saying that the German and Italian military attachés admitted Dreyfus's guilt. As soon as he heard of it, Schneider from Vienna telegraphed his denial of what he claimed to be a forgery. By that time Mercier's statement had been accepted. On a statement by Freystaetter that a shell had been mentioned in the biographical note on Dreyfus, Mercier turned the question on to the mention of a particular shell. At the same time he did his utmost to blacken the honour of the honest Freystaetter. On the statement of another officer that he had lent Esterhazy a primitive form of director in 1894, Mercier turned up with a director of 1899 to demonstrate that anyone could procure one. Fertile in invention, resourceful, *rusé*, he continually widened the battle-front, staging ambushes, mounting counter-attacks, always in the breach. The yellow, lined face never quivered, never expressed disturbance. The thin lips never hesitated. The slow, passionless monotone of the voice never changed. Unscrupulous as he had been, he never flinched; he remained what he was, a bold soldier and a monomaniac. Perhaps his adherents recognised a touch of lunacy in the unshakeable fighter. "He sees nothing," remarked one journalist, "lost in endless reflection." By now he believed what he had scarcely believed five years earlier. At the end of his first morning's evidence he turned towards Dreyfus and said: "If the slightest doubt had entered my mind, I should be the first to declare and say before you, to Captain Dreyfus, that I was mistaken in good faith." Dreyfus rose and cried: "That's what you ought to do!" and on Mercier attempting to continue, said huskily: "It's your duty!" Amid the excited hubbub of the audience Mercier coldly repeated his sentence. By that small demonstration, early in the proceedings, he put the trial in its true perspective. The verdict must be for Dreyfus or for Mercier.

One card only he did not play, the famous photograph of the annotated *bordereau*. The anti-Dreyfusard editors, Drumont, Rochefort, Meyer of the *Gaulois*, all called on him to produce it. He did nothing. If—which is doubtful—the photograph existed, Mercier was certainly wise enough to know that it would be destroyed as evidence in half an hour: much better allow it to live on in rumour.

4

Only those who knew the case intimately could have drawn any conclusions from the chaos of facts, fictions, truths, half-truths, opinions, suppositions and contradictions. Sometimes the audience heard evidence of fact, sometimes evidence of conjecture, sometimes evidence of evidence of an opinion. English journalists, used to the strict interpretation by High Court judges of what is and is not permissible, sat aghast as hearsay of hearsay was poured out by garrulous witnesses. The audience heard of the secret dossier, documents from it were quoted or misquoted, but its contents still remained a mystery. The proceedings were without reality.

Jouast, secretly convinced that Dreyfus was innocent, and therefore more indulgent to the witnesses for the prosecution than to those for the defence, failed to keep the hearing to the point. No doubt he was unskilled, but he was not helped by counsel. Labori was absent for the second week. In the early morning of August 14, while on his way to the court, accompanied by Picquart, he was shot in the back by an unknown man, who fled before hands could be laid on him and vanished into the country. The wound was not severe and Labori was able to return on August 22. His subsequent conduct of cross-examinations was not calculated either to bring out the truth or persuade the judges. His attacks on witnesses, his apostrophes, undoubtedly rubbed them up the wrong way. Demange, quieter, more deeply read in the case than Labori, secured better results. "Like a *maître d'hôtel* offering the turbot, he presented his remarks to Zurlinden and Chanoine, who did not see the trap beneath the parsley, and when he had shown them the horror in the dish, with what an air of good temper he drew the attention of the judges " (12, 173). The transcript of the proceedings reveals that neither counsel was a skilled cross-examiner. It may well be that the mediation of the judge between counsel and witness, as Lord Russell remarked, often made their questions ineffective, yet a skilled cross-examiner could have done much better than they in fact did. But the root of their failure lay in their permanent disagreement as to strategy, Labori wishing to dominate and bully the hostile witnesses and demonstrate to the audience that they were liars, Demange aiming to throw such doubt into the minds of the seven judges that they would find the charges not proven.

Day after day Dreyfus sat patiently listening to witness after witness. He was a sick man. He could eat little and lived chiefly on milk. He was often shaken by fever. And it is probable that his battered mind often failed to follow the bewildering nonsense which was being retailed from the witness-box. Once or twice he was driven to protest against some wilful distortion. Once (it was on the question of whether he had attended German manœuvres) he asked for a question to be repeated, hesitated over his reply, and, according to Steevens, left an impression of imperfect frank-ness.

In the fifth week little was left except small fragments of argument between experts on minor points. Labori, theatrical as ever, attempted to secure the testimony of Schwartzkoppen and Panizzardi, and receiving no replies, telegraphed to the German Emperor. All that was returned was an official note drawing attention to the formal denials of Münster and Bülow in 1894, 1895 and 1898, that at no time had any German agent had contact with the accused.

On September 7 Carrière for the prosecution asked for a verdict of Guilty. Labori gave up his right to plead. Demange addressed the court on September 8 and 9. "Before he had spoken two sentences," wrote Steevens, "you saw that here was a master. Not a great emotional orator, but a great pleader, a master of his business, which is to persuade." He spoke for seven hours and was never monotonous. Russell of Killowen (40, 320–21) thought that Demange was mistaken in treating the evidence as honest; that to confine himself to treating the question of Dreyfus's guilt as not proven was unjustifiable, and that he should have appealed to public opinion. Russell was surely wrong. Courts-martial, as much in England as in France, up to 1914 and after, were travesties of judicial tribunals, and moreover at Rennes the appeal, the real appeal, was not to any public, but to seven army officers whose minds were burdened with army sentiment.

Demange ended at noon on September 9. Carrière asked to reply and spoke after lunch. It is said that Carrière consulted Jules Auffray, and that he, guessing that the judges, or a majority of them, would shrink from sending Dreyfus back to The Devil's Island, and would therefore acquit, suggested to Carrière a middle course. Thus in his reply, instead of merely asking for the usual sentence, which would have sent Dreyfus back to The Devil's Island, Carrière reminded the judges that they could, if they wished, add a rider of extenuating circumstances.

Demange made a brief rejoinder. Dreyfus, asked by Jouast if he had anything to add, could only utter a few broken sentences: he was innocent . . . the honour of his children. . . . The court retired.

Only those versed in the case could have given a decisive verdict of Not Guilty. The French in the audience were partisans, their minds already long made up. Among the neutral observers Russell seems to have thought the prosecution's case not proven, Liebknecht believed Dreyfus guilty, Steevens was unable to make up his mind. The judges had listened through five weeks to the confused medley of testimony. They were not lawyers, they were not even skilled, as were the reporters, in listening and observing. Now they must declare. On all sides they had been watched. It was known that de Bréon had been worked on by his Dreyfusist brother, the priest; he was seen frequently going to church to pray: he was known to be racked by conscience: his old friend, one of the leading Royalists, Villebois-Marueil, had attempted to reason with him. Major Merle was in tears at the end of Demange's speech. Major Profilet, on the other hand, although a poor man with three daughters, was believed by the anti-Dreyfusards to be perfectly reliable: "We are sure of him, although he's poor." Jouast throughout had shown himself favourable to the prosecution witnesses and rough with those of the defence.

After the judges retired there was a long pause. Everyone knew that the verdict was in doubt. What in fact occurred is known from Captain Beauvais, who about the middle of 1901 confided in a friend, who passed the story on to Syveton (11, 213). There appears to have been no discussion before voting. Jouast started, according to convention, with the junior officers. Beauvais, a dyed-in-the-wool anti-Dreyfusard, and Parfait voted Guilty. So did Merle and Profilet. De Bréon: Not Guilty. Brongniart then said Guilty. Jouast had apparently expected Brongniart to vote the other way. He burst out: "What! you think there are proofs? You think there are even indications?" and himself put down Not Guilty. Parfait, it is said, then suggested that they should start again. Jouast refused, since it would be illegal; but he at once took up the question of extenuating circumstances. Beauvais—rightly, since he believed Dreyfus to be guilty of treason—fought fiercely for twenty years' imprisonment, Jouast for five, which would have meant immediate release. At the end of an hour's heated discussion, Jouast secured five votes for the rider of extenuating circumstances, and an agreed penalty of ten years' detention.

They returned to the courtroom a little before five. Scarcely able to master his voice, Jouast delivered the verdict—Guilty by a majority of five to two. The audience seemed stunned; there was no demonstration. Demange and Labori burst into tears. Dreyfus, waiting in another room, was informed of the verdict by Labori, Demange being too overwrought. He said simply: "Console my wife."

5

It has been suggested by Reinach that those who voted Guilty were swayed by the introduction in secret, by or through Mercier, of the photograph of the *bordereau* with the notes and initial of the German Emperor. In support of this (47, VI, 203, *et seq.*) he cites the accounts given to Mornard and Jaurès by a Dr Dumas, of conversations with Major Merle in 1902. Even though one refrains from calling in question the bona fides of Merle's questioner, who was a passionate Dreyfusard, nothing solid emerges from the conversations. Merle admitted that what had led him to a conviction of Dreyfus's guilt was not entirely the facts that had appeared *"au grand jour."* The phrase might apply merely to those parts of the evidence heard *in camera*, and have no reference to the photograph. Dumas relates (47, VI, 211) that he spoke of the photograph and that Merle seemed "stunned and frightened" and answered: "Nothing of that kind should be mentioned; it might get abroad"; and: "Don't talk about it: I don't wish to speak of it." (*"Il ne faut pas parler d'une affaire pareille; elle pourrait surmonter sur l'eau"* . . . *"Ne parlez pas de cela; je ne veux pas en parler."*) Merle in his deposition of 19 May 1904 gave a somewhat contrary version of the conversations.

There is, however, no need to go deeply into the allegation. The answer lies in the behaviour of the court itself. If the photograph was shown to the judges and accepted as genuine, how was it that Jouast and de Bréon voted for acquittal, and how then did Jouast persuade three others to join with him in the rider of extenuating circumstances? The account of what happened, given by Beauvais (11, 211–13), implies that the usual court-martial procedure was followed; that is, the president without discussion passed immediately to the vote. There is no place here for the insinuation of the photograph; nor does Beauvais, the hot anti-Dreyfusard on the court, mention it. The only alternative possibility is that it was shown to a few uncommitted judges privately outside the walls of the court, but strangely in that case it was not shown to the obviously wobbly de Bréon. Furthermore, why was Auffray so uncertain at lunch-time on the last day that he persuaded Carrière to draw the attention of the judges to the possibility of extenuating circumstances?

Again, the rider of extenuating circumstances—what extenuating circumstances could there be for a guilty traitor?—could have been accepted by Brongniart, Merle and Parfait only if in their hearts they knew that they had voted from motives other than those of pure justice.

It is unlikely that the evidence, either that which was true or that which was false, played an influential part in the condemnation. The verdict sprang from the inescapable dilemma which faced the judges: Dreyfus or Mercier. The ethos of the Army lay in the belief that one's senior is always right and must be implicitly obeyed. Whatever their personal feelings, they must vote for Mercier.

Moreover there were personal considerations. There was the pressure of wives, dreading the social ostracism that would follow acquittal. Jouast was on the point of retirement: he had nothing to fear. All the others knew that their future careers depended on the verdict they gave; on it depended accelerated or delayed promotion. Beauvais in his account said that Profilet, in spite of being a poor man with three daughters, could be reckoned on to vote against acquittal: Profilet voted for condemnation and against

extenuating circumstances. It is said that the Army was influenced by religion. This Republican opinion is denied by both
officers and priests; and the one judge who was a sincerely religious
man, de Bréon, voted Not Guilty.

The pressure on the judges to recondemn Dreyfus came not
from any weight of evidence, but from their fear of inculpating
senior officers. Soldiers, filled with the spirit of hierarchy and
solidarity, filled too perhaps with hatred of the civilians who
attacked the Army, they could only vote for Mercier. They
should not be blamed. The case, as Sorel says, was vitiated by
its very nature.

6

Of the many interested parties not present at Rennes, none
waited for the verdict more anxiously than Galliffet and Waldeck-
Rousseau. Galliffet, receiving a daily report from his representative,
Colonel Chamoin, had foretold a condemnation almost from the
beginning. "I believe that Labori, by his continuous outbursts,
has done his client the worst of service. All my reports confirm
this impression. . . . In the judgment, Dreyfus matters little to me;
you know that I've never known anything about his case, and he
has never seemed to me a sympathetic character. What alarms
me is that France will be condemned by Europe: it will be painful
to me to think that the cradle of every liberty will be accused of not
tolerating one" (46, 340). It is said that Waldeck-Rousseau desired an acquittal. As an individual he may have done so: he
certainly dropped well-intentioned remarks to Reinach, but perhaps they should be discounted. For, as Prime Minister, however
much he may have believed in Dreyfus's innocence, he could see the
consequences of a verdict of Not Guilty. Galliffet had already
written to Princess Radziwill that he would support Mercier in all
circumstances, but Lebret's letter of June 5 to the President of the
Chamber, containing the charges against Mercier, had only been
adjourned pending the decision at Rennes. If the Government,
faced by an acquittal, reopened, as it must do, the case against
Mercier, Galliffet would resign and the Government would then

be defeated, with incalculable consequences. The best, indeed the only, solution likely to bring peace was the "condemnation of favour," that is condemnation by four votes to three, which would permit the prisoner's liberation and bar attempts to reopen the case. It might be an injustice; it would at least solve the political problem.

On the day before the verdict—Friday, September 8—Galliffet wrote to the Prime Minister at length on the consequences of a second condemnation (47, VI, 579–80). What he said may be briefly resumed as follows. If Dreyfus is condemned by a large majority, the revising court, in case of appeal, will, from solidarity with the Army, refuse to recognise errors of law or procedure. If, as Waldeck seems to think, the matter then goes to the civil Courts of Appeal, there will be the verdict of two courts-martial against the verdict of two Courts of Appeal. Every foreign country will condemn us with extreme severity, but many revisionists, tired of the struggle, will accept the verdict. "Let us not forget that in France the majority is anti-semite." Thus on one side there will be the whole Army, the majority of Frenchmen (leaving apart the Senators and Deputies) and all the agitators; on the other, the Cabinet, the Dreyfusards and the foreigner.

Neither Galliffet nor anyone else could have known whether the majority of Frenchmen was anti-semite: indeed, the great majority, outside what may be called more or less intellectual circles, seems to have been indifferent. It was, however, at once made very clear that the foreigner was anti-French. The Italian and German Foreign Offices had already shown their resentment at some of Mercier's allegations against their representatives. "It is just to say," wrote Lord Russell (40, 317), "that, in its comments during the actual sitting of the court, the British press, from *The Times* upward or downwards, almost without exception have indulged in such partisan comment as would have earned for their editors at the hands of English judges prompt committal to prison, had any such comments been made during a trial pending in England." The Germans, Dutch, Belgians, Italians were no less explosive. In many foreign cities French consulates were besieged and stoned.

A number of hostile journals suggested that the Paris Exhibition of 1900 should be boycotted. The French began to think that their only friends in the world were the Russians, and even they were doubtful. In England, Valentine Chirol, under the pseudonym of "Verax," himself of Catholic upbringing, started a correspondence in *The Times* with a violent attack on the Catholic Church and Catholic education. In the United States Mr Dooley gave his friend Hennessy an uproariously funny travesty of the "historic night" of General Mercier.

7

Waldeck-Rousseau's problem was not one of justice. Dreyfus's counsel had considered filing an application to appeal on a number of legal grounds. It was perfectly certain that it would be rejected by the military revising court. After that an application to the Appeal Courts could come only from the Minister of Justice. But this would at once demonstrate that the Government was taking sides, and, as Galliffet had already pointed out, such action would merely restart the whole weary circle of trials: "a third court-martial would condemn him six to one, a fourth unanimously. It is in the state of mind of the Army; one can't hide it from oneself" (46, 220). The War Minister was moreover highly disturbed by the general unrest and indiscipline among the officers: whatever solution was found, it must be one that did not inflict a further injury on their *amour-propre*.

Waldeck consulted Lucie Dreyfus's counsel, Mornard, as to whether there was any means of quashing the verdict without recourse to a third trial. Regretfully they could find no method. The only release possible was by way of pardon. Would it be politically possible? On this same morning the members of the court-martial met and unanimously agreed to forward a memorial to President Loubet asking that the ceremonial degradation, required by the law, should not be repeated.

On this same Sunday a group of Dreyfusards met at the office of Ranc's *Radical*. Reinach, knowing nothing of the consultation of Mornard by Waldeck, said that the only way out was by Presidential pardon. Clemenceau and Jaurès were bitterly opposed; they wanted the prisoner to appeal and endure his trials until an impartial court appeared. Clemenceau declared that when the whole people had been roused in defence of justice, it was immoral to ask it to be satisfied with an act of mercy. Reinach was supported by several journalists returned from Rennes, who said the soldiers expected pardon and were not hostile to the idea. On the next day Mathieu Dreyfus, now back from Rennes, said that his brother would not survive his sentence and that an immediate pardon was necessary.

Reinach and Mathieu therefore sought the Prime Minister. Waldeck welcomed their approach and agreed to a pardon as soon as possible, provided Dreyfus withdrew his appeal. Mathieu at first refused on the ground that his brother would be left open to the charge that he had accepted a just condemnation. Millerand, who now became the link with the Cabinet, persuaded him to yield. Jaurès, under the weight of the solid proletarian common sense of his party-paper's editor, Gérault-Richard, gave way, and in the end Clemenceau, growling, surrendered.

One further difficulty had to be overcome. Loubet, in a speech on August 24, when he thought an acquittal certain, had rashly said that all would accept the verdict. Naturally he shrank from so precipitate a *volte-face*. The pardon was postponed for a week. Galliffet also insisted that, while he would propose the act of clemency, there must be initiated a bill of amnesty for the generals and other officers involved. Otherwise he would not answer for what might occur in the Army.

On September 19, in response to a formal letter from the Minister of War, Loubet remitted the balance of the sentence on Alfred Dreyfus and cancelled the order for his degradation. To the disgust of the Dreyfusards, the Minister's letter foreshadowed an amnesty for the other actors in the case.

On the same evening Dreyfus was brought by the Director of the Sûreté to Nantes, where he met Mathieu. A day or so later he reached the house of one of his sisters near Carpentras, to begin his convalescence. In accepting the President's act of clemency, he nevertheless claimed the right to use every means in his power to establish his innocence.

Also on the same day Scheurer-Kestner, who had given so much to the cause of justice, died at Luchon.

Two days later, on September 21, Galliffet, without consulting the Cabinet, sent directly to the corps commanders and to the newspapers a manifesto:

> The incident is closed! The military judges, surrounded by the respect of all, have given their verdict in complete independence. Unreservedly we defer to their judgment. Equally we defer to the action which a sentiment of deep pity had dictated to the President of the Republic. There should be no question of reprisals whatever.
>
> Therefore, I repeat, the incident is closed. I ask you, and if it were necessary I should order you, to forget the past so that you may think only of the future. With all my comrades I heartily cry, "*Vive l'Armée*," which belongs to no party, but to France alone.

The incident was far from being closed, as a large number of people hastened to tell him.

CHAPTER SEVENTEEN

The Politics of Liquidation

1

AT Carpentras, Dreyfus endured a slow convalescence from the physical and mental ordeal to which he had been subjected. He was racked with rheumatic pains; for two years he suffered from fevers and nightmare. To the anger of the majority of the Dreyfusards, he refused to lend himself to the campaign against the generals or the Army. His single desire was to be acquitted by his peers and to be reincorporated in the service. He had given Mathieu Dreyfus permission to withdraw his appeal against the Rennes verdict only after much argument, and he intended to pursue his rehabilitation with all the means open to him. The more violent Dreyfusards, whether crusaders or opportunists, were disgusted that, by his reluctance to be made the spearhead, he was denying and deserting his supporters. Clemenceau, exasperated that his principles and his ambitions should both be thwarted, was outraged: "Dreyfus may busy himself with Dreyfus; well and good. We, we think of our country dying under the implacable evil of the Roman sect and under the imbecile brutality of a sword which is powerless against the foreigner." For the younger idealists from the University, who had fought the anti-semite gangs in the street, Charles Péguy wrote bitterly: "We might have died for Dreyfus; Dreyfus has not died for Dreyfus" (41, 95–96). Dreyfus refused to be either bullied or persuaded to abandon his aloof and dignified stoicism. To Julien Benda he once remarked: "These people who are always groaning over my sufferings oppress me. What I like is to talk objectively about my case." And, adds Benda: "I understood his condemnation" (13, 202). Far more important for the victim than this summons to violence was the need to discover one new fact which would permit him to lodge an

appeal to the civil Appeal Courts. Only after long and cruel dis-
appointments was he to discover the clue that would lead him
through the maze of legal procedure befogged by politics, and reach
the centre.

2

The pardon was no more than the preliminary act in the process
of cleaning up the Affair. During September Galliffet and Waldeck-
Rousseau were carrying out a number of operations for which no
parliamentary sanction was necessary. The Prime Minister rejected
Méline's request that he should summon the Chambers. There was
urgent work to be done. Moreover he must study the new situation
and settle his policy.

Before the conclusion of the Rennes trial Galliffet had considered the suppression of the Statistical Section. Lauth and Junck
were back with their regiments: the officers who had succeeded
them had become inoculated with their tradition, now sanctified
by the martyrdom of Henry; their practices had been divested of
all respectability by the revelations of Mercier, Roget and Gonse
at Rennes. Furthermore, in what they believed to be the interests
of the service, they had monkeyed with the funds at their disposal;
they had financed the abduction of Bastian before the Rennes trial,
and they had played some part in the introduction of the lunatic
buffoon Cernusky. Faced with dissolution, they put up a strong
case for survival, and Galliffet, to his subsequent mortification,
was persuaded to allow the Section to live. He contented himself
with minor reforms. On September 13 he relieved Henry's successor, Rollin, of his duties and replaced him by his junior,
François. On the same day he handed the duties of counter-
espionage over to the Sûreté, where they were given to Commissioner Tomps, the hated detective who had refused to enter into
Henry's schemes. The Section was henceforward confined to the
business of providing information regarding foreign military developments, but was forbidden to deal directly with foreign
agents. Furthermore Galliffet prohibited any future touching of
the Dreyfus case.

A fortnight later, on September 29, he published a decree stating that, in future, promotion to the rank of general was reserved to the War Minister alone. Formally it was merely the reaffirmation of the earlier practice. Galliffet's action was intended not only to cow the senior officers, but also to reassure Republicans of his own unimpeachable republicanism.

On the day before Loubet signed Dreyfus's pardon, Waldeck laid before the Senate the cases of the men arrested on August 12. In their preliminary examination the Senators decided that there was sufficient evidence to warrant the charge of an attempt against the State by some twenty of the prisoners; the other forty-five were released. The trial took place before the High Court of the Senate between November 9 and January 4, in a series of noisy hearings. It was soon evident that there was no substance in the plot, and that no serious preparations had been made except by the adventurer Guérin. Déroulède, his friends and witnesses, all joined in a long and dreary act of *cabotinage*, insulted the Senators and behaved like ill-bred children. In the end the great majority of the "conspirators" were acquitted, somewhat contemptuously. Déroulède and André Buffet were condemned to ten years' exile, and Marcel Habert, who surrendered in December and was tried later, to five. Guérin, the Duc d'Orléans's mercenary, the only formidable member of the group, was given ten years' imprisonment. It was the end of Déroulèdism as a force: it survived as a minor idea to be kept academically alive through the discussions of Charles Maurras as to whether a *coup de force* was still possible.

On November 11 the police moved into both the central and provincial offices of *La Croix*, seizing in the Paris house, among other things, nearly two million francs, the political war-chest of the Assumptionists. A full examination of the activities of this Order was put in hand.

3

Superficially the situation of the Cabinet appeared precarious. Its majority in June had been very narrow. Since then nothing had occurred that seemed calculated to increase it. The correspondence of Galliffet shows that he at least believed that the Government could not survive: "formed of sectaries such as Millerand and Monis —I speak of the most sectarian—from the moment the Chambers are summoned it cannot last." Save Waldeck, not one of the Ministers had any parliamentary following, while the enormous range from the conservatism of Galliffet to the socialism of Millerand made the Cabinet highly vulnerable. To weld a majority in the Chamber it was necessary to take account of the claims of the Socialists and to make some concessions to social welfare. It was no less necessary to smooth the susceptibilities of the Radicals with their insistence on individualism and the principle of private property. At the same time, since the support of the Progressists who had backed the Government in June had been given rather from disgust at the blunders of Méline and Dupuy than from love of the Cabinet, it was necessary to avoid taking up any of the peculiar doctrines of the Radicals and Socialists, for example the adoption of income-tax.

On the other hand, the Cabinet had been put in to clear up the Affair and to bring the restless army officers back to normal behaviour; the Army also must be soothed and brought to order. Pacification of a kind might be secured by a general amnesty covering the generals, but the restoration of discipline could not be achieved in a moment: "Little subalterns," wrote Galliffet, "say they won't obey such or such a general because he has submitted to War Office orders." He himself was far from being loved. His rough sallies over many years had made him enemies. His outspoken contempt for Boulanger had not endeared him to the Nationalists. His comments on soldier politicians, such as Billot, were well known. His well-advertised belief that the Army was rotten did not encourage corps commanders to love him. His no less well-advertised distrust of the Russian Army and the Russian alliance could not fail to make him odious to the circles in which Freycinet and Hanotaux moved. He had relieved two generals, Négrier and Zurlinden, of their commands. He had sent Roget to a garrison far away from Paris: "General Roget talks well, but he talks too much," he told the Chamber in November, and it is unlikely that he minced his words in private—he did not in his letters—in speaking of the Right's hero, Mercier, "this raving lunatic." By the Left this aristocrat, this executioner of the Communards, would be supported only just so long as he remained the enemy of the Right.

A further difficulty was Millerand. In spite of his undoubted capacity, he had been given no better a portfolio than that of Commerce, regarded as a technical rather than a political Ministry. The intention had been to secure the support of the Socialists without frightening the other groups, but over the appointment the Socialists had already shown that they were divided. Millerand had to prove at once that he was still a Socialist and yet not one. His embarrassment was demonstrated in October by two contradictory speeches at Limoges and Lille. In the first he warned his audience against believing that Socialism could be brought about by the stroke of a magic wand; it lay in the future through evolution and could not be hastened by force or violence. At Lille he produced a new edition of his notorious speech at Saint-Mandé in 1896, assuring his hearers that Socialism was advancing day by day and would finally be achieved by the conquest of public powers. Neither speech was intrinsically revolutionary, but in the ears of many Deputies, perhaps of the majority, the mere suggestion that Socialism might succeed was revolutionary, and on the lips of a member of the Government menacing.

Yet the situation was less insecure than it appeared. In spite of their divisions over Millerand, the Socialists perceived that they could for the first time become part of the Government forces. The Case had done much for them. As Reinach remarks with great truth: "There sprang up a whole bourgeois Socialism, a whole university Socialism, which dates, which emerges, from the Affair." They could look forward to becoming a Government party, and to everything that goes with that position. "Never did men adopt quicker the good and bad practices which are contracted on the fringes of power, when power's responsibilities and profits are shared. As long as their association with the Republicans lasted, never were politicians more politic, never opportunists more opportunistic" (47, VI, 26). Although three months later the delegate at the Socialist Congress voted the resolution that no Socialist should participate in a bourgeois Government, the party in the Chamber would not fail for another five years to uphold a Government of the class enemies. "Everything," wrote the disillusioned Dreyfusard Charles Péguy, "everything begins with a *mystique* and ends with politics. The founders come first, but the profiteers come after them" (41, 204).

Much the same was to be said of the Radicals. On the one side they hated the Socialist doctrine. "If the Collectivist society became a reality," said Camille Pelletan, "I should be the first to escape from it." They remained impenitently individualists, and as individualists their tendencies were divergent. As has been seen, between moderate Radicals and advanced Republicans there was little difference; similarly between Socialist Radicals and Socialists the difference lay in the extent of Socialist aims. In reality few Radicals were embarrassed by questions of doctrine. Their electors were not the proletariat of the great industrial cities, but the shopkeepers, artisans and peasants of the country towns, who would vote for the man they knew and would accept from him the vaguest of declarations. The one persistent doctrine of Radicalism was anti-clericalism. Waldeck-Rousseau was undoubtedly anti-clerical, so too were most of the members of the Cabinet. If Waldeck-Rousseau were beaten, it was almost certain that a Progressist Cabinet based on Right and Nationalist support would succeed. Hence Radical tactics must be to support the Government and urge it towards anti-clerical measures. "Good policy," said Sorel, "consisted in preparing in secret for the 1902 elections and meeting them with a programme against the congregations" (54, 40). They could look forward with some confidence. Until Méline's Government the Freemasons had as a rule put their organisation, such as it was, at the service of the Republicans, but Méline's tacit acceptance of the support of the Liberal Republicans, the Ralliés and clericals of the Right—in fact of the whole policy of the Ralliement—had forfeited their support; they switched to Radicalism. How effective were the Grand Orient and the other

Rites it is perhaps impossible to estimate; but the Grand Orient alone had forty thousand members in five hundred lodges, and it was the only body with an organisation able to serve a political party.

There was thus between the Ministry and the two Left-wing groups a mutual interest in the Cabinet's survival. The Tartuffes of 1898-99 had become the most militant of Dreyfusards. A programme which conveyed any hint of Socialism, or led out the Radicals' favourite hobby-horse, income-tax, would result in the desertion of the Left Republicans. The terrain chosen for the fight was therefore the old battleground of Public Instruction, and here the religious orders would once more be challenged. As has been remarked, "Old General Hokum leads an unbeatable army."

Thus, on facing the Chamber on November 16, Waldeck-Rousseau put forward what amounted to a very moderate programme. While disclaiming any intention of attacking the secular Church, he proposed to deal with the many unauthorised congregations. He would not suppress the free schools, almost all of which were supported by the subscriptions of devout Catholics, but for the future all candidates for public service would have to have attended a State secondary school for three years; this would deprive the Jesuit colleges of the candidates for Saint-Cyr and the Polytechnic. There would be amendments of a liberal nature in the regulation of trade unions, and Millerand would examine the case for pensions for working-men. For the Army, in future common-law crimes would be tried, not by courts-martial, but by the ordinary civil courts, while appeals from the verdict of courts-martial would be laid before the civil Appeal Courts.

During the debate he was challenged on Millerand's recent Lille speech, which his interpellator claimed was in direct contradiction to his own declarations against Socialism. Waldeck replied that he required no member of his Cabinet to sacrifice his own personal opinions, that he himself had not changed his, and that the Cabinet would be judged by its acts. Méline vainly accused him of selling the pass he had sworn to hold, but the Chamber gave him a vote of confidence by a majority of upwards of a hundred, four times greater than the vote of June.[1]

Having obtained his vote of confidence, Waldeck now proceeded to what he hoped would be the liquidation of the Dreyfus case. On November 17, in the Senate, he tabled an amnesty bill; or rather since an amnesty bill for a number of minor crimes, put forward in the previous year by Dupuy's Government, was still under consideration by the Senate committee, he tacked on to it a supplementary paragraph covering all crimes and misdemeanours connected with the Dreyfus case, or included in a prosecution relative to any of the trials. Further he added another clause to extinguish all pending legal actions connected with the case.

As would appear later, it was a casual, almost skulking method of proceeding. Moreover it was grossly unjust, since it covered all the illegalities and irregularities of the past five years, but deprived the most injured of all means of redress. As if to underline the

---

[1] A comparison of the voting on June 26 and November 16 shows that some 120 members changed sides. The two main groups were Socialists and Progressists. Some seventeen of the former who had registered their disapproval of Galliffet by abstaining, chiefly Vaillant's followers, now voted for the Government. Some twenty Progressists, who had either voted against the Government or abstained, now voted for it, while a dozen more who had voted against it now abstained. However, the Deputies for a number of hitherto unimpeachably Republican departments would not support Waldeck. Almost all the fourteen Deputies from Meurthe-et-Moselle, Vosges and Belfort, the frontier constituencies, were hostile, and to a lesser degree those of Meuse and Haute-Saône, while the members for the highly conservative Republican Seine-Inférieure, outraged by the inclusion of Millerand, persisted in their refusal to support the Cabinet. The vote of November 16 registered the schism in the Republican Party which had ruled France since 1877. The more conservative and Catholic members joined the Opposition and formed the Republican Federation (1902), while Waldeck-Rousseau's supporters joined the Républicains de Gauche formed by Poincaré in the spring, later to be known as the Ministerial Republicans, of which the extra-parliamentary body would be the Alliance Démocratique formed in 1902.

Léon Blum in his *Souvenirs sur l'Affaire* (16, 105–8) severely but rightly criticises the Radicals for their attitude from January 1898 to June 1899, but he is wrong in saying that their internal divisions nearly caused the defeat of Waldeck-Rousseau on his first appearance as Prime Minister. Half of his supporters were Radicals, and not more than twenty-five per cent of the party abstained or voted against him. At the same time Blum excuses the Guesdists and Vaillant's Blanquists for exactly the same attitude, on the ground that they considered this the correct parliamentary tactic. In that case it is a little difficult to see how they differed from the Radicals.

odiousness of the proposal, all cases of Dreyfusards against civil parties were immediately adjourned: Reinach's case with the widow Henry, Picquart's against Vervoort of the *Jour* for printing a faked photograph of him in conversation with Schwartzkoppen. From the Dreyfusards went up a howl of protest, immediately answered by another from the anti-Dreyfusards, since Waldeck-Rousseau refused a suggestion from a member of the Senate committee that the amnesty should be extended to Déroulède and his co-defendants, now appearing before the High Court of the Senate. The project indeed resembled the Act of Forgiveness and Oblivion of Charles II, forgiveness of enemies and oblivion of friends. Regardless of the fact that all the Dreyfusard journalists were fulminating, the anti-Dreyfusards developed the theme that Picquart and Reinach were the authors of the scheme.

In January 1900 were held the elections for the renewal of a third of the Senate. Mercier was invited to stand by the Right politicians who practically controlled the electorate in Loire-Inférieure. With characteristic audacity he accepted the invitation, but made it a condition that he should not be expected to join in the ordinary party struggles: he would stand as a Nationalist and patriotic candidate. The Breton nobility, Royalist and Catholic, with behind them a century of rebellion against the Republic, humbly accepted the terms of the arrogant Republican and free-thinking general. He obtained some seventy per cent of the votes. His election was perhaps less significant than the defeat of three Dreyfusist Senators, Ranc, Thévenet and Jules Siegfried. The country was not yet converted to Dreyfusism.

In this same month the Assumptionists were dissolved by order of the court, but the dissolution was deferred until the government bill on the congregations became law. There was little sympathy for the Fathers. They had been disavowed by the Archbishops of Rouen, Tours and Avignon, whose diocesan authority they had refused to recognise. Unfortunately the Archbishop of Paris, Cardinal Richard, modest, ascetic and mystical, unwisely offered publicly his condolences to the brotherhood. Leo XIII, through the mouth of Monsignor Touchet, Bishop of Orléans, found it necessary to deprecate such manifestations, which were likely to be looked on as meddling in politics. Some of the more bellicose prelates ignored the warnings from Rome, made public protests and were in consequence temporarily deprived of their salaries. The astute directors of *La Croix* and their other paying publications had already formed a lay company to take over the press. Under Paul Féron Vrau *La Croix* continued to flourish, but the more dubious activities of the society were abandoned. Possibly more than any other body the Assumptionists had contributed to the failure of the Ralliement. They had created the impression that democratic Catholicism could exist only by the encouragement of the grossest superstition, lending weight to Renan's dictum that Catholicism causes transcendent mysticism to flourish by the side of ignorance. On the other hand the prosecution was unwise. It made martyrs of a group which deserved no sympathy. The same result might have been achieved by negotiation with the Vatican.

The Senate, its hands full with the Déroulède case, did not hurry itself over the amnesty proposal, and after the New Year the Budget, as usual not passed by the beginning of the financial year, occupied most of its time. Waldeck-Rousseau, having succeeded in getting the legal actions touching on the Affair adjourned, did not press the matter, it may be from his distaste for the inevitable irritation its discussion would cause. The Senate committee, however, at the end of February discovered a flaw in the procedure which effectively prevented the tacking of the Dreyfus amnesty clauses on to the earlier bill. Further, it was pointed out that an amnesty applied only to the already condemned, not to the innocent. Thus on March 1 Waldeck laid a new bill which extinguished all proceedings on criminal charges, other than murder, but did not cover civil cases. "The question," he said, "is not to judge or absolve actions accomplished; it merely prevents parties from reviving a painful conflict." Picquart and Reinach once more protested that they, innocent of crimes, would get no redress, while Dreyfus from Carpentras memorialised the chairman of the committee that the extinction of the actions meant that evidence which might reveal a new fact, permitting him to lodge an appeal, would never come to light.

By now the public, weary of the Affair, indifferent whether justice were done or not, was looking forward to the opening of the Paris Exhibition in April. The Senate committee agreed with the public, and with one dissentient accepted the bill. They too were getting bored.

Before the bill could be discussed by the Senate, there were changes in the political situation. On May 1 were held the municipal elections. Although in the provinces the new councils were almost wholly Republican, in Paris there was a landslide to the Right, or rather to the Nationalists. This may have been due to the generally bad administration of the hitherto favoured Radicals and Socialists, who quarrelled on principle with the Préfets of the Seine and of the Police, found jobs for their friends, and raised the cost of living by adding to the level of the *octroi* dues. Or it may have been the reward of extensive bribery by two Nationalists, Edmond Archdeacon, railway director and racehorse-owner, who popularised his political speeches by giving racing tips in the peroration, and Boniface de Castellane, who had married Anna Gould and enjoyed spending the Gould millions. In the upshot, of the eighty seats on the municipal council forty-five were won by Nationalists, a fact which added gall to the repeated Nationalist claim that the Government did not represent France.

In the same month a more unpleasant crisis arose. The Statistical Section, anti-Dreyfusard to a man, had ignored Galliffet's injunction against meddling in the Affair. By chance they had run across the fact that Commissioner Tomps was in touch with a group of foreign agents, and after much involved negotiation succeeded in getting hold of two letters written by Tomps which might be interpreted as indicating that, in an attempt to defame the General Staff, he was busying himself in the Dreyfus case at the very moment when the Government was preaching appeasement. François tried to get his seniors to take up the matter, but Lacroix, Gonse's successor, thought the letters unimportant, and having in turn reported to his chief, Delanne, told François to file the

documents and do no more. Furious at their failure, the officers
of the Section ignored his orders and pursued the matter.

A second attempt by François had no better luck. Delanne again
said the case had no interest and dropped Francois's report on the
fire. As it happened, one of the foreign agents involved, arrested
and threatened with extradition, applied to the Minister of the
Interior, Waldeck-Rousseau, who communicated with Galliffet.
The latter at once realised that his orders were being disobeyed,
and that the Section must be cleaned out. He immediately returned François and another to their regiments, and maintained
Captain Fritsch only to hand over to their successors. Fritsch,
another man to be poisoned by the Dreyfus virus, had photographs taken of the two Tomps letters and handed prints to Le
Hérissé, Deputy for Rennes, one of Boulanger's former adherents,
now a Nationalist. The Right, the Nationalists and Méline's
followers believed they had enough matter to detach sufficient
Deputies from the Government majority to bring about the defeat
of the Cabinet. On May 22 a formal accusation was made that the
Government intended to reopen the Affair. After Waldeck-
Rousseau had replied, the question was brought to a head by a
motion inviting the Government to oppose any reopening, from
whatever quarter the proposal might come. During the debate
Humbert charged the Government with lying, and brought up
what had been learned from the officers of the Statistical Section,
and finally referred to the Tomps letters, of which both Waldeck
and Galliffet were in ignorance. The motion was passed, and later
Galliffet was shown the photographs by Le Hérissé. He promptly
ordered an investigation. Delanne interrogated Fritsch, who now
realised what he had done, burst into tears and cried: "I have committed an act of madness." He was at once relieved of his appointment, but Galliffet had to meet the Senate and the Chamber. With
the former he had no trouble: he explained what he called
Fritsch's crime and there was no debate. He came before the
Chamber on May 28.

Already, as has been seen, Galliffet had had doubts as to the
survival of the Government. The doubts had grown. As recently

as May 16 he had written to a friend of the dangers arising from the cleverness of the Nationalists in showing up the weaknesses of the Government, its sympathy for the Dreyfusards, its lack of persistence in pressing for the amnesty, its minor but irritating persecution of the Church. He ended: "The Cabinet has suffered the consequences of the association of Millerand with Galliffet. It should have got rid of one or the other at the reopening of the Chambers in November . . . The departure of either would have indicated the definite orientation of the Ministry" (46, 345).

On May 28 he apologised to the Deputies for his ignorance at the previous session of the two Tomps letters. He assumed full responsibility, declined to follow the interpretations which had been put on the documents, and condemned Fritsch for dereliction of duty. He desired that the Army should be kept remote from politics. "It still suffers from the fact that fifteen years ago an adventurer [Boulanger] was forced on it: it will not let another be imposed." "If you need someone responsible, let it be me."

After the usual calumnious and insolent attacks of the Nationalists, Waldeck-Rousseau spoke in support of his War Minister. No doubt tired, no doubt bored with the humbug of this unworthy farce, he allowed himself to drop the word "felony" in connection with Fritsch's conduct—Fritsch in a less tumultuous season would have been awaiting court-martial. Galliffet took umbrage at the word. "There are things a soldier can say, which he cannot bear to be said by a civilian," he wrote to a friend the next day. He scribbled a note of resignation and hobbled out of the Chamber; thereafter he was seen no more. As he explained to his correspondent, he could not rebuke the Prime Minister, but he could not in the circumstances remain in office. "My authority, laboriously and progressively built up over eleven months, would have been too much weakened . . . while to accept the public apologies of Waldeck-Rousseau and give way to Loubet's persuasion would be to return to a hostile Chamber, the Right hostile from ingrown habit, the Left because I could not be forgiven for my departure yesterday . . . Waldeck-Rousseau, who at first was in agreement with me, has fallen under the destructive influence of Millerand;

he gets daily more deeply under it. Every day the need to hold his majority together obliges him to take a step forward in the programme of the Socialists and Anarchists" (46, 345).

For an hour it looked as if the Government would be beaten. Bourgeois, realising the emergency, rallied the weakened morale of the ministerial forces by calling on them to defend the Republic, to unite against "the eternal enemies of civil liberties." He proposed a vote of confidence, which was carried by a small but sufficient majority, but it was noticeable that Barthou voted with the Right, and that Poincaré scrupulously abstained.

Nevertheless the Chamber, save for the small intractable body of Dreyfusards, had made it abundantly clear that it was unwilling to reconsider the Dreyfus case, or to make any move towards helping the victims of military justice to vindicate their honour or obtain redress.

Waldeck-Rousseau may have been wrong in delaying to press for the amnesty. The error, if it was an error, is understandable. As a private person he was convinced that at least two judicial crimes had been committed, which he wished to see repaired: but as Prime Minister his duty was to prevent the anti-parliamentary forces from creating parliamentary anarchy, and in all circumstances legality must be preserved, even if justice could not. He could get no support from the Right; he must lean, unwillingly, on the Left. It was not, as Galliffet complained, that he was influenced by Millerand, but that he must have the Socialist support: he was therefore willing to accept reforms proposed by his Socialist colleague so far as they were purely administrative developments, and not revolutionary measures. He would, for example, support Millerand's bill for shorter working hours for women and children, because legislation on these lines had been several times voted by Parliament, though in practice it had been ineffective. On the other hand, he would not countenance Millerand's proposals to enforce arbitration in strikes between owners and employees, because that would be both novel and contrary to prevailing opinion. Forced to prefer order to justice, he was thus impotent to act towards the victims of military justice as he would have liked.

Raison d'état, as much as his own sentiments, made him desire revision of the case. *Raison d'état* equally forbade him to reopen it.

On the suggestion of Bourgeois and Brisson, the Commandant of the Polytechnic, General André, was appointed to succeed Galliffet. From the Radical point of view he was all that could be desired: Republican, Positivist, and anti-clerical, though not a Freemason. As a Minister, and particularly as Minister of War, he was entirely unsuitable. Far more widely read than most soldiers, he was at the same time muddle-headed, unmethodical, self-confident and obstinate. He looked on himself as a reformer; indeed, some of his reforms—the raising of the pay of junior officers, the putting in hand of heavy guns—were admirable: but his intention to republicanise the Army, which was impossible and perhaps undesirable, required a man of tact and presence. He had no tact, and his odd, gloomy features and tall, ill-balanced body were comic rather than impressive. Clemenceau nicknamed him the spouting whale.

4

The amnesty bill was discussed by the Senate on June 1 and 2. Waldeck defended it simply on the ground of necessity. "The amnesty," he said, "does not judge, it does not accuse, it does not acquit; it ignores." In the tiny minority against the bill only four Republicans voted, on the ground that innocent men were being deprived of justice: they were all old men from the days when the Republic was untried and unstained. The *affichage* of Waldeck's speech was voted by a huge majority.

The Chamber, having, only six weeks earlier, urged the rapid passage of the bill, now dilly-dallied. The committee disagreed and the bill was held over until after the summer recess. It did not reach the order of the day until December, when it occupied four confused sittings. The Right demanded the inclusion of the Déroulède group and the exclusion of Reinach and Picquart, the authors of all the ill, while the defenders of justice also asked for their exclusion on the ground that they were innocent. Some of the Left attacked the generals, others Méline. Waldeck spoke three times. In his last speech he said: "I know well the sentiments which some among you have obeyed. The wound inflicted by some acts, either too arbitrary or too inhuman, has reopened, and you have listened only to the inspiration of your conscience and the counsel of your indignation. . . . I do not condemn these reactions, which I myself have felt. . . . But there are moments when one must turn to the future and take less account of the aspects which impugn the guilty than of the state of affairs which has created the guilty." The bill was carried at 2 a.m. on December 19 in an almost empty House. A few days later the amended bill passed the Senate.

CHAPTER EIGHTEEN

The Dreyfusian Revolution

1

SAYS Sorel (54, 40) "The one-time brutalities of *coups d'état* are no longer needed for a rapid change of direction." In November 1897 no one could have foreseen the transformation of the political scene which would take place within eight years, could have foretold that the apparently impregnable Republican Party would be split into two weak fractions, and that the cement of the Ralliement would have crumbled to dust. Up to the end of 1897 the issue of Alfred Dreyfus had been concentrated in two small and narrow groups of interests: on the one side those of the handful of Dreyfusists, on the other those of the Ministers of War, the Chiefs of Staff and the Statistical Section. Their conflict had extended to, and now occupied, the whole political arena. The clever neutrals of 1898–99, who would not be Dreyfusist, were now wholly Dreyfusard. Had the Affair been, as it should have been, confined to Mercier, Sandherr and the Section, it could have been decently wound up. Its extension to the political and religious spheres had rekindled the dying embers of mutual antipathy between the Republicans and the professional soldiers. As Jules Delafosse, an Independent Deputy of Nationalist leanings, wrote: "The Republican is the moral antithesis of the soldier; he can neither understand nor love him."

The long-term effects of political Dreyfusardism were almost wholly evil. The following wave of anti-militarist and politically conscious pacifism was not the most regrettable of them. More demoralising to the national life and unity was the revenge the anti-clericals took on the religious Orders and the Church. But for the Affair, would Combes ever have been given the chance to do what he did? True, the separation of Church and State had a revivifying effect on the Church, but the bitterness born of the struggle can have done the country no good. Nor is it possible either to measure or to deny the ill effects on the military efficiency of the French Army of the course set by André.

The Affair raised a crop of critics of the Army very different from the Hermants, Descaves and Courtelines. From January 1898, under the stimulus of *J'Accuse*, attacks on the military as military had begun. Clemenceau had not hesitated to abuse the General Staff on the score of its incompetence over many years, but he never verged on anti-militarism. The new enemies went much further: Anarchists and Socialists attacked the French Army and armies in general as institutions, denounced national frontiers and savaged the French army officer in particular as an aspirant praetorian. The earliest of these violent critics was a former Monarchist, the journalist Urbain Gohier. From early 1898 onwards, with the persistence of the fanatic he had become, he delivered a series of violent indictments against the army officers. In *L'Armée de Condé* he claimed to expose those whose ancestors had served against France during the Revolution and to imply that they were again ready to betray. *L'armée contre la Nation* and *l'Histore d'une Trahison* followed. Gohier asserted that he had raised the Affair above the particular instance of Dreyfus to the general level. So venomous, so outrageous did his articles become that Reinach publicly rebuked him, and Clemenceau resigned from the *Aurore* rather than appear on the same page as such a colleague.

The effect of Gohier's violence was to rally the army officers against the Dreyfusards, and since the slanderer was acquitted on the one occasion he was prosecuted, the attacks merely raised, in the ordinary professional officer, a hatred of the press and the Dreyfusard cause. The temper and discipline of the Army were affected and the authority of the Minister of War weakened. In the Army, known Dreyfusists, such as those who gave evidence at Rennes on behalf of the accused, were treated as pariahs. Officers who read the wrong newspapers were taken to task by their generals.

Had Gohier been alone in his fanaticism he might gradually have faded out, but his attacks were reinforced by other men and widened to include militarism in general. An emotional school-master at Sens, Gustave Hervé, published, from 1901 onwards, a series of anti-militarist, anti-patriotic articles, inviting the troops to mutiny, to lay down their arms, to insult the flag and so forth, with the usual wealth of cheap facetiousness and abuse; his pamphlets were circulated in the barracks. He was prosecuted in the autumn of 1901 for attempts to suborn the soldiers. Defended by Aristide Briand, now rising under the wing of Jaurès, Hervé was acquitted. Extolled by the *Petite République*, he became a public figure, preaching the general strike against war: "Civil wars are the only wars in which the people have something to gain. . . . You owe the country neither devotion nor obedience." Nothing analyses the transformation of Dreyfusism more clearly than a passage from Charles Péguy's *Notre Jeunesse* (41, 186): "Founded on the same postulate, starting from the same postulate, we spoke the same language. The anti-Dreyfusards said, treason by a soldier is a crime, and the soldier Dreyfus has betrayed. We said, treason by a soldier is a crime, and Dreyfus has not betrayed. Since Hervé came, all that has changed. In appearance, the same conversation goes on; the Affair moves. But it is not the same Affair, the same conversation. . . . It is something infinitely other, be-cause the basis of the debate has shifted. Hervé is a man who says, one must betray. . . ."

Hervé was the most prominent of the anti-militarists, but the whole body of State teachers became infected with the same disease, the teachers' magazines incessantly carried articles denouncing chauvinism and the degradation of barrack life. Sorel in his *Reflections on Violence* pointed out that the Army was the centre of the bourgeois State; strike the Army first, and the bourgeois State will crumble. Further support for anti-patriotism was brought by Gustave Téry, the founder of *l'Œuvre*, an ex-Normalien, who, writing from the furthest edge of the Left, borrowed the weapons of Drumont, the incitement to hatred, the denigration, the mockery of all civic virtue.

The Confédération Générale du Travail had indeed passed

pacifist resolutions annually since 1897. In 1906, at the Amiens Congress, the resolution laid down that anti-militarist and anti-patriotic propaganda should become more intense and bolder; "in every war the working class is duped and sacrificed to the profit of the employers, parasitic and bourgeois." But the resolution was passed by only 488 votes to 310, which demonstrates that the sentiment was far from universal. Pacifism is an intellectual concept. What the workers resented was the fact that, owing to the smallness of the police forces, the military were often called in to supplement them. The Army was thus the employers' weapon. Between 1890 and 1908, before the trade unions were well organised, on a number of occasions there were bloody clashes between strikers and soldiers, particularly in 1907 and 1908. The anti-militarism was directed against strike-breaking rather than against war.

Yet, all in all, the long anti-militarist campaign seems to have had little effect on the conscripts. The only instance of serious collective indiscipline was the refusal of the 17th Infantry Regiment to act against the insurgent and despairing wine-growers of the Midi in 1907, and for that there were good local reasons. In the provinces, among the peasants, anti-militarism had no roots. In 1914 the conscripts did not fail to report at their depots. And Hervé and Téry both became militant patriots.[1]

2

Although allied with the anti-clericals against the Right, Waldeck-Rousseau had no intention of making a destructive attack on the religious Orders, let alone the secular Church. It would seem that his intention at most was to eliminate from employment in the State schools teachers from the Orders, to control rather than to disperse the congregations, and if liquidation of any such religious body became necessary, to force its dissolution through fiscal pressure. He intended to bring them within the State and, to this end, to circumscribe them within the Association Law of

[1] Téry died in 1928 and the *Œuvre* passed into other hands. Hervé was still living in 1940: he became a Pétainist. He was the author of *C'est Pétain qu'il nous faut*, 1936.

1884—the law legalising the formation of trade unions, of which he himself had been the author. He put forward a new bill involving all associations whether lay or clerical, and freeing the unions from some irksome restrictions laid down in 1884.

At Toulouse in October 1900, possibly as a counter-blast to a recent speech by Millerand at Lens once more championing Social-ism, he had accused the free—i.e. the Catholic—schools of dividing the youth of France into two bodies, neither of which knew the other, and about the same time he spoke very hotly on the subject of the trading Orders. It has been suggested that he would have been wiser to postpone the introduction of his bill, but since it was bound to entail a long-drawn-out debate, its presentation could hardly have been postponed beyond the spring of 1901, with the general elections falling in April and May 1902.

The bill itself made no mention whatever of the religious congre-gations. It proposed the fullest freedom for all associations, pro-vided their objects were not forbidden by law; it granted them legal personality and the right to receive and own property. But for each association composed partly of foreigners or directed from abroad, or whose members lived in common, the authorisation of the Conseil d'Etat would be required. The religious Orders, being directly under the Vatican, fell under this head, but so too did the International Working-men's Association. The prospect of having this organisation submitted to the control of a hostile Parliament alarmed the Socialists.

The Chamber committee entrusted with the examination of the bill, of which the majority were Radicals and Socialists, was less concerned to control the congregations than to suppress them. It amended the bill out of recognition and presented the Chamber with an additional series of regulations directed against the enemy. The main novelty was the withdrawal of the duty of authorisation from the Conseil d'Etat and the addition of the requirement that each congregation must apply to Parliament for authority, which would be embodied in a separate bill and debated. Further, the com-mittee added an article forbidding members of unauthorised con-gregations to be employed in teaching. Waldeck-Rousseau was unable to resist the committee's amendments without defeat. The debates, which lasted through the spring, were stormy, but the bill in its new form was passed by a majority of a hundred. The Senate accepted most of the provisions, and reduced from six to three months the period within which the congregations must apply. The bill became law on 1 July 1901.

Owing to the inexplicit drafting of the text, a grave difficulty remained. First, if one of the Chambers refused authorisation, must the congregation at once be dissolved? The Conseil d'Etat, when the question was referred to it, replied that the decision of the other Chamber must be awaited. If the second Chamber then authorised the congregation, the bill must return to the Chamber which had rejected it for re-examination. Since the Chambers were notoriously slow in dealing with, and even capable of burying, matters which they disliked, the congregation might remain indefinitely neither authorised nor unauthorised.

Furthermore, in order to clarify the position of the unauthorised teaching establishments of authorised congregations, the Government decreed that only schools opened after the date of the Act required authorisation.

In spite of the fierceness with which the bill had been fought by de Mun and the Catholics, the Pope did not forbid the congregations to seek the shelter of the law. By October sixty-four of the 147 unauthorised congregations of men, and 482 of the 606 women's congregations, had filed their applications. The rest disappeared, at least in their former guise; many merely changed their clothes to those of laymen.

3

Before the elections of May 1902 a considerable change had occurred in the grouping and organisation of the Socialists in the Chamber. In the Socialist group the quarrel over Millerand's acceptance of office had not died down. It had been covered up at the Paris Congress of December 1899 by ambiguous and contradictory resolutions, but the Guesdists had no intention of surrendering their position. In the following June a strike at Châlon-sur-

Saône took a violent turn; troops were called out and bloodshed followed. The Nationalists, in the hope of bringing the Government down, persuaded the Guesdists to support them in a demand for an enquiry, which Waldeck-Rousseau resisted. He would have been beaten but for the fact that the Jaurèsists, in spite of their interest in the matter, stood by the Government. The Guesdist action added further bitterness to the struggle. But Jaurès was now the dominant figure, and at the International Congress in Paris during September 1900, under the presidency of Kautsky, he succeeded in securing the passage of a motion that in certain circumstances participation in a bourgeois Government might be admissible. Therefore, at the French annual Congress in December, Guesde and his followers walked out, to be imitated in the following May at the Lyon Congress by Vaillant and his Blanquists. The break was confirmed by the founding of two Socialist parties: the French Socialist Party, composed of the followers of Jaurès and Allemane with Briand as its secretary, and the Socialist Party of France, formed by Guesdists, Blanquists and a number of autonomous federations. Henceforward it would be the ideas of Jaurès which would predominate.

The auguries pointed to a fiercely fought election. For the first time since 1885 both Right and Left did their utmost to eliminate rival candidatures within their own framework. For the first time since the Ralliement, Monarchists and Ralliés came to terms. It is probable that the Government put all its weight behind Left candidates. In the more conservative departments the task of the Préfets was difficult. In Seine-Inférieure, whose eleven Republican Deputies, as has been seen, voted against Waldeck in November 1899, the popular Préfet Hendlé found himself helpless. The Government did not scruple to support Jaurèsists against Guesdists, to which intervention the hitherto unlucky candidate, Aristide Briand, owed his election at Saint-Etienne. The results of the voting were heavily in favour of the Left, and at the expense of the Progressists, who lost some twenty seats. The only gainers on the Right were the Nationalists, who captured thirteen seats in Paris, among them one by Syveton, whom the Chamber was later to

unseat. The Socialists lost a few seats, but Jaurès recovered his at
Carmaux, defeating both the sitting member and a Guesdist.
Guesde, on the other hand, once more failed to recapture Roubaix.
The Ministerial Republicans, like the Progressists, lost twenty con-
stituencies. The winners were the Radicals and Socialist Radicals,
who came back two hundred strong, the biggest party in the
Chamber.

Nevertheless, in spite of the preponderance of the Left in numbers, the Government's strength depended on its ability to maintain its union. If either the Ministerial Republicans or the Socialists
deserted, the Government would be defeated.

4

Before the Chamber met, Waldeck-Rousseau resigned, an un-
precedented action in a Prime Minister who had just won an election. His motives remain conjectural. He alleged reasons of health,
and it is true that he had expended himself to the full in his long
Ministry—the longest so far in the annals of the Third Republic.
It may be also that he had inklings of the disease which was to
bring about his death within three years. At the same time he may
have felt that as Prime Minister he would be unable to contain the
anti-clerical zealots of the new Chamber, whose passions had
already been roused by the campaign of the previous year. Possibly he believed that as a private member of the Senate he would
have a greater influence than as a Minister.

Both Brisson and Bourgeois flinched from the unwelcome succession. In the circumstances it could only be a Radical Cabinet,
and with the Association Law of July 1901 not yet completed by
the consideration of the requests for authorisation of such congregations as had applied, a Radical Prime Minister was indicated.
Loubet invited Emile Combes, Senator for Charente-Inférieure and
chairman of the Senate committee on the Association Law, to form
a Ministry.

Rarely has a Prime Minister with so superficial a familiarity
with government been selected to lead a country. His only
Cabinet experience had been as Minister of Public Instruction in

the short-lived Bourgeois government in 1895–96, during which he picked a quarrel with the Vatican over the wording of the appointment of bishops. Trained for the Church, he had rejected its teachings and turned to medicine; unfrocked, he remained a fanatical anti-clerical. He had one and only one idea, the battle with the Church. For matters of finance, of foreign policy, of defence, of social welfare, he cared nothing. His sole policy was to keep his Radicals in hand. He had no difficulty in forming his Ministry, but he made no invitation to the Socialists. The Cabinet was formed for the most part of Radicals-of-all-work of little distinction. He kept Delcassé at the Foreign Office, André at the War Office, and in order to keep the support of the Ministerial Republicans offered the Ministry of Finance to Maurice Rouvier, whose antipathy to income-tax was sufficient to appease those who had not forgiven his connection with the Panama Company. Rouvier accepted. The single Radical in the new Cabinet who had Radicalism in the blood was Camille Pelletan, noted for the humour and unintelligibility of his speeches; he took over the Marine. Combes himself went to the Interior, to which office he added that of Public Worship.

That this small, dapper, obstinate, bustling and tyrannous old man of seventy, *le père* Combes, meant business was immediately made clear. Hitherto Governments, while in emergency using the methods of Bonapartism, had slowly modified them, leaving much of the administration to the good sense and local knowledge of the Préfets. Combes at once made it clear that he proposed to reverse the process. He published an astounding circular to the Préfets, directing that in future those "favours of which the Republic disposes" should be granted only to friends of the Government. Further he ordered that, in parishes of which the Maire was a member of an Opposition party, there should be a delegate selected from the local politicians of the Left to advise the Préfet on local appointments. It was the first step in a policy of spying and delation which, though in the long run it brought the Cabinet down, was to leave a permanent blot on the political system.

The next and no less repugnant innovation was the formation

of the Delegation of the Left, a committee of Deputies chosen by
each of the majority groups in the Chamber to establish what in
England would be known as a Whips' Office. These set themselves
to the task with all the zest and cunning they had learned in the
rural constituency committees. No action appears to have been
too base to bring errant Deputies up to scratch; their private lives
were spied on and threats of scandal employed. The most influential member of this Committee of Public Safety was none other
than Jaurès, who, further, had been elected a vice-president of the
new Chamber. In this rôle, which he filled during most of the
period of the Socialist schism, lasting to the end of 1904,[1] he displayed little ardour for the cause, and it is questionable whether he
was ever more than a Socialist of sentiment. As Emile Vandervelde
wrote: "At bottom, Marxism always remained to him something ad-
ventitious, added later like a graft. To this peasant of genius, this man
from a region [Tarn] where factory chimneys are few, this intellectual,
this parliamentarian, who had never plunged into the working-class
milieu, Socialism was an ideal; but to make it a reality he counted
much more on the action of united democracy than on the isolated
action of the proletariat" (58, 160). It is inescapable that, like many
Socialist leaders, he was a bourgeois, and a comfortably situated
bourgeois. The things he valued had little interest for the mass of
the workers. Like other bourgeois Socialists, he wanted to trans-
form them into simulacra of himself, concerned for what he would
call the higher values. His Socialism had nothing in common with
that of Guesde on the one hand or, on the other, of the *étatistes*
Millerand, Briand and Thomas, three men who in spite of their
apostasy did the workers meritorious service. There are no reforms
to which the name of Jaurès is attached. Nothing save eloquence.
During the period, 1902–4, when he was covertly organising the
majority behind Combes, no social reform was carried. The

---

[1] The reunion of the two wings came about through the rejection, at the
Amsterdam Congress of August 1904, of the rider passed by the International on
opportunist collaboration with a bourgeois Government. Jaurès submitted, and
the two wings fused in April 1905, becoming the Section Française de l'International Ouvrière (S.F.I.O.), or United Socialist Party. A number of Jaurès's
followers refused to surrender and became Independents.

minority group of Socialists became thoroughly dissatisfied with his direction. They had expected tangible rewards for their support of the anti-clerical campaign, to which they were indifferent and which, with Guesde, they believed was an astute manœuvre to save capitalism. When, in March 1904, Millerand attacked the Government on its failure to produce a bill on workers' pensions, which had been the subject of study for nearly five years, a number of Socialists voted against Combes, who survived only by a tiny majority.

That Combes in his fanaticism planned to despatch the congregations once and for all was immediately made clear by his declaration that the Law of Associations would be rigorously executed "without tiresome regard to certain juridical interpretations." The phrase meant that he would ignore Waldeck-Rousseau's guarantee of the existing unauthorised schools of authorised congregations. In July the closing of the schools of teaching sisters was begun, and from a servile Chamber and Senate Combes obtained approval of his actions. He further forced the Conseil d'Etat to go back on its earlier interpretation and to hold that a negative vote by one Chamber alone would be sufficient to refuse authorisation to an unauthorised congregation. Then, having laid before the Senate bills authorising five congregations of men, he tabled in the Chamber bills rejecting applications from fifty-four more. The Chamber committee, which contained a Radical majority, knowing that the Chamber majority would support Combes, decided to avoid what would be useless discussion. They packed all the fifty-four applications into one bill recommending authorisation: thus a mere negative vote by the Chamber would dispose of the men's congregations in the shortest time. It is fair to say that Combes opposed such cavalier treatment of the matter, but he was not prepared to make a stiff stand. Waldeck protested in the Senate, as did some of the Left Republicans. The only concession was the division of the congregations into three groups, the teaching bodies, the preachers and the traders. In the middle of the following March (1903) all three bills were rejected. The police at once closed the houses in question and the occupiers were dispersed.

All this high-handed procedure had not passed without trouble. The Papal Nuncio, Lorenzelli, had protested in vain. There had been manifestations and minor riots. In Brittany the closing of some free primary schools and the removal of the teaching sisters had roused the peasantry, and in places the troops had been called in to maintain order. Possibly the most spectacular battle was of indirect origin, when in the spring of 1903 Combes was invited to unveil the statue of Renan at Tréguier in north Brittany. The proceedings developed into a pitched battle between clericals and anti-clericals. Peasants swarmed into the town and, warmed with drink, fought in the square below the former cathedral from which the bells continued, as at the sack of Antwerp, to toll throughout the day, while the anti-clericals chanted:

> *Viens, père Combes, viens!*
> *Viens à Tréguier*
> *Pour chasser les curés!*

The women's congregations were treated similarly but even more expeditiously. All four hundred applications from them were rejected in June. Once again, but too late, Waldeck-Rousseau protested to the Senate against the transformation of his law of control into a law of exclusion. He pointed out that the exclusion of the teaching Orders would inevitably add to the already over-burdened budget of the Minister of Public Instruction, who had not yet even completed the Law of 1886, and that the additions to the Budget would cripple the national finances and preclude the promised Old Age Pensions scheme. Goblet, formerly one of the hottest anti-clericals, was disgusted at the attempt to enforce the educational dictatorship of the State.

Combes was incorrigible, and from the middle of 1903 proceeded to lay about him with reckless inconsequence, so long as each morning he could have his tumbril-full of monks and nuns. That summer Leo XIII died, having seen the approaching ruin of his policy of reconciling the Republic with Catholicism. His successor, Pius X, with little if any experience of administration or diplomacy, was a fighter. Combes, early in 1904, quarrelled with the Holy See over the appointment of bishops. At the same time he arranged for Loubet to make a State visit to the Italian Court, but to ignore the Vatican. Pius X was not prepared to overlook such studied discourtesy and circulated to the Catholic powers a confidential protest. Delcassé, anxious that diplomatic relations with the Vatican should not be broken, insisted that the protest be withheld from publication. The Prince of Monaco, however, gave it privately to Jaurès, who at once printed it in his new paper, *Humanité*. Combes, unwilling to lose face, withdrew Nisard, the French Ambassador, from the Vatican (May 1904) but maintained a *chargé d'affaires*. The Vatican promptly recalled the Nuncio, Lorenzelli.

But the reaction to Combes had started. Even Radicals began to be irked by their crooked and zealous leader. In January Jaurès failed to secure re-election to the vice-presidency of the Chamber. Both the Democratic Alliance and the Radical Party split into Combists and anti-Combists. Clemenceau, who had been elected to the Senate for Var on a by-election in April 1902, though he was anti-clerical, was incensed by the methods of the Delegation of the Left.

5

In the meantime a further controversy had broken out with the Vatican. The Bishops of Laval and Dijon had been summoned to appear at Rome before the Holy Office. Combes forbade them to go. The Vatican stood by its action, and on July 30 the French Government broke off diplomatic relations and closed the Embassy to the Holy See, which was not reopened until 1921. A Chamber committee was set up to consider ways and means of bringing about the separation of Church and State. Combes produced a bill in November, but by the time it came before the Chamber he himself had vanished. The Government survived to the end of the year. In January 1905, when the Chamber officers were re-elected by secret vote, the dissident Radical Doumer was chosen over Brisson: it signified the end of the Government. Combes struggled on for a few days, scrambling along with tiny majorities of six or eight, but on January 14 he resigned in an open letter to the President, full of rancour and vanity. He was succeeded by his Minister of Finance, Rouvier, who, except for three Ministers, among them the now almost permanent Delcassé, produced a wholly new team, much further to the Right than its predecessor—"more like a board of directors than a cabinet," said Clemenceau.

Here the matter of the Church may be left. In due course the law separating the Church from the State was passed and, after much complicated negotiation, a working arrangement ensued. At the same time the dissolved congregations were slowly liquidated, but instead of the expected millions from their property, only about a tenth was recovered. The Orders, which had many friends among the lawyers and in government offices, had taken steps to put their property out of reach of the Exchequer. The Concordat now broken, the secular Church was no longer the salaried servant of the State, but, though it suffered financially, it had liberty. The bishops could no longer be disciplined by the Conseil d'Etat. Their appointment could no longer be refused by an anti-clerical Minister. The Director of Public Worship, Charles Dumay, retired, and having nothing to do, promptly died. In spite of new difficulties, both internal and external, the Church in its freedom renewed its life and continued to grow in strength and influence, how greatly may be seen from the reports of the secretary of the Grand Orient at the present day.

6

Parallel with their resolve to abolish the congregations and coerce the Church, the majority had determined to deal with the Army. So long as Galliffet remained at the War Office this was difficult. It is noteworthy that when in February 1900 Pelletan, as *rapporteur* of the War Office budget, made severe criticisms of army administration, of the squandering of men and money, and the Socialist Allard moved for an enquiry, the Chamber gave the Minister an overwhelming vote of support. But Galliffet passed on, and the Republican André succeeded. It now became possible to take action to destroy the autonomy the Army had hitherto enjoyed, and to end what was thought to be a State within the State.

It is unfair to André to consider him a fool. His hope was to break down the isolation in which the professional Army had hitherto existed, to make of it a living body which grew as part of the body of the nation. It was a task to which many officers had given their minds during the past forty years. André set on foot a variety of schemes in the expectation of benefitting the non-commissioned officers and soldiers in the direction of their education and leisure. He raised the miserable pay of subalterns and captains; he suppressed the requirement that the bride of an officer should bring a dowry of 1,200 francs a year. On the side of equipment, he put in hand the construction of heavy artillery; it was the fault of his successors that the French Army was not so equipped in 1914.

On the other hand, he did away with a number of very ancient privileges concerning officers' servants, their use of carriages and shooting-brakes, all of which actions were naturally looked on as attacks on military prestige.

Then he lent himself to a favourite Republican project, the reduction of military service from three to two years. A private bill to this end had been laid before the Senate in 1898, but nothing had come of it. With André's appointment, the question was revived and semi-official conversations took place between the army committee of the Senate and the Minister of War. As it happened, in earlier discussions the only general who had approved of the reduction had been André's own corps commander, Mercier. André thus felt fortified in accepting the principle, provided the strength of the Army was maintained at 575,000. Under the Law of 1889 the annual contingent was larger than could be incorporated, and there had been dispensations from service in certain categories. Under the new scheme there would be a deficiency in numbers. It was therefore proposed to fill the gap by the suppression of dispensations and by an increase in the numbers of re-engaged N.C.O.s and privates. At last, said the Left, the great democratic principle of equality of sacrifice will be realised. The discussion of the bill began in June 1902, but the final text was not passed until 21 April 1905. Jaurès claimed that it was only a step toward substituting a militia on the Swiss model for a standing army.

The law was a political manœuvre, a half-capitulation to antimilitarism, a sop to the electorate. In practice the re-engaged volunteers were too few to make good the deficit; there was no money available to make any serious improvement in the soldiers' pay. At the same time the infantry was again and again drained to find men for the newly-created artillery and engineer units; the establishment of infantry companies had to be lowered. Finally the growing menace of war with Germany, coupled with the increases in the German Army, alarmed the Government. In 1912 Poincaré, then Prime Minister, brought in a bill for the re-establishment of three years' service. It was fought strenuously by the Socialist Radicals and Socialists. Nevertheless the bill became law in 1913.

André's fall came through his desire to republicanise the Army. His formula, he said, was "to adapt the Army to modern ideas, modern manners and modern institutions" (9, 24), and his method to purge the Army of clerical officers, beginning with the Staff: in other words, taking the reprisals which Galliffet had refused to take. Within a short time of his arrival at the Rue Saint-Dominique he had replaced three senior officers, one of whom was the Catholic de Castelnau, later known as "*le capucin botté.*" These transfers had led to the resignation of General Delanne, the Chief of Staff, and General Jamont, chairman of the Conseil Supérieure de la Guerre. André's next move was to suppress the promotion committees and take the matter into his own hands. "The substitution of the responsible Minister for an irresponsible committee means that the promotion of officers is now in the hands of Parliament," he told the Chamber. He had informed Waldeck-Rousseau that he proposed to invite lists for promotion two or three times longer than in the past, and to make his own choices. Waldeck-Rousseau agreed, but warned the Minister that in doing justice to Republicans he must not do injustice to others. Since, however, it was quite impossible for André to know the political views or religious sentiments of the twenty-odd thousand officers, and he would not rely on the recommendations of Catholic and perhaps anti-Republican officers, he must go elsewhere. He therefore invited the members of the Bloc des Gauches to report to him on officers in their constituencies; he requested information from Préfets and the Sûreté, and, worst of all, he asked the help of political bodies, among others of the Freemasons. One of his personal staff named Mollin, son-in-law to Anatole France, got into touch with the secretary-general of the Grand Orient, Vadecard, who thereon circularised the masonic lodges. The Ligue des Droits de l'Homme was also mobilised in the same service. During nearly four years some twenty-five thousand notes (*fiches*) from every kind of source —ardent anti-clericals, retired and even active officers with a grudge, butchers, bakers, grocers and the master-shoemaker of a regiment in Clermont-Ferrand—were sent through the Grand Orient to the War Office. Promotion to a large degree passed from the hands of the Minister of War into those of Vadecard. Waldeck-Rousseau, hearing about it from André's *chef de cabinet*, General Percin, warned Combes that he would rue it, but the infatuated Prime Minister ignored the warning. André later insisted that he himself took little notice of the reports and promoted on military efficiency only. He printed in his book thirty examples of hostile *fiches*, of which the subjects had been promoted to general. It is somewhat difficult to think that any Minister could indeed have taken notice of these trivial and unsupported charges.

It was inevitable that sooner or later these proceedings would come to light. In the autumn of 1904 Vadecard's assistant, Bidegain, sold some important letters from Mollin and a batch of several hundred *fiches* to the Nationalist Deputies, Syveton and Guyot de Villeneuve, an officer who had been retired by Galliffet. In full session on October 28 Guyot de Villeneuve challenged one of André's statements and then read samples of the delations. André, taken aback, returned an evasive answer. Combes briskly flung himself into the debate, and asserted that André's action was both logical and legal, and that, when the Nationalists' friends were

at the War Office, they had not scrupled to apply to their co-religionists. The indignation came from the Right and Centre. The
Radicals remained silent, except for Vazeille, "the best of the
Dreyfusards" (42, 97), who expressed his horror. Combes would have
been defeated but for Jaurès, who begged the Republicans not to
lose their heads, not to help "the Caesarians, the promoters of war
and adventure, to overthrow the Government." A Radical moved
a resolution which would allow André time to make his dispositions.
It was carried by a majority of four: all the Ministers and under-
secretaries voted with the majority.

André could not escape. Clemenceau, who had now purchased
the *Aurore*, denounced his methods as a replica of those practised
by the War Office in the Affair, and the Freemasons as mere lay
Jesuits. But the Ligue des Droits de l'Homme refused to pronounce
against delation. When on November 4 André made his defence,
a lame one, he could scarcely be heard for the interruptions.
Jaurès once more made an extravagant speech of defiance, full of
contradictions and abuse of his interrupters. Combes asked that
the Army should not be left to the chances of a change of Government. He was attacked by Ministerial Republicans, old followers
of Waldeck-Rousseau, by dissident Radicals and by Leygues and
Millerand. For the moment Combes was saved by Syveton,
who crossed the floor and smacked André's face. As the Papal
chargé d'affaires wrote to Rome: "The Opposition invariably in
one way or another plays the Government's game" (39, 120).
Ten days later André either resigned or was dismissed by Combes,
who replaced him by the Radical stockbroker, Berteaux.

The effect of the so-called *affaire des fiches* had both immediate
and more remote consequences. In the Army there was fury against
real or suspected delators. Every promotion of the last four years
seemed tainted. To add to this exasperation, the soldiers were
called on to assist the civil power in implementing the law separating the Church from the State, to sweep away the crowds of the
faithful vainly attempting to prevent inventories of Church
property being taken in the now State-owned churches. Some
officers refused to obey and were broken: others resigned rather

than carry out their orders. Some generals, who were thought to have ordered on the duty officers known to be believing and practising Catholics in order to test their Republicanism, earned the hatred of their subordinates. Rancour and distrust were the fruit of five years' struggle to republicanise an army which had never desired to meddle in politics. From five years' struggle were to emerge political generals. "Officers know that they will no longer find in their superiors the defenders on whom they could formerly count," wrote an officer in 1911 (d'Arbeux, see 75, 265).

The further consequence of these tensions was that the Army was gradually looked on less and less as a career. To the low pay, the slow promotion, the vegetation in dull provincial towns, the pointless formalism, the uninspiring routine, had now been added bitterness. The sons of the old families who had come back after 1870 once more held back. The candidatures for Saint-Cyr fell year by year. In 1897 there had been 1,920; in 1900, 1,870; in 1907, 982; in 1912, 872. From 1905 the resignations of officers from the Polytechnic was no less significant: of sixty-five entering the artillery in 1905, only thirty remained in 1910; of the seventy-one of 1906, only forty-three, and of the seventy-five of 1907, only thirty-eight. Furthermore, the proportion of Saint-Cyriens and Polytechniciens in relation to rankers was declining, and under André's decree of 18 June 1904, which gave adjutants the right to ten per cent of the vacancies for commissions each year without passing through a military school, the proportion of these promotions from the ranks had risen to nearly twenty per cent.

It is possible, though there is little evidence, that the appointment of Picquart to the War Office by Clemenceau in 1906 played some part in the general malaise, which was not improved by the succession of General Brun, his Chief of Staff, on Picquart's resignation, since Brun discounted all possibility of war. The depression began to lift about 1911, partly as the threat of war became more apparent, partly with the appointment of first Messimy and then Millerand as Ministers, the reorganisation of the War Office and the appointment of Joffre. At least it is clear that from about 1911 to 1912 a healthier spirit invaded the Army, which, if its consequences were not wholly happy, at least brought about a revival of morale.

7

The real Dreyfusian revolution, if the term be accepted, occurred in the Chamber of Deputies. Sorel (54, 72) says that it liquidated the former Republican aristocracy and replaced it by a regime not very different from that of the early years of the Second Empire. The comparison with the Empire is a trifle fanciful, nor is the statement wholly accurate as regards the liquidation of the Republicans.

The crisis came with the publication of the names of the Waldeck-Rousseau Cabinet in June 1899. It is clear from the voting that without the forty-odd votes of the Socialists the Government would not have survived its first appearance. Waldeck-Rousseau knew, after his first failure to construct a Cabinet, that he could not count on as much as half the Republican vote, and must therefore secure the extreme Radicals and the Socialists.

But the Republican schism was not wholly over Millerand. True, it is to-day forgotten how acute was the fear of Socialism in western Europe, in England as much as in France, "that bourgeois dread which for a century has never failed to throw Joseph Prudhomme into the arms of Catiline," says Monsieur Jacques Madaule. But keen as was the economic fear, it is possible that fears for the Army and the Church, especially when the strength of the Radical vote was seen, were stronger. The vote of the Deputies representing the frontier departments is some evidence on the Army question, while for the Church it is significant that Aynard, the Catholic Lyonnais banker, who did so much to save Waldeck in June 1899, did not support him in November and, in spite of the appointment of his son-in-law, Jonnart, to the governorship of Algeria, went back into opposition. Some writers have thought the split a resumption of the old quarrel between the Right and Left Centres, but the Centre had changed. If the Alliance Démocratique, formed by the Ministerial Republicans, has any significance, it is that this group was alive to a new trend in France. The clericalised Republic dreamed of by Leo XIII had disappeared. The Ministerial Republicans hoped that by adapting themselves to the new circumstances they would control whatever forces were coming into existence.

In spite of their outcry on the publication of the members of the Cabinet, the Radicals rapidly changed their mind. It was their vote which formed the bulk of Waldeck-Rousseau's majority in both June and November 1899. It is possible that it was Ranc who showed them that they could, if they supported this conservative-minded Prime Minister, make themselves indispensable. They had played a shoddy part in the Affair for the past eighteen months, and their opportunism was rewarded. From November onwards they controlled the Cabinet; they got their reward, the dissolution of the congregations. From 1902 they secured a firm grip on local government, on the internal administration of the country—the number of Radicals who held the portfolio of the Interior in Cabinets headed by men of other parties is remarkable—on the Army, the Judiciary and the University.

With the separation of Church and State their ideas were at an end. The Radical and Socialist-Radical Party, the party of small borough and village politics, the party of the masonic lodges, of Gambetta's "new social stratum," were without a policy and became a party of negation: "We are opposed to the idea that large-scale industrial production should assume the character of a new feudalism." On the other hand, "What separates us from the Collectivists is our passionate attachment to personal property, the suppression of which we wish neither to begin nor even to prepare." Their creed was summed up in the old phrase, "neither reaction nor revolution"; in effect, "neither increase of taxes nor public loans." After the fall of Combes they were without leaders. Clemenceau, the Jacobin, was of a colour unrecognisable by the Radical of the Café de Commerce and the masonic lodge. Otherwise they drew indifferently from Right and Left: Poincaré, Briand, Caillaux, Barthou, Viviani, all came from either the Republicans or the Socialists. They existed by allying themselves with other groups, shifting from Right to Left, betraying each in turn, until they drowned themselves in the waters of Vichy on 9 July 1940.

CHAPTER NINETEEN

The End of the Affair

1

NEITHER Dreyfus nor Picquart had subscribed to the amnesty; but, while Dreyfus contented himself with stating that he would continue to pursue the establishment of his innocence, Picquart took up a public attitude of extreme hostility to Waldeck-Rousseau. The Prime Minister wished the Conseil d'Etat to deal immediately with the appeal which Picquart had lodged in February 1898, in order that he could be restored to the Army, promoted to the rank he would now have reached, and given a command. Picquart replied by withdrawing his appeal, and published an open letter in which he forcefully restated his grievances, claiming his right to be retried by court-martial, asserting that the interests of the country required that he should have justice. Like so many others, he had by now become poisoned with the Affair: he accused Waldeck of bargaining for Dreyfus's pardon, hinted that the Prime Minister knew more about the attempt on Labori's life than had been made public, while at the same time he was letting "the real enemies of the country" escape unscathed.

From now (December 1900) onwards the Dreyfusist group fell out among themselves. Labori had taken umbrage that Mathieu Dreyfus had accepted his proffered renunciation to plead at Rennes, and protested that if he had been allowed to speak the verdict would have been an acquittal. He quarrelled with Mathieu who, after a long struggle to reason with the vain lawyer, broke with him. Later Labori quarrelled with Reinach, who gave up employing him. Labori took to saying that he had been ill-paid for his trouble, and finally allied himself with Picquart. Alfred Dreyfus had come to Paris in November and had written Picquart a letter asking to be permitted to thank him in person for all he had done.

Picquart would not even acknowledge the letter. His former anti-semitism stirred in him; it is said that he took to reading the *Libre Parole*.[1] He associated only with Clemenceau and Labori, who was planning to reopen the Affair in order to satisfy his political aspirations and to make trouble for Waldeck-Rousseau. In an attempt to heal the breach between his brother and his counsel, Alfred Dreyfus called on Labori on December 22. Picquart was present. He and Labori were harsh and insisted that Dreyfus should no longer accept the advice of Mathieu or Demange but put his case in their hands. Otherwise he could no longer look for their support. Disillusioned, Dreyfus refused.

2

The prime difficulty in the way was the legal point that, to win an appeal, a new fact, vital to the decision of the judges at Rennes and unknown to them, must be submitted. Search as they would, the Dreyfus brothers and Reinach could discover no new fact. They had hoped, by enquiry of the judges at Rennes, to discover that the famous annotated *bordereau* had either been shown or at least spoken of in secret. Jouast refused to speak. Merle, as has been seen, dodged the question and denied the words attributed to him by the Dreyfusard emissary. All that existed was the current rumour that Mercier had a photograph of the document in his possession, and a volume of newspaper paragraphs, none of which could be adduced as influencing the verdict.

Mathieu's patient detective work wasted much time. It was not until the spring of 1903 that a move was made. The action then arose out of the elections of May 1902. Syveton, treasurer of the Ligue de la Patrie Française, had been elected over a prominent Radical in the Paris Bourse constituency. During the campaign Lemaître, picking up the rags of a falsified quotation from the letter Galliffet had written to Waldeck-Rousseau at the end of the Rennes trial (cf. p. 301), had produced a poster referring to the

[1] Barrès (11, 209), though giving no authority, states that Clemenceau exclaimed: "Ah, if it were not for Drumont, what a fine anti-semitic paper Picquart and I would run." If true, it is probably no more than one of Clemenceau's habitual brutal jests. He had far more interesting enemies than the Jews.

Government as "the foreigners' Government." On these grounds a
parliamentary enquiry into the conduct of the election was set up.
The report of the committee, which favoured the validation of
Syveton, came to the Chamber in April 1903. Jaurès had been told
of Mathieu Dreyfus's search. Now the power on the Delegation of
the Left, he saw in the debate on the Syveton report an opportunity to raise the question of the annotated *bordereau*. "He saw,
as an artist," wrote Reinach, "the fine speech he would make, which
would go echoing round the world and down to history, and the
fine scene, while as a politician he calculated the effects of his
action: Nationalism definitely conquered and dishonoured, and a
thrust to the heart of the Church party." Unfortunately for his
plan, and for Dreyfus, the Chamber were thoroughly sick of the
Affair they had hoped was safely buried

The debate on Syveton began on April 6. By working in the
wording of the election poster, Jaurès successfully reached the
discussion of the annotated *bordereau*, but none of the Nationalists,
not even Millevoye, who had first publicly given the terms of the
letter, accepted the challenge. Nothing emerged, and the debate
wandered. There were sharp passages of arms between Cavaignac
and Brisson over the resignation of Pellieux, much noise from the
Left; and Lasies once more trotted out Cuignet's obsession that the
Foreign Office had falsified the Panizzardi telegram. The single
relief was a promise by André to have a further War Office enquiry
into the Dreyfus documents. In deep boredom the Chamber
unseated Syveton.[1]

Unfortunately Jaurès tried to carry the matter further. Once
again a storm blew up. The Radicals were restive at Jaurès's
persistence. On the eve of the day on which Jaurès was to speak
Ferdinand Buisson came to see Dreyfus. "He told me of the disquiet of many minds in the Chamber over Jaurès's intervention.

---

[1] Syveton was re-elected in June. As has been seen, in November 1904 he
smacked André's face in the Chamber. Charged with assault, he stated that
his action was premeditated. While awaiting trial, he found himself involved
in certain scabrous charges and committed suicide. It is said that he had made
away with some hundred thousand francs of the Ligue's money, which his widow
returned.

The Left groups were far from happy over the importance he was acquiring and the fact that he wished to drag them in his train without consulting them" (27, 353). The Socialists and Radicals thus welcomed a resolution to leave the case within the judicial sphere. But by ventilating the question of the annotated *bordereau* Jaurès had succeeded in demonstrating that the mythical document had no existence, and thus deprived it of its character as a possible "new fact." Nevertheless, on the advice of his counsel, Mornard, Dreyfus himself applied to André for an enquiry into this and also into the Cernusky evidence.

3

André entrusted the investigation to a member of his personal staff, Major Targe. For the first time since the War Office had occupied the Rue Saint-Dominique, a thorough search of its files was carried out. That alone occupied six months, but it brought its reward. A number of reports to the Statistical Section tending to demonstrate Dreyfus's innocence, which the Section had carefully suppressed, were discovered, of which the most important was a letter of April 1895 from a spy Lajoux, giving a recognisable description of Esterhazy as the officer in the pay of the German War Office. Several notes from Schwartzkoppen came to light, relating to the purchase, at twenty francs each, of sections of the large-scale plans. Further it was discovered that, to hide the identity of certain agents, Henry, with the aid of Gribelin, who now decided that truth was the better part of discretion, had falsified the registers, that he had amassed a secret fund to be employed on unavowable ends, and that from Guénée's notes he had put together a file on the characters of leading politicians, generals and journalists.[1] It was also discovered that on the charge-sheets against Esterhazy given to the president and vice-president of his court-martial the date of 1894 had been erased with the intention of absolving him of the accusation for all time. One document on artillery, which had disappeared, and was therefore presumed to

---

[1] This secret fund had been discovered immediately after Henry's death, but nothing had been said about it: the money had simply been put back to the War Office general secret fund.

have been handed to the Germans by Dreyfus, turned up in the private file of a deceased officer. But possibly the most revealing discoveries were: (a) true copies, made by Gribelin and signed by Sandherr on the very day of its receipt, of the letter from Panizzardi, stating that he was about to receive details of the French railway organisation, showed it to have been written on 28 March 1895, three months after Dreyfus had been condemned, whereas the date of the original had been removed by Henry, and March 1894 substituted: (b) a true copy of the letter from Panizzardi, quoted by Cavaignac in his speech to the Chamber in July 1897, saying that "D" had brought many interesting things, showed that the original initial was not "D" but "P." Now for the first time the file of documents dealing with the case was put together complete and in order.

It was not until October 19 that André submitted to Combes a full report, in which he was careful to make no recommendation. Combes promptly handed it over to the Minister of Justice, who at once sent it to the consultative committee. The committee unanimously decided that there were grounds for revision, and on Christmas Day the Procureur-Général was instructed to submit the Rennes verdict to the Court of Criminal Appeal.

Baudouin, the Procureur-Général, approached his task with an open mind, expecting to find at least some reasonable ground for Dreyfus's second conviction. As Picquart had been staggered in 1896, so now was Baudouin. Yet his task was an involved one: it was not until 3 March 1904 that he was able to produce his summary before the Criminal Appeal Court, now presided over by Bard. The court decided in favour of full revision.

Once more the witnesses were summoned. Once more they were cross-examined by the judges—Mercier, Gonse, Du Paty, Picquart and the rest. Some witnesses who had never yet been seen were secured. Maurice Weil, much suspected of being Esterhazy's accomplice, who had carefully avoided appearing at Rennes, was somewhat roughly handled: his dossier from the War Office showed him to be a coward and a parasite but contained nothing criminal, and nothing of interest came out. Old Bastian, no longer protected by the Statistical Section, half-witted, illiterate and wildly anti-semitic, made scenes, but her evidence was valueless. She, however, produced a series of letters from Henry making appointments. There came the hitherto unknown Brücker, who professed to be uncertain whether he was the stealer and carrier of the *bordereau* to the War Office: "I did not read all the papers that came through my hands. I know nothing about this *bordereau*" (8, I, 450). Albert I, Prince of Monaco, recounted a private conversation with the Kaiser, who had once more reiterated the statement that the Germans had never dealt with Dreyfus. Finally two committees of experts examined the relevant documents. One, of senior artillery officers, affirmed that no gunner could have written the *bordereau* and that the famous secret manual was in fact not confidential. The other, composed of savants including the great mathematician Henri Poincaré, destroyed once and for all Bertillon's system, and established Esterhazy as the writer of the *bordereau*. It was nearly the end of November before the last witness was heard. It remained for one of the judges to write and present the report on the evidence.

4

One of the more puzzling questions at the end of the Affair is that of the enormous lapse of time between the setting up of the War Office enquiry by André in April 1903 and the delivery of the judgment of the united Appeal Courts in July 1906. Is it to be accounted for by the normal "law's delays"? While the period up to the conclusion of the evidence is not unreasonable, the nineteen months between November 1904 and June 1906 are not explained by the fact that the first two *rapporteurs* appointed by the Criminal Appeal Court fell sick. There is a gap of more than twelve months between the appointment of the last *rapporteur*, Moras, and the meeting of the united Courts.

Georges Sorel in his pamphlet review of Reinach's history (54, Ch. V) suggests that the obstacle was Cavaignac. But by the end of 1904 Cavaignac was wholly discredited and moreover was a dying man: he died on 25 September 1905. Even if Sorel's belief were true, there remain nine months between the death of Cavaignac and the first meeting of the united Courts on 18 June 1906.

Sorel's second suggestion seems more realistic, that during much of the time private argument was going on as to whether the courts should send Dreyfus for a third court-martial or break the Rennes verdict once and for all. By this time no one could trust a court-martial, however competent its members. The Army had not only retained its former prejudices, but had now, as a result of the case, suffered both the scandalous operations of André's staff and the Two-Year Service Law. A new court-martial with a sixth rehearing of the hundred witnesses would revive all the old hatreds. On the other hand, there was the legal question whether the united Appeal Courts could produce technical grounds for refusing to return Dreyfus to military justice. The sole ground on which they could do so was if no crime had been committed, or, materially, if the despatch of the *bordereau* to Schwartzkoppen was in itself not a crime. Baudouin attempted to adopt this thesis by accepting Esterhazy's statement that he had written the document on the order of Sandherr. The united Courts, when they came to deliver judgment, rejected Baudouin's proposition. Sorel suggests that it was Reinach who would not accept the expedient of there being no crime, but in view of Reinach's many failures in other directions to make his weight felt, it seems unlikely. It is more probable that the judges felt the justice of the plea, put forward by Mornard on behalf of Dreyfus, that it was absurd that the verdict of a junior tribunal composed of extemporary judges, who, without being required to state their reasons, merely said Guilty or Not Guilty, should be placed above the reasoned judgment and verdict of the highest court in the land.

It is still more probable that the delay was prompted by political considerations. The year 1905 was occupied with the unpleasant conflict with Germany over Morocco, which in June led to the virtual dismissal of Delcassé from the Foreign Office and the even more difficult negotiations leading up to the Algeciras Conference. There is no doubt that Rouvier, the Prime Minister, who took over Delcassé's office, was considerably agitated: the last thing he can have desired was a revival of the Affair. Further, at the same time Parliament was struggling with the Law of Separation. The Dreyfus case would add fuel to a raging fire. By the end of 1905 a general election was once more in view. Until this, which would take place in May 1906, was out of the way, it would be most impolitic to allude to the case. It is surely significant that the united Courts began their sittings within a month of the conclusion of the election.

This may be purely fanciful. The delay may have been due merely to administrative difficulties which no official was in a hurry to solve. Certainly during the three months before the elections the judges were fully occupied in dealing with a mass of voters' registration appeals. The answer will perhaps never be known.

5

During the long delay Clemenceau in the *Aurore* and Picquart in the *Gazette de Lausanne* continued to campaign for pure justice: Dreyfus must not be judged by civilians but by his peers, and if his peers once more condemned him, so much the worse for the Army and for France, and the fight for yet a fourth court-martial would begin. Picquart had now become a bitter anti-semite: "the better share of the booty [of the Affair] has gone to the Jews—they have been pushed up, particularly in the Army." No Nationalist could have gone further: Picquart even achieved quotation by Drumont.

So far as Clemenceau was concerned, he lost interest in Dreyfus as a stick with which to beat the Government. In March 1906, two months before the election, Rouvier was defeated and resigned. Armand Fallières, who had succeeded Loubet in the Presidency of the Republic in January, found an interim Prime Minister in the ageing Radical, Brisson's Minister of Justice, Sarrien, "the post to which the Car of State is hitched when the horses are tired." Sarrien invited Clemenceau to join the Cabinet—the first time such an invitation had ever been extended to him.[1] He took as

---

[1] In 1887 he had been invited to form a Government by Grévy who was being forced out of the Presidency by the Chamber, and had refused.

of right the Ministry of the Interior, at the moment the key Ministry, and at once his opinions were transformed: he wanted no rekindling of fires on the eve of the election. "While I am Minister," he said, "not a church in France shall be closed." The elections passed off quietly, with an increase in the Radicals and a heavy defeat for the Nationalists.

The three Appeal Courts met on June 18 and continued to sit until July 7, the Criminal Court presided over by Bard, the Court of Petitions by Tanon, who had led and persuaded the united Courts in 1899, and the Civil Court by Sarrut, who had been one of Scheurer-Kestner's advisers. On this occasion there was no first-night crowd, just a few old Dreyfusists and the journalists: above all there were no police. In turn Baudouin the Procureur-Général, the *rapporteur* Moras, and Mornard for Alfred Dreyfus, made their long submissions. Moras held that the writing and delivery of the *bordereau* was a crime and that Dreyfus was not the criminal. He submitted to the judges three new facts as a basis for revision: the substitution of the letter "D" for "P," the falsification of the date of the Panizzardi letter on railway organisation, and the recovery of the missing report on artillery. He claimed that Dreyfus had not written the *bordereau*, had not confessed to Lebrun-Renaud, that the annotated *bordereau* had no existence, and that the Foreign Office version of the Panizzardi telegram was correct. Nevertheless, he proposed that Dreyfus should once more be tried by court-martial.

As soon as it was published in the press, his report was greeted with a yell of protest from the minor participants in the Affair—Cuignet, Du Paty, Gribelin and Gonse. (The last incidentally challenged Picquart: they met on July 6, Gonse missed, and Picquart did not fire.) Boisdeffre and Mercier were silent. Drumont summoned the latter to speak—to reveal, as he hoped, the photograph of the annotated *bordereau*. Mercier wrote a long letter protesting against minor details in Baudouin's speech; it had no fire, and Drumont replied bitterly: "You have not spoken; you have made a pretence of speaking."

On July 12 Ballot-Beaupré, the *rapporteur* of 1899, on behalf of the judges read their full reasoned judgment. Each fact was examined, document after document analysed, charge after charge rebutted. Not a fragment of the original accusation was left in existence. The courts therefore broke and annulled the verdict of the Rennes court-martial, which had been erroneously and wrong-fully delivered. It was noted that Dreyfus had declared that he would forgo any pecuniary indemnity which the Code allowed him; further, that the judgment of the courts should be printed at the public expense and posted up in Paris and Rennes.[1]

6

By the anti-Dreyfusards the verdict was accepted with sneers and resignation. Drumont groaned: "To think that I have battled for years for the Staff and General Mercier! I really do not know why so many Dreyfusard civilians have seemed to take military men for great captains." Among the politicians the Left at once adopted postures of justified virtue. The Senate, which had formerly treated Scheurer-Kestner and Trarieux with hostility and contempt, passed a vote recognising the civic excellence of the two dead members, and decreed that their busts should be set up in the lobby. It is fair to say that the Right opposed and the Centre abstained.

As for Dreyfus and Picquart, the Cabinet was perplexed what to do with them. Obviously reparation must be made, but not exaggerated. Dreyfus, who had refused to make himself a political symbol, was to be promoted to the rank of major, which he would normally have reached in 1903, and given the fourth grade of the Legion of Honour. Since he had refused a financial indemnity, this reparation was scurvy. Picquart's was a more difficult case. Unlike Dreyfus, he had taken to political journalism. During 1903–4 André had made an effort to restore him by a special bill in the Chamber, and had failed. The new Minister of War, Etienne,

---

[1] It is doubtful if the annulment without retrial could be justified in law. It is severely criticised in *Recueil Sirey* for 1907 (pp. 1–49). A defence of the judg-ment appeared in Dalloz, *Jurisprudence Générale*; the author is believed to have been Sarrut, President of the Civil Appeal Court, and therefore prejudiced. But surely, if ever *raison d'état* was justified, this was the occasion.

proposed to promote him to the rank of Brigadier-General as from 10 July 1903, which would place him in the seniority he would probably have reached. Special laws for the reintegration of both men were necessary. Etienne introduced them in the Chamber on the day before the recess, July 13. Both bills were passed by majorities of over four hundred. Except for one speech—that of the only intelligent member of the Right, Denys Cochin—the debates were commonplace. Cochin took up some violent criticism of the anti-revisionist Right, uttered by the *rapporteur* Messimy, and pointed out that the great number of the Deputies who had opposed revision were not, like himself and his party, opponents of the Government and the regime, but dyed-in-the-wool Republicans. Were not Dupuy, Cavaignac, Billot, Méline, defenders of the Republic? Was General Mercier a Jesuit? He protested at the campaign against the Army, the volume of abuse of the whole officer body. In vain the Left tried to shout him down and threw insults at individuals; he was telling them what they wished to forget—that for political gains neither Radicals nor Socialists had dared to declare for the cause of justice, that they had accepted Cavaignac, that even after Henry's confession and suicide, when it was plain to reasonable men that revision, which did not imply recognition of innocence, was necessary, they had by their votes confirmed Dupuy's tergiversations. It was true, and now these late-comers had ridden to power on disreputable calculation. The righting of an injustice had been due, not to them, but to the patient and courageous obstinacy of a handful of men who had undergone obloquy for their refusal to accept *raison d'état*. Founders lead, but the profiteers are on their heels.

In the Senate the debate took a different turn. Mercier, defeated, still fought on. He asked to be allowed to explain why he could not vote for the reintegration of Dreyfus. He claimed that the united Appeal Courts had acted irregularly in that they did not know, could not have read, all the evidence. When indignant exclamations smothered his words and the President invited the assembly to allow the General to offer his defence, he at once riposted that he was not an accused, and that his conscience—the word raised cries of derision—did not allow him to vote for the bill. He was answered by one of the early Dreyfusards, Delpech. "If we desired to extend our need for justice, there is one man who should take the prison cell of the honourable victim whose innocence, after long and terrible sufferings, was yesterday confirmed. That man, sir, is you." Mercier attempted to continue the struggle, but the patience and courtesy of the Senators were worn out. He was shouted down and the bills restoring Dreyfus and Picquart were passed.

On July 22 a small parade was held in one of the minor courts of the Ecole Militaire. In the presence of a few friends, under the eyes of a guard of honour, Dreyfus was decorated with the Legion of Honour.

7

It had taken nearly twelve years from the arrival of the *bordereau* at the Rue Saint-Dominique to establish the innocence of one accused man. During that time a number of men who had worked either for or against revision had passed away—Scheurer-Kestner, Trarieux, Waldeck-Rousseau, Grimaux, Cavaignac, Cordier were dead. Billot followed them in 1907, Galliffet in 1909. Déroulède, after vain struggles to re-enter Parliament at the end of his exile, died in 1914. Guérin of the Anti-Semitic League, such is the irony of our existence, died in 1910 of pneumonia resulting from his attempt to save a drowning boy from the Seine floods.

Roget was refused promotion and retired in January 1908. He stood for the Chamber as a Nationalist in 1914 and was defeated. He died in 1917. Both Lauth and Cuignet retired. Both were living in 1935, still convinced that Dreyfus was a traitor; Cuignet even published a book about the case. André died in 1913, but Boisdeffre lived on in silence until 1919. Mercier, the indomitable, got himself re-elected to the Senate in 1906 and remained a member until 1920: a year later he died, at the age of eighty-eight. Du Paty, retired from the Army, was restored at the end of 1912 to the command of a territorial regiment by Millerand, now Minister of War. The protests that rose from the Left forced the rash Minister to resign. In 1914 Du Paty was offered a lines-of-communication appointment. He refused and enlisted in the 16th Chasseurs à pied. He was then given back his rank and commanded an infantry regiment with skill and great gallantry. In September 1916 he died of wounds received in action, aged sixty-three.

Schwartzkoppen had retired in 1908. In October 1914 he was given command of a brigade and took part in the heavy fighting at Notre-Dame-de-Lorette in the following spring. Owing to a serious fall from a horse in October 1915, he was on the sick list for a year, after which he was appointed to the command of a division on the eastern front. Here he was taken ill and brought to Berlin, where he died on 8 January 1917. On his deathbed he suddenly cried: "Frenchmen, hear me! Dreyfus is innocent! It was all just intrigue and forgery. Dreyfus is innocent" (53, 242–43 and viii).

Drumont lost his influence. Anti-semitism went out of fashion: the aristocracy no longer relished his puritanism, and were now marrying more and more into Jewish families. The circulation of the *Libre Parole* declined. Tentative offers to buy it were made by Charles Maurras, the rising hope of the enemies of the Republic, but the negotiations came to nothing. In the winter of 1917–18 Drumont died in poverty.

Bertillon was an obstinate man. Long before his death the finger-print method for the identification of criminals had been adopted by the police of western Europe. Bertillon resisted any change in France and maintained his own anthropometric system. Similarly he refused to admit he had made any error in his attribution of the *bordereau* to Dreyfus. It is said that in consequence of his attitude, he was never given the Legion of Honour, to which his long service and his reforms in police administration had undoubtedly entitled him. He died in February 1914, and the Préfecture of Police promptly went over to the finger-print method.

The career of Esterhazy followed its fantastic and obscure course. Having been condemned to three years' imprisonment in 1899 on Christian Esterhazy's charge of false pretences, he did not return to France. At intervals from London he abruptly intervened with letters to notabilities, but he was no longer useful.

For some time he lived with a Frenchwoman who kept a *maison de rendezvous*, but in the end she turned him out, and he disappeared from view. At some time in 1904 Etienne Lamy, the very Catholic editor of the *Correspondant*, put Judet, now editor of the *Eclair*, in touch with a man called Fitzgerald, who, as a good Irishman, hated the English. Judet, himself anglophobe and detesting Delcassé's *rapprochement* with the British Government, went to London and arranged with Fitzgerald for a series of articles under the heading *l'Angleterre Inconnue*. He apparently failed to recognise in Fitzgerald the famous Esterhazy, and thus for some time, under Judet and his successor Trogan, the Uhlan continued to lambast the country which sheltered him (61, 345–47). About 1906 he retired to Harpenden, where he acquired a house and assumed the name and style of Comte Jean-Marie de Voilemont. He also acquired a wife and is said to have lived by selling foreign tinned foods. He survived until 1923 when on May 21 he expired and was buried in the parish churchyard.

Two months after his restoration to the Army, Picquart was appointed to command an infantry division, but a month later, in October 1906, Clemenceau succeeded Sarrien as Prime Minister and remained in office for three years of chaotic opportunism. With characteristic levity, he appointed Picquart Minister of War. No great reforms can be attributed to his term of office. Those he attempted appear to have been met with the hostility of his brother generals and often ignored. His own resentments still swayed him. He held back the promotion of the luckless orderly officer of Pellieux, Ducassé, who had merely carried out his superior's instructions. He refused to promote Roget. He would do nothing for Dreyfus. He never lived down his past and always suffered embarrassment when faced by officers who could not forgive him. He was eventually appointed to command the Second Army Corps at Amiens, where in January 1914 he was thrown from his horse and a few days later died. He was a brave and honourable man, but he was also a prig.

Joseph Reinach did not easily live down the reputation his enemies attached to him for his share in the case. He did not win back his constituency of Digne until 1906, and lost it for good in 1914. During the war he became the military commentator of the *Figaro* under the pseudonym of Polybe, much in favour with that Catholic, patriotic and combatant general, Charles Mangin, but regarded by British G.H.Q. as a pestilent nuisance. He died in 1921. Long before that his *éloge* had been written in shining words by a Catholic Dreyfusist, who himself died in battle. In *Notre Jeunesse* Charles Péguy wrote: "Alone he [Reinach] was of a political and social depth, of an order of greatness at least equal to that of Jaurès. . . . Of our whole headquarters, we see that he alone did not weaken before the Dreyfusist demagogy . . . never bowed the knee . . . to the demagogy of the Combes tyranny. And this is even more remarkable in that he has throughout his career been a politician. He was the only one who opposed the delations of the Ligue des Droits de l'Homme. . . . It is surprising, and this is the highest praise I know of a man . . . that this politician, wealthy and powerful, had at many turns the political virtues of a poor man. Of what non-Jew can so much be said?" (41, 226).

Dreyfus remained what he had always been, a strictly honourable soldier. He had never lent himself to political adventurers. He was even heard to say that the abuse of Mercier was exaggerated (28, 314). After a short period in the Army, he resigned and went on to the reserve. During the 1914–18 war he was recalled to service and commanded an ammunition column with efficiency. He died in 1935, a quiet old gentleman. During his later years he liked to play bridge. One evening his partner remarked that a certain X had been arrested for espionage, and then, realising the tactlessness of his remark, added that he did not suppose there was anything in it. Dreyfus, calmly dealing, rejoined: "Oh, I don't know; after all, there's no smoke without fire."

Conclusion

MANY theories have been propounded, many generalisations presented, as to the meaning of the Affair, usually with a moral tang. Few deserve to survive. The more the evidence is examined, the less heroic and the less odious do the leading actors become. The case was not a battle between good and evil, and such a view simplifies it to meaninglessness.

It passed through three phases. The first concerns only the soldiers and the scattered handful of early revisionists—the victim's family, Reinach and Lazare alarmed at the inflammation of anti-semitism, Picquart and Leblois, Scheurer-Kestner and Ranc. The accusers, with the single exception of Henry, were acting in good faith. That they were precipitate is true, but in 1894 they had good reason, at the moment when the defence plans were being completely redrawn and the new 75-millimetre quick-firing field-gun, the best in Europe, was on the point of being produced. That the leading staff officers persisted in error is excusable, in that Picquart could offer no serious evidence against Esterhazy other than the handwriting, which was controverted by the experts, while on paper Esterhazy had an excellent record. That they were deceived may argue foolishness but not bad faith. There is no evidence of a "plot," even as regards their depositions at the Zola trial and the subsequent proceedings. The transcripts of the evidence demonstrate fully that no serious consultation had taken place between the generals. As for the famous conspiracy against the Republic, which Dreyfusard literature wearisomely repeats, no officer's name has ever been mentioned except Pellieux's, and that by Déroulède after the General's death.

Anti-semitism appears to have played no part in the case until Drumont and the Assumptionists took advantage of the fact that Dreyfus was a Jew. And, as Mazel remarks (64, 204), anti-semitism throughout was no more than an accessory. Anti-semitic prejudice existed both before and after the case—there are anti-semites to-day in all Western countries—but the fury died away, and Socialist critics as much as clerical lamented that the Jews were in fact the profiteers from the misfortunes of their co-religionist. Except for Reinach, Bernard Lazare and a few young intellectuals as yet of small importance—Marcel Proust, the Halévy brothers, Léon Blum, the Natansons, the circles of Mme Caillavet and Mme Strauss (Bizet's widow)—the Jews were at best neutral, and on the whole hostile to the cause of revision. Léon Blum speaks of the egotistic and timorous prudence of Jewish society. "The rich Jews, the middle bourgeoisie, the Jewish public servants, were afraid of the fight . . . they thought only of going to ground and hiding" (16, 24–6).

In fact, a cool examination of the case shows that in its origins it arose partly from genuine error or deception, partly from mistaken loyalty. I have myself no doubt that Sandherr was convinced of Dreyfus's guilt. Had he had doubts he would never have rested until he discovered the real traitor; he would not have recommended that the papers should not be re-examined. Henry may have believed Dreyfus guilty, but he also knew that his deposition to the first court-martial was false. That he feared the appearance of new evidence seems clear from the fact that, six months before Picquart came on Esterhazy's name, he wrote the "Blenheim" letter: none other than he had an interest in sending it. His subsequent forgeries and manipulations were pursued in the spirit of loyalty to the Army and the Statistical Section and with the intention of stiffening his superiors. That such conduct was not unique is shown by André, who in his memoirs (9, 325) quotes letters from his personal secretariat which indicate that they were pushing him forward by acting behind his back. As for Henry, the actions of a single cunning, stupid man, with his own conception of loyalty, precipitated a political crisis of great magnitude, in which he involved his chiefs and in the end brought about the dissolution of the department he was striving to fortify.

The second phase of the Affair turns on the Zola trial. This led to the entry of the intellectuals, particularly the teachers and students of the Ecole Normale Supérieure. I have no doubt in my own mind, although the only evidence is that of his biographer, Charles Andler, that the real fomenter of the tumult was Lucien Herr, the School's librarian, the mentor and inspirer of Jaurès. The reactions of this group are not invariably as would be expected. Barrès, as Benda acutely saw (14, 418–19), by turning anti-revisionist denied both his past and his nature. He had not been a devotee of order as preferable to justice, but "the cultivator of anti-social individualism." In consequence "he never felt completely happy, as if he were poisoned by the bitterness of a secret betrayal, treachery to himself." In contrast to Barrès, Clemenceau, temperamentally authoritarian, who within ten years of his adoption of Dreyfus's cause was showing himself the ruthless adept of *raison d'état*, fought with indomitable spirit on the side which his ruling passion must have told him was wrong because it was against authority.

The third phase is that of the professional politicians. Throughout they behaved with the familiar opportunism of politicians: but opportunism is a natural part of politics. In the early period they no more than the general public could penetrate the truth. Practically the whole Chamber thankfully accepted Cavaignac's assurances. But after Henry's suicide they displayed all the *canaillerie* of opportunism, and their later assumption of virtue is as revolting as their unscrupulous attacks on the Church and the Army and the creation of the fantasy of a clerico-military plot. How little they were concerned with the justice they talked of is to be seen in their behaviour after the pardon of 1899, when for more than three years the majority blocked every move to reopen the case.

The political consequences of the Affair horrified many of the early revisionists. Reinach, while remaining a faithful fighter for Dreyfus, shows in his sixth volume, written after the final rehabilitation, his distress at Dreyfusardism and its aftermath. Like many others, he had hoped to avoid the consequences of his actions. It was not to be, and no one has more clearly summed up the Dreyfusist blindness than Julien Benda (14, 423–24). "Those who persist in dissociating the judicial Dreyfus case from the political do not wish to see that if they in all sincerity made the dissociation, the mob did not, could not make it, with the result that their judicial action, whether they desired it or not, became inevitably a political action. The single coherent attitude for the non-revolutionary Dreyfusist was to say *either*: 'I put justice before all, and *with death in my soul* accept the political consequences of my act of justice'; *or* 'I put order above everything, and *with death in my soul* renounce an act of justice which will inevitably bring in its train such and such social consequences.' As for claiming to carry out the act which they believed just, while avoiding the social troubles, it was, if done in good faith, a demonstration, as Maurras clearly saw, of blindness very near to weakness of mind."

In his reminiscences, Lord Morley remarked that it was difficult to see how Acton reconciled the view that history is a matter of broad general principles with his other view that the real prize of the historian is the episode on the back-stairs. The Affair illustrates the reconciliation. The secret actions of a minor executive official began a movement which ended in a great transformation of the political scene. Yet, even so, chance played an enormous part, intervening on more than one occasion with shattering effect. But for chance, Dreyfus would have died on The Devil's Island, a dishonoured man. As the old police agent in Nizan's *La Conspiration* says: "Little chances and little men manufacture great events. The masses and the professors never see the true relationship because the causes have no visible proportion to the consequences and all the tracks are blurred. Everyone is blind to the turns and twists of chance and the secret of little men."

Again, the Affair illustrates the influence of propaganda on history. Nine-tenths of the literature of the case is Dreyfusard; the Dreyfusard view, with its crude blacks and whites, has passed into history. The anti-Dreyfusard versions, such as they are, are no less propagandist, but since their side was defeated, the writers have been ineffective. Both versions are distorted. It is only by examining the case in detail that a picture emerges, not of virtue at grips with villainy, but of fallible human beings pulled this way and that by their beliefs, their loyalties, their prejudices, their ambitions and their ignorance. "*Rien ne vit que par le détail.*"

APPENDIX I : *Esterhazy*

(a)

Schwartzkoppen's account of his transactions with Esterhazy has been called in question by Mazel (64), and while Mazel's own theory is far from acceptable, his criticisms have some pertinence. Münster stated that he did not think Esterhazy was employed by the attaché before 1893, but claimed he knew less than anybody about their relations. Cuers, the spy, also told Lauth that an officer, certainly by description resembling Esterhazy, had been in Schwartzkoppen's pay from 1893 (cf. p. 122). Furthermore, it would seem that Esterhazy had been selling information for some time: otherwise his interest in artillery is inexplicable, since he offered no evidence of being a zealous officer. Neither the Austrian nor the Italian attaché had heard of him. Was he working for the Russians? Reinach (47, II, 69, f.n. 3) says he was denounced in 1892 to General Brault, then head of the secretariat of Freycinet, the Minister of War. The information was passed to the Military Government of Paris, but nothing came of it. Reinach also says that the Russian general, Annenkoff, the builder of the Trans-Siberian railway, who committed suicide in January 1899, had related that both Henry and Esterhazy had been in Russian pay "before the alliance," which I take to mean the military convention of 1893–94. The statement is possible as regards Esterhazy, but it is surely unrealistic as regards Henry. As Town Major of Péronne in 1890–92, Henry could scarcely have had any information of value; at the best he could have begun only after he joined the Statistical Section in January 1893. In any case there is nothing to support Annenkoff's statement.

Major-General Sir Reginald Talbot, the British Military Attaché in Paris from 1889 to 1895, later Sirdar of Egypt, told Galliffet (6, I, 217) that when he was in Paris it was common knowledge among the military attachés that Esterhazy could be bought for a thousand francs. But Talbot denied personal knowledge of Esterhazy.

As to Schwartzkoppen's evidence, there is, on the other hand, the crumpled note of January 1894, "*Zweifel—Beweise—Patent*" (cf. p. 84), which certainly implies some approach by a French officer. It may be that, with the signature of the military convention at this time, the Russians dismissed so unreliable an agent as Esterhazy, since they could now obtain openly from the French War Office as much as he could probably give them, and Esterhazy may have made a first approach to Schwartzkoppen at this time and been rebuffed. Then in July, by now desperately in need of money, he made his bold *ad hominem* approach.

It is difficult to see why, as Mazel holds, Schwartzkoppen should have written, apparently for his own private satisfaction, a false account of what occurred.

(b)

At the several trials and enquiries, controversy arose as to whether Esterhazy had seen the new 120-millimetre gun fired at Châlons. The defenders of Dreyfus attempted to show that he had, the witnesses for the Army that he had not. The guns were not fired on the range until August 16. Cavaignac, among other witnesses, said that Esterhazy left Châlons on August 10, went to his house at Dommartin-la-Planchette, near Sainte-Menehould, and returned to Rouen by way of Paris on August 13. This is partly confirmed by Schwartzkoppen, who on returning to Paris on August 6 found a letter from Esterhazy saying that he would be at Châlons until August 10, then at Dommartin until August 12, and then "at my usual residence." Then, says Schwartzkoppen, Esterhazy called on him at 10 p.m. on August 13 and again on the 15th.

Against this, there was shown to the Criminal Appeal Court a letter from Esterhazy written on the 11th from Châlons, saying he would remain there for five more days. This, no doubt, is one of the letters mentioned in *l'Aurore* of 28 August 1899, in an article, "Esterhazy en 1894" (57), in which the contributor, Adolphe Tabarant, claimed to have traced Esterhazy for 305 days during the year from six hundred letters, telegrams and *petits bleus* written by him. According to Tabarant, he was at Châlons from August 3 to 9, when he went to Paris; at Dommartin on August 10 and 11, but he returned on August 12 to Châlons where he remained until the 17th, when he returned to Rouen, where he stayed until September 7. These dates conflict with those given by Schwartzkoppen of Esterhazy's visits, viz. September 1, 5 and 6, but Rouen was within easy reach of Paris. It seems strange that no notice was taken of Tabarant's article by the defence.

The conflict of evidence as to his presence at Châlons on August 16 may, however, be less irresolvable when it is seen that Dommartin-la-Planchette is only twenty kilometres from Suippes, the southern point of the Châlons *champ de tir*, and connected by railway.

What, however, none of the French witnesses knew was that, on some date between August 16 and 31, Esterhazy attended another firing practice at the Sissonne artillery ranges, near Laon (53, 11). These then are the "manœuvres" referred to in the last line of the *bordereau*. It is probable that it was at Sissonne that he saw the new 120-millimetre gun in action, since he gave Schwartzkoppen a description on September 1. This would place the delivery of the *bordereau* not earlier than the last week of August. I have put 27th, but the exact date is of no consequence. This leaves less than a month between the leaving of the *bordereau* at the Embassy and its appearance on Henry's desk, and during a part of that time Henry seems to have been on leave, returning to the War Office on September 25.

It seems probable that Esterhazy paid yet another visit to look at the guns. According to Tabarant, he was at Evreux from October 7 to 14, when he was presumed to have gone to Dommartin until the end of the month. But on October 29 Schwartzkoppen wrote to Berlin that he had received information from a good source on manœuvres at, *inter alia*, Vanjours, a fort some twenty-four kilometres east of Paris on the Ourcq canal, to which two batteries of the new guns had been sent, a fact to which the German War Office had drawn his attention. It is possible that the "good source" was Esterhazy. Schwartzkoppen's letter appears to have reached the French War Office by the "ordinary route," but since Dreyfus had been under lock and key for a fortnight, the letter could not refer to him. The document was therefore filed. It was shown *in camera* to the judges at the Rennes trial in 1899, and referred to by Labori; but it was not disclosed until the final investigation of 1904.

APPENDIX II : *The Arrival of the* Bordereau *at the War Office*

As to which of the two versions of this incident is correct, there is considerable but conflicting evidence. Of the first version the only narrative is that given by Brücker's uncle, who lived with Bastian, to Puybaraud, political director to the Police Préfecture, as coming from his nephew. Puybaraud retailed this to Reinach on 30 November 1899, in the presence of the playwright Sardou and his son-in-law, Robert de Flers. Puybaraud and Brücker's uncle were both dead before the final investigation of 1904, while at that date Brücker professed to know nothing about the matter, which is scarcely credible if the uncle's story is correct (8, I, 450).

According to the uncle's narrative, on seeing the substance of the letter, Brücker at once recognised its value and carried it to Henry. Henry, having glanced at it, said: "It doesn't seem to be any better than what you have brought me of late," and began to tear the paper, which was then intact. Brücker stopped him and said: "If you think the letter worthless, I don't. Give it me back. I shall find others who will think it more important than you do." On which Henry said: "Well, leave it. I'll look at it, and after I've seen what it's worth, I'll send for you." About this there is first the difficulty that Schwartzkoppen says that

Esterhazy personally brought him the documents on four different dates, one of which was before the end of the Châlons trials. But the wording of the *bordereau* indicates it as a covering letter, and according to the Brücker version there was also in Schwartzkoppen's pigeon-hole a packet presumably but not certainly the documents. The only certainty is that the *bordereau* never reached Schwartzkoppen.

Secondly, if Henry did retain the *bordereau* when it was handed to him by Brücker, why did he not show it to anyone in the Statistical Section before September 27, a month later? It is probable that Henry in fact did not see Bastian on "the ordinary route" before September 26, since a letter dated September 25, indicating that he had just returned to the War Office from leave, was among the papers handed over by Bastian to the Criminal Appeal Court in 1904 (8, III, 344). Further, General Roget stated to the Criminal Appeal Court in 1899 (6, I, 74) that in the same delivery there were an official document of August 4, and four private letters dated August 21, 25, 26 and September 2, which implies a long interval since the previous delivery. There are thus over three weeks to be accounted for. From the evidence of Mme Henry, who is above suspicion, her husband was undoubtedly working on the reconstruction of the *bordereau* on the night before he handed it to Sandherr.

The only point that supports the Brücker version is that the letter was not, as were the usual papers from Schwartzkoppen's waste-paper basket, torn and crumpled, but almost intact. As Picquart said to the united Courts in 1899, was it credible that a letter of this nature could have been thrown, practically undamaged, into the waste-paper basket? Reinach, whose object is to convict Henry of being Esterhazy's accomplice, argues that Henry recognised the handwriting as Esterhazy's but, fearing what Brücker would do if he destroyed or hid the letter, eventually brought it to Sandherr. But it is unrealistic to suppose that a disgraced agent could have blackmailed a bold man such as Henry, who would have laughed in his face. There is no serious evidence that Henry and Esterhazy were in conspiracy to betray. To General Roget on 30 August 1899, twenty-four hours before his death, Henry insisted that the *bordereau* arrived on the "ordinary route." If Brücker had any hand in the matter at all, it seems possible that he stole the letter, tore it and gave it to the illiterate Bastian to deal with as usual.

APPENDIX III: *The* Libre Parole *Disclosure of* 29 *October* 1894

This episode is one of the most baffling. On the evening of October 27 Papillaud, during Drumont's absence in Brussels acting editor of the *Libre Parole*, found under the door of his private apartment a note which ran:

My dear friend, you were quite right. It is Captain Dreyfus, the one who lives at 6 Avenue du Trocadéro, who was arrested on 15th for espionage, and is in prison at the Cherche-Midi. He is said to be travelling, but this is a lie, because they want to hush up the case. All Jewry is roused.

Yours, Henry.

Do get that little enquiry of mine answered as soon as possible.

According to Reinach (47, I, 190–92, and VI, 351–52), a copy of this letter was given by Papillaud to a friend, who passed it to a contributor to *Le Siècle*: it appeared in that paper on 2 April 1899, seven months after the death of Henry, and during the re-examination of the case by the Cour de Cassation. On April 3 there appeared a full story of what had occurred, given by Papillaud to Yvonne Leclaire, a contributor to the revisionist *La Fronde*, a paper run entirely by women journalists and edited by Marguérite Durand. According to this, Papillaud "towards the end of October" (date unspecified) had the letter. On the following morning, Papillaud, together with Commandant Biot, military correspondent of the *Libre Parole*, called at Dreyfus's house. They were told that Dreyfus was away and Mme Dreyfus had just gone out. They told the maid, an Alsatian, that her master had been arrested. She said she knew nothing, but that Madame had done nothing but cry since two gentlemen had called two days earlier—an odd statement, for Lucie Dreyfus had known of the arrest and the charge since October 15. Papillaud said that he and Biot then went to the War Office, where after some trouble they saw Henry, who claimed the letter was a forgery and said that an enquiry must be set on foot. Papillaud retained the letter, but allowed Henry to take a copy. Nothing more was heard of the matter. Biot, in *Le Temps* of 4 August 1903, said he had never seen or spoken with Henry and had had no relations with him.

In the *Libre Parole* of 3 April 1899, Papillaud wrote that the note had no greater importance for him than any other anonymous letter, since he did not know the signature. Nevertheless he had printed his "fishing" enquiry in the paper. Later he insisted to the Court of Appeal that the letter had not come from Henry. When asked to produce it, he said it was no longer in his possession.

Neither Picquart nor Cuignet believed the letter to be Henry's: it would have been far too dangerous for him, and in any case Henry was not as yet directly interested. The *Fronde* article stated: "Well-informed people affirm that it is the work of Col. Du Paty de Clam"; but such an action is not at all in Du Paty's style of idiocy. I myself am inclined to think that the whole thing was an elaborate mystification on the part of Papillaud, partly to cover the real betrayer of the information, partly to embroil the case still further.

APPENDIX IV: *The Commentaries*

How many so-called commentaries were there? The discussion in Reinach (47, I, App. xii, pp. 603–11) reaches no conclusion, save that the judges of 1894 saw a commentary which was not that made by Du Paty. As has been seen, Du Paty's dealt only with the memo "Zweifel Beweise," the Davignon letter and the *canaille de D* letter. It was handed back to him by Sandherr and produced by Du Paty before the Cour de Cassation in 1899.

It is clear, from Freystaetter's evidence at Rennes, that the commentary or biographical notice seen by the judges in 1894 bore no relation to Du Paty's commentary. Du Paty in 1904 (8, I, 239–40) said emphatically: "The commentary which I have already produced is not that of which a copy was destroyed in 1897 (i.e. the copy of the biographical notice Sandherr retained). . . . It was not my commentary; this differed in appearance and in details from the commentary I have tabled. . . . It was not my commentary which was communicated to the judges, but the commentary of which I saw a copy in 1897." Later in the same examination he said (p. 243): "The commentary [mine] once corrected and *recopied* [author's italics] was taken from me by Sandherr."

From this it appears that there were not three documents, as Reinach surmises, but four, viz:—

(1) Du Paty's original draft, in his keeping, produced in 1899.

(2) A copy of (1), "taken from me by Sandherr."

(3) The biographical notice in fair copy, shown to the judges in 1894 and destroyed by Mercier between December 22 and the day he quitted the War Office, 27 January 1895.

(4) The draft of (3), seen by Du Paty in 1897, and then given, perhaps by Gonse, to Mercier, who destroyed it.

This would seem to solve the difficulty, but for the fact that Picquart stated to the Criminal Appeal Court (6, I, 135) that when he first saw the secret file in August 1896, he found in it a commentary "which may have been written by Du Paty," i.e. No. 2. Since they had been working in the Third Bureau, he should have been familiar with Du Paty's writing, but he merely adds "from what Col. Sandherr said to me." Moreover, according to his own evidence—given, it is true, more than eighteen months later—the commentary he had read said nothing about the Bourges Explosives School or the Ecole de Guerre course. If it is accepted that Picquart's memory was accurate and that Du Paty was telling the truth when he said that the document he saw in 1897 was not his commentary, it is clear that between November 1896, when Picquart left the War Office, and December 1897, biographical notice No. 4 was substituted for Du Paty's commentary (No. 2), which then disappeared. The only person who could have done this was Henry. The reason for the substitution would no doubt be that the biographical note was a more cogent piece, more likely to convince Gonse than Du Paty's unintelligible essay. But how did he come to have it, as he must have had it, from Sandherr? And why was it not put into the Secret File in December 1894?

APPENDIX V: *The* Petit Bleu

At Rennes, Emile Picot, the distinguished librarian and critic and a member of the Institut, stated on oath the story he had had from the Austrian military attaché, Colonel Schneider, in May 1899, concerning the *petit bleu*. Schwartzkoppen had broken with Esterhazy. Esterhazy pressed Schwartzkoppen, saying he was about to enter the War Office. It was in answer to this that Schwartzkoppen dictated the *petit bleu* to a lady with whom he had a liaison and who was at the moment in his office. She took it down in a somewhat, though not wholly, disguised hand. Then, thinking the matter over, he said, "No! One can't have dealings with a man like that," and tore the letter into fragments.

On the other hand Schwartzkoppen says (53, 90) that he believes he wrote the *petit bleu* himself and posted it. He therefore thinks that he must have been followed and the letter seized in transit. But it certainly was not in his handwriting and, since it bore no stamp, it is improbable that it had been posted.

A further version is given by Princess Radziwill in a letter of 2 May 1899. According to this, Schwartzkoppen put the *petit bleu* in the pocket of his overcoat when he went out to dinner, intending to post it at some distance from the Embassy. He left the coat in the cloakroom at Durand's (today Thomas Cook's office by the Madeleine), and while he dined it was stolen and brought to Picquart. Picquart tore it in fragments to conceal the fact that it had been stolen (46, 197). If this is true, it follows that Henry's statement that he had not seen it in the bags he took from Bastian (47, II, 242 *et seq.*) is also true.

APPENDIX VI: *Selected Documents*

1. The "Canaille de D" Letter. Schwartzkoppen to Panizzardi (p. 52)

Je regrette bien de ne pas vous avoir vu avant votre départ: du reste je serai de retour dans huit jours. Ci-joint douze plans directeurs de Nice que ce canaille de D. m'a remis pour vous. Je lui ai dit que vous

n'aviez pas l'intention de reprendre des relations. Il prétend qu'il y a
malentendu et qu'il ferait tout son possible pour vous satisfaire. Il dit
qu'il s'était entêté et que vous ne lui en voulez pas. Je lui ai repondu
qu'il était fou et que je ne croyais pas que vous reprendriez les relations avec lui. Faites ce que vous voudrez. Au revoir, je suis très
pressé.   Alexandrine

Undated. Cordier believed it of 1892, Lauth claimed to have recon-
stituted it in December 1893. Not photographed until October 1894.
Shown in secret to the court-martial of 1894. Read by Cavaignac to
the Chamber of Deputies 7 July 1898.
Dated by someone in the Statistical Section "16 April 1894" after
October of that year.

2. *The* Bordereau (p. 56)

Sans nouvelles m'indiquant que vous désirez me voir, je vous adresse
cependant, Monsieur, quelques renseignements intéressants:

1. Une note sur le frein hydraulique du 120 et la manière dont
   s'est conduite cette pièce;
2. Une note sur les troupes de couverture (quelques modifications seront apportées par le nouveau plan);
3. Une note sur une modification aux formations de l'artillerie;
4. Une note relative à Madagascar;
5. Le projet de manuel de tir de l'artillerie de campagne (14
   mars 1894).

Ce dernier document est extrêmement difficile à se procurer et je ne
puis l'avoir à ma disposition que très peu de jours. Le ministère de la
Guerre en a envoyé un nombre fixe dans les corps, et ces corps en sont
responsables. Chaque officier détenteur doit remettre le sien après les
manoeuvres.
Si donc vous voulez y prendre ce qui vous intéresse et le tenir à ma
disposition après, je le prendrai. A moins que vous ne vouliez que je
fasse copier in extenso et ne vous en adresse la copie.
Je vais partir en manœuvres.

3. *The Panizzardi Telegram to Rome of 2 November 1894* (pp. 81-2)

The original Italian version, so far as I am aware, is not available,
though it might be found in an Italian newspaper of August–September
1899.
The first trial of the ciphered telegram produced no more than certainty
of the name "Dreyfus," together with a hypothesis that the sentence
ran: "Arrestato capitano Dreyfus che non avuto relazione con Ger-
mania. . . ." (Captain Dreyfus arrested who has not had relations with

Germany.) The rest was more sketchy: "uffiziale rimane prevenuto emissario," which the Foreign Office cryptographer said was impossible. This was the version seized by Sandherr and carried over to the War Office, where it was copied and possibly further distorted.

The correct version was not passed by the Foreign Office until some date between November 7 and 13, when it was transmitted to Sandherr. This ran: "If Captain Dreyfus has not had relations with you, it would be well to order the Ambassador to publish an official denial, in order to avoid press comment."

The War Office embellishers appear to have added to the trial version: "precautions taken, emissary warned." This seems to have been the version, either as a document or in the commentary, which was shown to the court-martial of 1894, since Freystaetter at Rennes in 1899 believed this was what he had read or heard, though he would not swear to the phrase "precautions taken" etc. The same version was sworn to by Mercier, Boisdeffre and Gonse. There can be no doubt that Sandherr was the author of the additions.

4. *The Davignon Letter. Panizardi to Schwartzkoppen* (p. 84)

Je viens encore d'écrire au colonel Davignon; si vous avez occasion de parler de la question avec votre ami, faites-le particulièrement, en façon que Davignon ne vienne pas à le savoir. Du reste, il n'y répondrait pas. Car il faut jamais faire voir qu'un agent s'occupe de l'autre.

Probably of December 1893–January 1894. Shown in secret to the court-martial of 1894.

5. *The Schwartzkoppen Memorandum* (p. 84)

The original German is nowhere given *in toto*.

"Doute [*Zweifel*]. Preuves [*Beweise*]. Lettre de service [*Patent*]. Situation dangéreuse pour moi, relations avec un officier français. Ne pas conduire personellement les négociations. Apporter ce qu'il a. Absolute (*Ge*......)... Bureau des Renseignements [in French]. Aucunes relations corps de troupes. Important seulement sortant du Ministère. Deja quelquepart ailleurs."

Generally accepted as of January 1894 in reply to a telegram of 25 December 1893: "Choses aucun signe d'état-major."
Examined by Du Paty in his commentary, but not shown to court-martial of 1894.

Appendix VII

From December 1893

	Prime Minister	Justice	Foreign Office	Interior	Finance	War
3 Dec 1893	Casimir-Perier	Dubost	Casimir-Perier	Raynal	Burdeau	General Mercier
30 May 1894	Dupuy	Guérin	Hanotaux	Dupuy	Poincaré	General Mercier
27 Jan 1895	Ribot	Trarieux	Hanotaux	Leygues	Ribot	General Zurlinden
2 Nov 1895	Bourgeois	Ricard	Berthelot	Bourgeois	Doumer	Cavaignac
29 Apr 1896	Méline	1 Darlan 2 Milliard	Hanotaux	Barthou	Cochery	General Billot
28 Jun 1898	Brisson	Sarrien	Delcassé	Brisson U/S Vallé	Peytral	1 Cavaignac 2 General Zurlinden 3 General Chanoine
3 Nov 1898	Dupuy	Lebret	Delcassé	Dupuy	Peytral	1 Freycinet 2 Krantz
23 Jun 1899	Waldeck-Rousseau	Monis	Delcassé	Waldeck-Rousseau	Caillaux	1 General de Galliffet 2 General André
7 Jun 1902	Combes	Vallé	Delcassé	Combes	Rouvier	1 General André 2 Berteaux
24 Jan 1905	Rouvier	Chaumié	1 Delcassé 2 Rouvier	1 Etienne 2 Dubief	1 Rouvier 2 Merlou	1 Berteaux 2 Etienne
13 Mar 1906	Sarrien	Sarrien	Bourgeois	Clemenceau	Poincaré	Etienne
19 Oct 1906	Clemenceau	Guyot-Dessaigne	Pichon	Clemenceau	Caillaux	General Picquart

Presidents of the Republic

3 Dec 1887	Sadi Carnot
27 Jun 1894	Jean Casimir-Perier
17 Jan 1895	Félix Faure
18 Feb 1899	Emile Loubet
17 Jan 1906	Armand Fallières

Ministries

to October 1906

Marine	Public Instruction	Public Worship	Public Works	Commerce	Agriculture	Colonies
Admiral Lefévre	Spuller	Dubost	Jonnart	Marty	Viger	Boulanger
Félix Faure	Leygues	Dupuy	Barthou	Lourtice	Viger	Delcassé
Admiral Besnard	Poincaré	Poincaré	Dupuy-Dutemps	André Lebon	Gadaud	Chautemps
Lockroy	Combes	Combes	Guyot-Des-saigne	Mesureur	Viger	Guieysse
Admiral Besnard	Rambaud	Rambaud	Turrel	Boucher	Méline	André Lebon
Lockroy	Léon Bour-geois	Sarrien	Tillaye	Maruéjouls	Viger	Trouillot
Lockroy	Leygues	Dupuy	1 Krantz 2 Monestier	Delombre	Viger	Guillain
de Lanessan	Leygues	Leygues	Baudin	Millerand	Jean Dupuy	Decrais
Pelletan	Chaumié	Combes	Maruéjouls	Trouillot	Mougeot	Doumergue
Thomson	Bienvenu-Martin	Bienvenu-Martin	Gauthier	1 Dubief 2 Trouillot	Ruau	Clémentel
Thomson	Briand	Briand	Barthou	Doumergue	Ruau	Leygues
Thomson	Briand	Guyot-Des-saigne	Barthou	Doumergue	Ruau	Milliès-Lacroix

APPENDIX VIII: *Calendar of Events*

1893

Jan 13 — Henry enters Statistical Section.

1894

January	Arrival of memo *"Zweifel, Beweise, Patent"* at War Office.
May 17	W.O. circular that second-year staff learners will not go on manœuvres.
„ 30	Second Dupuy Ministry.
June 24	Assassination of President Carnot.
„ 27	Casimir-Perier elected President of the Republic.
June–July	Staff ride attended by Dreyfus.
July 20	First interview Schwartzkoppen–Esterhazy.
„ 27	Second interview Schwartzkoppen–Esterhazy.
Aug 3–16	Artillery demonstrations at Châlons-sur-Marne.
„ 3–25	Inter-services committee on Madagascar expedition.
„ 15	Third interview Schwartzkoppen–Esterhazy.
„ 20–30(?)	Artillery demonstrations at Sissonne.
Sep 1	Fourth interview Schwartzkoppen–Esterhazy.
„ 5	Fifth interview Schwartzkoppen–Esterhazy.
„ 6	Esterhazy leaves note on Madagascar at German Embassy.
„ 26	*Bordereau* arrives at Statistical Section.
Oct 6	Fourth Bureau suspects Dreyfus.
„ 15	Dreyfus arrested.
„ 18	Du Paty's first interrogation of Dreyfus.
„ 29	*Libre Parole* announces an arrest.
Nov 2	Panizzardi's telegram to Rome seized.
„ 3	Ormeschville appointed *rapporteur* of case.
Dec 3	Ormeschville submits his report to Saussier.
„ 19–22	First court-martial.
„ 31	Du Paty invites Dreyfus to confess.

1895

Jan 5	Degradation of Dreyfus.
„ 6	Interview of Münster with Casimir-Perier.
„ 14	Dupuy resigns.
„ 15–16	Casimir-Perier resigns.
„ 17	Félix Faure elected president of the Republic.
„ 28	Third Ribot Ministry.

Feb 21	Dreyfus despatched to The Devil's Island.
March 28	Panizzardi's letter re railway organisation reaches War Office.
July 1	Sandherr retires from Statistical Section, Picquart takes over.
Oct 20	Fall of Ribot Ministry.
Nov 2	Léon Bourgeois Ministry.

1896

March	Schwartzkoppen breaks with Esterhazy.
,, 15–20	Arrival of *petit bleu* at War Office.
April 23	Fall of Bourgeois Ministry.
,, 30	Méline Ministry.
Aug 5	Picquart speaks of Esterhazy to Boisdeffre.
,, 6	Henry and Lauth meet Cuers at Bâle.
Sep 4	*Weyler* forgery reaches Colonial Ministry.
,, 14	*Eclair* article on Dreyfus and Secret File.
Nov 1	Henry forges Panizzardi letter, the *faux Henry*.
,, 6	Lazare publishes first pamphlet, *La Vérité sur l'Affaire Dreyfus*.
,, 10	*Matin* prints facsimile of the *bordereau*.
,, 15–16	Picquart hands over to Gonse and leaves War Office.
,, 18	Castelin interpellation.
Dec 12	Picquart ordered to North Africa.

1897

June 7	Picquart receives Henry's letter of accusation.
,, 20–27	Picquart in Paris talks to Leblois.
July 14	Scheurer-Kestner makes his first statement.
Oct 18	Henry warns Esterhazy by anonymous letter.
,, 23	Last interview Schwartzkoppen–Esterhazy. Du Paty, Gribelin and Henry meet Esterhazy at Montsouris Park.
Nov 9	Mathieu Dreyfus puts facsimile of *bordereau* on sale.
,, 12	Schwartzkoppen's final departure from Paris.
,, 15	Mathieu Dreyfus denounces Esterhazy.
,, 17–20	First Pellieux examination. Picquart recalled from Africa.
,, 24–Dec 3	Second Pellieux examination.
Dec 4	Order to prosecute Esterhazy. Méline in Chamber speaks of *res judicata*.
,, 7	Scheurer-Kestner interpellates in Senate.
,, 8–30	Ravary instruction.

1898

Jan 7	*Siècle* publishes Ormeschville's report of 1894.
„ 10–11	Esterhazy's court-martial.
„ 13	*Aurore* prints Zola's *J'Accuse.*
	Picquart placed under arrest.
„ 17	Anti-semite riots begin.
Feb 1	Enquiry on Picquart.
„ 7–23	Zola trial.
„ 24	Foundation of Ligue des Droits de l'Homme.
„ 26	Picquart dismissed the service.
March 3	Death of Lemercier-Picard.
April 7	Parliament rises.
May 8 & 22	General election.
June 14	Fall of Méline Ministry.
„ 28	Second Brisson Ministry.
July 7	Cavaignac's declaration.
„ 9	Picquart's open letter to Cavaignac.
„ 18	First interview Bertulus–Henry.
	Panizzardi recalled to Italy.
Aug 12	Picquart arrested and sent to Santé.
„ 13	Cuignet discovers Henry forgery.
„ 30	Henry's confession and arrest.
„ 31	Henry's suicide. Esterhazy flees to Belgium.
	Esterhazy dismissed the service.
	Boisdeffre resigns.
Sep 3	Cavaignac resigns, Zurlinden appointed.
„ 4	Mme Dreyfus files appeal to Minister of Justice.
„ 17	Zurlinden resigns. Chanoine appointed.
„ 19	Meeting of Kitchener with Marchand at Fashoda.
„ 21	Picquart removed from Santé to Cherche-Midi.
„ 23	Consultative committee on revision disagrees.
„ 25	Déroulède reconstitutes Ligue des Patriotes.
„ 27	Minister of Justice lays case before Criminal Appeal Court.
„ 29	Criminal Appeal Court accepts case.
Oct 25	Parliament reopens. Fall of Brisson Ministry.
Nov 3	Third Dupuy Ministry, Freycinet at War Office.
„ 28	Poincaré's speech in support of revision.
Dec 31	Foundation of Ligue de la Patrie Française.

1899

Feb 16	Death of Félix Faure.
„ 18	Emile Loubet elected President of the Republic.
„ 23	Déroulède demonstration at Faure funeral.
„ 28	Senate passes law sending Dreyfus case to united Appeal Courts.
May 5	Freycinet resigns, Krantz takes over War Office.
„ 12	Cuignet put on half-pay.
„ 31	Déroulède acquitted.
June 3	Judgment of united Appeal Courts. Du Paty arrested and sent to Cherche-Midi.
„ 4	Auteuil demonstration.
„ 9	Picquart released. Dreyfus leaves The Devil's Island.
„ 11	Longchamps counter-demonstration.
„ 12	Fall of Dupuy Ministry.
„ 24	Waldeck-Rousseau Ministry.
„ 26	Confidence motion carried 262–237.
July 4	Parliament rises.
Aug 7	Second court-martial begins at Rennes.
„ 10–11	Arrest of Déroulède and others.
„ 14	Maître Labori wounded.
Sep 9	Rennes trial verdict.
„ 15	Dreyfus withdraws appeal.
„ 19	Dreyfus pardoned and goes to Carpentras.
„ 21	Galliffet's Order of the Day.
Nov 14	Parliament reassembles.
„ 16	Vote of Confidence in Waldeck-Rousseau's Government carried 317–211.

1900

Jan 4	Sentences pronounced on Déroulède, Buffet and Guérin.
„ 22	Assize Court orders dissolution of the Assumptionists.
„ 28	Mercier elected to Senate.
May 5	Municipal elections: Nationalists win Paris.
„ 28	Galliffet resigns. André appointed to War Office.
Oct 10	Chamber vote against reopening the Dreyfus case.
Dec 18	Amnesty law carried in Chamber.
„ 24	Amnesty law carried in Senate.

1901

| July 1 | Law of Associations passed. |

1902

Apr 27 & May 11	General election.
June 10	Combes Ministry.
,, 19	Opening of debate on Two-Year Service Bill in Senate.
,, 27	Decree closing 120 Church schools.

1903

April 6	Debate on Syveton election.
May–October	War Office examination of the Dreyfus case papers.
Nov 26	Dreyfus petitions for revision.

1904

March 5	Dreyfus petition accepted.
Mar 5–Nov 19	Courts of Appeal take evidence.
Oct 28	*Affaire des fiches* begins.
Nov 15	André resigns from War Office. Berteaux appointed.

1905

Jan 14	Resignation of Combes Ministry.
,, 23	Second Rouvier Ministry.
Dec 9	Law of Separation of Church and State.

1906

March 13	Sarrien Ministry.
May 6 & 20	General election.
July 12	Judgment of Appeal Courts quashing Rennes verdict.
,, 15	Bills reinstating Dreyfus and Picquart passed by Parliament.
,, 22	Dreyfus decorated with the Légion d'Honneur.
Oct 19	First Clemenceau Ministry.

BIBLIOGRAPHY

The numbers preceding the titles are used in the text to indicate the reference. Unless otherwise stated, the place of publication is Paris.

1. Desachy, Paul. *Bibliographie de l'Affaire Dreyfus.* Cornély, 1905.
   Records practically all the contemporary material, including translations up to the date of publication. Most of it, however, is little better than polemic.

2. Guyot, Yves, *La Révision du Procès Dreyfus: faits et documents juridiques.* Stock, 1898.
   There is no transcript of the proceedings of the court-martial of 1894. This book contains the *rapport* of Bexon d'Ormeschville. It also contains a transcript of the public part of the court-martial on Esterhazy in 1898.

3. *Le Procès Zola devant la Cour d'Assises et la Cour de Cassation.* 2 vols., Le Siècle et Stock, 1898.

4. *L'Instruction Fabre et les Décisions Judiciaires Ultérieures.* Stock, 1899.

5. *L'Affaire Picquart devant la Cour de Cassation.* Stock, 1899.
   Contains in addition a number of annexed pieces including Siben's *rapport* on the minor charges against Picquart and Leblois.

6. *La Révision du Procès Dreyfus [devant la Cour de Cassation].* Vol. I, *Instruction de la Chambre Criminelle:* Vols. II and III, *Instruction des Chambers Réunies, Débats.* Stock, 1899.
   In Vol. II will be found again Bexon d'Ormeschville's *rapport* of 1894, together with the proofs of evidence of the witnesses for the prosecution at the first court-martial.

7. *Le Procès Dreyfus devant le Conseil de Guerre de Rennes.* 3 vols., Stock, 1900.

8. *Révision du Procès de Rennes. Enquête de la Chambre Criminelle de la Cour de Cassation.* 3 vols, Ligue Français pour le Défense des Droits de l'Homme et du Citoyen, 1908.

Writings by Contemporaries

8a. Andler, Charles, *La Vie de Lucien Herr (1864–1926).* Rieder, 1932.

9. André, Gen. L. J. N. *Cinq Ans de Ministère.* Michaud, 1907.

10. Bard, A. *Six Mois de Vie Judiciaire.* Jouve, 1927.

11. Barrès, Maurice. *Cahiers*, Vol. II. Plon, 1930.

12. Barrès, Maurice. *Scènes et Doctrines du Nationalisme*, Vol. I, Juven, 1902.

13. Benda, Julien. *La Jeunesse d'un Clerc.* Gallimard, 1936.

14. Benda, Julien. *"Regards sur le Monde Passé"* in 264 *Nouvelle Revue Française*, 1 September 1935, pp. 413–24.

15. Bidegain, Jean. *Le Grand Orient de France: ses doctrines et ses actes* Librairie Anti-Sémite, 1905.

16. Blum, Léon. *Souvenirs sur l'Affaire.* Gallimard, 1935.

17. Brisson, Henri. *Souvenirs: Affaire Dreyfus, avec documents* etc. Cornély, 1908.

18. Brunetière, Ferdinand. *"Après le Procès"* in *Revue des Deux Mondes*, 15 March 1898.

19. Cambon, Paul. *Correspondance, 1870–1924*, Vol. I. Grasset, 1945.

20. Chaîne, Chanoine Léon. *Les Catholiques Français et leurs Difficultés Actuelles.* Stock, 1903.

21. Claretie, Jules. *Souvenirs du Diner Bixio.* Charpentier, 1924.

22. Clemenceau, Georges. *L'Iniquité.* Stock, 1899.

23. Clemenceau, Georges. *Vers la Réparation.* Stock, 1899.
    (Both contain reprints of articles from *L'Aurore.*)

24. Combarieu, Abel. *Sept Ans à l'Elysée avec le President Loubet.* Hachette, 1932.

25. Dreyfus, Alfred. *Cinq Ans de ma Vie.* Fasquelle, 1901.

26. Dreyfus, Alfred. *Lettres d'un Innocent.* Stock, 1898.

27. Dreyfus, Alfred. *Souvenirs et Correspondance.* Grasset, 1936.

28. Dutrait-Crozon, H. (ps. of Cols. Larpent and F. Delebecque). *Joseph Reinach, historien:* préface de Charles Maurras. Savaète, 1905.

29 Dutrait-Crozon, H. (ps.) *Précis de l'Affaire Dreyfus.* Nouvelle Librairie Nationale, 1909, and 3rd edition, 1938.
   The anti-revisionist case

30. Esterhazy, Major Walsin-. *Les Dessous de l'Affaire Dreyfus.* Fayard, 1898.

31. France, Jean. *Souvenirs de la Sûreté-générale: Autour de l'Affaire Dreyfus.* Rieder, 1936.

32. Jaurès, Jean. *Les Preuves.* Petite République, 1898.

33. Lazare, Bernard. *La Vérité sur l'Affaire Dreyfus.* Brussels, Imprimerie Monnom, 1896.

34. Lazare, Bernard. *Une Erreur Judiciare.* Stock, 1897.

35. Leblois, Louis. *L'Affaire Dreyfus: l'Iniquité, la Réparation, les principaux faits et documents.* Quillet, 1929.
    The most valuable single volume on the case, with a very thorough selection of documents. It is from the Picquartien standpoint.

36. Leyret, Henry. *Lettres d'un Coupable* [Esterhazy]. Stock, 1898.

37. Louzon, Robert. *"La Faillite du Dreyfusisme, ou le Triomphe du Parti Juif"* in *Mouvement Socialiste*, Ser. 2, vol. 6. Cornély, 1906.

38. Millaud, Edouard. *Journal d'un Parlementaire*, Vol. II, Oudin, 1914; Vol. III, Nouvelle Revue, s.d. [1919]; Vol. IV, Cheberre, 1925.

39. [Montagnini, Mgr]. *Les Fiches Pontificales de Monsignor Montagnini.* E. Nourrey, 1908.

40. O'Brien, R. Barry. *Lord Russell of Killowen.* London, Smith Elder, 1901.

41. Péguy, Charles. *Notre Jeunesse* in 4 *Oeuvres Complètes*, Gallimard, 1916.

42. Péguy, Charles. *L'Argent* (suite) in 14 *Oeuvres Complètes*, Gallimard, 1932.

43. Pichot, Abbé. *La Conscience Chrétienne et l'Affaire Dreyfus.* Soc. d'éditions littéraires, 1899.

44. Pichot, Abbé and Jorrand, Louis. *La Conscience Chrétienne et la Question Juive.* Soc. d'éditions littéraires, 1899.

45. Pimodan, C. E. H. M. Rarecourt de la Vallée, Comte de, *Simples Souvenirs.* Plon, 1908.

46. [Radziwill, Princesse, née de Castellane]. *Lettres de la Princesse Radziwill au Général de Robilant.* 4 vols., Bologna, Zanichelli, 1934.
    Contains a section in Vol. II of letters from Galliffet written during the period he was at the War Office from June 1899 to May 1900. The text refers to this volume.

47. Reinach, Joseph. *Histoire de l'Affaire Dreyfus.* 7 vols., of which the last contains a full index and sixty pages of corrections and additions. Fasquelle, 1901–8.
    Indispensable, but to be treated with caution. The first five volumes were issued before the final revision of the case, and

being directed to this end, are less frank about the revisionists **than** Vol. VI. Further, since Reinach was convinced that Henry was the central traitor, a belief shared by no writer nowadays, many of his interpretations are distorted. Again, he over-emphasises the anti-semitic side in both the Army and the Church. On the other hand, as an early and leading revisionist, his information, especially on the political side, is of immense value, and no one has ever gone through the contemporary newspapers so thoroughly.

48. Reinach, Joseph. *Tout le Crime.* Stock, 1900.

49. Saint-Aulaire, vicomte de. *Confessions d'un Vieux Diplomate.* Flammarion, 1953.

50. Anon [François Simiand]. *Histoire des Variations de l'Etat-Major.* Bellais, 1899.

51. S[mith], S. F. "The Jesuits and the Dreyfus Case" in 93 *The Month,* Feb 1899, pp. 113–34.

52. S[mith], S. F. "Mr Conybeare Again" *ib.*, April 1899, pp. 405–12.

53. Schwertfeger, Bernard. *The Notebooks of Colonel von Schwartz-koppen,* translated from the German by E. W. D. London, Putnam, 1931.

Gives precise information on the military attaché's dealings with Esterhazy in 1894. It is doubtful when these notes were written, certainly not before Schwartzkoppen left Paris, and possibly, since Reinach is drawn on, not before 1901 or 1902.

54. Sorel, Georges. *La Révolution Dreyfusienne.* Marcel Rivière, 1909.

55. Steed, H. Wickham. *Through Thirty Years,* Vol. I. London, Heinemann, 1924.

56. Steevens, G. W. *The Tragedy of Dreyfus.* London and New York, Harper, 1899.

57. Tabarant, Adolphe. "*Esterhazy en 1894*" in *l'Aurore,* 28 Aug 1899.

58. Vandervelde, Emile. *Souvenirs d'un Militant Socialiste.* Denoël, 1939.

Later Commentaries

59. Charensol, G. *L'Affaire Dreyfus et la Troisième République.* Kra, 1930

60. Charpentier, Armand. *Les Côtés Mystérieux de l'Affaire Dreyfus.* Rieder, 1937.

The author believes that Sandherr was told by the Alsatian ironmaster, Kuhlmann, that someone named Dreyfus had betrayed the signature of the Franco-Russian military convention of 1893–94 to Schwartzkoppen, and jumped to the conclusion that it was the Dreyfus in the War Office. Having no evidence, since Kuhlmann could not be uncovered, Sandherr did get Esterhazy to forge the *bordereau*, which in fact never left the War Office. There is no serious evidence to support this thesis.

61. Foucault, André. *"Un Nouvel Aspect de l'Affaire Dreyfus"* in 205 *Oeuvres Libres*, 1938, pp. 310 et seq.

62. Kohler, Max James. "Some New Light on the Dreyfus Case" reprinted from the Freidus Memorial Volume. Vienna, University Press, 1937.

63. Locard, Edmond (Director of the Laboratoire de Police Technique de Lyon). *L'Affaire Dreyfus et l'Expertise des Documents Ecrits.* Lyon, Desvigne, 1937.

64. Mazel, Henri. *Histoire et Psychologie de l'Affaire Dreyfus.* Boivin, 1934.

Mazel holds that the *bordereau* was in fact written by Schwartzkoppen in order to be revenged on Sandherr, who through Esterhazy had been selling him bogus documents. Horrified at the fate of Dreyfus, the attaché then tried to right matters by deliberately putting the *petit bleu* in Picquart's way. It is a persuasive and amusing thesis until tested, when it is found that awkward points are avoided. Mazel, who claims to be a Dreyfusist but an anti-Dreyfusard, and has moreover no liking for Jews, has nevertheless written an extremely interesting book, full of minor but valuable criticisms.

65. Zévaès, Alexandre. *L'Affaire Dreyfus.* Editions Sphinx, 1931.

Largely on the theme of the nobility of the Socialists, but the author fails to mention that he himself was for some time a hot anti-Dreyfusist.

Anti-Semitism

66. Drumont, Edouard. *La France Juive.* 2 vols., Marpon et Flammarion, 1886.

67. Drumont, Edouard. *La Fin d'un Monde.* Dentu, 1889.

68. Levaillant, Isaïe. *"La Génèse de l'Anti-Sémitisme sous la Troisième République"* in 53 *Revue des Etudes Juives*, 1907, *Actes et conférences*, pp. lxxvi–c.

69. Roblin, Michel. *Les Juifs de Paris.* A. et J. Picard, 1952.

The Catholic Church in France

70. Dansette, Adrien. *Histoire Réligieuse de la France Contemporaine sous la Troisième République.* Flammarion, 1951.

71. Lecanuet, R. P. *L'Eglise de France sous la Troisième République.* Alcan, 1930.

72. Lecanuet, R. P. *Les Signes Avant-Coureurs de la Séparation.* Alcan, 1930.

The French Army

73. *Les Armées Françaises dans la Grande Guerre*, Tome I. Vol, i. Imprimerie nationale, 1922.

74. Anon [Hubert Lyautey]. *"Du rôle social de l'officier dans le service militaire universel"* in *Revue des Deux Mondes*, 15 March 1891.

75. Girardet, Raoul. *La Société Militaire dans la France Contemporaine, 1815–1939.* Plon, 1953.

76. Monteilhet, J. *Les Institutions Militaires de la France*, 2nd edition. Alcan, 1932.

Other Works

77. Siegfried, André. *Tableau Politique de la France de l'Ouest.* Plon, 1913.

78. Bataille, Albert. *Causes Criminelles et Mondaines.* Dentu, annual.

79. Daniel, André (ps. André Lebon). *Année Politique.* Annual.

80. *Annales de la République.*

81. *Journal Officiel.*

82. *Revue Politique et Parlementaire.*

Le Temps, L'Aurore, La Fronde, Le Figaro, La Libre Parole.

Index

398   I<small>NDEX</small>

279–80; deals with Déroulède, etc.,
283–84; his view on the trial, 300;
policy on pardon, 302–03; refuses to
recall Parliament, 306; begins proceedings against Déroulède, 307; situation
of Cabinet, 307–11; programme, 311;
vote of confidence, 312 and f.n.;
amnesty bill, 312–13; second bill, 314;
and Tomps affair, 316–18; his political
manoeuvres, 318; appoints André to
War Office, 319; and amnesty, 319–20;
and religious Orders, 324–26; speech at
Toulouse, 325; resignation, 328; protests against Combes's policy, 331 and
332; warns André, 336; and Combes,
337; death, 353

Weil, Maurice:
Saussier's orderly officer, recommends
Esterhazy to Calmon, 123–24; receives
anonymous letter, 136; confers with
Esterhazy, 136; before Criminal Appeal
Court, 1904, 346

"Weyler" letter:
126–27; Cuignet on, 248

William II, Emperor:
anger, 85; alleged correspondence with

Dreyfus, 86, 148–49, 149 f.n., 171, 198,
259, 278; 294; 298, 345; Hohenlohe's
note, 101; visits French ambassador,
184; allegation against, 290; assurances to Prince of Monaco, 347

Zévaès, Alexandre Bourson, dit:
and Lazare, 135

Zola, Emile:
character, 178–79; writes "J'Accuse,"
179; trial of, 185–97; to England, 197
f.n.

Zurlinden, Gen. Emile (1840–1929):
Minister of War, 109; Military Governor of Paris; and Henry's arrest 225,
226; and Pellieux's resignation, 227;
War Minister, 230–31; resigns, 231;
proposes enquiry into petit bleu, 231–
32; on Picquart's prosecution, 233;
as Military Governor of Paris, orders
court-martial on Picquart, 241; consequences, 242–43; at Faure's funeral,
256; orders arrest of Du Paty, 263;
promises not to re-arrest Picquart, 269;
dismissed from command, 280; and
proceedings against Du Paty, 281